MARGINS
of Philosophy

D0946259

Jacques Derrida   MARGINS
of Philosophy

Translated, with
Additional Notes,
by Alan Bass

The University of Chicago Press

The University of Chicago Press, Chicago 60637
The Harvester Press Limited, Brighton, Sussex
© 1982 by The University of Chicago
All rights reserved. Published 1982
Paperback edition 1984
Printed in the United States of America
10 09 08 07 06 05 04 03 02 01   10 11 12 13

This work was published in Paris under the title *Marges de la philosophie,* © 1972, by Les Editions de Minuit.

Library of Congress Cataloging-in-Publication Data

Derrida, Jacques.
  Margins of philosophy.

  Translation of: Marges de la philosophie.
  1. Philosophy. 2. Languages—Philosophy. 3. Heidegger,
Martin, 1889–1976. Sein und Zeit. 4. Ontology.
5. Space and time. 6. Valéry, Paul, 1871–1945.
7. Hegel, George Wilhelm Friedrich, 1770–1831. I. Title.
B53.D4613 1982   190   82-11137
ISBN 0-226-14326-0 (pbk.)

❂ The paper used in this publication meets the minimum
requirements of the American National Standard for
Information Sciences—Permanence of Paper for Printed
Library Materials, ANSI Z39.48-1992.

Contents

Translator's Note	vii
Tympan	ix
Différance	1
Ousia and *Grammē:* Note on a Note from *Being and Time*	29
The Pit and the Pyramid: Introduction to Hegel's Semiology	69
The Ends of Man	109
The Linguistic Circle of Geneva	137
Form and Meaning: A Note on the Phenomenology of Language	155
The Supplement of Copula: Philosophy before Linguistics	175
White Mythology: Metaphor in the Text of Philosophy	207
Qual Quelle: Valéry's Sources	273
Signature Event Context	307

Translator's Note

Many of these essays have been translated before. Although all the translations in this volume are "new" and "my own"—the quotation marks serving here, as Derrida might say, as an adequate precaution—I have been greatly assisted in my work by consulting:

"*Différance*," trans. David Allison, in *Speech and Phenomena* (Evanston: Northwestern University Press, 1973).

"Ousia and Grammē," trans. Edward Casey, in *Phenomenology in Perspective*, ed. F. Joseph Smith (The Hague: Nijhoff, 1970).

"The Ends of Man," trans. Edouard Morot-Sir, Wesley C. Puisol, Hubert L. Dreyfus, and Barbara Reid, *Philosophy and Phenomenological Research* 30, no. 1 (1969).

"Form and Meaning," trans. David Allison, in *Speech and Phenomena*.

"The Supplement of Copula," trans. James S. Creech and Josué Harrari, *The Georgia Review* 30 (1976).

"White Mythology," trans. F. C. T. Moore, *New Literary History* 6, no. 1 (1974).

"Signature Event Context," trans. Samuel Weber and Jeffrey Mehlman, *Glyph: Johns Hopkins Textual Studies* 7 (1977).

Although I read it after completing the work on this volume, I believe that Philip Lewis's "Vers la traduction abusive" (in *Les fins de l'homme—à partir du travail de Jacques Derrida*, Paris: Galilée, 1981) contains the criteria by which all translations of Derrida will be judged.

ALAN BASS
New York City
July 1982

Tympan

The thesis and antithesis and their proofs therefore represent nothing but the opposite assertions, that a *limit is (eine Grenze ist)*, and that the limit equally is only a *sublated (aufgehobene [relevé])* one; that the limit has a beyond with which however it stands in relation (*in Beziehung steht*), and beyond which it must pass, but that in doing so there arises another such limit, which is no limit. The *solution* of these antinomies, as of those previously mentioned, is transcendental, that is.

Hegel, *Science of Logic*

The essence of philosophy provides no ground (*bodenlos*) precisely for peculiarities, and in order to attain philosophy, it is necessary, if its body expresses the sum of its peculiarities, that it cast itself into the abyss *à corps perdu* (*sich* à corps perdu *hineinzustürzen*).

Hegel, *The Difference between the Fichtean and Schellingian Systems of Philosophy*

The need for philosophy can be expressed as its presupposition if a sort of vestibule (*eine Art von Vorhof*) is supposed to be made for philosophy, which begins with itself.

Ibid.

To tympanize[1]—philosophy.

Being at the limit: these words do not yet form a proposition, and even less a discourse. But there is enough in them, provided that one plays upon it, to engender almost all the sentences in this book.

Does philosophy answer a need? How is it to be understood? Philosophy? The need?

Ample to the point of believing itself interminable, a discourse that has *called itself* philosophy— doubtless the only discourse that has ever intended to receive its name only from itself, and has never ceased murmuring its initial letter to itself from as close as possible—has always, including its own, meant to say its limit. In the familiarity of the languages called (instituted as) natural by philosophy, the languages elementary to it, this discourse has always insisted upon assuring itself mastery over the limit (*peras, limes, Grenze*). It has recognized, conceived, posited, declined the limit according to all possible modes; and therefore by the same token, in order better to dispose of the limit, has transgressed it. *Its own limit* had not to remain foreign to it. Therefore it has appropriated the concept for itself; it has believed that it controls the margin of its volume and that it thinks its other.

Philosophy has always insisted upon this: thinking its other. Its other: that which limits it, and from which it derives its essence, its definition, its production. To think its other: does this amount solely to *relever*[2] (*aufheben*) that from which it derives, to head the procession of its method only

"And I have chosen, as the sign beneath which to place them, the entirely floral and subterranean name of *Persephone*, which is thus extracted from its dark terrestrial depths and lifted to the heavens of a chapter heading.

The acanthus leave copied in school when, for better or for worse, one learns to use the fusain, the stem of a morning glory or other climbing plant, the helix inscribed on the shell of a snail, the meanders of the small and the large intestine, the sandy serpentine excreted by an earth worm, the curl of childish hair encased in a medallion, the putrid simulacrum

---

1. Translator's note (hereafter abbreviated as "TN"). In French, *tympaniser* is an archaic verb meaning to criticize, to ridicule publicly. I have transliterated it here.
2. TN. On Derrida's translation of the Hegelian term *aufheben* as *relever*, see below, "La différance," note 23, for a system of notes. There is an untranslatable play of words here: "Penser son autre: cela revient-il seulement à *relever* (*aufheben*) ce dont elle *relève* . . . ?"

x

by passing the limit? Or indeed does the limit, obliquely, by surprise, always reserve one more blow for philosophical knowledge? Limit/passage.

In propagating this question beyond the precise context from which I have just extracted it (the infinity of the *quantum* in the greater *Logic* and the critique of the Kantian antinomies), almost constantly, in this book, I shall be examining the *relevance*[3] of the limit. And therefore relaunching in every sense the reading of the Hegelian *Aufhebung*, eventually beyond what Hegel, inscribing it, understood himself to say or intended to mean, beyond that which is inscribed on the internal vestibule of his ear. This implies a vestibule in a delicate, differentiated structure whose orifices may always remain unfindable, and whose entry and exit may be barely passable; and implies that the text—Hegel's for example—functions as a writing machine in which a certain number of *typed* and systematically enmeshed propositions (one has to be able to recognize and isolate them) represent the "conscious intention" of the author as a reader of his "own" text, in the sense we speak today of a mechanical reader. Here, the lesson of the finite reader called a philosophical author is but one piece, occasionally and incidentally interesting, of the machine. *To insist* upon thinking *its other:* its proper[4] other, the proper of its other, an other proper? In thinking it *as such,* in recognizing it, one misses it. One reappropriates it for oneself, one disposes of it, one misses it, or rather one misses (the) missing (of) it, which, as concerns the other,

drawn by a slight pressure of the fingers from a *père-la-colique,* *

the marblings that bloom on the edges of certain bound books,

the curved wrought iron, "modern style," of the Métro entries,

the interlace of embroidered figures on sheets and pillow cases,

the kiss-curl pasted with grease on the cheekbone of a prostitute in the old days of *Casque d'or,*

the thin and browner braid of the steel cable, the thick and blonder one of the string cable,

the cerebral convolutions exemplified by, when you eat it, mutton brains,

the corkscrewing of the vine, the image

---

* TN. A *père-la-colique* is a small porcelain toy representing an old man sitting on a toilet seat. When a certain product is put into it, it excretes.

3. TN. *Relevance* is not the English "relevance" but a neologism from the translation of *aufheben* as *relever.* Like *Aufhebung* it is a noun derived from a gerund.

4. TN. *Le propre* is one of the key terms of this book. In French, *propre* can mean both "proper" and "own," as here with *son propre autre,* its own other, the other proper to it. I have sometimes given simply "proper," and sometimes "own, proper" (e.g. "its own, proper other"). See also "La différance," note 1.

always amounts to the same. Between the proper of the other and the other of the proper.

If philosophy has always intended, from its point of view, to maintain its relation with the non-philosophical, that is the antiphilosophical, with the practices and knowledge, empirical or not, that constitute its other, if it has constituted itself according to this purposive *entente* with its outside, if it has always intended to hear itself speak, in the same language, of itself and of something else, can one, strictly speaking, determine a nonphilosophical place, a place of exteriority or alterity from which one might still treat *of philosophy?* Is there any ruse not belonging to reason to prevent philosophy from still speaking of itself, from borrowing its categories from the logos of the other, by affecting itself without delay, on the domestic page of its own tympanum (still the muffled drum, the *tympanon*, the cloth stretched taut in order to take its beating, to amortize impressions, to make the *types* (*typoi*) resonate, to balance the striking pressure of the *typtein*, between the inside and the outside), with heterogeneous percussion? Can one violently penetrate philosophy's field of listening without its immediately—even pretending in advance, by hearing what is said of it, by decoding the statement—making the penetration resonate within itself, appropriating the emission for itself, familiarly communicating it to itself between the inner and middle ear, following the path of a tube or inner opening, be it round or oval? In other words, can one puncture the tympanum of a philosopher and still be heard and understood by him?

To philosophize with a hammer. Zarathustra begins by asking himself if he will have to puncture them, batter their ears (*Muss man ihnen erst die Ohren zerschlagen*), with the sound of cymbals or tympani, the instruments, always, of some Diony-

of what later will be—once the juice has been bottled—the corkscrew (itself prefiguring the endless screw of drunkenness),

the circulation of the blood,

the concha of the ear, the sinuous curves of a path,

everything that is wreathed, coiled, flowered, garlanded, twisted, arabesque,

the spur (which for my purposes here I will imagine in a spiral) of an espadon, the twists of a ram's horn,

all this I believe uncovered in the name of Persephone, potentially, awaiting only an imperceptible click to set it off like the ribbon of steel tightly wound on itself in the midst of the pinions of a clockwork or the spring in the closed-cover box from which the bristly-bearded devil

sianism. In order to teach them "to hear with their eyes" too.

But we will analyze the metaphysical exchange, the circular complicity of the metaphors of the eye and the ear.

But in the structure of the tympanum there is something called the "luminous triangle." It is named in *Les Chants de Maldoror* (II), very close to a "grandiose trinity."

But along with this triangle, along with the *pars tensa* of the tympanon, there is also found the handle of a *"hammer."*

In order effectively, practically to transform what one decries (tympanizes), must one still be heard and understood within it, henceforth subjecting oneself to the law of the inner hammer?[5] In relaying the inner hammer, one risks permitting the noisiest discourse to participate in the most serene, least disturbed, best served economy of philosophical irony. Which is to say, and examples of this metaphysical drumming are not lacking today, that in taking this risk, one risks nothing.

From philosophy—to separate oneself, in order to describe and decry its law, in the direction of the absolute exteriority of another place. But exteriority and alterity are concepts which by themselves have never surprised philosophical discourse. *Philosophy by itself has always been concerned* with them. These are not the conceptual headings un-

has not yet emerged. Therefore, essentially, in question is a *spiraled* name—or more broadly: a *curved* name, but whose gentleness is not to be confused with the always more or less lenitive character of that which has been dulled, since—quite to the contrary—what is piercing and penetrating about it is confirmed by the rapprochement to be made between the syllables that compose its name and the syllables forming the civil status of the insect called [in French] *perce-oreille* (ear-piercer) [and in English, "earwig"]. For not only do "Per-

5. The hammer, as is well known, belongs to the chain of small bones, along with the anvil and the stirrup. It is placed on the *internal* surface of the tympanic membrane. It always has the role of mediation and communication: it transmits sonic vibrations to the chain of small bones, and then to the inner ear. Bichat recognized that it has another paradoxical function. This small bone protects the tympanum while acting upon it. "Without it, the tympanum would be affected painfully by vibrations set up by too powerful sounds." The hammer, thus, can weaken the blows, muffle them on the threshold of the inner ear. The latter—the labyrinth—includes a *vestibule*, the *semicircular canals*, a *cochlea* (with its two *spirals*), that is, two organs of balance and one organ of hearing. Perhaps we shall penetrate it more deeply later. For the moment, it suffices to mark the role of the middle ear: it tends to equalize the acoustic resistance of the air and the resistance of the labyrinthine liquids, to balance internal pressures and external pressures.

der which philosophy's border can be overflowed; the overflow is its object. Instead of determining some other circumscription, recognizing it, practicing it, bringing it to light, forming it, in a word *producing* it (and today this word serves as the crudest "new clothes" of the metaphysical denegation which accommodates itself very well to all these projects), in question will be, but according to a movement unheard of by philosophy, an other which is no longer *its other*.

But by relating it to something to which it has no relation, is one not immediately permitting oneself to be encoded by philosophical logos, to stand under its banner?[6] Certainly, except by writing this relationship following the mode of a nonrelationship about which it would be demonstrated simultaneously or *obliquely*—on the philosophical surface of the discourse—that no philosopheme will ever have been prepared to conform to it or translate it. This can only be written according to a deformation of the philosophical tympanum. My intention is not to extract from the question of metaphor—one of the most continuous threads of this book—the figure of the oblique. This is also, thematically, the route of *Dissemination*.[7] We know that the membrane of the tympanum, a thin and

sephone" and "*perce-oreille*" both begin with the same allusion to the idea of "piercing" (less decided in Persephone, because of the *s* which imparts something undulating and grassy, chimerical and fleeting, to the name, to the extent that one might be tempted, by executing an easy metathesis, to call her the Fay Person . . .), but the one and the other end with an appeal to the sense of hearing, which is overtly in play, for the insect, due to the enunciation of the word "ear" (that is,

6. Without an inventory of all the sexual investments which, everywhere and at all times, powerfully constrain the *discourse of the ear*, I shall give an example here to indicate the topics of the material left in the margins. The horn that is called *pavillon (papillon)* is a phallus for the Dogon and Bambara of Mali, and the auditory canal a vagina. [TN. *Pavillon* in French has multiple meanings. Here, the reference is to the end of the horn called the bell in English; it also designates the visible part of the ear. Further, both senses of *pavillon* just given derive from its older sense of "military tent," because of such tents' conic shape. Finally, *pavillon* can also mean flag or banner, as in the sentence above that ends with the phrase "stand under its banner (*pavillon*)."] Speech is the sperm indispensable for insemination. (Conception through the ear, all of philosophy one could say.) It descends through the woman's ear, and is rolled up in a spiral around the womb. Which is hardly very distant from Arianism (from the name Arius, of course, a priest from Alexandria, the father of Arianism, a heretical doctrine of the conception in the Trinity), from *homoousios*, and from all the records of the Nicene Council.

7. Cf. especially "La double séance." ['The Double Session,' in *Dissemination*, trans. Barbara Johnson (Chicago: University of Chicago Press, 1981).]

transparent partition separating the auditory canal from the middle ear (the *cavity*), is stretched obliquely (*loxōs*). Obliquely from above to below, from outside to inside, and from the back to the front. Therefore it is not perpendicular to the axis of the canal. One of the effects of this obliqueness is to increase the surface of impression and hence the capacity of vibration. It has been observed, particularly in birds, that precision of hearing is in direct proportion to the obliqueness of the tympanum. The tympanum squints.

Consequently, to luxate the philosophical ear, to set the *loxōs* in the *logos* to work, is to avoid frontal and symmetrical protest, opposition in all the forms of *anti-*, or in any case to inscribe *antism* and overturning,[8] domestic denegation, in an entirely other form of ambush, of *lokhos*, of textual maneuvers.

Under what conditions, then, could one *mark*, for a philosopheme in general, a *limit*, a margin that it could not infinitely reappropriate, *conceive* as its own, in advance engendering and interning the process of its expropriation (Hegel again, always), proceeding to its inversion by itself? How to unbalance the pressures that correspond to each

of the organ by means of which auditory sensations penetrate into us), and less directly in play for the goddess by means of the suffix *phone*, also found in "telephone" and "gramophone," the latter being an instrument for which is more appropriate than the former the very euphonic ending that beautifully defines it as a musical mechanism.

The insect whose principal work is to gnaw on the inside of fruit pits in order to take subsistence from them, and

8. On the problematic of overturning and displacement, see *Dissemination* and *Positions* (Chicago: University of Chicago Press, 1980). To luxate, to tympanize philosophical autism is never an operation *within* the concept and without some carnage of language. Thus it breaks open the roof, the closed spiral unity of the palate. It proliferates *outside* to the point of no longer being *understood*. It is no longer *a* tongue.

Hematographic music.
"Sexual jubilation is a choice of glottis,
of the splinter of the cyst of a dental root,
a choice of otic canal,
of the bad auricular ringing,
of a bad instillation of sound,
of current brocaded on the bottom carpet,
of the opaque thickness,
the elect application of the choice of the candelabra of chiselled string,
*   in order to escape the prolific avaric obtuse music*
without ram, or age, or ramage,
and which has neither tone nor age."
ARTAUD (December 1946)

other on either side of the membrane? How to block this correspondence destined to weaken, muffle, forbid the blows from the outside, the other hammer? The "hammer that speaks" to him "who has the third ear" (*der das dritte Ohr hat*). How to interpret—but here interpretation can no longer be a theory or discursive practice of philosophy—the strange and unique property of a discourse that organizes the *economy* of its representation, the law of its proper weave, such that *its* outside is never its *outside*, never surprises it, such that the logic of its heteronomy still reasons from within the vault of its autism?

For this is how *Being* is understood: its proper. It assures without let-up the *relevant* movement of reappropriation. Can one then *pass* this singular limit which is not a limit, which no more separates the inside from the outside than it assures their permeable and transparent continuity? What form could this play of limit/passage have, this logos which posits and negates itself in permitting its own voice to well up? Is this a well-put question?

The analyses that give rise to one another in this book do not answer this question, bringing to it neither an *answer* nor *an* answer. They work, rather, to transform and deplace its statement, and toward examining the presuppositions of the question, the institution of its protocol, the laws of its procedure, the headings of its alleged homogeneity, of its apparent unicity: can one treat of philosophy itself (metaphysics itself, that is, ontotheology) without already permitting the dictation, along with the pretention to unity and unicity, of the ungraspable and imperial totality of an order? If there are margins, is there still *a* philosophy, *the* philosophy?

No answer, then. Perhaps, in the long run, not even a question. The copulative correspondence, the opposition question/answer is already lodged

which occasionally, so they say, perforates human tympanums with its pincers, has in common with the daughter of Demeter that it too buries itself in a subterranean kingdom. The deep country of hearing, described in terms of geology more than in those of any other natural science, not only by virtue of the cartilaginous cavern that constitutes its organ, but also by virtue of the relationship that unites it to grottoes, to chasms, to all the pockets hollowed out of the terrestrial crust whose emptiness makes them into resonating drums for the slightest sounds.

Just as one might worry about the idea of the tympanum, a fragile membrane threatened with perforations by the minute pincers of an insect—unless it had

xvi

in a structure, enveloped in the hollow of an ear, which we will go into to take a look. To find out how it is made, how it has been formed, how it functions. And if the tympanum is a limit, perhaps the issue would be less to displace a *given* determined limit than to work toward the concept of limit and the limit of the concept. To unhinge it on several tries.

But what is a *hinge* (signifying: to be reasoned in every sense)?

Therefore, what legal question is to be relied upon if the limit in general, and not only the limit of what is believed to be one very particular thing among others, the tympanum, is structurally oblique? If, therefore, there is no limit *in general*, that is, a straight and regular form of the limit? Like every *limus*, the *limes*, the short cut, signifies the oblique.

But indefatigably at issue is the ear, the distinct, differentiated, articulated organ that produces the effect of proximity, of absolute properness, the idealizing erasure of organic difference. It is an organ whose structure (and the suture that holds it to the throat) produces the pacifying lure of organic indifference. To forget it—and in so doing to take shelter in the most familial of dwellings— is to cry out for the end of organs, of others.

But indefatigably at issue is the ear. Not only the sheltered portico of the tympanum, but also the vestibular canal.[9] And the phoneme as the "phe-

already been broken by too violent a noise—it is equally permissible to fear for the vocal cords, which can be broken instantaneously when, for example, one screams too loudly, subjecting them to excessive tension (in the case of anger, grief, or even a simple game dominated by the sheer pleasure of shrieking), so that one's voice gets "broken." An accident my mother sometimes warned me against, whether she actually believed that it could happen, or whether—as I tend to believe—she used the danger as a scarecrow that might make me less noisy,

9. "Anatomical term. Irregular cavity that is part of the inner ear. Genital vestibule, the vulva and all its parts up to the membrane of the hymen exclusively. Also the name of the triangular space limited in front and laterally by the ailerons of the nymphs [small lips of the vulva], and in back by the orifice of the urethra; one enters through this space in practicing a vestibular incision. *E. Lat. vestibulum,* from the augmentative particle *ve,* and *stabulum,* place in which things are held (see *stable*), according to certain Latin etymologists. Ovid, on the contrary, more reasonably, it appears, takes it from *Vesta* because the *vestibule* held a fire lit in the honor of Vesta [goddess of the proper, of familiarity, of the domestic hearth, etc.]. Among the moderns, Mommsen says that *vestibulum* comes from *vestis,* being an entryway in which the Romans left the toga (*vestis*)." Littré.

nomenon of the labyrinth" in which *Speech and Phenomena*, from its epigraph and very close to its false exit, had introduced the question of writing. One might always think, of course, in order to reassure oneself, that "labyrinthic vertigo" is the name of a well-known and well-determined disease, the local difficulty of a particular organ.

 This is—another tympanum.

at least for a while. Marginal to Perse-phone and *perce-or-eille*,   soldered together by a cement of   relationships hardened—in broad daylight—by their

---

Lodged in the vestibule, the labyrinthic receptors of balance are named *vestibular receptors*. These are the *otolithic* organs (utricle and saccule) and the *semicircular* canals. The utricle is sensitive to the head's changes of direction, which displace the otoliths, the ear's stones, small calcified granulations modifying the stimulation of the ciliary cells of the macula (the thick part of the membraneous covering of the utricle). The function of the saccule in the mechanisms of balance has not yet been definitely ascertained. The semicircular canals, inside the labyrinth, are sensitive to all the movements of the head, which create currents in the liquid (endolymph). The reflex movements which result from this are indispensable for assuring the stability of the head, the direction and balance of the body in all its movements, notably in walking upright.

Tympanum, Dionysianism, labyrinth, Ariadne's thread. We are now traveling through (upright, walking, dancing), included and enveloped within it, never to emerge, the form of an ear constructed around a barrier, going round its inner walls, a city, therefore (labyrinth, semicircular canals—warning: the spiral walkways do not hold) circling around like a stairway winding around a lock, a dike (dam) stretched out toward the sea; closed in on itself and open to the sea's path. Full and empty of its water, the anamnesis of the concha resonates alone on a beach. [TN. There is an elaborate play on the words *limaçon* and *conque* here. *Limaçon* (aside from meaning snail) means a spiral staircase and the spiral canal that is part of the inner ear. *Conque* means both conch and concha, the largest cavity of the external ear.] How could a breach be produced, between earth and sea?

By means of the breach of philosophical identity, a breach which amounts to addressing the truth to itself in an envelope, to hearing itself speak inside without opening its mouth or showing its teeth, the bloodiness of a disseminated writing comes to separate the lips, to violate the embouchure of philosophy, putting *its* tongue into movement, finally bringing it into contact with some other code, of an entirely other kind. A necessarily unique event, nonreproducible, hence illegible as such and, when it happens, inaudible in the conch, between earth and sea, without signature.

Bataille writes in "The Structure of the Labyrinth": "Emerging from an inconceivable void in the play of beings as a satellite wandering away from two phantoms (one bristling with beard, the other, sweeter, its head covered with a chignon), it is first of all in the father and mother who transcend it that the minuscule human being encounters the illusion of sufficiency. (. . .) Thus are produced the relatively stable gatherings whose center is a city, similar in its primitive form to a corolla enclosing like a double pistil a sovereign and a king. (. . .) The universal god destroys rather than 'supports the human aggregations which erect its phantom. He himself is only dead, whether a mythical delirium proposes him for adoration like a cadaver pierced with wounds, or whether by his very universality he becomes more than any other incapable of opposing to the loss of being the breached walls of *ipseity*."

If Being is in effect a process of reappropriation, the "question of Being" of a new type can never be percussed without being measured against the absolutely coextensive question of the proper. Now this latter question does not permit itself to be separated from the idealizing value of the *very-near*, which itself receives its disconcerting powers only from the structure of hearing-oneself-speak. The *proprius* presupposed in all discourses on economy, sexuality, language, semantics, rhetoric, etc., repercusses its absolute limit only in sonorous representation. Such, at least, is the most insistent hypothesis of this book. A quasi-organizing role is granted, therefore, to the motif of sonic vibration (the Hegelian *Erzittern*) as to the motif of the proximity of the meaning of Being in speech (Heideggerian *Nähe* and *Ereignis*). The logic of the event is examined from the vantage of the structures of expropriation called *timbre (tympanum), style,* and *signature.* Timbre, style, and signature are the same obliterating division of the proper. They make every event possible, necessary, and unfindable.

What is the specific resistance of philosophical discourse to deconstruction? It is the infinite mastery that the agency of Being (and of the) proper seems to assure it; this mastery permits it to interiorize every limit as *being* and as being its own *proper.* To exceed it, by the same token, and therefore to preserve it in itself. Now, in its mastery and its discourse on mastery (for mastery is a signification that we still owe to it), philosophical power always seems to combine *two types.*

On the one hand, a *hierarchy:* the particular sciences and regional ontologies are subordinated to general ontology, and then to fundamental ontology.[10] From this point of view all the questions that solicit Being and the proper upset the order that submits the determined fields of science, its formal

names, a durable suture is thus formed between the throat and the tympanum, which, the one as much as the other, are subject to a fear of being injured, besides both belonging to the same cavernous domain. And in the final analysis caverns become the geometric place in which all are joined together: the chthonian divinity, the insect piercer of pits, the matrix in which the voice is formed, the drum that each noise comes to strike with its wand of vibrating air; caverns: obscure pipe-works reaching down into the most secret part of being in order to bring even to the totally naked cavity of our mental space the exhalations—of variable temperature, consistency, and ornamentation—that are

10. The putting into question of this ontological subordination was begun in *Of Grammatology* (Baltimore: Johns Hopkins University Press, 1978).

objects or materials (logic and mathematics, or semantics, linguistics, rhetoric, science of literature, political economy, psychoanalysis, etc.), to philosophical jurisdiction. In principle, then, these questions are prior to the constitution of a rigorous, systematic, and orderly theoretical discourse in these domains (which therefore are no longer simply domains, regions circumscribed, delimited, and assigned from outside and above).

On the other hand, an *envelopment:* the whole is implied, in the speculative mode of reflection and expression, in each part. Homogenous, concentric, and circulating indefinitely, the movement of the whole is remarked in the partial determinations of the system or encyclopedia, without the status of that remark, and the partitioning of the part, giving rise to any general deformation of the space.

These two kinds of appropriating mastery, hierarchy and envelopment, communicate with each other according to complicities we shall define. If one of the two types is more powerful here (Aristotle, Descartes, Kant, Husserl, Heidegger) or there (Spinoza, Leibniz, Hegel), they both follow the movement of the same wheel, whether it is a question, finally, of Heidegger's hermeneutical circle or of Hegel's ontotheological circle. ("White Mythology" deviates according to another wheel.) For as long as this tympanum will not have been destroyed, (the tympanum as also a hydraulic *wheel,* described minutely by Vitruvius),[11] which

propagated in long horizontal waves after rising straight up from the fermentations of the outside world.

On the one hand, therefore, is the outside; on the other hand, the inside; between them, the cavernous.

A voice is usually described as 'cavernous' to give the idea that it is low and deep, and even a bit too much so. For example: a *basse taille,*** in relation to a *basse chantante* with a higher register and also more supple line, whereas that of the *basse taille* rather would seem more proper—in that it seems rough, as if hewn with an ax—to the stone breaker, the

---

** TN. The *basse-taille* is the voice called in English and Italian the *basso profundo,* while the *basse chantante* is the voice usually called "bass" (between *basso profundo* and baritone). Leiris is playing on the *taille* in *basse-taille,* from the verb *tailler* meaning to hew, to cut, to chisel, etc.

11. In *De Architectura* Vitruvius described not only the water clock of Ctesibius, who had conceived *aquarum expressiones automatopoetasque machinas multaque deliciarum genera* ("First he made a hollow tube of gold, or pierced a gem; for these materials are neither worn by the passage of water nor so begrimed that they become clogged. The water flows smoothly through the passage, and raises an inverted bowl which the craftsmen call the cork or drum (*quod ab artificibus phellos sive tympanum dicitur*). The bowl is connected with a bar on which a drum revolves. The drums are wrought with equal teeth" (*On Architecture,* translated and edited

cannot be achieved by means of a simply discursive or theoretical gesture, for as long as these two types of mastery will not have been destroyed in their essential familiarity—which is also that of *phallocentrism* and *logocentrism*[12]—and for as long chiseler of funerary marbles, to the miner with his pick, to the gravedigger, the ditchdigger, and (if

by Frank Granger, New York: Putnam, 1934; Book IX, C. VIII, p. 259). One ought to cite all the "corks or drums" which follow. Vitruvius also describes the axle of the *anaphorical clock, ex qua pendet ex una parte phellos (sive tympanum) qui ab aqua sublevatur* ("On one end hangs a cork or drum raised by the water," ibid., p. 263), and the famous hydraulic wheel which bears his name: a drum or hollow cylinder is divided by wedges which are open on the surface of the drum. They fill up with water. Reaching the level of the axle, the water passes into the hub and flows out.

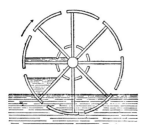

Instead of the wedges of *Vitruvius' tympanum, Lafaye's tympanum* has cylindrical partitions following the developables of a circle. The angles are economized. The water, entering into the wheel, no longer is lodged in the angles. Thus the shocks are reduced, and so, by the same token, is the loss of labor. Here, I am reproducing the perhaps Hegelian figure of Lafaye's tympanum (1717).

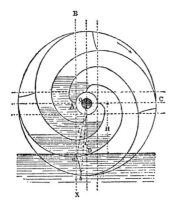

12. This *ecorché (Dissemination* too was to "skin the ear"), bares the *phallogocentric* system in its most sensitive philosophical articulations. [TN. An *ecorché* (from the verb *ecorcher,* to skin) is a model of a human or animal without its skin used to teach the techniques of life drawing.] Therefore, it pursues the deconstruction of the triangulocircular structure (Oedipus, Trinity, Speculative Dialectics) already long since begun, and does so explicitly in the texts of *Dissemination* and of *Positions.*

as even the philosophical concept of mastery will not have been destroyed, all the liberties one claims to take with the philosophical order will remain activated *a tergo* by misconstrued philosophical machines, according to denegation or precipitation, ignorance or stupidity. They very quickly, known or unknown to their "authors," will have been called back to order.

Certainly one will never prove *philosophically* that *one has* to transform a given situation and proceed to an effective deconstruction in order to leave irreversible marks. In the name of what and of whom in effect? And why not permit the dictation of the norm and the rule of law *a tergo* (viz. the tympanotribe)? If the displacement of forces does not effectively transform the situation, why deprive oneself of the pleasure, and specifically of the laughter, which are never without a certain repetition? This hypothesis is not secondary. With what is one to *authorize oneself*, in the last analysis, if not once more with philosophy, in order to disqualify naiveté, incompetence, or misconstrual, in order to be concerned with passivity or to limit pleasure? And if the value of authority remained fundamentally, like the value of the critique itself, the most naive? One can analyze or transform the desire for im-pertinence, but one cannot, within discourse, make it understand pertinence, and that

I can refer to a social situation which, strictly speaking, is no longer a profession) to the monk, pursued with weighty steps, down along cloistered corridors and through the years, by the slow voyage toward an internal prey.

Of this *basse taille*, with the idea attached to it, like a stone around its neck, of steps fashioned in the ground, as if in order to go to the basement or step by step to descend a certain number of meters below sea-level (. . .) to open up a passageway through the organs by burrowing

---

This structure, the mythology of the proper and of organic indifference, is often the architectural figure of the *tympanum*, the part of a pediment included in the triangle of the three cornices, sometimes shot through with a circular opening called an *oculus*. The issue here is not one of paying it the tribute of an oracular denegation or of a thesis without a strategy of writing that the phallogocentric order manipulates at every turn in its conceptual argumentation and in its ideological, political, and literary connotations. The issue, rather, is to mark the conceptual holds and turns of writing that the order cannot turn inside out in order to get its gloves back on or to start up once more. Here, margin, march, and demarcation pass between denegation (plurality of modes) and deconstruction (systematic unity of a spiral).

Speaking of the *écorché*, there are then at least two anatomy lessons, as there are two labyrinths and two cities. In one of them, a brain dissection, the surgeon's head remains invisible. It seems to be cut off by the painter with a line. In fact, it was burned, in 1723, along with a quarter of the painting.

one must (know how to) destroy what one destroys.

Therefore, if they appear to remain marginal to some of the great texts in the history of philosophy, these ten writings *in fact* ask the question of the margin. Gnawing away at the border which would make this question into a particular case, they are to blur the line which separates a text from its controlled margin. They interrogate philosophy beyond its meaning, treating it not only as a discourse but as a determined text inscribed in a general text, enclosed in the representation of its own margin. Which compels us not only to reckon with the entire logic of the margin, but also to take an entirely other reckoning: which is doubtless to recall that beyond the philosophical text there is not a blank, virgin, empty margin, but another text, a weave of differences of forces without any present center of reference (everything—"history," "politics," "economy," "sexuality," etc.—said not to be written in books: the worn-out expression with which we appear not to have finished stepping backward, in the most regressive argumentations and in the most apparently unforeseeable places); and also to recall that the *written* text of philosophy (this time in its books) overflows and cracks its meaning.

To philosophize *à corps perdu.*[13] How did Hegel understand that?

Can this text become the margin of a margin? Where has the body of the text gone when the margin is no longer a secondary virginity but an inexhaustible reserve, the stereographic activity of an entirely other ear?

through the canal of a wound narrow but deep enough to involve the innermost muscles; whether it is that of an artist from the opera, cut from the heart of the rock, or fashioned in the most supple steel if it is that of a singer, emerging from the moist earth of a hothouse or stretched out in breaking glass filament if that of one of the creatures more readily called *cantatrices* than *chanteuses* (even though *cantateur†* is an unknown species); or whether it is the most vulgar voice, issuing from the most insignificant being for the most insipid ballad or most trivial refrain, mysterious is the voice that sings, in relation to the voice that speaks.

The mystery—if

† *Cantatrice* has the sense of an opera singer, a diva (a hothouse, glass-breaking voice), while *chanteuse* is simply a female singer. There is no masculine form *cantateur* corresponding to *cantatrice.*

13. TN. See the second epigraph above for Hegel's use of the expression *à corps perdu.* It means impetuously, passionately.

Overflows and cracks: that is, on the one hand compels us to count in its margin more and less than one believes is said or read, an unfolding due to the structure of the mark (which is the same word as *marche*,[14] as limit, and as *margin*); and on the other hand, luxates the very body of statements in the pretensions to univocal rigidity or regulated polysemia. A lock opened to a double understanding no longer forming a single system.

Which does not amount to acknowledging that the margin maintains itself within *and* without. Philosophy says so too: *within* because philosophical discourse intends to know and to master its margin, to define the line, align the page, enveloping it in its volume. *Without* because the margin, *its* margin, *its* outside are empty, are outside: a negative about which there seems to be nothing to do, a negative without effect in the text *or* a negative working in the service of meaning, the margin *relevé (aufgehoben)* in the dialectics of the Book. Thus, one will have said nothing, or in any event done nothing, in declaring "against" philosophy that its margin is within or without, within and without, simultaneously the inequality of its internal spacings and the regularity of its borders. Simultaneously, by means of rigorous, philosophically *intransigent* analyses, *and* by means of the inscription of marks which no longer belong to philosophical space, not even to the neighborhood of its other, one would have to displace philosophy's alignment of its own types. To write otherwise. To delimit the space of a closure no longer analogous to what philosophy can represent for itself under this name, according to a straight or circular line enclosing a homogenous space. To determine, entirely against any philosopheme, the

we wish at any price, for the purposes of discourse, to give a figure of speech to that which by definition cannot have one—can be represented as a margin, a fringe surrounding the object, isolating it at the same time as it underlines its presence, masking it even as it qualifies it, inserting it into an untied harlequin of facts with no identifiable cause at the same time as the particular color that it dyes the object extracts it from the swampy depths in which ordinary facts are mixed up. Musical elocution, compared to ordinary elocution, appears to be endorsed with a similar irisation, a fairy's coat, which is the index of a connivance between that which could seem to

14. TN. Derrida often plays on the series *marque, marche, marge* (mark, step, margin).

intransigence that prevents it from calculating its margin, by means of a *limitrophic* violence imprinted according to new *types*. To eat the margin in luxating the tympanum, the relationship to itself of the double membrane. So that philosophy can no longer reassure itself that it has always *maintained* its tympanum. The issue here is the *maintenant* [maintaining, now]: it travels through the entire book. How to put one's hands [*mains*] on the tympanum and how the tympanum could escape from the hands of the philosopher in order to make of phallogocentrism an impression that he no longer recognizes, in which he no longer rediscovers himself, of which he could become conscious only *afterward* and without being able *to say to himself*, again turning on his own hinge: I will have anticipated it, with absolute knowledge.

This impression, as always, is made on some tympanum, whether resonating or still, on the double membrane that can be struck from either side.

As in the case of the *mystic writing pad*, I am asking in terms of the *manual printing press* the question of the writing machine which is to upset the entire space of the proper body in the unlimited enmeshing of machines-of-machines, hence of machines without hands.[15] The question of the machine is asked one more time, between the pit and the pyramid, in the margins (of the Hegelian text).

In terms of the printing press, therefore, the manual press, what is a tympan? We *must know this*, in order to provoke within the balance of the inner ear or the homogenous correspondence of the two ears, in the relation to itself in which philosophy understands itself to domesticate its march,

be only a human voice and the rhythms of the fauna and flora, that is, the rhythms of the mineral domain in which every velleity of gesture is transcribed into a frozen form. And when from spoken language—which is sufficiently enigmatic itself, since it is only from the instant in which it is formulated, in external fashion or not, that thought takes on its reality—one comes to sung language, what one encounters before one is an enigma of the second degree, seeing that the closer one is in a sense to the corporal structures (of which each note emitted has the appearance of being the direct fruit) and, consequently, the more certain one is of apparently stand-

15. As concerns the metaphysical concept of the machine, see, for what is questioned here, the piece on Hegel ("The Pit and the Pyramid," below); "Freud and the Scene of Writing," in *Writing and Difference*; and *Of Grammatology.*

some dislocation without measure. And, if the Hegelian wound (*Beleidigung, Verletzung*) always *appears* sewn up again, to give birth, from the lesion without suture, to some unheard-of partition.

In terms of the manual printing press, then, there is not one tympan[16] but several. Two frameworks, of different material, generally wood and iron, fit into one another, are lodged, if one can put it thus, in one another. One tympan in the other, one of wood the other of iron, one large and one small. Between them, the sheet of paper. Therefore, in question is an *apparatus,* and one of its essential functions will be the regular calculation of the margin. This apparatus is lowered onto the marble on which the inked form is found. A crank rolls the carriage under the platen, which is then, with the aid of the bar, lowered onto the small tympan. The carriage is rolled. The tympan and the frisket are lifted ("Frisket. Printing term. The piece of the hand-operated press that the printer lowers onto the sheet, both to keep it on the tympan and to prevent the margins and spaces from being soiled." Littré), and the sheet is then printed on one of its sides. From a treatise on typography: "The large *tympan* is a wood chassis with a piece of silk stretched over it; the points, the margin, and successively each of the sheets to be printed are placed on the tympan. The lever to which the frisket is attached is made of iron. The large *tympan* is attached to the drum in its lower part, that is to the right-hand end of the press; it is held by a double hinge called the couplets of the *tympan*. It is ordinarily of the same width as the drum. In each of the bars that extend along its width, the large *tympan* is pierced by two holes,

ing on firm ground, one finds oneself, in truth, in the grasp of the ineffable, the melodic line presenting itself as the translation, in a purely sonorous idiom, of that which could not be said by means of words. And even more so when the source of the song, rather than being a human mouth (that is, an organ with which we are more or less familiar), is a mechanical device adding to what is already strange in musical speech the surprise of being reproduced; one is then face to face with a mystery in the almost pure state. (. . .) I myself possessed a phonograph (. . .) not only were there no provisions for using it as a recording device,

---

16. TN. In French all the words whose senses Derrida plays on throughout this essay are *tympan*. In English they are all tympanum, with the single exception of the printing term, which is tympan (as in French). I have kept the original French title—*tympan*—of this essay.

one in the middle, the other two-thirds up, into which the screws of the points fit. The small *tympan* is a frame formed by four bands of rather thin iron, with a sheet or parchment glued underneath, or more usually a piece of silk flattened onto the four sides of the chassis. It is fitted into the large *tympan*, to which it is attached at the top by two thin, pointed nails, which penetrate between the wood and the silk, at the bottom by a hook, and at the sides by clasps. The platen falls directly onto the small tympan when it is lowered by the bar. The sheets of cloth (satin, or merino if a less dry impression is desired), the cardboard, and the carriage are inserted between the silk of the large and the small tympans. The *tympans* require careful maintenance, and must be renewed as soon as they have begun to deteriorate."

Will the multiplicity of these tympanums permit themselves to be analyzed? Will we be led back, at the exit of the labyrinths, toward some *topos* or commonplace named *tympanum?*

It may be about this multiplicity that philosophy, being situated, inscribed, and included within it, has never been able to reason. Doubtless, philosophy will have sought the reassuring and absolute rule, the norm of this polysemia. It will have asked itself if a tympanum is natural or constructed, if one does not always come back to the unity of a stretched, bordered, framed cloth that watches over its margins as virgin, homogenous, and negative space, leaving its outside outside, without mark, without opposition, without determination, and ready, like matter, the matrix, the *khōra*, to receive and repercuss type. This interpretation will have been *true*, the very history of the truth such as it is, in sum, recounted a bit in this book.

But certainly that which cannot be presented in the space of this truth, that which cannot lend itself to being heard or read, or being seen, even if in

but it could only be used for the cylinders of small or medium format, not for the large ones, such as those that could be heard on the other gramophone, which was fitted with bizarre accessories that tended to clutter up all the closets in the house, along with a vast series of 'rolls' (as we called the cylinders) that my father had recorded himself, and the still virgin wax rolls that had yet to be engraved.

When you wanted to listen to a roll of the medium format on the junior apparatus, which was freely available to me, you had to increase the size of the cylindrical motor; you obtained this result with the aid of a metal tube adapted to the motor, which could take only the smallest cylinders unless its diameter had been increased to the de-the "luminous triangle" or *oculus* of the tympanum, is that this thing, a tympanum, punctures itself or grafts itself. And *this*, however one writes it, resists the concepts of machine or of nature, of break or of body, resists the metaphysics of castration as well as its similar underside, the denegation of modern Rousseauisms, in their very academic vulgarity.

Will it be said, then, that what resists here is the unthought, the suppressed, the repressed of philosophy? In order no longer to be taken in, as one so often is today, by the confused equivalence of these three notions, a conceptual elaboration must introduce into them a new play of opposition, of articulation, of difference. An introduction, then, to *différance*. If there is a *here* of this book, let it be inscribed on these steps.

It has already begun, and all of this refers, cites, repercusses, propagates its rhythm without measure. But it remains entirely unforeseen: an incision into an organ made by a hand that is blind for never having seen anything but the here-and-there of a tissue.

What is then woven does not play the game of tight succession. Rather, it plays on succession. Do not forget that to weave (*tramer, trameare*) is first to make holes, to traverse, to work one-side-and-the-other of the warp. The canal of the ear, what is called the auditory meatus, no longer closes after being struck by a simulated succession, a secondary phrase, the echo and logical articulation of a sound that has not yet been received, already an effect of that which does not take place. "Hollow time, / a kind of exhausting void between the blades of cutting / wood, / nothingness calling man's trunk / the body taken as man's trunk," such is the "tympanon" of the Tarahumaras.

sired proportions by means of the addition just described. Linked to the horn‡ by a short rubber tube analogous to the joints of gas ovens and of a brick-reddish color, a diaphragm of the type ordinarily called "sapphire"—a small round box with a bottom made of a thin sheet of mica or some analogous material which bore the tiny hard appendix that was supposed to transmit the vibrations inscribed in the wax cylinder to the sensitive membrane—a diaphragm which, when taken apart, could fit in toto in the palm of your hand, did its best to transform into sound waves the oscillations communicated to by the roll, which seemed to be marked all over its surface (in a helicoid too tight

‡I.e. the bell-shaped horn, in French *pavillon*. See above, note 6, translator's interpolation.

This already enervated repercussion, of a kind that has not yet sounded, this timbered time between writing and speech, call for/themselves a *coup de donc.*

As soon as it perforates, one is dying to replace it by some glorious cadaver. It suffices, in sum, barely, to wait.

Prinsengracht, eight–twelve May 1972

to show anything other than the narrow, dense stripes) by the furrow of varying depth that the original waves had dug into it."

Michel Leiris§

§ Michel Leiris, *Biffures* (Paris: Gallimard), pp. 85ff.

Différance

Address given before the Société française de philosophie, 27 January 1968, published simultaneously in the *Bulletin de la société française de philosophie*, July–September 1968, and in *Théorie d'ensemble*, coll. Tel Quel (Paris: Editions du Seuil, 1968).

1

I will speak, therefore, of a letter.

Of the first letter, if the alphabet, and most of the speculations which have ventured into it, are to be believed.

I will speak, therefore, of the letter *a*, this initial letter which it apparently has been necessary to insinuate, here and there, into the writing of the word *difference*; and to do so in the course of a writing on writing, and also of a writing within writing whose different trajectories thereby find themselves, at certain very determined points, intersecting with a kind of gross spelling mistake, a lapse in the discipline and law which regulate writing and keep it seemly. One can always, de facto or de jure, erase or reduce this lapse in spelling, and find it (according to situations to be analyzed each time, although amounting to the same), grave or unseemly, that is, to follow the most ingenuous hypothesis, amusing. Thus, even if one seeks to pass over such an infraction in silence, the interest that one takes in it can be recognized and situated in advance as prescribed by the mute irony, the inaudible misplacement, of this literal permutation. One can always act as if it made no difference. And I must state here and now that today's discourse will be less a justification of, and even less an apology for, this silent lapse in spelling, than a kind of insistent intensification of its play.

On the other hand, I will have to be excused if I refer, at least implicitly, to some of the texts I have ventured to publish. This is precisely because I would like to attempt, to a certain extent, and even though in principle and in the last analysis this is impossible, and impossible for essential reasons, to reassemble in a *sheaf* the different directions in which I have been able to utilize what I would call provisionally the word or concept of *différance*, or rather to let it impose itself upon me in its neographism, although as we shall see, *différance* is literally neither a word nor a concept. And I insist upon the word *sheaf* for two reasons. On the one hand, I will not be concerned, as I might have been, with describing a history and narrating its stages, text by text, context by context, demonstrating the economy that each time imposed this graphic disorder; rather, I will be concerned with the *general system of this economy*. On the other hand, the word *sheaf* seems to mark more appropriately that the assemblage to be proposed has the complex structure of a weaving, an interlacing which permits the different threads and different lines of meaning—or of force—to go off again in different directions, just as it is always ready to tie itself up with others.

Therefore, preliminarily, let me recall that this discreet graphic intervention, which neither primarily nor simply aims to shock the reader or the grammarian, came to be formulated in the course of a written investigation of a question about writing. Now it happens, I would say in effect, that this graphic difference (*a* instead of *e*), this marked difference between two apparently vocal notations, between two vowels, remains purely graphic: it is read, or it is written, but it cannot be heard. It cannot be apprehended in speech, and we will see why it also bypasses the order of apprehension in general. It is offered by a mute mark, by a tacit monument, I would even say by a pyramid, thinking not only of the form of the letter when it is printed as a capital, but also of the text in Hegel's *Encyclopedia* in which the body of the sign is compared to the Egyptian Pyramid. The *a* of *différance*, thus, is not heard; it remains silent, secret and discreet as a tomb: *oikēsis*. And thereby let us anticipate the delineation of a site, the familial residence and tomb of the proper[1] in which is produced, by *différance*, the *economy of death*. This stone—provided that one knows how to decipher its inscription— is not far from announcing the death of the tyrant.[2]

And it is a tomb that cannot even be made to resonate. In effect, I cannot let you know through my discourse, through the speech being addressed at this moment to the French Society of Philosophy, what difference I am talking about when I talk about it. I can speak of this graphic difference only through a very indirect discourse on writing, and on the condition that I specify, each time, whether I am referring to difference with an *e* or *différance* with an *a*. Which will not simplify things today, and will give us all, you and me, a great deal of trouble, if, at least, we wish to understand each other. In any event, the oral specifications that I will provide—when I say "with an *e*" or "with an *a*"—will refer uncircumventably to a *written text* that keeps watch over my discourse, to a text that I am holding in front of me, that I will read, and toward which I necessarily will attempt to direct your hands and your eyes. We will be able neither to do without the passage through a written text, nor to avoid the order of the disorder produced within it—and this, first of all, is what counts for me.

The pyramidal silence of the graphic difference between the *e* and the *a* can function, of course, only within the system of phonetic writing, and within the language and grammar which is as historically linked to phonetic writing as it is to the entire culture inseparable from phonetic writing. But I would say that this in itself—the silence that functions within only a so-called phonetic writing—

1. TN. Throughout this book I will translate *le propre* as "the proper." Derrida most often intends all the senses of the word at once: that which is correct, as in *le sens propre* (proper, literal meaning), and that which is one's own, that which may be owned, that which is legally, correctly owned—all the links between proper, property, and propriety.
2. TN. The last three sentences refer elliptically and playfully to the following ideas. Derrida first plays on the "silence" of the *a* in *différance* as being like a silent tomb, like a pyramid, like the pyramid to which Hegel compares the body of the sign. "Tomb" in Greek is *oikēsis*, which is akin to the Greek *oikos*—house—from which the word "economy" derives (*oikos*—house—and *nemein*—to manage). Thus Derrida speaks of the "economy of death" as the "familial residence and tomb of the proper." Further, and more elliptically still, Derrida speaks of the tomb, which always bears an inscription in stone, announcing the death of the tyrant. This seems to refer to Hegel's treatment of the Antigone story in the *Phenomenology*. It will be recalled that Antigone defies the tyrant Creon by burying her brother Polynices. Creon retaliates by having Antigone entombed. There she cheats the slow death that awaits her by hanging herself. The tyrant Creon has a change of heart too late, and—after the suicides of his son and wife, his *family*—kills himself. Thus family, death, inscription, tomb, law, economy. In a later work, *Glas*, Derrida analyzes Hegel's treatment of the *Antigone*.

quite opportunely conveys or reminds us that, contrary to a very widespread prejudice, there is no phonetic writing. There is no purely and rigorously phonetic writing. So-called phonetic writing, by all rights and in principle, and not only due to an empirical or technical insufficiency, can function only by admitting into its system nonphonetic "signs" (punctuation, spacing, etc.). And an examination of the structure and necessity of these nonphonetic signs quickly reveals that they can barely tolerate the concept of the sign itself. Better, the play of difference, which, as Saussure reminded us, is the condition for the possibility and functioning of every sign, is in itself a silent play. Inaudible is the difference between two phonemes which alone permits them to be and to operate as such. The inaudible opens up the apprehension of two present phonemes such as they present themselves. If there is no purely phonetic writing, it is that there is no purely phonetic *phōnē*. The difference which establishes phonemes and lets them be heard remains in and of itself inaudible, in every sense of the word.

It will be objected, for the same reasons, that graphic difference itself vanishes into the night, can never be sensed as a full term, but rather extends an invisible relationship, the mark of an inapparent relationship between two spectacles. Doubtless. But, from this point of view, that the difference marked in the "differ( )nce" between the *e* and the *a* eludes both vision and hearing perhaps happily suggests that here we must be permitted to refer to an order which no longer belongs to sensibility. But neither can it belong to intelligibility, to the ideality which is not fortuitously affiliated with the objectivity of *theōrein* or understanding.[3] Here, therefore, we must let outselves refer to an order that resists the opposition, one of the founding oppositions of philosophy, between the sensible and the intelligible. The order which resists this opposition, and resists it because it transports it, is announced in a movement of *différance* (with an *a*) between two differences or two letters, a *différance* which belongs neither to the voice nor to writing in the usual sense, and which is located, as the strange space that will keep us together here for an hour, *between* speech and writing, and beyond the tranquil familiarity which links us to one and the other, occasionally reassuring us in our illusion that they are two.

What am I to do in order to speak of the *a* of *différance?* It goes without saying that it cannot be *exposed.* One can expose only that which at a certain moment can become *present,* manifest, that which can be shown, presented as something

---

3. TN. ". . . not fortuitously affiliated with the objectivity of *theōrein* or understanding." A play on words has been lost in translation here, a loss that makes this sentence difficult to understand. In the previous sentence Derrida says that the difference between the *e* and the *a* of *différence/différance* can neither be seen nor heard. It is not a sensible—that is, relating to the senses—difference. But, he goes on to explain, neither is this an intelligible difference, for the very names by which we conceive of objective intelligibility are already in complicity with sensibility. *Theōrein*—the Greek origin of "theory"—literally means "to look at," to *see;* and the word Derrida uses for "understanding" here is *entendement,* the noun form of *entendre,* to *hear.*

present, a being-present[4] in its truth, in the truth of a present or the presence of the present. Now if *différance* ̶i̶s̶ (and I also cross out the "̶i̶s̶") what makes possible the presentation of the being-present, it is never presented as such. It is never offered to the present. Or to anyone. Reserving itself, not exposing itself, in regular fashion it exceeds the order of truth at a certain precise point, but without dissimulating itself as something, as a mysterious being, in the occult of a nonknowledge or in a hole with indeterminable borders (for example, in a topology of castration).[5] In every exposition it would be exposed to disappearing as disappearance. It would risk appearing: disappearing.

So much so that the detours, locutions, and syntax in which I will often have to take recourse will resemble those of negative theology, occasionally even to the point of being indistinguishable from negative theology. Already we have had to delineate that *différance is not*, does not exist, is not a present-being (*on*) in any form; and we will be led to delineate also everything *that* it *is not*, that is, *everything;* and consequently that it has neither existence nor essence. It derives from no category of being, whether present or absent. And yet those aspects of *différance* which are thereby delineated are not theological, not even in the order of the most negative of negative theologies, which are always concerned with disengaging a superessentiality beyond the finite categories of essence and existence, that is, of presence, and always hastening to recall that God is refused the predicate of existence, only in order to acknowledge his superior, inconceivable, and ineffable mode of being. Such a development is not in question here, and this will be confirmed progressively. *Différance* is not only irreducible to any ontological or theological—ontotheological—reappropriation, but as the very opening of the space in which ontotheology—philosophy— produces its system and its history, it includes ontotheology, inscribing it and exceeding it without return.

For the same reason there is nowhere to *begin* to trace the sheaf or the graphics of *différance*. For what is put into question is precisely the quest for a rightful beginning, an absolute point of departure, a principal responsibility. The problematic of writing is opened by putting into question the value *arkhē*.[6] What I

4. TN. As in the past, *être* (*Sein*) will be translated as Being. *Etant* (*Seiendes*) will be either beings or being, depending on the context. Thus, here *étant-présent* is "being-present." For a justification of this translation see Derrida, *Writing and Difference*, trans. Alan Bass (Chicago: University of Chicago Press, 1978), Translator's Introduction, p. xvii.

5. TN. ". . . a hole with indeterminable borders (for example, in a topology of castration)." This phrase was added to "La Différance" for its publication in the French edition of this volume and refers to the polemic Derrida had already engaged (in *Positions;* elaborated further in *le Facteur de la vérité*) with Jacques Lacan. For Derrida, Lacan's "topology of castration," which assigns the "hole" or lack to a place—"a hole with determinable borders"—repeats the metaphysical gesture (albeit a negative one) of making absence, the lack, the hole, a transcendental principle that can be pinned down as such, and can thereby *govern* a theoretical discourse.

6. TN. The Greek *arkhē* combines the values of a founding principle and of government by a controlling principle (e.g. *arche*ology, mon*archy*).

will propose here will not be elaborated simply as a philosophical discourse, operating according to principles, postulates, axioms or definitions, and proceeding along the discursive lines of a linear order of reasons. In the delineation of *différance* everything is strategic and adventurous. Strategic because no transcendent truth present outside the field of writing can govern theologically the totality of the field. Adventurous because this strategy is not a simple strategy in the sense that strategy orients tactics according to a final goal, a *telos* or theme of domination, a mastery and ultimate reappropriation of the development of the field. Finally, a strategy without finality, what might be called blind tactics, or empirical wandering if the value of empiricism did not itself acquire its entire meaning in its opposition to philosophical responsibility. If there is a certain wandering in the tracing of *différance*, it no more follows the lines of philosophical-logical discourse than that of its symmetrical and integral inverse, empirical-logical discourse. The concept of *play* keeps itself beyond this opposition, announcing, on the eve of philosophy and beyond it, the unity of chance and necessity in calculations without end.

Also, by decision and as a rule of the game, if you will, turning these propositions back on themselves, we will be introduced to the thought of *différance* by the theme of strategy or the strategem. By means of this solely strategic justification, I wish to underline that the efficacity of the thematic of *différance* may very well, indeed must, one day be superseded, lending itself if not to its own replacement, at least to enmeshing itself in a chain that in truth it never will have governed. Whereby, once again, it is not theological.

I would say, first off, that *différance*, which is neither a word nor a concept, strategically seemed to me the most proper one to think, if not to master— thought, here, being that which is maintained in a certain necessary relationship with the structural limits of mastery—what is most irreducible about our "era." Therefore I am starting, strategically, from the place and the time in which "we" are, even though in the last analysis my opening is not justifiable, since it is only on the basis of *différance* and its "history" that we can allegedly know who and where "we" are, and what the limits of an "era" might be.

Even though *différance* is neither a word nor a concept, let us nevertheless attempt a simple and approximate semantic analysis that will take us to within sight of what is at stake.

We know that the verb *différer* (Latin verb *differre*) has two meanings which seem quite distinct;[7] for example in Littré they are the object of two separate articles. In this sense the Latin *differre* is not simply a translation of the Greek *diapherein*, and this will not be without consequences for us, linking our discourse to a particular language, and to a language that passes as less philosophical, less originally philosophical than the other. For the distribution of meaning in

---

7. TN. In English the two distinct meanings of the Latin *differre* have become two separate words: to defer and to differ.

7

the Greek *diapherein* does not comport one of the two motifs of the Latin *differre*, to wit, the action of putting off until later, of taking into account, of taking account of time and of the forces of an operation that implies an economical calculation, a detour, a delay, a relay, a reserve, a representation—concepts that I would summarize here in a word I have never used but that could be inscribed in this chain: *temporization*. *Différer* in this sense is to temporize, to take recourse, consciously or unconsciously, in the temporal and temporizing mediation of a detour that suspends the accomplishment or fulfillment of "desire" or "will," and equally effects this suspension in a mode that annuls or tempers its own effect. And we will see, later, how this temporization is also temporalization and spacing, the becoming-time of space and the becoming-space of time, the "originary constitution" of time and space, as metaphysics or transcendental phenomenology would say, to use the language that here is criticized and displaced.

The other sense of *différer* is the more common and identifiable one: to be not identical, to be other, discernible, etc. When dealing with *differen(ts)(ds)*, a word that can be written with a final *ts* or a final *ds*, as you will, whether it is a question of dissimilar otherness or of allergic and polemical otherness, an interval, a distance, *spacing*, must be produced between the elements other, and be produced with a certain perseverence in repetition.[8]

Now the word *différence* (with an *e*) can never refer either to *différer* as temporization or to *différends* as *polemos*.[9] Thus the word *différance* (with an *a*) is to compensate—economically—this loss of meaning, for *différance* can refer simultaneously to the entire configuration of its meanings. It is immediately and irreducibly polysemic, which will not be indifferent to the economy of my discourse here. In its polysemia this word, of course, like any meaning, must defer to the discourse in which it occurs, its interpretive context; but in a way it defers itself, or at least does so more readily than any other word, the *a* immediately deriving from the present participle (*différant*), thereby bringing us close to the very action of the verb *différer*, before it has even produced an effect constituted as something different or as *différence* (with an *e*).[10] In a conceptuality adhering

8. TN. The next few sentences will require some annotation, to be found in this note and the next two. In this sentence Derrida is pointing out that two words that sound exactly alike in French (*différents, différends*) refer to the sense of *differre* that implies spacing, otherness—difference in its usual English sense. *Les différents* are different things; *les différends* are differences of opinion, grounds for dispute—whence the references to allergy (from the Greek *allos*, other) and polemics.

9. TN. However, to continue the last note, *différence* (in French) does not convey the sense of active putting off, of deferring (*différance* in what would be its usual sense in French, if it were a word in common usage), or the sense of active polemical difference, actively differing with someone or something. ("Active" here, though, is not really correct, for reasons that Derrida will explain below.) The point is that there is no noun-verb, no gerund for either sense in French.

10. TN. Such a gerund would normally be constructed from the present participle of the verb: *différant*. Curiously then, the noun *différance* suspends itself between the two senses of *différant*—deferring, differing. We might say that it defers differing, and differs from deferring, in and of itself.

8

to classical strictures "*différance*" would be said to designate a constitutive, productive, and originary causality, the process of scission and division which would
produce or constitute different things or differences. But, because it brings us
close to the infinitive and active kernel of *différer, différance* (with an *a*) neutralizes
what the infinitive denotes as simply active, just as *mouvance* in our language
does not simply mean the fact of moving, of moving oneself or of being moved.
No more is resonance the act of resonating. We must consider that in the usage
of our language the ending *-ance* remains undecided *between* the active and the
passive. And we will see why that which lets itself be designated *différance* is
neither simply active nor simply passive, announcing or rather recalling something like the middle voice, saying an operation that is not an operation, an
operation that cannot be conceived either as passion or as the action of a subject
on an object, or on the basis of the categories of agent or patient, neither on the
basis of nor moving toward any of these *terms*. For the middle voice, a certain
nontransitivity, may be what philosophy, at its outset, distributed into an active
and a passive voice, thereby constituting itself by means of this repression.

Différance as temporization, *différance* as spacing. How are they to be joined?
Let us start, since we are already there, from the problematic of the sign and
of writing. The sign is usually said to be put in the place of the thing itself, the
present thing, "thing" here standing equally for meaning or referent. The sign
represents the present in its absence. It takes the place of the present. When we
cannot grasp or show the thing, state the present, the being-present, when the
present cannot be presented, we signify, we go through the detour of the sign.
We take or give signs. We signal. The sign, in this sense, is deferred presence.
Whether we are concerned with the verbal or the written sign, with the monetary
sign, or with electoral delegation and political representation, the circulation of
signs defers the moment in which we can encounter the thing itself, make it
ours, consume or expend it, touch it, see it, intuit its presence. What I am
describing here in order to define it is the classically determined structure of the
sign in all the banality of its characteristics—signification as the *différance* of
temporization. And this structure presupposes that the sign, which defers presence, is conceivable only on the *basis* of the presence that it defers and *moving
toward* the deferred presence that it aims to reappropriate. According to this
classical semiology, the substitution of the sign for the thing itself is both *secondary*
and *provisional:* secondary due to an original and lost presence from which the
sign thus derives; provisional as concerns this final and missing presence toward
which the sign in this sense is a movement of mediation.

In attempting to put into question these traits of the provisional secondariness
of the substitute, one would come to see something like an originary 'différance;
but one could no longer call it originary or final in the extent to which the values
of origin, archi-, *telos, eskhaton,* etc. have always denoted presence—*ousia, parousia.*[11] To put into question the secondary and provisional characteristics of the

11. TN. *Ousia* and *parousia* imply presence as both origin and end, the founding principle
(*arkhē-*) as that toward which one moves (*telos, eskhaton*).

9

sign, to oppose to them an "originary" *différance*, therefore would have two consequences.

1. One could no longer include *différance* in the concept of the sign, which always has meant the representation of a presence, and has been constituted in a system (thought or language) governed by and moving toward presence.

2. And thereby one puts into question the authority of presence, or of its simple symmetrical opposite, absence or lack. Thus one questions the limit which has always constrained us, which still constrains us—as inhabitants of a language and a system of thought—to formulate the meaning of Being in general as presence or absence, in the categories of being or beingness (*ousia*). Already it appears that the type of question to which we are redirected is, let us say, of the Heideggerian type, and that *différance seems* to lead back to the ontico-ontological difference. I will be permitted to hold off on this reference. I will note only that between difference as temporization-temporalization, which can no longer be conceived within the horizon of the present, and what Heidegger says in *Being and Time* about temporalization as the transcendental horizon of the question of Being, which must be liberated from its traditional, metaphysical domination by the present and the now, there is a strict communication, even though not an exhaustive and irreducibly necessary one.

But first let us remain within the semiological problematic in order to see *différance* as temporization and *différance* as spacing conjoined. Most of the semiological or linguistic researches that dominate the field of thought today, whether due to their own results or to the regulatory model that they find themselves acknowledging everywhere, refer genealogically to Saussure (correctly or incorrectly) as their common inaugurator. Now Saussure first of all is the thinker who put the *arbitrary character of the sign* and the *differential character* of the sign at the very foundation of general semiology, particularly linguistics. And, as we know, these two motifs—arbitrary and differential—are inseparable in his view. There can be arbitrariness only because the system of signs is constituted solely by the differences in terms, and not by their plenitude. The elements of signification function due not to the compact force of their nuclei but rather to the network of oppositions that distinguishes them, and then relates them one to another. "Arbitrary and differential," says Saussure, "are two correlative characteristics."

Now this principle of difference, as the condition for signification, affects the *totality* of the sign, that is the sign as both signified and signifier. The signified is the concept, the ideal meaning; and the signifier is what Saussure calls the "image," the "psychical imprint" of a material, physical—for example, acoustical—phenomenon. We do not have to go into all the problems posed by these definitions here. Let us cite Saussure only at the point which interests us: "The conceptual side of value is made up solely of relations and differences with respect to the other terms of language, and the same can be said of its material side . . . Everything that has been said up to this point boils down to this: in

language there are only differences. Even more important: a difference generally implies positive terms between which the difference is set up; but in language there are only differences *without positive terms*. Whether we take the signified or the signifier, language has neither ideas nor sounds that existed before the linguistic system, but only conceptual and phonic differences that have issued from the system. The idea or phonic substance that a sign contains is of less importance than the other signs that surround it."[12]

The first consequence to be drawn from this is that the signified concept is never present in and of itself, in a sufficient presence that would refer only to itself. Essentially and lawfully, every concept is inscribed in a chain or in a system within which it refers to the other, to other concepts, by means of the systematic play of differences. Such a play, *différance*, is thus no longer simply a concept, but rather the possibility of conceptuality, of a conceptual process and system in general. For the same reason, *différance*, which is not a concept, is not simply a word, that is, what is generally represented as the calm, present, and self-referential unity of concept and phonic material. Later we will look into the word in general.

The difference of which Saussure speaks is itself, therefore, neither a concept nor a word among others. The same can be said, a fortiori, of *différance*. And we are thereby led to explicate the relation of one to the other.

In a language, in the *system* of language, there are only differences. Therefore a taxonomical operation can undertake the systematic, statistical, and classificatory inventory of a language. But, on the one hand, these differences *play*: in language, in speech too, and in the exchange between language and speech. On the other hand, these differences are themselves *effects*. They have not fallen from the sky fully formed, and are no more inscribed in a *topos noētos*, than they are prescribed in the gray matter of the brain. If the word "history" did not in and of itself convey the motif of a final repression of difference, one could say that only differences can be "historical" from the outset and in each of their aspects.

What is written as *différance*, then, will be the playing movement that "produces"—by means of something that is not simply an activity—these differences, these effects of difference. This does not mean that the *différance* that produces differences is somehow before them, in a simple and unmodified—in-different—present. *Différance* is the non-full, non-simple, structured and differentiating origin of differences. Thus, the name "origin" no longer suits it.

Since language, which Saussure says is a classification, has not fallen from the sky, its differences have been produced, are produced effects, but they are effects which do not find their cause in a subject or a substance, in a thing in general, a being that is somewhere present, thereby eluding the play of *différance*.

12. TN. Ferdinand de Saussure, *Course in General Linguistics*, trans. Wade Baskin (New York: Philosophical Library, 1959), pp. 117–18, 120.

If such a presence were implied in the concept of cause in general, in the most classical fashion, we then would have to speak of an effect without a cause, which very quickly would lead to speaking of no effect at all. I have attempted to indicate a way out of the closure of this framework via the "trace," which is no more an effect than it has a cause, but which in and of itself, outside its text, is not sufficient to operate the necessary transgression.

Since there is no presence before and outside semiological difference, what Saussure has written about language can be extended to the sign in general: "Language is necessary in order for speech to be intelligible and to produce all of its effects; but the latter is necessary in order for language to be established; historically, the fact of speech always comes first."[13]

Retaining at least the framework, if not the content, of this requirement formulated by Saussure, we will designate as *différance* the movement according to which language, or any code, any system of referral in general, is constituted "historically" as a weave of differences. "Is constituted," "is produced," "is created," "movement," "historically," etc., necessarily being understood beyond the metaphysical language in which they are retained, along with all their implications. We ought to demonstrate why concepts like *production*, constitution, and history remain in complicity with what is at issue here. But this would take me too far today—toward the theory of the representation of the "circle" in which we appear to be enclosed—and I utilize such concepts, like many others, only for their strategic convenience and in order to undertake their deconstruction at the currently most decisive point. In any event, it will be understood, by means of the circle in which we appear to be engaged, that as it is written here, *différance* is no more static than it is genetic, no more structural than historical. Or is no less so; and to object to this on the basis of the oldest of metaphysical oppositions (for example, by setting some generative point of view against a structural-taxonomical point of view, or vice versa) would be, above all, not to read what here is missing from orthographical ethics. Such oppositions have not the least pertinence to *différance*, which makes the thinking of it uneasy and uncomfortable.

Now if we consider the chain in which *différance* lends itself to a certain number of nonsynonymous substitutions, according to the necessity of the context, why have recourse to the "reserve," to "archi-writing," to the "archi-trace," to "spacing," that is, to the "supplement," or to the *pharmakon*, and soon to the hymen, to the margin-mark-march, etc.[14]

13. TN. Ibid., p. 18.
14. TN. All these terms refer to writing and inscribe *différance* within themselves, as Derrida says, according to the context. The supplement (*supplément*) is Rousseau's word to describe writing (analyzed in *Of Grammatology*, trans. Gayatri Spivak [Baltimore: Johns Hopkins University Press, 1976]). It means *both* the missing piece and the extra piece. The *pharmakon* is Plato's word for writing (analyzed in "Plato's Pharmacy" in *Dissemination*, trans. Barbara Johnson [Chicago: University of Chicago Press, 1981]), meaning *both* remedy and poison; the hymen (*l'hymen*) comes from Derrida's analysis of Mallarmé's writing and Mallarmé's reflections on writing ("The Double Session" in *Dissemination*) and refers *both* to virginity and to consummation; *marge-marque-marche* is the series *en différance* that Derrida applies to Sollers's *Nombres* ("Dissemination" in *Dissemination*).

12

Let us go on. It is because of *différance* that the movement of signification is possible only if each so-called "present" element, each element appearing on the scene of presence, is related to something other than itself, thereby keeping within itself the mark of the past element, and already letting itself be vitiated by the mark of its relation to the future element, this trace being related no less to what is called the future than to what is called the past, and constituting what is called the present by means of this very relation to what it is not: what it absolutely is not, not even a past or a future as a modified present. An interval must separate the present from what it is not in order for the present to be itself, but this interval that constitutes it as present must, by the same token, divide the present in and of itself, thereby also dividing, along with the present, everything that is thought on the basis of the present, that is, in our metaphysical language, every being, and singularly substance or the subject. In constituting itself, in dividing itself dynamically, this interval is what might be called *spacing*, the becoming-space of time or the becoming-time of space (*temporization*). And it is this constitution of the present, as an "originary" and irreducibly nonsimple (and therefore, *stricto sensu* nonoriginary) synthesis of marks, or traces of retentions and protentions (to reproduce analogically and provisionally a phenomenological and transcendental language that soon will reveal itself to be inadequate), that I propose to call archi-writing, archi-trace, or *différance*. Which (is) (simultaneously) spacing (and) temporization.

Could not this (active) movement of (the production of) *différance* without origin be called simply, and without neographism, *differentiation?* Such a word, among other confusions, would have left open the possibility of an organic, original, and homogeneous unity that eventually would come to be divided, to receive difference as an event. And above all, since it is formed from the verb "to differentiate," it would negate the economic signification of the detour, the temporizing delay, "deferral." Here, a remark in passing, which I owe to a recent reading of a text that Koyré (in 1934, in *Revue d'histoire et de philosophie réligieuse*, and reprinted in his *Etudes d'histoire de la pensée philosophique*) devoted to "Hegel in Jena." In this text Koyré gives long citations, in German, of the Jena *Logic*, and proposes their translation. On two occasions he encounters the expression *differente Beziehung* in Hegel's text. This word (*different*), with its Latin root, is rare in German and, I believe, in Hegel, who prefers *verschieden* or *ungleich*, calling difference *Unterschied* and qualitative variety *Verschiedenheit*. In the Jena *Logic* he uses the word *different* precisely where he treats of time and the present. Before getting to a valuable comment of Koyré's, let us look at some sentences from Hegel, such as Koyré translates them: "The infinite, in this simplicity, is, as a moment opposed to the equal-to-itself, the negative, and in its moments, although it is (itself) presented to and in itself the totality, (it is) what excludes in general, the point or limit; but in its own (action of) negating, it is related immediately to the other and negates itself by itself. The limit or moment of the present (*der Gegen-wart*), the absolute 'this' of time, or the now, is of an absolutely negative simplicity, which absolutely excludes from itself all multiplicity, and, by virtue of this, is absolutely determined; it is not whole or a *quantum* which would be extended in itself (and) which, in itself, also would have an undetermined moment, a diversity which, as indifferent (*gleichgultig*) or exterior in itself, would be related to an other (*auf ein anderes bezöge*), but in this is a relation absolutely different from the simple (*sondern es ist absolut differente Beziehung*)." And Koyré most remarkably specifies in a note: "different Relation: *differente Beziehung*. One might say: 'differentiating relation.' " And on the next page, another text of Hegel's in which one can read this: "*Diese Beziehung ist Gegenwart, als eine differente Beziehung* (This relationship is [the] present as a different relationship)." Another note of Koyré's: "The term *different* here is taken in an active sense."[15]

Writing "*différant*"[16] or "*différance*" (with an *a*) would have had the advantage of making it possible to translate Hegel at that particular point—which is also an absolutely decisive point in his discourse—without further notes or specifications. And the translation would be, as it always must be, a transformation of one language by another. I contend, of course, that the word *différance* can also serve other purposes: first, because it marks not only the activity of "originary" difference, but also the temporizing detour of deferral; and above all because *différance* thus written, although maintaining relations of profound affinity with Hegelian discourse (such as it must be read), is also, up to a certain point, unable to break with that discourse (which has no kind of meaning or chance); but it can operate a kind of infinitesimal and radical displacement of it, whose space I attempt to delineate elsewhere but of which it would be difficult to speak briefly here.

Differences, thus, are "produced"—deferred—by *différance*. But *what* defers or *who* defers? In other words, *what is différance*? With this question we reach another level and another resource of our problematic.

What differs? Who differs? What is *différance*?

If we answered these questions before examining them as questions, before turning them back on themselves, and before suspecting their very form, including what seems most natural and necessary about them, we would immediately fall back into what we have just disengaged ourselves from. In effect,

15. TN. Alexandre Koyré, "Hegel à Iena," in *Etudes d'histoire de la pensée philosophique* (Paris: Armand Colin, 1961), pp. 153–54. In his translation of "La différance" (in *Speech and Phenomena* [Evanston: Northwestern University Press, 1973]), David Allison notes (p. 144) that the citation from Hegel comes from "Jensener Logik, Metaphysik, und Naturphilosophie" in *Sämtliche Werke* (Leipzig: F. Meiner, 1925), XVIII, 202. Allison himself translated Hegel's text, and I have modified his translation.

16. TN. The point here, which cannot be conveyed in English, is that Koyré's realization that Hegel is describing a "differentiating relation," or "different" in an active sense, is precisely what the formation of *différance* from the participle *différant* describes, as explained in notes 9 and 10 above. And that it is the *present* that is described as differing from and deferring itself helps clarify Derrida's argument (at the end of the essay) that presence is to be rethought as the trace of the trace, as *différance* differed-and-deferred.

if we accepted the form of the question, in its meaning and its syntax ("what is?" "who is?" "who is it that?"), we would have to conclude that *différance* has been derived, has happened, is to be mastered and governed on the basis of the point of a present being, which itself could be some thing, a form, a state, a power in the world to which all kinds of names might be given, a *what*, or a present being as a *subject*, a *who*. And in this last case, notably, one would conclude implicitly that this present being, for example a being present to itself, as consciousness, eventually would come to defer or to differ: whether by delaying and turning away from the fulfillment of a "need" or a "desire," or by differing from itself. But in neither of these cases would such a present being be "constituted" by this *différance*.

Now if we refer, once again, to semiological difference, of what does Saussure, in particular, remind us? That "language [which only consists of differences] is not a function of the speaking subject." This implies that the subject (in its identity with itself, or eventually in its consciousness of its identity with itself, its self-consciousness) is inscribed in language, is a "function" of language, becomes a *speaking* subject only by making its speech conform—even in so-called "creation," or in so-called "transgression"—to the system of the rules of language as a system of differences, or at very least by conforming to the general law of *différance*, or by adhering to the principle of language which Saussure says is "spoken language minus speech." "Language is necessary for the spoken word to be intelligible and so that it can produce all of its effects."[17]

If, by hypothesis, we maintain that the opposition of speech to language is absolutely rigorous, then *différance* would be not only the play of differences within language but also the relation of speech to language, the detour through which I must pass in order to speak, the silent promise I must make; and this is equally valid for semiology in general, governing all the relations of usage to schemata, of message to code, etc. (Elsewhere I have attempted to suggest that this *différance* in language, and in the relation of speech and language, forbids the essential dissociation of speech and language that Saussure, at another level of his discourse, traditionally wished to delineate. The practice of a language or of a code supposing a play of forms without a determined and invariable substance, and also supposing in the practice of this play a retention and protention of differences, a spacing and a temporization, a play of traces—all this must be a kind of writing before the letter, an archi-writing without a present origin, without archi-. Whence the regular erasure of the archi-, and the transformation of general semiology into grammatology, this latter executing a critical labor on everything within semiology, including the central concept of the sign, that maintained metaphysical presuppositions incompatible with the motif of *différance*.)

17. TN. Saussure, *Course in General Linguistics*, p. 37.

One might be tempted by an objection: certainly the subject becomes a *speaking* subject only in its commerce with the system of linguistic differences; or yet, the subject becomes a *signifying* (signifying in general, by means of speech or any other sign) subject only by inscribing itself in the system of differences. Certainly in this sense the speaking or signifying subject could not be present to itself, as speaking or signifying, without the play of linguistic or semiological *différance*. But can one not conceive of a presence, and of a presence to itself of the subject before speech or signs, a presence to itself of the subject in a silent and intuitive consciousness?

Such a question therefore supposes that, prior to the sign and outside it, excluding any trace and any *différance*, something like consciousness is possible. And that consciousness, before distributing its signs in space and in the world, can gather itself into its presence. But what is consciousness? What does "consciousness" mean? Most often, in the very form of meaning, in all its modifications, consciousness offers itself to thought only as self-presence, as the perception of self in presence. And what holds for consciousness holds here for so-called subjective existence in general. Just as the category of the subject cannot be, and never has been, thought without the reference to presence as *hupokeimenon* or as *ousia*, etc., so the subject as consciousness has never manifested itself except as self-presence. The privilege granted to consciousness therefore signifies the privilege granted to the present; and even if one describes the transcendental temporality of consciousness, and at the depth at which Husserl does so, one grants to the "living present" the power of synthesizing traces, and of incessantly reassembling them.

This privilege is the ether of metaphysics, the element of our thought that is caught in the language of metaphysics. One can delimit such a closure today only by soliciting[18] the value of presence that Heidegger has shown to be the ontotheological determination of Being; and in thus soliciting the value of presence, by means of an interrogation whose status must be completely exceptional, we are also examining the absolute privilege of this form or epoch of presence in general that is consciousness as meaning[19] in self-presence.

Thus one comes to posit presence—and specifically consciousness, the being beside itself of consciousness—no longer as the absolutely central form of Being but as a "determination" and as an "effect." A determination or an effect within a system which is no longer that of presence but of *différance*, a system that no longer tolerates the opposition of activity and passivity, nor that of cause and effect, or of indetermination and determination, etc., such that in designating

18. TN. The French *solliciter*, as the English *solicit*, derives from an Old Latin expression meaning to shake the whole, to make something tremble in its entirety. Derrida comments on this later, but is already using "to solicit" in this sense here.

19. TN. "Meaning" here is the weak translation of *vouloir-dire*, which has a strong sense of willing (*voluntas*) to say, putting the attempt to mean in conjunction with speech, a crucial conjunction for Derrida.

consciousness as an effect or a determination, one continues—for strategic reasons that can be more or less lucidly deliberated and systematically calculated—to operate according to the lexicon of that which one is de-limiting.

Before being so radically and purposely the gesture of Heidegger, this gesture was also made by Nietzsche and Freud, both of whom, as is well known, and sometimes in very similar fashion, put consciousness into question in its assured certainty of itself. Now is it not remarkable that they both did so on the basis of the motif of *différance?*

Différance appears almost by name in their texts, and in those places where everything is at stake. I cannot expand upon this here; I will only recall that for Nietzsche "the great principal activity is unconscious," and that consciousness is the effect of forces whose essence, byways, and modalities are not proper to it. Force itself is never present; it is only a play of differences and quantities. There would be no force in general without the difference between forces; and here the difference of quantity counts more than the content of the quantity, more than absolute size itself. "Quantity itself, therefore, is not separable from the difference of quantity. The difference of quantity is the essence of force, the relation of force to force. The dream of two equal forces, even if they are granted an opposition of meaning, is an approximate and crude dream, a statistical dream, plunged into by the living but dispelled by chemistry."[20] Is not all of Nietzsche's thought a critique of philosophy as an active indifference to difference, as the system of adiaphoristic reduction or repression? Which according to the same logic, according to logic itself, does not exclude that philosophy lives *in* and *on différance*, thereby blinding itself to the *same*, which is not the identical. The same, precisely, is *différance* (with an *a*) as the displaced and equivocal passage of one different thing to another, from one term of an opposition to the other. Thus one could reconsider all the pairs of opposites on which philosophy is constructed and on which our discourse lives, not in order to see opposition erase itself but to see what indicates that each of the terms must appear as the *différance* of the other, as the other different and deferred in the economy of the same (the intelligible as differing-deferring the sensible, as the sensible different and deferred; the concept as different and deferred, differing-deferring intuition; culture as nature different and deferred, differing-deferring; all the others of *physis*—*tekhnē, nomos, thesis,* society, freedom, history, mind, etc.—as *physis* different and deferred, or as *physis* differing and deferring. *Physis* in *différance.* And in this we may see the site of a reinterpretation of *mimēsis* in its alleged opposition to *physis*). And on the basis of this unfolding of the same as *différance,* we see announced the sameness of *différance* and repetition in the eternal return. Themes in Nietzsche's work that are linked to the symptomatology that always diagnoses the detour or ruse of an agency disguised in

20. Gilles Deleuze, *Nietzsche et la philosophie* (Paris: Presses Universitaires de France, 1970), p. 49.

its *différance;* or further, to the entire thematic of active interpretation, which substitutes incessant deciphering for the unveiling of truth as the presentation of the thing itself in its presence, etc. Figures without truth, or at least a system of figures not dominated by the value of truth, which then becomes only an included, inscribed, circumscribed function.

Thus, *différance* is the name we might give to the "active," moving discord of different forces, and of differences of forces, that Nietzsche sets up against the entire system of metaphysical grammar, wherever this system governs culture, philosophy, and science.

It is historically significant that this diaphoristics, which, as an energetics or economics of forces, commits itself to putting into question the primacy of presence as consciousness, is also the major motif of Freud's thought: another diaphoristics, which in its entirety is both a theory of the figure (or of the trace) and an energetics. The putting into question of the authority of consciousness is first and always differential.

The two apparently different values of *différance* are tied together in Freudian theory: to differ as discernibility, distinction, separation, diastem, *spacing;* and to defer as detour, relay, reserve, *temporization.*

1. The concepts of trace (*Spur*), of breaching (*Bahnung*),[21] and of the forces of breaching, from the *Project* on, are inseparable from the concept of difference. The origin of memory, and of the psyche as (conscious or unconscious) memory in general, can be described only by taking into account the difference between breaches. Freud says so overtly. There is no breach without difference and no difference without trace.

2. All the differences in the production of unconscious traces and in the processes of inscription (*Niederschrift*) can also be interpreted as moments of *différance,* in the sense of putting into reserve. According to a schema that never ceased to guide Freud's thought, the movement of the trace is described as an effort of life to protect itself by *deferring* the dangerous investment, by constituting a reserve (*Vorrat*). And all the oppositions that furrow Freudian thought relate each of his concepts one to another as moments of a detour in the economy of *différance.* One is but the other different and deferred, one differing and deferring the other. One is the other in *différance,* one is the *différance* of the other. This is why every apparently rigorous and irreducible *opposition* (for example the opposition of the secondary to the primary) comes to be qualified, at one moment or another, as a "theoretical fiction." Again, it is thereby, for example (but such an example governs, and communicates with, everything),

21. TN. Derrida is referring here to his essay "Freud and the Scene of Writing" in *Writing and Difference.* "Breaching" is the translation for *Bahnung* that I adopted there: it conveys more of the sense of breaking open (as in the German *Bahnung* and the French *frayage*) than the Standard Edition's "facilitation." The *Project* Derrida refers to here is the *Project for a Scientific Psychology* (1895), in which Freud attempted to cast his psychological thinking in a neurological framework.

that the difference between the pleasure principle and the reality principle is only *différance* as detour. In *Beyond the Pleasure Principle* Freud writes: "Under the influence of the ego's instincts of self-preservation, the pleasure principle is replaced by the reality principle. This latter principle does not abandon the intention of ultimately obtaining pleasure, but it nevertheless demands and carries into effect the postponement of satisfaction, the abandonment of a number of possibilities of gaining satisfaction and the temporary toleration of unpleasure as a step on the long indirect road (*Aufschub*) to pleasure."[22]

Here we are touching upon the point of greatest obscurity, on the very enigma of *différance*, on precisely that which divides its very concept by means of a strange cleavage. We must not hasten to decide. How are we to think *simultaneously*, on the one hand, *différance* as the economic detour which, in the element of the same, always aims at coming back to the pleasure or the presence that have been deferred by (conscious or unconscious) calculation, and, on the other hand, *différance* as the relation to an impossible presence, as expenditure without reserve, as the irreparable loss of presence, the irreversible usage of energy, that is, as the death instinct, and as the entirely other relationship that apparently interrupts every economy? It is evident—and this is the evident itself—that the economical and the noneconomical, the same and the entirely other, etc., cannot be thought *together*. If *différance* is unthinkable in this way, perhaps we should not hasten to make it evident, in the philosophical element of evidentiality which would make short work of dissipating the mirage and illogicalness of *différance* and would do so with the infallibility of calculations that we are well acquainted with, having precisely recognized their place, necessity, and function in the structure of *différance*. Elsewhere, in a reading of Bataille, I have attempted to indicate what might come of a rigorous and, in a new sense, "scientific" *relating* of the "restricted economy" that takes no part in expenditure without reserve, death, opening itself to nonmeaning, etc., to a general economy that *takes into account* the nonreserve, that keeps in reserve the nonreserve, if it can be put thus. I am speaking of a relationship between a *différance* that can make a profit on its investment and a *différance* that misses its profit, the *investiture* of a presence that is pure and without loss here being confused with absolute loss, with death. Through such a relating of a restricted and a general economy the very project of philosophy, under the privileged heading of Hegelianism, is displaced and reinscribed. The *Aufhebung—la relève*—is constrained into writing itself otherwise. Or perhaps simply into writing itself. Or, better, into taking account of its consumption of writing.[23]

22. TN. *The Standard Edition of the Complete Psychological Works* (London: Hogarth Press, 1950 [hereafter cited as *SE*]), vol. 18, p. 10.
23. TN. Derrida is referring here to the reading of Hegel he proposed in "From Restricted to General Economy: A Hegelianism Without Reserve," in *Writing and Difference*. In that essay Derrida began his consideration of Hegel as the great philosophical *speculator*; thus all the economic metaphors of the previous sentences. For Derrida the deconstruction of

For the economic character of *différance* in no way implies that the deferred presence can always be found again, that we have here only an investment that provisionally and calculatedly delays the perception of its profit or the profit of its perception. Contrary to the metaphysical, dialectical, "Hegelian" interpretation of the economic movement of *différance*, we must conceive of a play in which whoever loses wins, and in which one loses and wins on every turn. If the displaced presentation remains definitively and implacably postponed, it is not that a certain present remains absent or hidden. Rather, *différance* maintains our relationship with that which we necessarily misconstrue, and which exceeds the alternative of presence and absence. A certain alterity—to which Freud gives the metaphysical name of the unconscious—is definitively exempt from every process of presentation by means of which we would call upon it to show itself in person. In this context, and beneath this guise, the unconscious is not, as we know, a hidden, virtual, or potential self-presence. It differs from, and defers,

metaphysics implies an endless confrontation with Hegelian concepts, and the move from a restricted, "speculative" philosophical economy—in which there is nothing that cannot be made to make sense, in which there is nothing *other* than meaning—to a "general" economy—which affirms that which exceeds meaning, the excess of meaning from which there can be no speculative profit—involves a reinterpretation of the central Hegelian concept: the *Aufhebung*. *Aufhebung* literally means "lifting up"; but it also contains the double meaning of conservation and negation. For Hegel, dialectics is a process of *Aufhebung*: every concept is to be negated and lifted up to a higher sphere in which it is thereby conserved. In this way, there is nothing from which the *Aufhebung* cannot profit. However, as Derrida points out, there is always an effect of *différance* when the same word has two contradictory meanings. Indeed it is this effect of *différance*—the excess of the trace *Aufhebung* itself—that is precisely what the *Aufhebung* can never *aufheben:* lift up, conserve, and negate. This is why Derrida wishes to constrain the *Aufhebung* to write itself otherwise, or simply to write itself, to take into account its consumption of writing. Without writing, the trace, there could be no words with double, contradictory meanings.

As with *différance*, the translation of a word with a double meaning is particularly difficult, and touches upon the entire problematics of writing and *différance*. The best translators of Hegel usually cite Hegel's own delight that the most speculative of languages, German, should have provided this most speculative of words as the vehicle for his supreme speculative effort. Thus *Aufhebung* is usually best annotated and left untranslated. (Jean Hyppolite, in his French translations of Hegel, carefully annotates his rendering of *Aufheben* as both *supprimer* and *dépasser*. Baillie's rendering of *Aufhebung* as "sublation" is misleading.) Derrida, however, in his attempt to make *Aufhebung* write itself otherwise, has proposed a new translation of it that *does* take into account the effect of *différance* in its double meaning. Derrida's translation is *la relève*. The word comes from the verb *relever*, which means to lift up, as does *Aufheben*. But *relever* also means to relay, to relieve, as when one soldier on duty relieves another. Thus the conserving-and-negating lift has become *la relève*, a "lift" in which is inscribed an effect of substitution and difference, the effect of substitution and difference inscribed in the double meaning of *Aufhebung*. A. V. Miller's rendering of *Aufhebung* as "supersession" in his recent translation of the *Phenomenology* comes close to *relever* in combining the senses of raising up and replacement, although without the elegance of Derrida's maintenance of the verb meaning "to lift" (*heben, lever*) and change of prefix (*auf-, re-*). Thus we will leave *la relève* untranslated throughout, as with *différance*. For more on *la relève*, see below "*Ousia* and *Grammē*," note 15; "The Pit and the Pyramid," note 16; and "The Ends of Man," note 14.

itself; which doubtless means that it is woven of differences, and also that it sends out delegates, representatives, proxies; but without any chance that the giver of proxies might "exist," might be present, be "itself" somewhere, and with even less chance that it might become conscious. In this sense, contrary to the terms of an old debate full of the metaphysical investments that it has always assumed, the "unconscious" is no more a "thing" than it is any other thing, is no more a thing than it is a virtual or masked consciousness. This radical alterity as concerns every possible mode of presence is marked by the irreducibility of the aftereffect, the delay. In order to describe traces, in order to read the traces of "unconscious" traces (there are no "conscious" traces), the language of presence and absence, the metaphysical discourse of phenomenology, is inadequate. (Although the phenomenologist is not the only one to speak this language.)

The structure of delay (*Nachträglichkeit*) in effect forbids that one make of temporalization (temporization) a simple dialectical complication of the living present as an originary and unceasing synthesis—a synthesis constantly directed back on itself, gathered in on itself and gathering—of retentional traces and protentional openings. The alterity of the "unconscious" makes us concerned not with horizons of modified—past or future—presents, but with a "past" that has never been present, and which never will be, whose future to come will never be a *production* or a reproduction in the form of presence. Therefore the concept of trace is incompatible with the concept of retention, of the becoming-past of what has been present. One cannot think the trace—and therefore, *différance*—on the basis of the present, or of the presence of the present.

A past that has never been present: this formula is the one that Emmanuel Levinas uses, although certainly in a nonpsychoanalytic way, to qualify the trace and enigma of absolute alterity: the Other.[24] Within these limits, and from this point of view at least, the thought of *différance* implies the entire critique of classical ontology undertaken by Levinas. And the concept of the trace, like that of *différance* thereby organizes, along the lines of these different traces and differences of traces, in Nietzsche's sense, in Freud's sense, in Levinas's sense—these "names of authors" here being only indices—the network which reassembles and traverses our "era" as the delimitation of the ontology of presence.

Which is to say the ontology of beings and beingness. It is the domination of beings that *différance* everywhere comes to solicit, in the sense that *sollicitare*, in old Latin, means to shake as a whole, to make tremble in entirety. Therefore, it is the determination of Being as presence or as beingness that is interrogated by the thought of *différance*. Such a question could not emerge and be understood unless the difference between Being and beings were somewhere to be broached. First consequence: *différance* is not. It is not a present being, however excellent,

24. TN. On Levinas, and on the translation of his term *autrui* by "Other," see "Violence and Metaphysics," note 6, in *Writing and Difference*.

unique, principal, or transcendent. It governs nothing, reigns over nothing, and nowhere exercises any authority. It is not announced by any capital letter. Not only is there no kingdom of *différance*, but *différance* instigates the subversion of every kingdom. Which makes it obviously threatening and infallibly dreaded by everything within us that desires a kingdom, the past or future presence of a kingdom. And it is always in the name of a kingdom that one may reproach *différance* with wishing to reign, believing that one sees it aggrandize itself with a capital letter.

Can *différance*, for these reasons, settle down into the division of the ontico-ontological difference, such as it is thought, such as its "epoch" in particular is thought, "through," if it may still be expressed such, Heidegger's uncircumventable meditation?

There is no simple answer to such a question.

In a certain aspect of itself, *différance* is certainly but the historical and epochal *unfolding* of Being or of the ontological difference. The *a* of *différance* marks the *movement* of this unfolding.

And yet, are not the thought of the *meaning* or *truth* of Being, the determination of *différance* as the ontico-ontological difference, difference thought within the horizon of the question *of Being*, still intrametaphysical effects of *différance*? The unfolding of *différance* is perhaps not solely the truth of Being, or of the epochality of Being. Perhaps we must attempt to think this unheard-of thought, this silent tracing: that the history of Being, whose thought engages the Greco-Western *logos* such as it is produced via the ontological difference, is but an epoch of the *diapherein*. Henceforth one could no longer even call this an "epoch," the concept of epochality belonging to what is within history as the history of Being. Since Being has never had a "meaning," has never been thought or said as such, except by dissimulating itself in beings, then *différance*, in a certain and very strange way, (is) "older" than the ontological difference or than the truth of Being. When it has this age it can be called the play of the trace. The play of a trace which no longer belongs to the horizon of Being, but whose play transports and encloses the meaning of Being: the play of the trace, or the *différance*, which has no meaning and is not. Which does not belong. There is no maintaining, and no depth to, this bottomless chessboard on which Being is put into play.

Perhaps this is why the Heraclitean play of the *hen diapheron heautōi*, of the one differing from itself, the one in difference with itself, already is lost like a trace in the determination of the *diapherein* as ontological difference.

To think the ontological difference doubtless remains a difficult task, and any statement of it has remained almost inaudible. Further, to prepare, beyond our *logos*, for a *différance* so violent that it can be interpellated neither as the epochality of Being nor as ontological difference, is not in any way to dispense with the passage through the truth of Being, or to "criticize," "contest," or misconstrue its incessant necessity. On the contrary, we must stay within the difficulty of this passage, and repeat it in the rigorous reading of metaphysics, wherever metaphysics normalizes Western discourse, and not only in the texts of the "history of philosophy." As rigorously as possible we must permit to appear/disappear the trace of what exceeds the truth of Being. The trace (of that) which can never be presented, the trace which itself can never be presented: that is, appear and manifest itself, as such, in its phenomenon. The trace beyond that which profoundly links fundamental ontology and phenomenology. Always differing and deferring, the trace is never as it is in the presentation of itself. It erases itself in presenting itself, muffles itself in resonating, like the *a* writing itself, inscribing its pyramid in *différance*.

The annunciating and reserved trace of this movement can always be disclosed in metaphysical discourse, and especially in the contemporary discourse which states, through the attempts to which we just referred (Niètzsche, Freud, Levinas), the closure of ontology. And especially through the Heideggerean text.

This text prompts us to examine the essence of the present, the presence of the present.

What is the present? What is it to think the present in its presence?

Let us consider, for example, the 1946 text entitled *Der Spruch des Anaximander* ("The Anaximander Fragment").[25] In this text Heidegger recalls that the forgetting of Being forgets the difference between Being and beings: ". . . to be the Being *of* beings is the matter of Being (*die Sache des Seins*). The grammatical form of this enigmatic, ambiguous genitive indicates a genesis (*Genesis*), the emergence (*Herkunft*) of what is present from presencing (*des Anwesenden aus dem Anwesen*). Yet the essence (*Wesen*) of this emergence remains concealed (*verbogen*) along with the essence of these two words. Not only that, but even the very relation between presencing and what is present (*Anwesen und Anwesendem*) remains unthought. From early on it seems as though presencing and what is present were each something for itself. Presencing itself unnoticeably becomes something present . . . The essence of presencing (*Das Wesen des Anwesens*), and with it the distinction between presencing and what is present, remains forgotten. *The oblivion of Being is oblivion of the distinction between Being and beings*" (p. 50).

In recalling the difference between Being and beings (the ontological difference) as the difference between presence and the present, Heidegger advances a proposition, a body of propositions, that we are not going to use as a subject for criticism. This would be foolishly precipitate; rather, what we shall try to do is to return to this proposition its power to provoke.

Let us proceed slowly. What Heidegger wants to mark is this: the difference between Being and beings, the forgotten of metaphysics, has disappeared without leaving a trace. The very trace of difference has been submerged. If we maintain that *différance* (is) (itself) other than absence and presence, if it *traces*,

25. TN. Martin Heidegger, *Holzwege* (Frankfurt: V. Klostermann, 1957). English translation ("The Anaximander Fragment") in *Early Greek Thinking*, trans. David Farrell Krell and Frank Capuzzi (New York: Harper and Row, 1975). All further references in the text.

then when it is a matter of the forgetting of the difference (between Being and beings), we would have to speak of a disappearance of the trace of the trace. Which is indeed what the following passage from "The Anaximander Fragment" seems to imply: "Oblivion of Being belongs to the self-veiling essence of Being. It belongs so essentially to the destiny of Being that the dawn of this destiny rises as the unveiling of what is present in its presencing. This means that the history of Being begins with the oblivion of Being, since Being—together with its essence, its distinction from beings—keeps to itself. The distinction collapses. It remains forgotten. Although the two parties to the distinction, what is present and presencing (*das Anwesende und das Anwesen*), reveal themselves, they do not do so as distinguished. Rather, even the early trace (*die frühe Spur*) of the distinction is obliterated when presencing appears as something present (*das Anwesen wie ein Anwesendes erscheint*) and finds itself in the position of being the highest being present (*in einem höchsten Anwesenden*)" (pp. 50–51).

Since the trace is not a presence but the simulacrum of a presence that dislocates itself, displaces itself, refers itself, it properly has no site—erasure belongs to its structure. And not only the erasure which must always be able to overtake it (without which it would not be a trace but an indestructible and monumental substance), but also the erasure which constitutes it from the outset as a trace, which situates it as the change of site, and makes it disappear in its appearance, makes it emerge from itself in its production. The erasure of the early trace (*die frühe Spur*) of difference is therefore the "same" as its tracing in the text of metaphysics. This latter must have maintained the mark of what it has lost, reserved, put aside. The paradox of such a structure, in the language of metaphysics, is an inversion of metaphysical concepts, which produces the following effect: the present becomes the sign of the sign, the trace of the trace. It is no longer what every reference refers to in the last analysis. It becomes a function in a structure of generalized reference. It is a trace, and a trace of the erasure of the trace.

Thereby the text of metaphysics is *comprehended*. Still legible; and to be read. It is not surrounded but rather traversed by its limit, marked in its interior by the multiple furrow of its margin. Proposing *all at once* the monument and the mirage of the trace, the trace simultaneously traced and erased, simultaneously living and dead, and, as always, living in its simulation of life's preserved inscription. A pyramid. Not a stone fence to be jumped over but itself stonelike, on a wall, to be deciphered otherwise, a text without voice.

Thus one can think without contradiction, or at least without granting any pertinence to such a contradiction, what is perceptible and imperceptible in the trace. The "early trace" of difference is lost in an invisibility without return, and yet its very loss is sheltered, retained, seen, delayed. In a text. In the form of presence. In the form of the proper. Which itself is only an effect of writing.

Having stated the erasure of the early trace, Heidegger can therefore, in a contradiction without contradiction, consign, countersign, the sealing of the trace. A bit further on: "However, the distinction between Being and beings, as something forgotten, can invade our experience only if it has already unveiled itself with the presencing of what is present (*mit dem Anwesen des Anwesenden*); only if it has left a trace (*eine Spur geprägt hat*) which remains preserved (*gewahrt bleibt*) in the language to which Being comes" (p. 51).

Still further on, while meditating on Anaximander's *to khreon*, which he translates as *Brauch* (usage), Heidegger writes this: "Enjoining order and reck (*Fug und Ruch verfügend*), usage delivers to each present being (*Anwesende*) the while into which it is released. But accompanying this process is the constant danger that lingering will petrify into mere persistence (*in das blosse Beharren verhärtet*). Thus usage essentially remains at the same time the distribution (*Aushändigung:* dis-maintenance) of presencing (*des Anwesens*) into disorder (*in den Un-fug*). Usage conjoins the dis (*Der Brauch fügt das Un-*)" (p. 54).

And it is at the moment when Heidegger recognizes *usage* as *trace* that the question must be asked: can we, and to what extent, think this trace and the *dis* of *différance* as *Wesen des Seins*? Does not the *dis* of *différance* refer us beyond the history of Being, and also beyond our language, and everything that can be named in it? In the language of Being, does it not call for a necessarily violent transformation of this language by an entirely other language?

Let us make this question more specific. And to force the "trace" out of it (and has anyone thought that we have been tracking something down, something other than tracks themselves to be tracked down?), let us read this passage: "The translation of *to khreon* as 'usage' has not resulted from a preoccupation with etymologies and dictionary meanings. The choice of the word stems from a prior crossing *over* (*Über-setzen;* trans-lation) of a thinking which tries to think the distinction in the essence of Being (*im Wesen des Seins*) in the fateful beginning of Being's oblivion. The word 'usage' is dictated to thinking in the experience (*Erfahrung*) of Being's oblivion. What properly remains to be thought in the word 'usage' has presumably left a trace (*Spur*) in *to khreon*. This trace quickly vanishes (*alsbald verschwindet*) in the destiny of Being which unfolds in world history as Western metaphysics" (p. 54).

How to conceive what is outside a text? That which is more or less than a text's *own, proper* margin? For example, what is other than the text of Western metaphysics? It is certain that the trace which "quickly vanishes in the destiny of Being (and) which unfolds . . . as Western metaphysics" escapes every determination, every name it might receive in the metaphysical text. It is sheltered, and therefore dissimulated, in these names. It does not appear in them as the trace "itself." But this is because it could never appear itself, *as such*. Heidegger also says that difference cannot appear as such: "Lichtung des Unterschiedes kann deshalb auch nicht bedeuten, dass der Unterschied als der Unterschied erscheint." There is no essence of *différance*; it (is) that which not only could never be appropriated in the *as such* of its name or its appearing, but also that which threatens the authority of the *as such* in general, of the presence of the thing itself in its essence. That there is not a proper essence[26] of *différance* at this point, implies that there is neither a Being nor truth of the play of writing such as it engages *différance*.

For us, *différance* remains a metaphysical name, and all the names that it receives in our language are still, as names, metaphysical. And this is particularly the case when these names state the determination of *différance* as the difference between presence and the present (*Anwesen/Anwesend*), and above all, and is already the case when they state the determination of *différance* as the difference of Being and beings.

"Older" than Being itself, such a *différance* has no name in our language. But we "already know" that if it is unnameable, it is not provisionally so, not because our language has not yet found or received this *name*, or because we would have to seek it in another language, outside the finite system of our own. It is rather because there is no *name* for it at all, not even the name of essence or of Being, not even that of "*différance*," which is not a name, which is not a pure nominal unity, and unceasingly dislocates itself in a chain of differing and deferring substitutions.

"There is no name for it": a proposition to be read in its *platitude*. This unnameable is not an ineffable Being which no name could approach: God, for example. This unnameable is the play which makes possible nominal effects, the relatively unitary and atomic structures that are called names, the chains of

---

26. *Différance* is not a "species" of the genus *ontological difference*. If the "gift of presence is the property of Appropriating (*Die Gabe von Anwesen ist Eigentum des Ereignens*)" ["Time and Being," in *On Time and Being*, trans. Joan Stambaugh, New York: Harper and Row, 1972; p. 22], *différance* is not a process of propriation in any sense whatever. It is neither position (appropriation) nor negation (expropriation), but rather other. Hence it seems—but here, rather, we are marking the necessity of a future itinerary—that *différance* would be no more a species of the genus *Ereignis* than Being. Heidegger: ". . . then Being belongs into Appropriating (*Dann gehört das Sein in das Ereignen*). Giving and its gift receive their determination from Appropriating. In that case, Being would be a species of Appropriation (*Ereignis*), and not the other way around. To take refuge in such an inversion would be too cheap. Such thinking misses the matter at stake (*Sie denkt am Sachverhalt vorbei*). Appropriation (*Ereignis*) is not the encompassing general concept under which Being and time could be subsumed. Logical classifications mean nothing here. For as we think Being itself and follow what is its own (*seinem Eigenen folgen*), Being proves to be destiny's gift of presence (*gewahrte Gabe des Geschickes von Anwesenheit*), the gift granted by the giving (*Reichen*) of time. The gift of presence is the property of Appropriating (*Die Gabe von Anwesen ist Eigentum des Ereignens*)." (*On Time and Being*, pp. 21–22.)

Without a displaced reinscription of this chain (Being, presence, -propriation, etc.) the relation between general or fundamental onto-logy and whatever ontology masters or makes subordinate under the rubric of a regional or particular science will never be transformed rigorously and irreversibly. Such regional sciences include not only political economy, psychoanalysis, semiolinguistics—in all of which, and perhaps more than elsewhere, the value of the *proper* plays an irreducible role—but equally all spiritualist or materialist metaphysics. The analyses articulated in this volume aim at such a preliminary articulation. It goes without saying that such a reinscription will never be contained in theoretical or philosophical discourse, or generally in any discourse or writing, but only on the scene of what I have called elsewhere the text in general (1972).

substitutions of names in which, for example, the nominal effect *différance* is itself *enmeshed*, carried off, reinscribed, just as a false entry or a false exit is still part of the game, a function of the system.

What we know, or what we would know if it were simply a question here of something to know, is that there has never been, never will be, a unique word, a master-name. This is why the thought of the letter *a* in *différance* is not the primary prescription or the prophetic annunciation of an imminent and as yet unheard-of nomination. There is nothing kerygmatic about this "word," provided that one perceives its decapita(liza)tion. And that one puts into question the name of the name.

There will be no unique name, even if it were the name of Being. And we must think this without *nostalgia*, that is, outside of the myth of a purely maternal or paternal language, a lost native country of thought. On the contrary, we must *affirm* this, in the sense in which Nietzsche puts affirmation into play, in a certain laughter and a certain step of the dance.

From the vantage of this laughter and this dance, from the vantage of this affirmation foreign to all dialectics, the other side of nostalgia, what I will call Heideggerian *hope*, comes into question. I am not unaware how shocking this word might seem here. Nevertheless I am venturing it, without excluding any of its implications, and I relate it to what still seems to me to be the metaphysical part of "The Anaximander Fragment": the quest for the proper word and the unique name. Speaking of the first word of Being (*das frühe Wort des Seins: to khreon*), Heidegger writes: "The relation to what is present that rules in the essence of presencing itself is a unique one (*ist eine einzige*), altogether incomparable to any other relation. It belongs to the uniqueness of Being itself (*Sie gehört zur Einzigkeit des Seins selbst*). Therefore, in order to name the essential nature of Being (*das wesende Seins*), language would have to find a single word, the unique word (*ein einziges, das einzige Wort*). From this we can gather how daring every thoughtful word (*denkende Wort*) addressed to Being is (*das dem Sein zugesprochen wird*). Nevertheless such daring is not impossible, since Being speaks always and everywhere throughout language" (p. 52).

Such is the question: the alliance of speech and Being in the unique word, in the finally proper name. And such is the question inscribed in the simulated affirmation of *différance*. It bears (on) each member of this sentence: "Being / speaks / always and everywhere / throughout / language."

Ousia and Grammē: Note on a Note from Being and Time

Originally published in *L'endurance de la pensée: Pour saluer Jean Beaufret* (Plon, 1968).

Am bedrängendsten zeigt sich
uns das Weitreichende des Anwesens dann, wenn wir be-
denken dass auch und gerade
das Abwesen durch ein bis-
weilen ins Unheimliche ge-
steigertes Anwesen bestimmt
bleibt.

Heidegger, *Zeit und Sein*

Its execution directed at the question of the meaning of Being, the "destruction" of classical ontology first had to shake the "vulgar concept" of time. This
is a condition for the analytic of *Dasein*, which *is there* through the opening to
the question of the meaning of Being, through the precomprehension of Being;
temporality constitutes the "Being of a Being-there (*Dasein*) which comprehends
Being," and it is the "ontological meaning of care" as the structure of Dasein.
This is why temporality alone can provide the horizon for the question of Being.
Thus the task assigned to *Being and Time* is to be understood as both preliminary
and urgent. Not only is the formulation of temporality to be delivered from the
traditional concepts that govern both everyday language and the history of
ontology from Aristotle to Bergson, but also the possibility of this vulgar con-
ceptualization is to be taken into account, and its "rightful due"[1] acknowledged.
    Traditional ontology, then, can be destroyed only by repeating and interro-
gating its relation to the problem of time. In what way has a certain determination
of time implicitly governed the determination of the meaning of Being in the
history of philosophy? Heidegger announces the question from the sixth section
of *Being and Time*. He announces it only, and does so on the basis of what he
still considers but a sign, a point of reference, an "outward evidence" (p. 47).
This outward evidence is "the treatment of the meaning of Being as *parousia* or
ousia, which signifies, in ontologico-Temporal terms, 'presence' (*Anwesenheit*).
Beings[2] are grasped in their Being as 'presence' (*Anwesenheit*); this means that
they are understood with regard to a definite mode of time—the '*Present*' (*Gegenwart*)"[3] (p. 47).

1. TN. Martin Heidegger, *Being and Time*, trans. John Macquarrie and Edward Robinson
(New York: Harper and Row, 1962), p. 39. All references are to this edition. All German
interpolations in the text are Derrida's.
    2. TN. Macquarrie and Robinson translate *Seiend* as "entity"; I consistently modify it to
"being" or "beings."
    3. The same question, in the same form, inhabits the center of *Kant and the Problem of
Metaphysics*. This should cause no surprise, since the latter work envelops *Sein und Zeit*.
A result of the lectures given in 1925–26, it was also to correspond, in its content, with
the second, unpublished part of *Sein und Zeit*. Thus, in elaborating the "aim of fundamental
ontology," and the necessity for the analytic of *Dasein* and for the exposition of "care as
temporality," Heidegger writes, for example: "What is the significance of the fact that

31

The privilege of the present (*Gegenwart*) already marked the *Poem* of Parmenides. *Legein* and *noein*[4] were to grasp a present under the heading of that which endures and persists, near and available, exposed to vision or given by hand, a present in the form of *Vorhandenheit* [presence-at-hand]. This presence is presented, is apprehended in *legein* or in *noein*, by means of a process whose "Temporal structure" is one of "pure 'making-present,' " of pure maintaining[5] (*reinen "Gegenwärtigens"*). "Those beings which show themselves in this [making-present] and for it, and which are understood as beings in the most authentic sense (*das eigentliche Seiende*), thus get interpreted with regard to the Present (*Gegen-wart*); that is, they are conceived as presence (*ousia* [*Anwesenheit*])" (p. 48).

This chain of interdependent concepts (*ousia, parousia, Anwesenheit, Gegenwart, gegenwärtigen, Vorhandenheit*) is *deposited* at the entry to *Being and Time:* both posited and provisionally abandoned. And even if the category of *Vorhandenheit,* of beings in the form of substantial and available objects, in effect never ceases to be at work and to have the value of a theme, the other concepts remain hidden until the end of the book. We must await the final pages of *Being and Time* (of its first, and only published, part) for the chain to be displayed anew, and this time without ellipsis and as the very concatenation of the history of ontology. For at this point there is an explicit analysis of the genesis of the vulgar

---

ancient metaphysics determines the *ontōs on*—the being which is in the highest degree— as *aiei on?* The Being of beings is obviously understood here as *permanence* and *persistence* (*Beständigkeit*). What project lies at the basis of this comprehension of Being? The *project relative to time,* for even eternity, taken as the *nunc stans,* for example, is *thoroughly* conceivable as 'now' and 'persistent' only on the basis of time. What is the significance of the fact that a being in the proper sense of the term (*das eigentlich Seiend*) is understood as *ousia, parousia,* i.e. basically as 'presence' (*das 'Anwesen'*), the immediate and always present possession, (*gegenwärtigen Besitz*), the 'having' (*Habe*)? This project reveals that 'Being' is synonymous with *permanence in presence.* In this way, therefore, i.e. in the spontaneous comprehension of Being, temporal determinations are accumulated. Is not the immediate comprehension of Being developed entirely from a primordial but self-evident *projection of Being relative to time? . . .* The essence (*Wesen*) of time as it was fixed—and, as it turned out, decisively—for the subsequent history of metaphysics by Aristotle does not provide an answer to this question. On the contrary, it would be easy to show that it is precisely Aristotle's conception of time that is inspired by a comprehension of Being which—without being aware of its action—interprets Being as permanent and as present (*Gegenwart*), and consequently determines the 'Being' of time from the point of view of the *now (Jetzt),* i.e. from the character of time which in itself is always *present (anwesend),* and thus properly *is,* in the ancient sense of the term." Martin Heidegger, *Kant and the Problem of Metaphysics,* trans. James S. Churchill (Bloomington: Indiana University Press, section 44, pp. 248–50 [translation modified]). On the relationship between *Anwesen* and *Gegenwärtigen,* see also *Being and Time.*

4. TN. The reference is to Parmenides' saying (*Khrē to legein te noein eon emmenai*), which is usually translated "One should both say and think that Being is." Heidegger has commented upon and retranslated this saying in several contexts, including *Being and Time* (p. 48) and *What Is Called Thinking?*

5. TN. In French "now" is *maintenant,* which makes it easy to translate *Gegenwärtigen* as *maintenance,* which I have given here as "maintaining." The *main* of *maintenance* is also related to the *hand* of Heidegger's concept of *Vorhandenheit*—being present at hand.

concept of time, from Aristotle to Hegel. Now, although the Hegelian concept of time is submitted to scrutiny, and several pages are devoted to it, Heidegger grants only a footnote to the pertinent traits that assign a Greek, and very precisely an Aristotelian, origin to this concept. The footnote invites several readings. Here we do not aspire to undertake such readings, or even to sketch them out. Rather, we are simply underlining the fact that they are indicated, and then opening the texts that Heidegger signals, marking their pages. Our only ambition in commenting on this note is to attempt to extend it a bit, and to do so according to two motifs.

1. To read in it, such as it is announced in highly determined form,[6] the Heideggerian question about *presence* as the ontotheological determination of

6. The following pages may be read as timid prologomena to a problem of translation. But who better than Heidegger has taught us to think what is involved in such a problem? Here, the question would be the following: how to transfer into, or rather what transpires when we transfer into the single Latin word *presence* the entire differentiated *system* of Greek and German words, the entire *system of translation* in which Heideggerian language (*ousia, parousia, Gegenwartigkeit, Anwesen, Anwesenheit, Vorhandenheit*, etc.) is produced? And all this taking into account that the two Greek words, and the words associated with them, already have translations charged with history (essence, substance, etc.)? Above all, how to transfer into the single word *presence*, both too rich and too poor, the *history* of the Heideggerian text which associates or disjoins these concepts in subtle and regular fashion throughout an itinerary that covers more than forty years? How to translate into French [English] or translate French [English] into the play of these displacements? To take only one example—but one which has a privileged status here—"The Anaximander Fragment" (1946) rigorously dissociates concepts which all signify presence, and which, in the text of *Being and Time* that we have just cited, were aligned as synonyms, or in any case without pointing out any pertinent trait of difference. Let us cut out a page from "The Anaximander Fragment." We will cite it in translation, inserting the German words which bear the burden of the difficulties even in places where the translator might not be obliged to do so: "The first point we gather from this poetic phrase is that *ta eonta* is distinguished from *ta essomena* and *pro eonta*. Thus *ta eonta* designates being in the sense of the present (*das Seiende im Sinne des Gegenwärtigen*). When we moderns speak of 'the present,' we either mean what is 'now' (*das Jetzige*)—which we represent as something within time (*etwas innerzeitiges*), the 'now' serving as a phase in the stream of time—or we bring the 'present' into relation with the 'objective' (*zum Gegenständigen*). As something objective (*das Objective*), an object is related to a representing subject. However, if we employ 'present' (*das 'gegenwärtig'*) for the sake of a closer determination of *eonta*, then we must understand 'the present' (*das 'gegenwärtig'*) from the essence (*Wesen*) of *eonta* and not vice versa. Yet *eonta* is also what is past and what is to come. Both are ways of presencing (*des Anwesenden*), i.e. the presencing of what is not presently present (*des ungegenwärtig Anwesenden*). The Greeks also named more precisely what is presently present (*das gegenwärtig Anwesende*) *ta pareonta, para* meaning 'alongside' (*bei*), in the sense of coming alongside in uncon-cealment (*Unverborgenheit*). The *gegen* in *gegenwärtig* (presently) does not mean something over against a subject, but rather an open expanse of unconcealment (*die offene Gegend der Unverborgenheit*), into which and within which whatever comes along lingers (*das Beige-kommene verweilt*). Accordingly, as a characteristic of *eonta*, 'presently' (*gegenwärtig*) means as much 'having arrived to linger awhile in the expanse of unconcealment.' Spoken first, and thus emphasized, *eonta* which is expressly distinguished from *proeonta* and *essomena*, names for the Greeks what is present (*das Anwesende*) insofar as it has arrived in the designated sense, to linger within the expanse of unconcealment. Such a coming is proper arrival, the presencing of what is properly present. (*Solche Angekommenheit ist die eigentliche*

33

the meaning of Being. Is not to transgress metaphysics, in the sense understood by Heidegger, to unfold a question which turns back on this strange limit, on this strange epochē of Being hiding itself in the very movement of its *presentation?* Hiding itself in its presence and in consciousness (that modification of presence), in representation or in self presence? From Parmenides to Husserl, the privilege of the present has never been put into question. It could not have been. It is what is self-evident itself, and no thought seems possible outside its element. Nonpresence is always thought in the form of presence (it would suffice to say simply in the *form*),[7] or as a modalization of presence. The past and the future are always determined as past presents or as future presents.

2. To indicate, from afar and in a still quite undecided way, a direction not opened by Heidegger's meditation: the hidden passageway that makes the problem of presence communicate with the problem of the written trace.[8] By means of this simultaneously concealed and necessary passageway, the two problems *give onto, open onto* each other. This is what appears, and yet is elided, in the texts of Aristotle and of Hegel. Although he urges us to reread these texts, Heidegger detaches from his thematic certain concepts which seem to require greater emphasis that they have been given thus far. The reference to the *gramme* (*grammē*) leads us back both to a center and a margin of Aristotle's text on time (*Physics IV*).[9] A strange reference and a strange situation. Are they already

---

Ankunft, ist das Anwesen des eigentlich Anwesenden.) What is past and what is to come also become present (*Anwesendes*) namely as outside the expanse of unconcealment. What presents itself as non-present is what is absent. (*Das ungegenwärtig Anwesende ist das Abwesende.*) As such it remains essentially related to what is presently present (*das gegenwärtig Anwesende*), inasmuch as it either comes forward into the expanse of unconcealment or withdraws from it. Even what is absent is something present (*Auch das Abwesende ist Anwesendes*), for *as* absent from the expanse, it presents (*anwesend*) itself in unconcealment. What is past and what is to come are also *eonta*. Consequently *eon* means becoming present in unconcealment (*Anwesen in die Unverborgenheit*).

"The conclusion of this commentary on *eonta* is that also in Greek experience what comes to presence (*das Anwesende*) remains ambiguous, and indeed necessarily so. On the one hand, *ta eonta* means what is presently present (*das gegenwärtig Anwesende*); on the other, it also means all that becomes present (*alles Anwesende*), whether at the present time or not (*das gegenwärtig und das ungegenwärtig Wesende*)." From *Early Greek Thinking,* trans. David Farrell Krell and Frank Capuzzi (New York: Harper and Row, 1975), pp. 34–35.

7. See "Form and Meaning," below.

8. See "The Ends of Man," below.

9. TN. I have followed Derrida's practice of transliterating all Greek terms throughout this essay. It should be noted, however, that there is a difference between the Greek *grammē* and the French *gramme*. Thus, for example, the title of this essay is "*Ousia and Grammē,*" roughly "presence and line," while the last two subtitles are "*Gramme* and Number" and "The Closure of the *Gramme* and the Trace of *Différance.*" Derrida uses "*gramme,*" which of course "derives" from *grammē* (line, trace), and reminds us of *gramma* (letter), as a neologism related to the concept of *différance,* as is evident in the last subtitle, which makes this relationship specific. Like *différance* it is best left untranslated. Thus, whenever Derrida has spoken of *ligne* I have translated it as "line," while *grammē* is given as *grammē,* that is, as a transliterated term from Aristotle, as in Derrida's text. What in French appears as "gramme" here is given as *gramme* in order to indicate its neologistic

34

included, implied, dominated by the concepts that Heidegger has fixed as the decisive ones in Aristotle's text? We are not certain, and our reading will follow this incertitude.

The Note

It is only a footnote, but it is by far the longest in *Being and Time*, pregnant with developments that are announced and held back, necessary but deferred. We will see that it already promises the second volume of *Being and Time*, but that it does so, we might say, by *reserving* the second volume, both as something still to be unfolded and as the definitive enveloping of the first.

The Note belongs to the next to last section of the last chapter ("Temporality and Within-Time-ness as the Source of the Ordinary Conception of Time"). Time is usually considered as that *in which* beings are produced. Within-time-ness, intratemporality, is taken to be the homogenous medium in which the movement of daily existence is reckoned and organized. This homogeneity of the temporal medium becomes the effect of a "leveling off of primordial time" (*Nivellierung der ursprünglichen Zeit*), and constitutes a world time more objective than the object and more subjective than the subject. In affirming that history—that is, spirit, which alone has a history—*falls into time (. . . fällt die Entwicklung der Geschichte in die Zeit)*,[10] is not Hegel thinking in terms of the vulgar concept of time? Heidegger claims to be in agreement with Hegel on this proposition in its "results" (*im Resultat*), and to the extent that it concerns the temporality of *Dasein* and the co-belonging that links *Dasein* to world time (p. 457).[11] But Heidegger agrees only with the proposition in its results, and Hegel himself has taught us that results are nothing without their becoming, outside the locus which assigns to them an itinerary or a method. Now, Heidegger wants to show in what way his project of fundamental ontology *displaces* the meaning of this result, thus making the Hegelian proposition appear as the "most radical" formulation of the vulgar concept of time. He is concerned not with "criticizing" Hegel but with sharpening the difference between fundamental ontology and classical or

---

use related to *différance*. See also the interview "Semiology and Grammatology" for a discussion of *gramme* as *différance*. *Grammē* is from Aristotle's *Physics*, a work cited extensively here. I have used the translation by R. P. Hardie and G. K. Gaye (Oxford: Oxford University Press, 1930); all following references are to this edition.

10. Hegel, *Die Vernunft in der Geschichte, Einleitung in die Philosophie der Weltgeschichte*, in *Sämtliche Werke*, ed. G. Lasson (Leipzig: F. Meiner, 1923), vol. 8, p. 133.

11. We will have occasion to ask whether or not this agreement about the "results," which keeps to a description of "fallen temporality," engages Heidegger in something beyond the limits that he seeks to mark here. Despite the reinterpretation to which he submits the *Verfallen* (for example at the end of section 82), it will be asked whether the single distinction—whatever its restructuration and originality—between proper and improper temporality, authentic, orginary and nonoriginary, etc., is not itself a tributary of Hegelianism, of the idea of a "fall" into time. And, consequently, a tributary of the "vulgar" concept of time.

vulgar ontology, and with doing so by restoring the radicality of a formulation "which has received too little attention" and by showing this formulation to be at work and at the center of the most profound, the most critical, and the most encompassing thought of metaphysics.

This section contains two subsections, and its several pages are articulated around the following propositions.

1. Hegel's interpretation of the relation between time and spirit operates on the basis of a concept of time elaborated in the second part of the *Encyclopedia*, that is, in a *philosophy of nature*. This concept belongs to an ontology of nature, and has the same milieu and characteristics as the Aristotelian concept of time such as it is constructed in *Physics IV*, in the course of a reflection on place and movement.

2. The "leveling" of which Heidegger speaks is due here to the exorbitant privilege of the form of the "now" and the "point." As Hegel himself says: "The now has a tremendous right (*ein ungeheures Recht*); it *is* nothing as the individual Now, for as I pronounce it, this proudly exclusive Now dissolves, flows away and falls into dust."[12]

3. The entire system of concepts organized around Hegel's fundamental assertion—according to which time is the existence (*Dasein*) of the concept, absolute spirit in its automanifestation, in its absolute disquietude as the negation of negation—depends upon a vulgar determination of time, and therefore upon a determination of *Dasein* itself conceived on the basis of the now of leveling, that is, *Dasein* in the form of *Vorhandenheit*, of presence *maintained* in availability.

The Note cuts this sequence in two. It intervenes at the end of the subsection devoted to the Hegelian exposition of the concept of time in the philosophy of nature and before the subsection of "Hegel's Interpretation of the Connection between Time and Spirit." Let us follow its translation:

> The priority which Hegel has given to the 'now' which has been levelled off, makes it plain that in defining the concept of time he is under the sway of the manner in which time is *ordinarily* understood; and this means that he is likewise under the sway of the *traditional* conception of it. It can even be shown that his conception of time has been drawn *directly* from the 'physics' of Aristotle.
>
> In the *Jena Logic* (Cf. G. Lasson's 1923 edition), which was projected at the time of Hegel's habilitation, the analysis of time which we find in his *Encyclopedia* has already been developed in all its essential parts. Even the roughest examination reveals that the section on time (pp. 202 ff.) is a *paraphrase* of Aristotle's essay on time. In the *Jena Logic* Hegel has already developed his view of time within the framework of his philosophy of

---

12. *Hegel's Philosophy of Nature (Encyclopedia Part Two)*, trans. A. V. Miller (Oxford: Clarendon Press, 1970), sec. 258, p. 36. All following references are to this edition, abbreviated as "*Enc.*"

Nature (p. 186), the first part of which is entitled 'System of the Sun' (p. 195). Hegel discusses the concept of time in conjunction with defining the concepts of aether and motion. Here too his analysis of space comes later (*nachgeordnet*). Though the dialectic already emerges, it does not have as yet the rigid schematic form which it will have afterward, but still makes it possible to understand the phenomena in a fairly relaxed manner. On the way from Kant to Hegel's developed system, the impact of the Aristotelian ontology and logic has again been decisive. The Fact of this impact has long been well known. But the kind of effect it has had, the path it has taken, even its limitations, have hitherto been as obscure as the Fact itself has been familiar. A *concrete philosophical* Interpretation comparing Hegel's *Jena Logic* with the 'physics' and 'metaphysics' of Aristotle will bring new light. For the above considerations, some rough suggestions will suffice.

Aristotle sees the essence of time in the *nun*, Hegel in the 'now' (*jetzt*). Aristotle takes the *nun* as *oros;* Hegel takes the 'now' as 'boundary' (*Grenze*). Aristotle understands the *nun* as *stigmē;* Hegel interprets the 'now' as a point. Aristotle describes the *nun* as *tode ti;* Hegel calls the 'now' the 'absolute this' (*das 'absolute Dieses'*). Aristotle follows tradition in connecting *khronos* with *sphaira;* Hegel stresses the 'circular course' (*Kreislauf*) of time. To be sure, Hegel escapes the central tendency of the Aristotelian analysis—the tendency to expose a foundational connection (*akolouthein*) between the *nun*, the *oros*, the *stigmē* and the *tode ti.*

In its result, Bergson's view is in accord with Hegel's thesis that space 'is' time, in spite of the very different reasons they have given. Bergson merely says the reverse: that time (*temps* [in French in the text in order to oppose *temps*, time, to *durée*, duration]) is space. Bergson's view of time too has obviously arisen from an Interpretation of the Aristotelian essay on time. That a treatise of Bergson with the title *Quid Aristoteles de loco senserit* should have appeared at the same time as his *Essai sur les données immédiates de la conscience,* where the problem of *temps* and *durée* is expounded, is not just a superficial literary connection. Having regard to Aristotle's definition of time as the *arithmos kinēseōs,* Bergson prefaces his analysis of time with an analysis of *number.* Time as space (Cf. *Essai,* p. 69) is *quantitative* Succession. By a counter-orientation (*Gegenorientierung*) to this conception of time, duration gets described as a *qualitative* Succession. This is not the place for coming to terms critically (*Auseinandersetzung*) with Bergson's conception of time or with other Present-day views of it. So far as anything essential has been achieved in today's analyses which will take us beyond Aristotle and Kant, it pertains more to the way time is grasped and to our 'consciousness of time'. We shall come back to this in the first and third divisions of Part Two. [The preceding

37

sentence has been deleted in the later editions of *Being and Time*, giving the Note its full charge of meaning.]

In suggesting a direct connection between Hegel's conception of time and Aristotle's analysis, we are not accusing Hegel of any 'dependence' on Aristotle, but are calling attention to the *ontological import which this filiation has in principle* for the *Hegelian logic* (p. 500, n. xxx).

An enormous task is proposed here. The texts pointed out are doubtless among the most difficult and most decisive of the history of philosophy. And yet, is not what Heidegger designates beneath these points of reference that which is most simple? Not only self-evident, but the very milieu, the element of self-evidence outside of which it seems that thought itself must suffocate? Has not the entire history of philosophy been authorized by the "extraordinary right" of the present? Have not meaning, reason, and "good" sense been produced within this right? And also that which joins ordinary discourse to speculative discourse, Hegel's in particular? How could one think Being and time *otherwise* than on the basis of the present, in the form of the present, to wit a certain *now in general* from which no *experience*, by definition, can ever depart? The experience of thought and the thought of experience have never dealt with anything but presence. Thus, for Heidegger it is not a question of proposing that we think otherwise, if this means to think some *other thing*. Rather, it is thinking that which could *not* have been, *nor* thought, *otherwise*. There is produced in the thought of the impossibility of the otherwise, in this *not otherwise*, a certain difference, a certain trembling, a certain decentering that is not the position of an other center. An other center would be an other now; on the contrary, this *displacement* would not envisage an *absence*, that is an other presence: it would *replace* nothing. Therefore we must—and in saying this we are already in sight of our problem, already have some footing on it—think our relation to (the entire past of) the history of philosophy otherwise than in the style of dialectical negativity, which—as a tributary of the vulgar concept of time—posits an other present as the negation of the present past-retained-uplifted in the *Aufhebung*, where it yields its *truth*. It is precisely a question of something entirely other: it is the tie between truth and presence that must be thought, in a thought that henceforth may no longer need to be either *true* or *present*, and for which the meaning and value of truth are put into question in a way impossible for any intraphilosophical moment, especially for skepticism and everything that is systematic with it. The dialectical negativity which has granted so many profound renewals to Hegelian speculation thus would remain within the metaphysics of presence, of *maintenance*, the metaphysics of the vulgar concept of time. It would only reassemble the enunciation of this metaphysics in its *truth*. Moreover, did Hegel ever wish to do anything else? Does he not often declare that he is rendering to dialectics the truth that is still hidden, although revealed, in Plato and in Kant?

38

There is no chance that within the *thematic* of metaphysics anything might have budged, as concerns the concept of time, from Aristotle to Hegel. The founding concepts of substance and cause, along with their entire system of connected concepts, suffice by themselves—whatever their differentiation and their internal problematics—to ensure (us of) the transmission and uninterrupted continuity—however highly differentiated—of all the moments of Metaphysics, Physics, and Logic, passing through Ethics. If one does not acknowledge this powerful, systematic truth, one no longer knows what one is talking about in allegedly interrupting, transgressing, exceeding, etc., "metaphysics," "philosophy," etc. And, without a rigorous critical and deconstructive acknowledgment of the system, the very necessary attention to differences, disruptions, mutations, leaps, restructurations, etc., becomes ensnarled in slogans, in dogmatic stupidity, in empiricist precipitation—or all of these at once; and in any event lets the very discourse it believes it is putting into question be dictated to itself *a tergo*. It is true that the pleasure one might have in doing so (in repetition) ultimately cannot be called to appear before the tribunal of any law. It is precisely the limit of such a tribunal—philosophy—that is in question here.

The Exoteric

First let us reestablish contact. The contact of the concept of *vulgarity* or ordinariness in the expression the "ordinary concept of time" with the stated point of departure of the Aristotelian interpretation. Precisely with the point of its *exotericness*.

In *Physics IV* Aristotle begins by proposing a conundrum, an *aporia*. He does so in the form of an exoteric argument (*dia tōn exōterikōn logōn*). First it is asked if time belongs to beings or nonbeings; and then what its nature, its *physis* might be. *Prōton de kalōs ekhei diaporēsai peri autou [khronou] kai dia tōn exōterikōn logōn, poteron tōn ontōn estin ē tōn mē ontōn, eita tis hē physis autou.*

The aporetic is an exoteric. It is opened and closed on this dead end: time is that which "is not," or which "is barely, and scarcely" (*holōs ouk estin ē molis kai amudrōs*). Now how is it to be thought that time is what is not? By giving in to the obvious, that time is, that time has as its essence, the *nun*, which is most often translated as *instant*, but which functions in Greek like our word "now" (*maintenant*). The *nun* is the form from which time cannot ever depart, the form in which it cannot not be given; and yet the *nun*, in a certain sense, is not. If one thinks time on the basis of the now, one must conclude that it is not. The now is given simultaneously as that which is *no longer* and as that which is *not yet*. It is what it is not, and is not what it is. *To men gar autou gegone kai ouk esti, to de mellei kai oupō estin.* "In one sense it has been and is no longer, and in another sense, it will be and is not yet" (217b). Thereby time is *composed* of nonbeings. Now, that which bears within it a certain *no-thing*, that which accommodates nonbeingness, cannot participate in presence, in substance, in *be-ingness* itself (*ousia*).

This first phase of the *aporia* involves thinking time in its divisibility. Time is divisible into parts, and yet none of its parts, no now, is *in the present*. Let us pause here before considering the other phase of the *aporia* on the beingness or nonbeingness of time. There Aristotle will maintain the inverse hypothesis: the now is not a part, time is not composed of *nun*.

What we will retain from the first hypothesis, is that time is defined according to its relation to an elementary part, the now, which itself is affected—as if it were not already temporal—by a time which negates it in determining it as a past now or a future now. The *nun*, the element of time, in this sense is not in itself temporal. It is temporal only in becoming temporal, that is, in ceasing to be, in passing over to no-thingness in the form of being-past or being-future. Even if it is envisaged as (past or future) nonbeing, the now is determined as the intemporal kernel of time, the nonmodifiable nucleus of temporal modification, the inalterable form of temporalization. Time is what overtakes this nucleus, in affecting it with no-thing. But in order to be, in order to be a being, it must not be affected by time, it must not become (past or future). To participate in beingness, in *ousia,* therefore is to participate in being-present, in the presence of the present, or, if you will, in presentness. Beings are what *is*. *Ousia* therefore is thought on the basis of *esti*. The privilege of the third person present of the indicative here yields all its historial significance.[13] Beings, the present, the now, subtance, essence, are all linked in their meaning to the form of the present participle. And it could be shown that the passage to the noun form supposes the recourse to the third person. And later it will be likewise for the form of presence that *consciousness* itself is.

The Paraphrase: Point, Line, Plane

At least twice, Heidegger reminds us, Hegel paraphrased *Physics IV* by analyzing time in a "philosophy of nature." In effect, the first phase of the exoteric is reproduced in the "Philosophy of Nature" in the *Jena Logic*. The first part of this "Philosophy of Nature," devoted to the "system of the sun," defines time within an elaboration of the "concept of movement." Although Aristotle is never cited—this kind of fundamental self-evidence is beyond reference—one finds in this passage formulations which *comment* upon the first phase of the exoteric. Thus, for example:

The limit (*Grenze*), or the moment of the *present (Gegenwart)*, the absolute *this* of time (*das absolute Dieses der Zeit*) or the now (*das Jetzt*) is the abso-

13. Heidegger underlines, from another point of view, the historical dominance of the third person of the present indicative of the verb *to be* in the *Introduction to Metaphysics* [trans. Ralph Manheim (New Haven: Yale University Press, 1959), p. 92]. On this problem, see "The Supplement of Copula," below.

lutely negatively simple; as entirely excluding from itself all multiplicity, and thereby absolutely determined . . . as an act of negation (*als Negieren*), it is also absolutely related to its contrary, and its activity, its simple act of negating, is related to its contrary: the now is immediately the contrary of itself, the act of negating itself . . . The now has its nonbeing (*Nichtsein*) in itself and becomes immediately something other than itself, but this other, the future, into which the present develops [transports, transforms itself], is immediately the other-than-itself, for it is now present (*denn sie ist jetzt Gegenwart*) . . . This essence which is its own (*Dieses sein Wesen*) is its non-being (*Nichtsein*).[14]

But the *dialectical* repetition of the Aristotelian *aporia* is perhaps articulated both more rigorously and more rigidly in the *Encyclopedia* ("Philosophy of Nature," section 257). Further, this is at the beginning of the "Mechanics," in the first part, in which space and time are considered as fundamental categories of nature, that is, as categories of the Idea as exteriority, the Idea as juxtaposition or separation, Being-outside-itself (*Aussereinander, Aussersichsein*). Space and time are the fundamental categories of this exteriority as immediate, that is, as abstract and undetermined (*das ganz abstrakte Aussereinander*).

Nature is the Idea outside itself. Space is this Being-outside-itself, is this nature to the extent that nature itself is itself outside itself, that is, to the extent that it is not yet related to itself, to the extent that it is not yet for-itself. Space is the abstract universality of this Being-outside-itself. Nature, as "absolute space" (this is the expression found in the *Jena Logic;* it does not reappear in the *Encyclopedia*, doubtless for essential reasons), not in relation to itself, knows no mediation, no difference, no determination, no discontinuity. It corresponds to what the *Jena Logic* called ether: the element of ideal transparency, of absolute indifferentiation, of undetermined continuity, of absolute juxtaposition, that is, the element without interior relations. In it, nothing is yet related to anything. Such is the origin of nature.

It is only on the basis of this origin that the following question could be asked: how do space, how do nature, in their undifferentiated immediacy, receive difference, determination, quality? Differentiation, determination, qualification can only overtake pure space as the negation of this original purity and of this initial state of abstract indifferentiation which is properly the spatiality of space. Pure spatiality is determined by negating properly the indetermination that constitutes it, that is, by itself negating itself. By *itself* negating itself: this negation has to be a determined negation, a negation *of* space *by* space. The first spatial negation of space is the POINT. "The difference (*Unterschied*) of space is, however, essentially a determinate, qualitative difference. As such it is first the *negation of space itself*, because this is immediate, *differenceless (unterschiedlose)* self-externality: the point" (*Enc.*, sec. 256, p. 31). The point is the space that does not

14. G. W. F. Hegel, *Gesammelte Werke*, vol. 7, *Jenaer Systementwürfe* II, ed. Rolf-Peter Horstmann and Johann Heinrich Trede (Hamburg: Meiner Verlag, 1971), pp. 194–95.

take up space, the place that does not take place; it suppresses and replaces the place, it takes the place of the space that it negates and conserves. It spatially negates space. It is the first determination of space. As the first determination and first negation of space, the point spatializes or *spaces* itself. It negates itself by itself in its relation to itself, that is, to another point. The negation of negation, the spatial negation of the point is the LINE. The point negates and retains itself, extends and sustains itself, lifts itself (by *Aufhebung*) into the line, which thus constitutes the *truth* of the point. But secondarily this negation is a negation of *space*, that is, itself is spatial; to the extent that essentially it is this relationship, that is, to the extent that it retains itself by suppressing itself (*als sich aufhebend*), the point is the *line*, the first Being-other, that is, the Being-spatial of the point (ibid.).

According to the same process, by *Aufhebung* and negation of negation, the truth of the line is the PLANE: "The truth of the other-Being is, however, negation of negation. The line consequently passes over into the plane, which, on the one hand, is a determinateness opposed to line and point, and so surface, simply as such, but, on the other hand, is the sublated negation of space (*die aufgehobene Negation des Raumes*). It is thus the restoration (*Wiederherstellung*) of the spatial totality which now contains the negative moment within itself . . ." (ibid.).

Space, therefore, has become concrete in having retained the negative within itself. It has become space in losing itself, in determining itself, in negating its original purity, the absolute indifferentiation and exteriority that constituted itself in its spatiality. Spatialization, the accomplishment of the essence of spatiality, is a despatialization and vice versa. *And vice versa:* this movement of the production of the surface as the concrete totality of space is circular and reversible. Inversely, then, one could demonstrate that the line is not composed of points, since it is made of negated points, of points outside-themselves; and that for the same reason the surface is not composed of lines. Henceforth the concrete totality of space will be considered as at the beginning, with the surface as its first negative determination, the line its second, the point its last. The indifferent abstraction is indifferently the founding principle and the end of the circle. Etc.

Despite its interest, we must leave aside the discussion of Kantian concepts which is interlaced with this demonstration in a series of *Remarks*. We must come to the question of time.

Is it still to be asked? Is it still to be asked how time appears on the basis of this genesis of space? In a certain way it is always too late to ask the question of time. The latter has already appeared. The Being-no-longer and the Being-still which related the line to the point, and the plane to the line—this negativity in the structure of the *Aufhebung* already was time. At each stage of the negation, each time that the *Aufhebung* produced the truth of the previous determination, time was requisite. The negation at work in space or as space, the spatial negation of space, time is the truth of space. To the extent that it *is*, that is, to the extent

42

that it becomes and is produced, that it manifests itself in its essence, that it *spaces* itself, in itself relating to itself, that is, in negating itself, space is time. It temporalizes itself, it relates itself to itself and mediates itself as time. Time is *spacing*. It is the relation of space to itself, its for-itself. "Negativity, as point, relates itself to space, in which it develops its determinations as line and plane; but in the sphere of self-externality, negativity is equally *for itself*, and so are its determinations; [i.e. in the being-for itself of negativity] . . . Negativity, thus posited for itself, is Time" (*Enc.*, sec. 257, p. 34). Time *relève* ["relifts"][15] space.

In recalling this development, Heidegger underlines that in this way space is only *thought* as time (p. 482). Space is time to the extent that space is determined on the basis of the (first or last) negativity of the point. "According to Hegel, this negation of the negation as punctuality is time" (p. 482). Time, therefore, is thought on the basis of, or looking toward, the point, and the point is thought on the basis of, or looking toward, time. Point and time are thought in this circularity which relates them one to the other. And the very concept of *speculative* negativity (the *Aufhebung*) is possible only by means of this infinite correlation or *reflection*. The *stigmē*, punctuality, therefore is the concept which, in Hegel as in Aristotle, determines nowness (*nun, jetzt*). Therefore it is not surprising that the first aporetic phase of *Physics IV* informs or preforms the first figure of time in Hegel's *Philosophy of Nature*. By the same token this aporia prefigures the relations between spirit and time, since nature is the Being-outside-itself of spirit, and time the first relation of nature to itself, the first emergence of its for-itself, spirit relating itself to itself only by negating itself and *falling* outside itself.

Here the Aristotelian aporia is understood, thought, and assimilated into that which is properly *dialectical*. It suffices—and it is necessary—to take things in the other sense and from the other side in order to conclude that the Hegelian dialectic is but the repetition, the paraphrastic reedition of an exoteric aporia, the brilliant formulation of a vulgar paradox.[16] To be persuaded of this it suffices

15. TN. In note 23 of "La Différance," above, I explained Derrida's translation of *Aufhebung* as *relève*. Here Derrida is using the verb form—"le temps *relève* l'espace"—again in order to make *aufhebt* rewrite itself. Note that Derrida's playful translation of *aufhebt* (third person singular of *Aufheben*) keeps the *hebt* (*lève*, lifts), but changes the *auf-* (up) to a *re-*. As in note 23 to "La Différance," the stress is on the effect of substitution and difference, of *repetition*, that is inscribed in *aufhebt*. Further, the *auf-* is related to *negation*-and-preservation in a *higher* sphere; the *re-* questions the metaphysics of negation, the theology implicit in dialectical negation as a raising *up*.

16. Hegel conceived his relation to the Aristotelian exoteric or to the Eleatic paradoxes in an entirely other category than that of the "paraphrase" of which Heidegger speaks. Or at least he conceives the possibility of the "paraphrase" on the basis of concepts which involve the very essence of logos. His "repetition" of the thought of time does not fall into the particular and rhetorical category of the *paraphrase*. (What is to *paraphrase* in philosophy?) The *past*, for Hegel, was both an ingenious anticipation of speculative dialectics and the teleological necessity of an "already-not-yet" that he will develop in the *Logic*, where one may read, for example, among pages that should be cited *in extenso:* "Infinitely more ingenious and profound than the Kantian antinomy with which we have just concerned ourselves are the dialectical examples of the ancient Eleatic school, especially

to consider the passage from Aristotle already cited (218a) along with this def-inition of time in section 258 of the *Encyclopedia:* "Time, as the negative unity of self-externality, is similarly an out-and-out abstract, ideal being. It is that being which, inasmuch as it *is*, is *not*, and inasmuch as it *is not, is:* it is Becoming *directly intuited* (*das* angeschaute *Werden*); this means that differences, which admittedly are purely momentary, i.e. directly self-sublating (*unmittelbar sich aufhebenden Unterschiede*), are determined as *external*, i.e. as external to them-selves" (p. 34).

This definition has at least three direct consequences in Hegel's text considered as a paraphrase of Aristotle.

1. The Kantian concept of time is reproduced in it, or rather is deduced from it. The necessity of such a deduction would show, then, that the Kantian rev-olution did not displace what Aristotle had set down but, on the contrary, settled down there itself, changing its locale and then refurbishing it. Further on we will come to suggest this from another point of view. In effect, "intuited becom-ing" in *itself*, without empirical sensory content, is the *purely sensory*, the formal sensory free from all sensuous matter, without whose discovery no Copernican revolution would have taken place. What Kant discovered is the "non-sensuous sensuous" that here reproduces the "paraphrase" of Aristotle: "Time, like space, is a *pure form* of sense or of *intuition*, the non-sensuous sensuous (*das unsinnliche Sinnliche*)" (*Enc.*, sec. 258, Remark, p. 34). In alluding to this "nonsensuously sensuous,"[17] Heidegger does not relate the Hegelian concept to its Kantian equiv-alent; it is well known that he considered Hegel to have covered over and erased Kant's audaciousness in many respects. Are we not justified here, *Heidegger notwithstanding*, in placing Kant in the *direct line* which, *according to Heidegger*, leads from Aristotle to Hegel?

2. According to an elaboration which resembles that found in *Kant and the Problem of Metaphysics* (and consequently, *Being and Time*), Hegel concludes from his definition:

a) "Time is the same principle as the I = I of pure self-consciousness" (ibid.). We would have to relate—although we cannot do so here—the entire Remark of section 258 of the *Encyclopedia*, which demonstrates this last proposition, to section 34 of Heidegger's *Kant*, particularly to the section on "Time as Pure Self-Affection and the Temporal Character of the Self." Does not Heidegger repeat the Hegelian gesture when he writes, for example, "Time and the 'I think' are

---

with respect to movement . . . The solutions given by Aristotle to these dialectical for-mations merit the highest praise; they are contained in his truly speculative notions of time, space and movement . . . Even a lively intelligence (which Aristotle himself pos-sessed to an unrivalled degree) does not suffice to comprehend and judge these speculative notions and to see what is obtuse in Zeno's argumentation." *Science of Logic*, trans. W. H. Johnston and L. G. Struthers (London: Allen and Unwin, 1929), vol. 1, pp. 212–13). See also the entire problematic of sensible certitude [in the *Phenomenology of Spirit*].

17. *Being and Time*, p. 480.

no longer opposed to one another as unlike and incompatible; they are the same. Thanks to the radicalism with which, in the laying of the foundation of metaphysics, Kant for the first time subjected time and the 'I think,' each taken separately, to a transcendental interpretation, he succeeded in bringing them together in their primordial sameness (*ursprüngliche Selbigkeit*)—without, to be sure, having seen this sameness expressly as such."[18]

b) ". . . it is not *in* time (*in der Zeit*) that everything comes to be and passes away, rather time itself is the *becoming*, this coming-to-be and passing away" (*Enc.*, sec. 258, p. 35). Hegel takes multiple precautions of this type. By opposing them to all the metaphorical formulations that state the "fall" into time (which, moreover, are not to be denied all dignity),[19] one could exhibit an entire Hegelian critique of intratemporality (*Innerzeitigkeit*). This critique not only would be analogous to the one developed in *Being and Time*, it also would have to accommodate itself, as in *Being and Time*, to the thematic of the fall or of the decline, the *Verfallen*. We will come back to this concept that no precaution—and Hegel took no fewer precautions than Heidegger—can lift from its ethicotheological orb. Unless, in the void, the term of the orb in question is itself redirected toward a *point of falling* still further off.[20]

3. According to a fundamentally Greek gesture, this Hegelian determination of time permits us to think the present, the very form of time, as eternity. Eternity is not the negative abstraction of time, nontime, the outside-of-time. If the elementary form of time is the present, eternity could be outside of time only by keeping itself outside of presence. It would not be presence; it would come before or after time, and in this way would become again a temporal *modification*. Eternity would be made into a moment of time. Everything in Hegelianism that receives the predicate of eternity (the Idea, Spirit, the True) therefore must not be thought outside of time (any more than in time).[21] Eternity as presence is neither temporal nor intemporal. Presence is intemporality in time

18. TN. *Kant and the Problem of Metaphysics*, p. 197. Translation modified.
19. See "White Mythology," below.
20. See "The Double Session," in *Dissemination*.
21. Here, we can only cite and situate several texts on which our examination would have to bear down, patiently. For example: "The real (*das Reelle*) is certainly distinct from time, but is also essentially identical with it. What is real is limited (*beschränkt*), and the Other to this negation is *outside* it; therefore, the determinateness in it is self-external and is consequently the contradiction of its being; the abstraction of this externality and unrest (*Unruhe*) of its contradiction is time itself. The finite is perishable and *temporal* because, unlike the Notion, it is not in its own self total negativity . . . The Notion, however, in its freely self-existent identity as I = I, is in and for itself absolute negativity and freedom. Time, therefore, has no power over the Notion, nor is the Notion in time or temporal (*ein Zeitliches*); on the contrary, *it* is the power over time (*die Macht der Zeit*), which is this negativity only *qua* externality. Only the natural, therefore, is subject to time insofar as it is finite; the True, on the other hand, the Idea, Spirit, is eternal. But the notion of eternity must not be grasped negatively as abstraction from time, as existing, as it were, outside of it of time; nor in a sense which makes eternity come *after* time, for this would turn eternity into futurity, one of the moments of time" (*Enc.*, sec. 258, p. 35).

45

or time in intemporality: this, perhaps, is what makes anything like an originary temporality impossible. Eternity is another name of the presence of the present. Hegel also distinguishes this presence from the present as now. A distinction analogous, but not identical, to the one proposed by Heidegger, because it calls upon the difference between the finite and the infinite.[22] An intra-ontic difference, Heidegger would say. And in effect this is where the entire question would have to reside.

What the Question Evades

Until now we have remained, in a way, *within* the first hypothesis of the Aristotelian aporetic, which began by paralyzing itself in the determination of time as *nun* and of *nun* as *meros* (part).

Our question, then, is the following: in overturning the hypothesis, in demonstrating that the now is not a part of time, does Aristotle extract the problematic

22. The difference between the finite and the infinite is proposed here as the difference between the now (*Jetzt*) and the present (*Gegenwart*). Pure presence, infinite parousia, according to Hegel, then, would not be governed by the now which Heidegger tells us limits and determines *parousia* from the *Physics* to the *Encyclopedia*. But, since Heidegger also is questioning a privilege of the *Gegenwart*, here we ought to delve into the differences between *Jetzt*, *Gegenwart*, *Anwesenheit*. Again under the rubric of a preliminary survey, let us be satisfied, here, with translating Hegel's text: "The dimensions of time, *present (Gegenwart), future,* and *past,* are the *becoming* of externality as such, and the resolution (*Auflösung*) of it into the differences of being as passing over into nothing, and of nothing as passing over into being. The immediate vanishing of these differences into *singularity* is the present as Now (*die Gegenwart als Jetzt*) which, as singularity, is *exclusive* of the other moments, and at the same time completely *continues* in them, and is only this vanishing of its being into nothing and of nothing into its being.

"The *finite* present (*die endliche Gegenwart*) is the Now as *being* and distinguished as the concrete unity, and hence as the affirmative, from what is *negative,* from the abstract moments of past and future; but this being is itself only abstract, vanishing into nothing. Furthermore, in Nature, where time is a Now, being does not reach the *existence* of the difference of these dimensions; they are of necessity only in subjective imagination (*Vorstellung*), in remembrance and *fear* and *hope*. But the past and future of time as being in Nature are space, for space is negated time; just as sublated (*aufgehobene*) space is immediately the point, which developed for itself is time" (*Enc.,* sec. 259, p. 37). These texts—and several others—seem both to confirm and to challenge the interpretation in *Being and Time*. The confirmation is evident. The challenge complicates things at the point at which the present is distinguished from the now, at which the now, in its purity, belongs only to nature and is not yet time, etc. In a word, it would be quite hasty and an oversimplification to say that the Hegelian concept of time is borrowed from a "physics" or from a "philosophy of nature," and that in this way it essentially passes unchanged into a "philosophy of spirit" or into a "philosophy of history." Time is also this passage itself. The reading of Aristotle already would raise analogous questions.

Every affirmation (here, Heidegger's) according to which a concept, in Hegel, belongs to the philosophy of nature (or, in general, to a determined, particular site of the Hegelian text) a priori is of limited pertinence due to the *relevant* [cf. *aufheben*] structure of the relations between nature and non-nature in speculative dialectics. Nature is outside spirit, but as spirit itself, as the position of its proper being-outside-itself.

of time from the "spatial" concepts of part and whole, from the predetermination of the *nun* as *meros* or even as *stigmē?* Let us recall Aristotle's two questions. 1. Is or is not time a part of *onta?* 2. After the aporias relative to the properties which amount to time (*peri tōn huparkhontōn*), it is asked what time is, and what its *physis* might be (*ti d'estin ho khronos kai tis autou hē physis*). The manner in which the first question is formulated indeed shows that the Being of time has been anticipated on the basis of the now, and of the now as part. And this occurs at the moment when Aristotle seems to overturn the first hypothesis and to contend instead that the now is not a part, or that time is not composed of nows (*to de nun ou meros . . . ho de khronos ou dokei sungkeisthai ek tōn nun*—218a). This second series of propositions belongs to an elaboration of the common-sense hypotheses whereby time may be thought of as not belonging to beings, or to beingness (*ousia*) in any pure and simple fashion. These initial exoteric hypotheses never will be put into question at another level, a nonexoteric level.[23] Having recalled why it may be thought that time is not a being, Aristotle leaves the question in suspense. From here on the *physis* of that whose belonging to being still remains undecidable will be examined. As has been noted,[24] there is here "a metaphysical problem that Aristotle in part, perhaps, has evaded," even if "nevertheless, he has clearly posed it." That the evaded question is properly metaphysical might be understood otherwise. What is metaphysical is perhaps less the evaded *question* than the *evaded* question. Metaphysics, then, may be posited by this omission. In repeating the question of Being in the transcendental horizon of time, *Being and Time* thus brings to light the omission which permitted metaphysics to believe that it could think time on the basis of a being already silently predetermined in its relation to time. If all of metaphysics is engaged by this gesture, *Being and Time*, in this regard at least, constitutes a decisive step beyond or within metaphysics. The question was evaded because it was put in terms of belonging to being or to nonbeing, being already determined as being-present. It is what the question evades that Heidegger puts back into play from the first part of *Being and Time* on: time, then, will be that on the basis of which the Being of beings is indicated, and not that whose possibility will be derived on the basis of a being already constituted (and in secret temporally predetermined), as a present being (of the indicative, as *Vorhandenheit*), that is, as substance or object.

That what is evaded in the question propagates its effects over the entire history of metaphysics, or rather constitutes this history as such, as the effect of the evasion, is recognizable not only in the massively evident fact that, until Kant, metaphysics held time to be the nothingness or the accident foreign to

23. This is the difference, in *Physics IV*, between the treatise on place and the treatise on time. Only the former adds a critical elaboration to the exoteric elaboration and explicates its articulation (210b).

24. J. Moreau, *L'espace et le temps selon Aristote* (Padua: Antenare, 1965), p. 92.

essence or to truth. That all of metaphysics, so to speak, has been sunk in this opening or, if you will, paralyzed in the aporia of the exoteric discourse of *Physics IV* is *still* to be seen in Kant. Not only in Kant's linking of the possibility of time to the *intuitus derivativus* and to the concept of a *derived* finitude or passivity, but above all in that which is most revolutionary and least metaphysical in his thought of time. This can be attributed, as you will, to the passive in Kant or to the active in Aristotle. It will have as little meaning in both cases.

In effect, *as Aristotle says*, it is because time does not belong to beings, is no more a part of them than it is a determination of them, and because time is not of (phenomenal or noumenal) being in general, that it must be made into a *pure* form of sensibility (the nonsensuous sensuous). This profound metaphysical fidelity *is organized and arranged* along with the break that recognizes time as the condition for the possibility of the appearance of beings in (finite) experience, *i.e., also along with that in Kant which will be repeated by Heidegger*. In principle, therefore, the text of Aristotle could always be submitted to what might be called the "generous repetition," the repetition from which Kant profits, but which is denied Aristotle and Hegel, at least at the period of *Being and Time*. At a certain point, then, the destruction of metaphysics remains within metaphysics, only making explicit its principles. This is a necessity that would have to be examined in terms of this example, and its *rule would have to be formalized*. Here, the Kantian break was prepared by *Physics IV*, and one could say as much for the Heideggerian "re-edition" of the Kantian gesture in *Being and Time* and in *Kant and the Problem of Metaphysics*.

In effect, if one compares the "Transcendental Exposition of the Concept of Time" to *Physics IV*, one quickly picks up this decisive common characteristic: "Time is not something which exists of itself, or which inheres in things as an objective determination, and it does not, therefore, remain when abstraction is made of all subjective conditions of its intuition."[25] It may be said that this characteristic—the nonbeingness in itself of time—is very general, and that the community of intention between Kant and Aristotle is quite limited. Let us consider, then, the narrower definition of time in the "Transcendental Exposition," not the definition of time as nonexistence in itself, nor as the "formal condition of all phenomena in general" (internal as well as external), but rather as the "form of inner sense."[26] The entire force of the break implied in this definition still seems rigorously prescribed in *Physics IV*. Examining the *physis* of time, Aristotle wonders—since time which is neither change nor movement *has a relationship* with *change* and *movement* (and this is precisely how the "Transcendental Exposition" begins)—*ti tēs kinēseōs estin* (219a), what of movement is time? And he remarks, not as is often and vaguely translated that "we perceive time in perceiving movement," but *hama gar kinēseōs aisthanometha kai khronou:*

25. TN. Kant, *Critique of Pure Reason,* trans. Norman Kemp Smith (New York: St. Martin's Press, 1965), p. 76.
26. TN. Ibid., p. 77.

"it is together that we have the sensation of movement and time." When we are in the dark, and are not affected by any body (*mēden dia tou sōmatos paskhōmen*), if a movement is produced in the soul (*en tēi psukhēi*), then it seems that a certain time has passed, and, by the same token, *together (hama)*, a certain movement seems to have occurred. Aristotle unites time and movement in *aisthēsis*. And does so such that no sensory exterior content, or objective movement, is necessary. Time is the form of that which can occur only *en tēi psukhēi*. The form of inner sense is also the form of all phenomena in general. The transcendental exposition of time places this concept in an essential relation with movement and change, even while rigorously distinguishing it from them.[27] And as in *Physics IV*, we shall see, it takes off from the possibility of the *analogy* constituted by *what is traced* determined as *line (grammē, Linie)*.[28]

What Aristotle has set down, then, is both traditional metaphysical security, and, in its inaugural ambiguity, the critique of this security. In anticipating the concept of the nonsensuous sensuous, Aristotle furnishes the premises of a thought of time no longer dominated simply by the present (of beings given in the form of *Vorhandenheit* and *Gegenwärtigkeit*). There is here both an instability and several possibilities of overturning; and we may wonder whether *Sein und Zeit* has not, in a way, arrested them. Whatever elements of the transcendental imagination that seem to escape the domination of the present given in the form of *Vorhandenheit* and *Gegenwärtigkeit* doubtless have been foreshadowed in *Physics IV*. The paradox would be the following, therefore: the originality of the Kantian

27. See also 223ab. Aristotle also thinks time in relation to movement (*kinēsis*) and change (*metabolē*), although he begins by demonstrating that time is neither the one nor the other. This is also the first moment of the *Transcendental Exposition of the Concept of Time*. "Here I may add that the concept of alteration (*Veränderung*), and with it the concept of motion (*Bewegung*), as alteration of place, is possible only through and in the representation of time; and that if this representation were not an *a priori* (inner) intuition, no concept, no matter what it might be, could render comprehensible the possibility of an alteration, that is, of a combination of contradictorily opposed predicates in one and the same object, for instance, the being and the non-being of one and the same thing (*Objekte*) in one and the same place. Only in time can two contradictorily opposed predicates meet in one and the same object, namely, *one after the other*. Thus our concept of time explains the possibility of that body of *a priori* synthetic knowledge which is exhibited in the general doctrine of motion, and which is by no means unfruitful" (*Critique of Pure Reason*, p. 76).

28. "Time is nothing but the form of inner sense, that is, of the intuition of ourselves and of our inner state. It cannot be a determination of outer appearances; it has to do neither with shape nor position, but with the relation of representations in our inner state. *And just because this inner intuition yields no shape, we endeavour to make up for this want by analogies. We represent the time-sequence by a line progressing to infinity (und stellen die Zeitfolge durch eine ins Unendliche fortgehende Linie vor)* in which the manifold constitutes a series of one dimension only; and we reason from the properties of this line to all the properties of time, with this one exception, that while the parts of the line are simultaneous the parts of time are always successive. From this fact also, that all the relations of time allow of being expressed in an outer intuition, it is evident that the representation is itself an intuition" (*Critique of Pure Reason*, p. 77).

breakthrough, such as it is repeated in *Kant and the Problem of Metaphysics*,[29] transgresses the vulgar concept of time only by making explicit something hinted at in *Physics IV*. Making explicit the evaded *question* always and necessarily keeps to the system of what is *evaded*. How does the predetermination of time on the basis of the *nun* evade the question? In one sense, Aristotle, in his exoteric, picks up Zeno's argument. While acknowledging that this argument clarifies nothing (218a), Aristotle repeats its aporia without deconstructing it. Time is not (among beings). It is nothingness because it is *is time, that is* a past or future now. Here, the *that is* supposes that I have somehow anticipated *what* time *is*, to wit, the nonpresent in the form of the now that is past or to come. The current now is not time, because it is present; time is not (a being) to the extent that it is not (present). This means that if it appears that one may demonstrate that time is no-thing (nonbeing), it is because one already has determined the origin and essence of no-thing as time, as nonpresent under the heading of the "not yet" or the "already no longer." Therefore, in order to state the no-thingness of time, one already has had to appeal to time, to a precomprehension of time, and, within discourse, to the self-evidence and functioning of the verb's tenses. Without *disclosing* it, one already has operated within the horizon of the meaning of

29. For example, in section 32 ("The Transcendental Imagination and Its Relation to Time"), which shows how the pure intuition of time, such as it is described in the "Transcendental Esthetic," is freed from the privilege of the present and the now. We must cite a long passage from section 32 that clarifies all the concepts of *Sein und Zeit*, a passage that interests us to the highest degree in this context: "We have shown how the transcendental imagination is the origin of pure sensible intuition. Thus, we have proved essentially that time as pure intuition arises from the transcendental imagination. However, a specific, analytical explication of the precise manner in which time is based upon the transcendental imagination is necessary.

"As the pure succession of the *now*-series (*Nacheinander der Jetztfolge*) time is 'in constant flux.' Pure intuition intuits this succession without making of it an object (*ungegenständtlich*). To intuit means: to receive that which offers itself. Pure intuition gives to itself, in the receptive act, that which is capable of being received.

"Reception of . . . is usually understood as the act of receiving something given (*Vorhandenen*) or present (*Anwesenden*). But this limited conception of the receptive act, a conception inspired by empirical intuition, must not be applied to pure intuition and its characteristic receptivity. It is easy to see that the pure intuition of the pure succession of *nows* cannot be the reception of something actually *present (Anwesenden)*. If it were, then it could at most only 'intuit' the actual *now (das jetzige Jetzt),* but never the *now*-sequence as such and the horizon which it forms. Strictly speaking, the simple act of receiving something actually present (*Gegenwärtigen*) could not even intuit a single *now (Jetzt),*) since each *now* has an essentially continuous extension in a *just passing* and *just coming (in sein Soeben und Sogleich).* The receptive act of pure intuition must in itself give the aspect of the now (*den Anblick des Jetzt*) in such a way that it *looks ahead (vorblickt)* to the just coming and back (*rückblickt*) to the *just passing.*

"We now discover, and in a more concrete way, why it is that pure intuition, which is the subject of the transcendental aesthetic, cannot be the reception of something 'present' (*Gegenwärtigen*). Pure intuition which, as receptive, gives itself its object is by nature not relative only to something present (*ein nur Anwesendes*), and least of all to a being actually given (*vorhändenes seiendes*)" (*Kant and the Problem of Metaphysics*, pp. 178–79; translation slightly modified).

time in order to think nonbeing as nonpresent, and being as present. Being has been determined temporally as being-present in order to determine time as nonpresent and nonbeing.

In effect, what is said *dia tōn exōterikōn logōn?* That "it [time] either does not exist at all, or exists barely and obscurely . . . One part of it has been and is no longer (*gegone kai ouk esti*); another part will be and is not yet (*mellei kai oupō estin*). Such are the components of time—of infinite time (*apeiros*) and of time considered in its incessant return (*aei lambanomenos*). Now it seems impossible that that which allows non-beings in its composition participates in beingness (*ousia*)."[30]

The *mē on*, the no-thingness of time, therefore, is accessible only on the basis of the Being of time. Time as nothing can be thought only according to the modes of time, the past and the future. Being is nontime, time is nonbeing insofar as being already, secretly has been determined as present, and beingness (*ousia*) as presence. As soon as being and present are synonymous, to say no-thingness and to say time are the same thing. Time is indeed the discursive manifestation of negativity, and Hegel, mutatis mutandis, will only make explicit what is said of *ousia* as presence.

Even before it is linked to the difficult analyses of the number—numbering or numbered—the Aristotelian dyad time-movement is conceived on the basis of *ousia* as presence. *Ousia* as *energeia*, in opposition to *dynamis* (movement, power), is presence. Time, which bears within it the already-no-longer and the not-yet, is a composite. In it, energy composes with power. This is why it is not, if you will,[31] "in act," and this is why it is not *ousia* (subsisting or substantial being, if you will). The determination of beingness (*ousia*) as *energeia* or *entelekheia*, as the act and end of movement, is inseparable from the determination of time. The *meaning* of time is thought on the basis of the present as nontime. And this could not be otherwise; *sense* (in whatever sense it is understood: as essence, as the meaning of discourse, as the orientation of the movement between *archē* and *telos*) has never been conceivable, within the history of metaphysics, otherwise than on the basis of presence and as presence. The concept of sense, of meaning, is governed by the entire system of determinations that we are pointing out here, and every time that a question of *meaning* is posed, it must be posed within the closure of metaphysics. To put it quite summarily, one seeks in vain to extract the question of meaning (the meaning of time, or of anything else) as such from metaphysics, or from the system of so called "vulgar" concepts. Such

30. TN. *Physics IV*, 217b–18a.
31. ". . . if you will, 'in act,' " because this is a problematical translation. That it does not go without saying is a problem that we cannot tackle here. We may refer, on the one hand, to "The Anaximander Fragment," which marks the distance between Aristotle's *energeia* and the *actualitas* or *actus purus* of medieval scholasticism; and on the other hand, to Pierre Aubenque, who emphasizes that "the modern translation of *act* is not a forgetting of the original sense, but for once remains faithful to it" (*Le Problème de l'être chez Aristote*, Paris: Presses Universitaires de France, 1962, p. 441, n. 1).

51

also would be the case, therefore, for a *question of Being* determined, as it is at the beginning of *Being and Time*, as a question of the *meaning of Being*, whatever the force, necessity, and value (irruptive as well as fundamental) of such a question. Heidegger doubtless would acknowledge that as a question of meaning, the question of Being is already linked, at its point of departure, to the (lexical and grammatical) discourse of the metaphysics whose destruction it has undertaken. In a sense, as Bataille gives us to think, the question of meaning, the project of *preserving* meaning, is "vulgar." This is his word too.

As for the meaning of time, therefore, its determination according to presence is as determining as it is determined: it tells us what time *is* (nonbeing as "no longer" or as "not yet"), but can do so only in order to *let itself be said*, by means of a concept implicit in the relation between time *and* Being: that time could *be* only a (in) *being*, that is, following this present participle, only a *present*. Consequently, time could be a (in) being only in not being what it is, that is, in being-present. Thus, because time, in its Being, is thought on the basis of the present, it is also strangely thought as nonbeing (or as an impure, composite being). In believing one knows what time is, in its *physis*, the question that will be asked only later has implicitly been answered and this permits the conclusion, in the exoteric aporia, of time's bare existence, that is, its nonexistence. One already knows, even if only in the naive practice of discourse, what time must be, what *past (gegone)* or *future (mellei)* mean, in order to reach the conclusion of time's bare existence or nonexistence. And past and future are thought as attenuating affections overtaking the presence which is known to be the meaning or essence of what is (beings). This is what will not budge from Aristotle to Hegel. The prime mover, as "pure act" (*energeia hē kath' hautēn*), is pure presence. As such, it animates all movement by means of the desire it inspires. It is the good, and the supremely desirable. Desire is the desire of presence. Eros is also thought on the basis of presence. Like movement. Hegel calls the *telos* that puts movement in motion, and that orients becoming toward itself, the absolute concept or subject. The transformation of parousia into *self*-presence, and the transformation of the supreme being into a subject thinking itself, and assembling itself near itself in knowledge, does not interrupt the fundamental tradition of Aristotelianism. The concept as absolute subjectivity itself thinks itself, is for itself and near itself, has no exterior, and it assembles, erasing them, its time and its difference in self-presence.[32] This may be put in Aristotle's language:

32. Time is the *existence* of the circle, of the circle of circles spoken of at the end of the *Logic*. Time is circular, but it is also that which, in the movement of the circle, dissimulates circularity; it is the circle in that itself it hides from itself its own totality, in that it loses in difference the unity of its beginning and its end. "But the method which thus becomes entwined in a circle cannot anticipate in a temporal development that the beginning as such is already derivative" (*Science of Logic*, vol. 2, p. 484). Therefore "the pure concept conceiving itself" is time, and nevertheless realizes itself as the erasure of time. It comprehends time. And if time has a meaning in general, it is difficult to see how it could be extracted from onto-theo-teleology (for example, of the Hegelian kind). It is not any given determination of the meaning of time that belongs to onto-theo-teleology, but it is the

noēsis noēseōs, the thought of thought, the pure act, the prime mover, the lord who, himself thinking himself, is subjugated to no objectivity, no exteriority, remaining immobile in the infinite movement of the circle and of the return to self.

The Pivot of Essence

Proceeding to the question of the *physis* of time, Aristotle first remarks that tradition has never answered such a question (a gesture that henceforth will be indefatigably repeated, even by Hegel and Heidegger). But afterward Aristotle only develops the aporia in its own terms, that is, in the concepts whose configuration is reconstituted by Heidegger (*nun, oros*—or *peras*—*stigmē, sphaira*, to which we should add *holon*, whole, *meros*, part, and *grammē*). The traditional form of the question is never fundamentally put back into question. What is this form?

Let us recall it. The first phase of the alternative (none of the parts of time is—present—therefore time in its totality *is* not—which means "is not *present*," "does not participate in *ousia*") supposed that time was composed of parts, to wit, of nows (*nun*). It is this presupposition that the second phase of the alternative contests: the now is not a part, time is not composed of nows, the unity and identity of the now are problematical. "If in fact the now is always other, and if none of the parts in time which are other are simultaneous (*hama*) . . .

anticipation of its meaning. Time already has been suppressed at the moment one asks the question of its meaning, when one relates it to appearing, truth, presence, or essence *in general*. The question asked at this moment is that of time's *realization*. Perhaps this is why there is no other possible answer to the question of the meaning or Being of time than the one given at the end of the *Phenomenology of the Mind:* time *is* that which erases (*tilgt*) time. But this erasure is a writing which gives time to be read, and maintains it in suppressing it. The *Tilgen* is also an *Aufheben.* Thus, for example: "*Time* is the very *concept* which *is there (der da ist),* presenting itself to consciousness as empty intuition. This is why spirit necessarily manifests itself in time, and it manifests itself in time as long as it does not *grasp* its pure concept, that is, does not eliminate time (*nicht de Zeit tilgt*). Time is the pure *exterior* self; it is the concept as merely intuited, *not grasped* by the self. When this concept grasps itself, it suppresses its temporal form (*hebt er seine Zeitform auf*), conceives the intuition, and is the intuition as conceived and conceiving. Thus, time manifests itself as destiny (*Schicksal*) and as the necessity of spirit which is not yet attained within itself." *Phenomenology of the Mind*, trans. J. B. Baillie (London: Allen and Unwin, 1931), p. 800. We have inserted the German words which show the unity of *Dasein* and of time, of the *Tilgen* and the *Aufheben.* However it is determined, Hegelian Being no more falls into time as into its *Da-sein*, than it *simply departs from time* to enter parousia.

That the circle for Aristotle is already the model of movement on which basis are thought time and the *grammē* is self-evident enough not to require reference. Let us underline only that this is made explicit with great precision in *Physics IV:* "Time appears as the movement of the sphere because other movements are measured by this one, as is time itself. This also explains the common saying that human affairs form a circle and that other things which have natural movement—e.g. generation and destruction—are also circular in character . . . even time itself is thought to be a certain circle . . . etc." (223b). See also Aubenque, p. 426.

and if the 'now' which is not, but formerly was, must have ceased to be or been destroyed at a certain moment, the 'nows' too cannot be simultaneous (*hama*) with one another, but the preceding 'now' must always have been destroyed" (218a).

How do the concepts of *number* (as the numbered or the numbering) and of *gramme* intervene in order to refurbish the same conceptuality in the same system?

In a rigorously *dialectical* fashion: not in the strictly Aristotelian sense, but already in the Hegelian sense. Aristotle affirms opposites, or rather defines time as a dialectic of opposites, and as the solution of the contradictions that arise in terms of space. As in the *Encyclopedia*, time is the line, the solution of the contradiction of the point (nonspatial spatiality). And yet it is not the line, etc. The contradictory terms posited in the aporia are simply taken up and affirmed together in order to define the *physis* of time. In a certain way, one might say that dialectics only always repeats the exoteric aporia by affirming it, by making of time the affirmation of the aporetic.

Thus Aristotle affirms that the now, in a certain sense, is the same, and in another sense, is the nonsame (*to de nun esti men hōs to auto, esti d' hōs ou to auto—* 219b); that time is continuous according to the now and divided according to the now (*kai sunekhēs te dē ho khronos tōi nun, kai diēirētai kata to nun*—220a).[33] And all these contradictory affirmations are reassembled in a dialectical manipulation of the concept of *gramme*. This dialectical manipulation is already—as it will be always—governed by the distinction between the potentiality and the act, the contradictions resolving themselves as soon as one takes into account the relationship under whose rubric they are considered: potentially or in act. And this distinction between the potentiality and the act evidently is not symmetrical, being itself governed by a teleology of presence, by the act (*energeia*) as presence (*ousia, parousia*).

It seems at first that Aristotle rejects the representation of time by the *gramme*, that is, here, by a linear inscription in space, just as he rejects the identification of the now with the point. His argumentation even then was traditional, and it remained so. It appeals to the noncoexistence of the parts of time. Time is distinguished from space in that it is not, as Leibniz will say, an "order of coexistences," but an "order of successions." The relationship of points between themselves cannot be the same as that of the nows between themselves. Points do not destroy each other reciprocally. But if the present now were not annulled by the following now, it would coexist with it, which is impossible. Even if it were annulled only by a now very distant from it, it would have to coexist with all the intermediate nows, which are infinite (indeterminate: *apeiros*) in number; and this too is impossible (218a). A now cannot coexist, as a current and present now, with another now as such. Coexistence has *meaning* only in the unity of

33. See also 222a.

a single, same now. This is *meaning*, sense itself, in what unites meaning to presence. One cannot even say that the coexistence of two different and equally present nows is impossible or unthinkable: the very signification of coexistence or of presence is constituted by this limit. Not to be able to coexist with an other (the same as itself), with an other now, is not a predicate of the now, but its essence as presence. The now, presence in the act of the present, is constituted as the impossibility of coexisting with an other now, that is, with an other-the-same-as-itself. The now *is* (in the present indicative) the impossibility of coexisting *with itself*: with itself, that is, with an other self, an other now, an other same, a double.

But it has already been remarked that this impossibility, when barely formulated, contradicts itself, is experienced as the possibility of the impossible. This impossibility implies in its essence, in order to be what it is, that the other now, with which a now cannot coexist, is also in a certain way the same, is also a now as such, and that it coexists with that which cannot coexist with it. The impossibility of coexistence can be posited as such only on the basis of a certain coexistence, of a certain *simultaneity* of the nonsimultaneous, in which the alterity and identity of the now are maintained together in the differentiated element of a certain same. To speak Latin, the *cum* or the *co-* of coexistence has meaning only on the basis of its impossibility, and vice versa. The impossible—the coexistence of two nows—appears only in a synthesis—taking this word neutrally, implying no position, no activity, no agent—let us say in a certain complicity or coimplication *maintaining* together several current nows [*maintenants*] which are said to be the one past and the other future. The impossible comaintenance of several present nows [*maintenants*] is possible as the maintenance of several present nows [*maintenants*]. Time is a name for this impossible possibility.

Conversely, the space of *possible coexistence*, precisely that which one believes is known by the name of *space*, the possibility of coexistence, is the space of the impossible coexistence. In effect, simultaneity can appear *as such*, can be simultaneity, that is, a *relating* of two points, only in a synthesis, a *complicity: temporally*. One cannot say that a point is *with* another point; and a point, whether one says it or not, cannot *be with* another point, there cannot be an *other* point with which, etc., without a temporalization. Which maintains together two different nows. The *with* of spatial coexistence arises only out of the *with* of temporalization. As Hegel shows: There is a *with* of time that makes possible the *with* of space, but which could not be produced as *with* without the possibility of space. (In pure *Aussersichsein* there is no more *determined* space than determined time.)

Truthfully, to state these propositions in this way is to remain naive. We are acting as if the difference between space and time were given as an obvious and constituted difference. Now, as Hegel and Heidegger remind us, one cannot treat space *and* time as two concepts or as two themes. We speak naively each time we give ourselves space and time as two possibilities to be compared and related. And especially each time we believe, in doing this, that we know what space or time *is*, or in general what the *essence* is, within whose horizon we believe we can ask the question of space and time. In this last case, we are supposing that a question on the essence of space and time is possible, without asking whether essence, here, can be the formal horizon of this question, and whether the essence of essence has not been predetermined secretly—as presence, precisely—on the basis of a "decision" concerning time *and* space. Therefore it cannot be a question of relating space *and* time, each of the terms *being* only what it is not, and consisting, first of all, only of the *com*-parison itself.

Now, if Aristotle gives himself the difference between time and space (for example, in the distinction between *nun* and *stigmē*) as a constituted difference, the enigmatic articulation of this difference is lodged in his text, hidden, sheltered, but operating within complicity, within the complicity of the same and the other, within the *with* or the *together*, with the *simul* in which Being-together is not a determination of Being, but the very production of Being. The entire weight of Aristotle's text comes down upon a word so small as to be hardly visible, and hardly visible because it appears self-evident, as discreet as that which goes without saying, a word that is self effacing, operating all the more effectively in that it evades thematic attention. That which *goes* without saying, making discourse play itself out in its articulation, that which henceforth will constitute the pivot [*cheville*] (*clavis*) of metaphysics, the small key that both opens and closes the history of metaphysics in terms of what it puts at stake, the clavicle on which the conceptual decision of Aristotle bears down and is articulated, is the small word *hama*. It appears five times in 218a. In Greek *hama* means "together," "all at once," both together, "*at the same time.*" This locution is first neither spatial nor temporal. The duplicity of the *simul* to which it refers does not yet reassemble, within itself, either points or nows, places or phases. It says the complicity, the common origin of time and space, appearing together [*com-paraître*] as the condition for all appearing of Being. In a certain way it says the dyad as the minimum. But Aristotle does not say it. He develops his demonstration in the unnoticed self-evidence of what the locution *hama* says. He says it without saying it, lets it say itself, or rather it lets him say what he says.

Let us verify this. If time, in the first hypothesis of the aporia, appears not to take part in pure *ousia* as such, it is that it is made of nows (time's parts), and that several nows cannot: (1) either follow each other by immediately destroying one another, for in this case there would be no time; (2) or follow each other by destroying each other in a not immediately consecutive way, for in this case the intervallic nows would be simultaneous, and again there would be no time; (3) or remain (in) the same now, for in this case things that occur at intervals of ten thousand years would be *together, at the same time*, which is absurd. It is this absurdity, denounced in the self-evidence of the "at the same time," that constitutes the aporia as aporia.

Thus, these three hypotheses make the *ousia* of time inconceivable. However, they themselves can be conceived and stated only by means of the temporal-intemporal adverb *hama*. Let us consider the sequence of nows. The preceding now, it is said, must be destroyed by the following now. But, Aristotle then points out, it cannot be destroyed "in itself" (*en heautōi*), that is, at the moment when it is (now, in act). No more can it be destroyed in an other now (*en allōi*): for then it would not be destroyed as now, itself; and, as a now which has been, it is (remains) inaccessible to the action of the following now. "One now cannot be related to another, any more than a point can be related to another point. If then the now is not immediately (*en tōi ephexēs*) destroyed in the next now but in another, it would exist at the same time (*hama*) as the innumerable nows between the two—which is impossible. But neither is it possible for the now to remain (*diamenein*) always the same. No determinate divisible thing has a unique limit, whether it is continuously extended in one or in more than one dimension; but the now is a limit, and it is possible to separate off a determinate time. Further, if being at the same time (*to hama einai*)—i.e. being neither anterior nor posterior—means to be in one and the same now, then, if both what is before and what is after are this same now, things which happened thousands of years ago would be simultaneous (*hama*) with what has happened today, and nothing would be before or after anything else" (218a).

Gramme and Number

Such, then, is the aporia. Despite its cinematic point of departure, it already prevents Aristotle's reflections from identifying time with the *gramme* representing movement, especially if this representation is of a mathematical nature: because nows are not "at the same time," as are points (218a); because time is not movement (218b); because *Physics IV* distinguishes between *gramme* in general and the mathematical line (222a; Aristotle speaks, here, of what happens *epi tōn mathēmatikōn grammōn* in which the points are always the same); and finally because, as we shall see, time, as the *numbered* number of movement, is not intrinsically of an arithmetic nature. For all these reasons, it is already evident that we are not dealing with the cinematographic concept of time so vigorously denounced by Bergson, and even less with a simple mathematicism or arithmeticism. And conversely, it appears that Bergson, in a sense perhaps different than the one indicated by Heidegger, is more Aristotelian than he himself believes.[34]

How does time *come into line* with the *Physics?*

34. Let us recall, for example, in order to keep things straight, the following passages, among so many others: "It is thus that we were led up to the idea of Time. There a surprise awaited us. In effect, we were very struck to see how real time, which plays a primary role in every philosophy of evolution, escapes mathematics. Its essence being to pass, none of its parts is still there when another presents itself . . . In the case of time, the idea of superimposition would imply an absurdity, for every effect of duration that would be superimposable with itself, and consequently measurable, would have as its essence not

57

1. Time is neither movement (*kinēsis*) nor change (*metabolē*). These exist solely in Being-moved or in changing-Being, and are more or less slow or rapid, which cannot be the case with time. On the contrary, time makes possible movement, change, their measurement, and differences of speed. Here time is what defines, and not what is defined (218b).

2. Nevertheless, there is no time without movement. It is here[35] that Aristotle links time to *experience* or to *appearing (dianoia, psykhē, aisthēsis)*. If time is not movement, we nevertheless cannot experience time except by feeling and determining a change or a movement. (Aristotle asserts that here the difference between movement and change is not pertinent and should not detain him—218b.) "Therefore it is clear that time neither *is* movement nor exists *without* it" (219a).

What is it then that relates time to what it is not, that is, to movement? What in movement determines time? One must seek in time *ti tēs kinēseōs estin*, that is, in sum, what relates time to space, and to changes of place. And one must find the concepts for this relationship.

Discreet, advanced without insistence, as if they went without saying, the fundamental categories, here, are those of *analogy* and *correspondence*. They lead back, by other names, and barely displacing it, to the *enigma* of the "at the same time," which both names and evades, states and obscures, the problem.

Magnitude is continuous. This is axiomatic here. Now, movement follows the order of magnitude, corresponds to this order (*akolouthei tōi megethei hē kinēsis*). Therefore it is continuous. Further, anterior and posterior are local situations (*en topōi*). As such, they are within magnitude, and therefore, according to the correspondence or the *analogy* of magnitude and movement (219a), they are also within movement. And within time, since "time and movement always correspond to each other" (*dia to akolouthein aei thaterōi thateron autōn*). It follows, finally, that time is continuous by analogy with movement and magnitude.

This leads to the definition of time as the number of movement following the before and the after (219ab). A definition made more specific, as is well known, by the distinction between the *numbered* number and the *numbering* number. The number is said in two ways (*dikhōs*): numbering number and numbered number (219b). Time is a numbered number (*oukh hōi arithmoumen all' ho arithmoumenos*).

---

to endure . . . The line is ready made, time is that which makes itself, and is even that which makes everything to make itself." And the following remark, which would be in agreement with a given passage from Heidegger's Note, if the latter precisely did not denounce a limit of the Bergsonian revolution: "Throughout the history of philosophy, time and space are put on the same level, and treated as things of the same genre. Thus, one studies space, determines its nature and function, and then transports the conclusions thus obtained onto time. The theory of space and the theory of time thus become symmetrical. To go from one to the other, it sufficed to change one word: 'juxtaposition' was replaced by 'succession.' " *La pensée et le mouvant* (Paris: Presses Universitaires de France, 1946), pp. 2, 3, 5ff.

35. See also 223a.

This means, paradoxically, that even if time comes under the rubric of mathematics or arithmetic, it is not in itself, in its nature, a mathematical being. It is as foreign to number itself, to the numbering number, as horses and men are different from the numbers that count them, and different from each other. *And different from each other,* which leaves us free to think that time is not a being among others, among men and horses. "The number of one hundred horses and one hundred men is one and the same number, but the things—the horses and men—for which there is a number are other" (220b).

There is time only in the extent to which movement has number, but time, in the rigorous sense, is neither movement nor number. It lets itself be numbered only insofar as it has a relation to movement according to the before and after. The unity of the measure of time numbered in this way is the now, which permits the distinction between before and after. And it is because movement is determined according to the before and the after that the graphic linear representation of time is simultaneously required and excluded by Aristotle. This determination according to the anterior and the posterior "corresponds," in effect, "in a certain manner to the point" (*akolouthei de kai touto pōs tēi stigmēi*). The point gives to length its *continuity* and its *limit.* The line is a continuity of points. And each point is both an *end* and a *beginning (arkhē kai teleutē)* for each part. Thus, one could be led to believe that the now is to time what the point is to the line. And that the essence of time can pass, intact and undamaged, into its linear representation, into the continuous, extended unfolding of punctuality.

Aristotle firmly indicates that this is not so. The spatial and linear representation, at least in this form, is inadequate. What is criticized, thereby, is not the relationship of time to movement, nor the numbered or numerable Being of time, but rather time's analogy with a certain structure of the *gramme.*

In effect, if one uses the point and the line to represent movement, one is manipulating a multiplicity of points which are both origin and limit, beginning and end; this multiplicity of immobilities, this series (if it can be called such), of successive arrests, *does not give time,* and when Aristotle recalls this, his language is indistinguishable from Bergson's: ". . . for the point both connects and limits the length—it is the beginning of one and the end of another. But if you consider the one point as two, an arrest or pause is necessary, if the same point is to be both beginning and end" (220a).

In this sense, the now is not the point, since it does not arrest time, is neither time's origin, end, or limit. At least it is not a limit *to the extent that* it belongs to time. The importance of the *to the extent that* henceforth will become more specific, and will do so unceasingly.

What is rejected, then, is not the *gramme* as such, but the *gramme* as a series of points, as a composition of parts each of which would be an arrested limit. But if one considers now that the point, as limit, does not exist *in act,* is not (present), exists only potentially and by accident, takes its existence only from the line in act, then it is not impossible to preserve the analogy of the *gramme:* on the condition that one does not take it as a series of potential limits, but as a line in act, as a line thought on the basis of its extremities (*ta eskhata*) and not of its parts (220a). Certainly this permits us to distinguish between, on the one hand, time and movement and, on the other, the *gramme* as a homogeneous series of point-limits unfolded in space; but, by the same token, this amounts to thinking time and movement on the basis of the *telos* of a *gramme* that is completed, in act, fully present, that keeps its *tracing* close to itself, that is, erases its tracing in a *circle.* The point can cease to immobilize movement, can cease to be both beginning and end, only if the extremities touch, and only if the *finite* movement of the circle regenerates itself *indefinitely,* the end indefinitely reproducing itself in beginning and the beginning in the end. In this sense the circle removes the limit of the point only by developing its potentiality. The *gramme* is *comprehended* by metaphysics between the point and the circle, between potentiality and the act (presence), etc.; and all the critiques of the spatialization of time, from Aristotle to Bergson, remain within the limits of this comprehension. *Time,* then, would be but the name of the limits within which the *gramme* is thus comprehended, and, along with the *gramme,* the possibility of the trace in general. *Nothing* other *has ever been* thought by the name of *time.* Time is that which is thought on the basis of Being as presence, and if something—which bears a relation to time, but is not time—is to be thought beyond the determination of Being as presence, it cannot be a question of something that still could be called *time.* Force and potentiality, *dynamics,* have always been thought, in the name of time, as an incomplete *gramme* within the horizon of an eschatology or a teleology that refers, according to the circle, to an archeology. Parousia is thought within the systematic movement of all these concepts. To criticize the manipulation or determination of any one of these concepts from within the system *always amounts,* and let this expression be taken with its full charge of meaning here, *to going around in circles:* to reconstituting, according to another configuration, the *same* system. Can this movement—which one must not hasten to denounce as useless restatement, and which has something essential to do with the movement of thought—be distinguished both from the Hegelian circle of metaphysics or ontotheology, and from that circle into which, Heidegger tells us so often, we must learn to enter *in a certain way?*

Whatever might be said about this circle, and the circle of circles, one may expect a priori, and in *the most formal* fashion, that the "critique"—or rather the denunciatory determination of a limit, the de-marcation, the *de-limitation*—which at any given moment is believed to be applicable to a "past" text is to be deciphered within it. More simply: every text of metaphysics carries within itself, for example, *both* the so-called "vulgar" concept of time *and* the resources that will be borrowed from the system of metaphysics in order to criticize that concept. And these resources are mandatory from the moment when the sign "time"—the unity of the word and the concept, of the signifier and signified "time" *in general*, whether or not it is limited by metaphysical "vulgarity"—begins to function in a discourse. It is on the basis of this formal necessity that one must reflect upon the conditions for a discourse exceeding metaphysics, supposing that such a discourse is possible, or that it announces itself in the filigree of some margin.

Thus, to keep to our Aristotelian anchorage, *Physics IV* doubtless confirms the Heideggerian de-limitation. Without a doubt, Aristotle thinks time on the basis of *ousia* as *parousia*, on the basis of the now, the point, etc. And yet an entire reading could be organized that would repeat in Aristotle's text *both* this limitation *and* its opposite. And which made it appear that the de-limitation is still governed by the same concepts as the limitation.

Let us sketch such a demonstration. Its development has been initiated several times in the itinerary that we have followed.

Like the point in relation to the line, the now, if it is considered as limit (*peras*), is *accidental* in relation to time. It is not time, but time's accident. *Hēi men oun peras to nun, ou khronos, alla sumbebēken* (220a). The now (*Gegenwart*), the present, therefore, does not define the essence of time. Time is not thought on the basis of the now. It is for this reason that the mathematization of time *has limits*. Let us take this in all possible senses. It is in the extent to which time requires *limits*, nows analogous to points, and in the extent to which the limits are always accidents and potentialities, that time cannot be made perfectly mathematical, that time's mathematization has limits, and remains, as concerns its essence, accidental. A rigorously Hegelian proposition: let us recall the difference between the present and the now.

On the other hand, the now, as limit, also serves to measure, to enumerate. Insofar as it enumerates, Aristotle says, it is number, *hēi d' arithmei, arithmos*. Now, the number does not belong to the thing numbered. If there are ten horses, the ten is not equine, is not of the essence of the horse, is elsewhere (*allothi*). In the same way, the now does not belong to the essence of time; it is elsewhere. That is, outside time, foreign to time. But foreign to it as its accident. And this foreignness, which might lift Aristotle's text from the Heideggerian delimitation, is comprehended within the system of the founding oppositions of metaphysics: foreignness is thought as accident, virtuality, potentiality, incompletion of the circle, weak presence, etc.

The now, therefore, is 1) a constitutive part of time and a number foreign to time; 2) a constitutive part of time and an accidental part of time. It can be considered *as such* or *as such*. The enigma of the now is dominated in the difference between act and potentiality, essence and accident, and the entire system of oppositions that follows from them. And the diffraction of the *to the extent thats* is made more specific, and is confirmed, the farther one goes in the text: in particular in 222a, where Aristotle reassembles the entire system of the various points of view one might have about the now, the entire system of the *to the extent thats*, the system according to which "the same things can be said in terms of potentiality and act" (*Physics I*, 191b, 27–29).

Here the plurality and distribution of significations is organized by the definition of movement as the "entelechy of that which, as such, exists potentially," such as this definition is produced in the decisive analysis of *Physics III* (201ab). The ambiguity of movement, the act of potentiality as potentiality, necessarily has a double consequence as concerns time. *On the one hand*, time, as the number of movement, is on the side of non-Being, matter, potentiality, incompletion. Being in act, energy, is not time, but eternal presence. Aristotle notes this in *Physics IV:* "Thus it is evident that eternal Beings (*ta aei onta*), as eternal, are not in time" (221b). But, *on the other hand*, time is not non-Being, and non-Beings are not in time. In order to be in time, something must have begun to be and to tend, like every potentiality, toward act and form:[36] "Thus it is evident that non-Being will not always be in time . . ." (221b).

Although understood on the basis of Being as presence in act, movement and time are neither (present) beings nor (absent) nonbeings. The categories of desire or movement as such, and the category of time as such, therefore are already or yet again *submitted* and *subtracted* in Aristotle's text, belonging as much to the de-limitation of metaphysics as the thought of the present, as to the simple overturning of metaphysics.

This play of submission and subtraction must be thought as a *formal rule* for anyone wishing *to read* the texts of the history of metaphysics. To read them, certainly, within the opening of the Heideggerian breakthrough, which is the only thought excess of metaphysics as such, but also to read them, occasionally, and faithfully, beyond certain propositions or conclusions within which the Heideggerian breakthrough has had to constrain itself, propositions or conclusions which it has had to call upon or take its support from. For example, the reading of Aristotle and Hegel during the epoch of *Being and Time*. And this formal rule must be capable of guiding our reading[37] of the entire Heideggerian text itself. In particular, it must permit us to pose the question of the inscription within it of the *epoch* of *Sein und Zeit*.

36. Even though Bergson criticizes the concept of the possible as possible, even though he makes neither of *duration* nor even of *tendency* a movement of the possible, and even though everything for him is "actual," it still remains that his concepts of duration, *élan*, and the ontological tension of the living oriented by a *telos* retain something of the Aristotelian ontology of time.

37. Only such a reading, on the condition that it does not give authority to the security or structural closing off of questions, appears to us capable of undoing *today, in France*, a profound complicity: the complicity which gathers together, in the same refusal to read, in the same denegation of the question, of the text, and of the question of the text, in the same reeditions, or in the same blind silence, the camp of Heideggerian devotion and the camp of anti-Heideggerianism. Here, political "resistance" often serves as a highly moral alibi for a "resistance" of an other order: *philosophical* resistance, for example, but there are other resistances whose political implications, although more distant, are no less determined.

The Closure of the Gramme
and the Trace of Difference

All this, in sum, in order to suggest:
1. That perhaps there is no "vulgar concept of time." The concept of time, in all its aspects, belongs to metaphysics, and it names the domination of presence. Therefore we can only conclude that the entire system of metaphysical concepts, throughout its history, develops the so-called "vulgarity" of the concept of time (which Heidegger, doubtless, would not contest), but also that an *other* concept of time cannot be opposed to it, since time in general belongs to metaphysical conceptuality. In attempting to produce this *other* concept, one rapidly would come to see that it is constructed out of other metaphysical or ontotheological predicates.

Was this not Heidegger's experience in *Being and Time?* The extraordinary trembling to which classical ontology is subjected in *Sein und Zeit* still remains within the grammar and lexicon of metaphysics. And all the conceptual pairs of opposites which serve the destruction of ontology are ordered around one fundamental axis: that which separates the authentic from the inauthentic and, in the very last analysis, primordial from fallen temporality. Now, as we have attempted to show, not only is it difficult simply to attribute to Hegel the proposition of a "fall of spirit into time," but in the extent to which it is possible, the de-limitation itself, perhaps, has to be *displaced.* The metaphysical or ontotheological limit doubtless consists less in thinking a fall *into time* (from a nontime, or an atemporal eternity, which has no meaning for Hegel), than in thinking a *fall* in general, even a fall of the kind *Being and Time* proposes as its fundamental theme and as its locus of greatest insistence, a fall from primordial into derivative time. For example, Heidegger writes at the end of section 82, devoted to Hegel: " 'Spirit' does not fall *into* time; but factical existence 'falls' as falling (*'fällt' als verfallende*) from primordial, authentic temporality (*aus der ursprünglichen, eigentlichen Zeitlichkeit*). But this 'falling' (*'Fallen'*) has its own existential possibility in a mode of its temporalizing—a mode which belongs to temporality."[38] And in closing *Being and Time* Heidegger wonders whether this primordial temporality constitutes the *horizon of Being,* if it leads to the *meaning of Being.*

Now, is not the opposition of the *primordial* to the *derivative* still metaphysical? Is not the quest for an *archia* in general, no matter with what precautions one surrounds the concept, still the "essential" operation of metaphysics? Supposing, despite powerful presumptions, that one may eliminate it from any other provenance, is there not at least some Platonism in the *Verfallen?* Why determine as *fall* the passage from one temporality to another? And why qualify temporality as authentic—or *proper (eigentlich)*—and as inauthentic—or improper—when every ethical preoccupation has been suspended? One could multiply such ques-

38. TN. *Being and Time,* p. 486.

tions around the concept of finitude, around the point of departure in the existential analytic of *Dasein*, justified by the enigmatic proximity[39] to itself or by the identity with itself of the questioning (section 5), etc. If we have chosen to examine the opposition that structures the concept of temporality, it is because the entire existential analytic leads back to it.

2. That the question we are asking remains within Heidegger's thought. It is not in closing but in interrupting *Being and Time* that Heidegger wonders whether "primordial temporality" leads to the meaning of Being. And this is not a programmatic articulation but a question and a suspension. The displacement, a certain lateralization, if not a simple erasure of the theme of time and of everything that goes along with it in *Being and Time*, lead one to think that Heidegger, without putting back into question the necessity of a certain point of departure in metaphysics, and even less the efficacity of the "destruction" operated by the analytic of *Dasein*, for essential reasons had to go at it otherwise and, it may be said literally, to *change horizons.*

Henceforth, along with the theme of time, all the themes that are dependent upon it (and, par excellence, those of *Dasein*, of finitude, of historicity) will no longer constitute the transcendental horizon of the question of Being, but in transition will be reconstituted on the basis of the theme of the epochality of Being.

What about presence then? We cannot easily think in the Latin word *presence* the movements of differentiation that are produced in the Heideggerian text. The task here is immense and difficult. Let us only locate a point of reference. In *Being and Time* and *Kant and the Problem of Metaphysics* it is difficult—we are tempted to say impossible—to distinguish rigorously between presence as *Anwesenheit* and presence as *Gegenwärtigkeit* (presence in the temporal sense of nowness). The texts that we have cited overtly assimilate them. Metaphysics, then, signified the determination of the meaning of Being as presence in both senses, and simultaneously.

Beyond *Being and Time*, it seems more and more that *Gegenwärtigkeit* (the fundamental determination of *ousia*) itself is only a restriction of *Anwesenheit*, which permits Heidegger to invoke, in *"Der Spruch des Anaximander"* ["The Anaximander Fragment"], an *"ungegenwärtig Anwesende."* And the Latin word *presence (Präsenz)* will connote, rather, another narrowing of *Anwesen* under the heading of subjectivity and representation. These linked determinations of presence *(Anwesenheit)*, which are the inaugural determination of the meaning of

39. The primordial, the authentic are determined as the *proper (eigentlich)*, that is, as the *near* (proper, *proprius*), the present in the proximity of self-presence. One could show how this value of proximity and of self-presence intervenes, at the beginning of *Sein und Zeit* and elsewhere, in the decision to ask the question of the meaning of Being on the basis of an existential analytic of *Dasein*. And one could show the metaphysical weight of such a decision and of the credit granted here to the value of self-presence. This question can propagate its movement to include all the concepts implying the value of the "proper."

64

Being by the Greeks, can specify both the question of Heidegger's reading of the texts of metaphysics and the question of our reading of Heidegger's texts. The Heideggerian de-limitation consists sometimes in appealing to a less narrow determination of presence from a more narrow determination of it, thereby going back from the present toward a more original thought of Being as presence (*Anwesenheit*), and sometimes in questioning this original determination itself, and giving us to think it as a closure, as *the* Greco-Western-philosophical closure. Along these lines, in sum, it would be a question of thinking a *Wesen*, or of making thought tremble by means of a *Wesen* that would not yet even be *Anwesen*. In the first case the displacements would remain within the metaphysics of presence in general; and the urgency or extent of the task explain why these intrametaphysical displacements occupy *almost* the entirety of Heidegger's text, offering themselves as such, which indeed is rare enough. The other gesture, the more difficult, more unheard-of, more questioning gesture, the one for which we are the least prepared, only permits itself to be sketched, announcing itself in certain calculated fissures of the metaphysical text.

Two texts, two hands, two visions, two ways of listening. Together simultaneously and separately.

3. The relationship between the two texts, between presence in general (*Anwesenheit*) and that which exceeds it before or beyond Greece—such a relationship can never offer itself in order to be read in the form of presence, supposing that anything ever can offer itself in order to be *read* in such a form. And yet, that which gives us to think beyond the closure cannot be simply absent. Absent, either it would give us nothing to think or it still would be a negative mode of presence. Therefore the sign of this excess must be absolutely excessive as concerns all possible presence-absence, all possible production or disappearance of beings in general, and yet, *in some manner* it must still signify, in a manner unthinkable by metaphysics as such. In order to exceed metaphysics it is necessary that a trace be inscribed within the text of metaphysics, a trace that continues to signal not in the direction of another presence, or another form of presence, but in the direction of an entirely other text. Such a trace cannot be thought *more metaphysico*. No philosopheme is prepared to master it. And it (is) that which must elude mastery. Only presence is mastered.

The mode of inscription of such a trace in the text of metaphysics is so unthinkable that it must be described as an erasure of the trace itself. The trace is produced as its own erasure. And it belongs to the trace to erase itself, to elude that which might maintain it in presence. The trace is neither perceptible nor imperceptible.

It is thus that the difference between Being and beings, the very thing that would have been "forgotten" in the determination of Being as presence, and of presence as present—this difference is so buried that there is no longer any trace of it. The trace of difference is erased. If one recalls that difference (is) itself other than absence and presence, (is) (itself) trace, it is indeed the trace of the

65

trace that has disappeared in the forgetting of the difference between Being and beings.

Is this not what "The Anaximander Fragment" seems to tell us at first? *"The oblivion of Being is oblivion of the distinction between Being and beings."*[40] "The distinction collapses. It remains forgotten. Although the two parties to the distinction, what is present and presencing (*das Anwesende und das An-wesen*), reveal themselves, they do not do so *as* distinguished. Rather, even the early trace (*die frühe Spur*) of the distinction is obliterated when presencing appears as something present (*das Anwesen wie ein Anwesendes erscheint*) and finds itself in the position of being the highest being present (*in einem höchsten Anwesenden*)" (pp. 50–51).

But at the same time, this erasure of the trace must have been traced in the metaphysical text. Presence, then, far from being, as is commonly thought, *what the sign signifies, what a trace refers to*, presence, then, is the trace of the trace, the trace of the erasure of the trace. Such is, for us, the text of metaphysics, and such is, for us, the language which we speak. Only on this condition can metaphysics and our language signal in the direction of their own transgression.[41] And this is why it is not contradictory to think *together* the *erased* and the *traced* of the trace. And also why there is no contradiction between the absolute erasure of the "early trace" of difference and that which maintains it as trace, sheltered and visible in presence. Thus Heidegger does not contradict himself when he writes further on: "However, the distinction between Being and beings, as something forgotten, can invade our experience only if it has already unveiled itself with the presencing of what is present (*mit dem Anwesen des Anwesendem*); only if it has left a trace (*eine Spur geprägt hat*) which remains preserved (*gewahrt bleibt*) in the language to which Being comes" (p. 51).

Henceforth it must be recognized that all the determinations of such a trace— all the names it is given—belong as such to the text of metaphysics that shelters the trace, and not to the trace itself. There is no trace *itself*, no *proper* trace. Heidegger indeed says the difference could not appear *as such*. (*Lichtung des Unterschiedes kann deshalb auch nicht bedeuten, dass der Unterschied als der Unterschied erscheint*: "Illumination of the distinction therefore cannot mean that the distinction appears as a distinction"—p. 51.) The trace of the trace which (is) difference above all could not appear or be named *as such*, that is, in its presence. It is the *as such* which precisely, and as such, evades us forever. Thereby the determinations which name difference always come from the metaphysical order. This holds not only for the determination of difference as the difference

40. TN. "The Anaximander Fragment" in *Early Greek Thinking*, trans. David Farrell Krell and Frank Capuzzi (New York: Harper and Row, 1975), p. 50. All further references are to this edition.

41. Thus Plotinus (what is his status in the history of metaphysics and in the "Platonic" era, if one follows Heidegger's reading?), who speaks of presence, that is, also of *morphē*, as the trace of nonpresence, as the amorphous (*to gar ikhnos tou amorphou morphē*). A trace which is neither absence nor presence, nor, in whatever modality, a secondary modality.

between presence and the present (*Anwesen/Anwesend*), but also for the determination of difference as the difference between Being and beings. If Being, according to the Greek forgetting which would have been the very form of its advent, has never meant anything except beings, then perhaps difference is older than Being itself. There may be a difference still more unthought than the difference between Being and beings. We certainly can go further toward naming it in our language. Beyond Being and beings, this difference, ceaselessly differing from and deferring (itself), would trace (itself) (by itself)—this *différance* would be the first or last trace if one still could speak, here, of origin and end.

Such a *différance* would at once, again, give us to think a writing without presence and without absence, without history, without cause, without *archia*, without *telos*, a writing that absolutely upsets all dialectics, all theology, all teleology, all ontology. A writing exceeding everything that the history of metaphysics has comprehended in the form of the Aristotelian *grammē*, in its point, in its line, in its circle, in its time, and in its space.

The Pit and
the Pyramid:
Introduction to
Hegel's Semiology

Paper presented at the Séminaire de Jean Hyppolite, Collège de France, 16 January 1968.
First published in the proceedings of the seminar, *Hegel et la pensée moderne* (P.U.F., coll.
Epimethée, 1971).

1. *"Since the real difference* (der reale Unterschied) *belongs to the extremes, this middle term is only the abstract neutrality, the real possibility of those extremes; it is, as it were, the* theoretical element *of the concrete existence of chemical objects, of their process and its result. In the material world* water *fulfills the function of this medium; in the spiritual world, so far as the analogue of such a relation has a place there, the* sign *in general, and more precisely* (näher) *language* (Sprache) *is to be regarded as fulfilling that function."*[1]

What is to be understood here by medium? By semiological medium? And more narrowly (näher) *by linguistic medium, whether it is a question, under the heading of* Sprache, *of speech or of language? Here, we are interested in the difference of this restriction, and no doubt will discover in it, en route, only a restriction of difference: the other name of the medium of the spirit.*

2. *In the* Encyclopedia *(Sec. 458), Hegel expresses his regret that in "logic and psychology, signs and language are usually foisted in somewhere as an appendix, without any trouble being taken to display their necessity and systematic place in the economy of intelligence" (p. 213).*

Despite appearances, then, the place of semiology is really at the center, and not in the margins or the appendix, of Hegel's Logic. *Thus are we authorized to inscribe an introduction to the Hegelian theory of the sign in a seminar devoted to the* Logic. *A prerequisite justification because, instead of remaining within the* Logic, *within the books bearing that title, we will proceed chiefly by detours, following the texts which more appropriately demonstrate the architectonic necessity of the relations between logic and semiology. Certain of these texts already having been examined by Jean Hyppolite in* Logique et existence,[2] *most notably in the chapter "Sens et sensible," we will be making an implicit and permanent reference to the latter.*

In determining Being as presence (presence in the form of the object, or self-presence under the rubric of consciousness), metaphysics could treat the *sign* only as a *transition.* Metaphysics is even indistinguishable from such a treatment of the sign. And neither has such a treatment somehow overtaken the concept of the sign: it has constituted it.

As the site of the transition, the bridge between two moments of full presence, the sign can function only as a *provisional* reference of one presence to another. The bridge can be *lifted [relevé].* The process of the sign has a history, and *signification* is even history *comprehended:* between an original presence and its circular reappropriation in a final presence. The self-presence of absolute knowledge and the consciousness of Being-near-to-itself in logos, in the absolute concept, will have been distracted from themselves only for the time of a detour

---

1. *Hegel's Science of Logic,* trans. A. V. Miller (London: George Allen and Unwin, 1969), p. 729. See also *Philosophy of Nature* (pt. 2 of *Encyclopedia of the Philosophical Sciences*), trans. William Wallace (Oxford: Clarendon Press, 1971), sec. 284. [All further references to the *Science of Logic* and the *Encyclopedia* are to these editions.]

2. Jean Hyppolite, *Logique et existence* (Paris: Presses Universitaires de France, 1961).

and for the time of a sign. The time of the sign, then, is the time of referral. It signifies self-presence, refers presence to itself, organizes the circulation of its provisionality. Always, from the outset, the movement of lost presence already will have set in motion the process of its reappropriation.

Within the limits of this continuum, breaks do occur, discontinuities regularly fissure and reorganize the theory of the sign. They reinscribe the concepts of this theory in original configurations whose specificity is not to be set aside. When taken up by other systems, these concepts certainly are no longer the same; and it would be more than foolish to erase the differences of these re-structurations in order to produce a smooth, homogenous, ahistorical, all-of-a-piece cloth, an ensemble of invariant and allegedly "original" characteristics. And would it be any less foolish, inversely, to overlook, not an origin, but long sequences and powerful systems, or to omit (in order to see them from too close a range, which is also from too far away) the chains of predicates which, even if not permanent, are still quite ample, not easily permitting themselves to be displaced or interrupted by multiple rupturing events, however fascinating and spectacular these events might be for the first unaccommodating glance? For as long as the great amplitude of this chain is not displayed, one can neither define rigorously the secondary mutations or order of transformations, nor account for the recourse to the *same word* in order to designate a concept both transformed and extirpated—within certain limits—from a previous terrain. (Unless one considers the order of language, words, and the signifier in general to be an accessory system, the contingent accident of a signified concept which might have its own autonomous history, its own displacements independent of the verbal tradition, independent of a certain semiological continuum, or of more ample sequences of the signifier; such an attitude also would derive from a philosophy, the most classical philosophy of the relations between sense and sign.) In order to mark *effectively* the displacements of the sites of conceptual inscription, one must articulate the systematic chains of the movement according to their proper generality and their proper period, according to their unevennesses, their in-equalities of development, the complex figures of their inclusions, implications, exclusions, etc. Which is something entirely other than going back to the origin or to the foundational ground of a concept, as if something of the sort could exist, even if such an inaugural and imaginary limit did not revive the reassuring myth of a transcendental signified, of an archeology before any trace and difference.

In the finite but relatively long sequence called metaphysics, it has been possible, then, for the sign to become the object of a *theory,* for the sign to be considered or to be regarded as something or on the basis of something, on the basis of that which is to be seen in intuition, to wit, being-present: a theory of the sign on the basis of being-present, but also, and by same token, *in sight* of being-present, in sight of presence, Being-in sight-of marking as much a certain theoretical authority of vision as it does the agency of a final goal, the *telos* of reappropriation, the coordination of the theory of the sign and the light of parousia. Which is also, as logic, a coordination with the invisible ideality of a logos which hears-itself-speak, a logos which is as close as possible to itself in the unity of concept and consciousness.[3]

It is the system of this coordination that we propose to analyze here. Its constraints have a highly general character. They are exercised, in constitutive fashion, over the entire history of metaphysics, and in general over the entirety of that which allegedly has been dominated by the metaphysical concept of history. It is often said that Hegelianism represents the fulfillment of metaphysics, its end and accomplishment. Thus, it is to be expected that Hegelianism would give to these constraints their most systematic and powerful form, taken to their limits.

Semiology and Psychology

An initial index of all this is to be found in an architectonic reading. In effect, Hegel grants to semiology a very determined place in the system of science.

In the *Encyclopedia of Philosophical Sciences,* the theory of the sign is to be found in the "Philosophy of Spirit," the third part of the work, which is preceded by the "Science of Logic" ("Lesser Logic") and the "Philosophy of Nature."

To what does this division correspond? Its meaning is assembled at the end of the Introduction (Section 18): "As the whole science, and only the whole, can exhibit what the Idea (*die Darstellung der Idee*) or system of reason is, it is impossible to give in a preliminary way a general impression (*eine vorläufige, allgemeine Vorstellung*) of a philosophy. Nor can a *division* of philosophy into its parts (*Einteilung*) be intelligible, except in connexion with the system. A preliminary division, like the limited conception from which it comes, can only be an anticipation (*etwas Antizipiertes*). Here however it is premised that the Idea turns out to be (*sich erweist*) the thought simply (*schlichthin*) identical with itself, and not identical simply in the abstract, but also in its action of setting itself over against itself, so as to gain a being of its own, and yet of being in full possession of itself while it is this other (*sich selbst, um für sich zu sein, sich gegenüber zu stellen und in diesem Andern nur bei sich selbst zu sein*). Thus philosophy is subdivided into three parts:

I. Logic: the science of the Idea in and for itself.

II. The Philosophy of Nature: the science of the Idea in its otherness.

III. The Philosophy of Spirit: the science of the Idea come back to itself out of that otherness" (*sec. 18*).

This schema, of course, is that of a living movement; and such a division would be unjustified, Hegel specifies, if it disarticulated and juxtaposed these three moments whose differences must not be substantialized.

3. TN. "La différance," note 3 (above), will help to explicate this passage.

The theory of the signs belongs to the third moment, to the third part, of the philosophy of spirit. It belongs to the science of the moment when the idea comes back to itself after having, if we may put it thus, lost awareness, lost the consciousness and meaning of itself in nature, in its Being-other. The sign, then, will be an agency or essential structure of the Idea's return to self-presence. If spirit is the Idea's Being-near-to-itself, one already may identify the sign by its first, most general determination: the sign is a form or a movement of the Idea's relation to itself in the element of spirit, a mode of the absolute's Being-near-to-itself.

Let us narrow our angle of vision. Let us situate the theory of the sign more precisely in the philosophy of spirit. The latter itself is articulated in three parts which correspond to the three movements of the development of spirit:

1. Subjective spirit: the spirit's relation to itself, an only ideal totality of the Idea. This is Being-near-to-itself in the form of only internal freedom.

2. Objective spirit, as a world to produce and produced in the form of reality, not only ideality. Freedom here becomes an existing, present necessity (*vorhandene Notwendigkeit*).

3. Absolute spirit: the unity, that is *in itself and for itself*, of the objectivity of the spirit and of its ideality or its concept, the unity producing itself eternally, spirit in its absolute truth—*absolute spirit* (sec. 385, p. 20).

The first two moments, then, are *finite* and transitory determinations of spirit. Now, the discourse on the sign derives from the science of one of these finite determinations: subjective spirit. If one recalls that, according to Hegel, "the finite *is not*, i.e., is not the truth, but merely a transition (*Übergegen*) and an emergence (*Übersichhinausgehen:* a transgression of itself)" (sec. 386, p. 23), then the sign indeed appears as a mode or determination of subjective and finite spirit as a mediation or transgression of itself, a transition within the transition, a transition of the transition. But this way out of itself is the obligatory route of a return to itself. It is conceived under the jurisdiction and in the form of dialectics, according to the movement of the true, and is watched over by the concepts of *Aufhebung* and negativity. "This finitude of the spheres so far examined is the dialectic that makes a thing have its cessation (*Vergehen*) by another and in another" (p. 23).

Let us define the place of this semiology more closely. Subjective spirit itself is:

1. *in itself or immediate:* this is the *soul* or *natural-spirit* (*Natur-Geist*), the object of the *anthropology* that studies man in nature;

2. *for itself or mediate,* as an identical reflection in itself and in the other, spirit in relation or particularization (*im Verhältnis oder Besonderung*), *consciousness,* the object of the phenomenology of spirit;

3. *spirit determining itself in itself,* as a subject for itself, the object of psychology (sec. 387, p. 25).

Semiology is a chapter in psychology, the science of spirit determining itself in itself as a subject for itself. Let us note, nevertheless—although this cannot detain us here—that semiology, as part of the science of the subject which is for itself, does not belong to the science of consciousness, that is, to phenomenology. This topical scheme, which inscribes semiology in a non-natural science of the soul, and properly in a psychology, in no way upsets a long traditional sequence, or at least does not do so in this way. The topical arrangement not only takes us back to the numerous semiological projects of the Middle Ages or the eighteenth century, which are all, directly or not, psychologies, but also to Aristotle. Aristotle is the model claimed by Hegel for his philosophy of spirit, and specifically for his psychology: "The books of Aristotle on the Soul, along with his discussions on its special aspects and states, are for this reason still by far the most admirable, perhaps even the sole, work of philosophical value on this topic. The main aim of a philosophy of mind [spirit] can only be to reintroduce unity of idea and principle into the theory of mind, and so reinterpret the lesson of those Aristotelian books" (sec. 378, p. 3).

It is Aristotle, precisely, who developed his interpretation of the voice in a treatise *Peri Psukhēs* (which will count for us in a moment), and who, in *Peri Hermeneias*, defined signs, symbols, speech and writing on the basis of the *pathēmata tēs psukhēs*, the states, affections or passions of the soul. Let us recall the well known opening of *Peri Hermeneias:* "Spoken words (*ta en tēi phōnēi*) are the symbols of mental experience and written words are the symbols of spoken words. Just as all men have not the same writing so all men have not the same speech sounds, but the mental experiences, which these directly symbolize [are signs of in the first place: *sēmeia protōs*] are the same for all [which is precisely what permits a science of them] as also are those things of which our experiences are the images. This matter has, however, been discussed in my treatise about the soul."[4]

The traditional repetition of the gesture by means of which semiology is made to proceed from psychology is not only the past of Hegelianism. Often that which purports to be a surpassing of Hegelianism, and sometimes a science free of metaphysics, still conforms to it.

This necessary gesture, which is properly metaphysical and governs an entire concatenation of discourses from Aristotle to Hegel, will not be challenged by the author considered as the founder of the first great project of general and scientific semiology, the model for so many modern, social sciences. Twice at least, in the *Course on General Linguistics,* Saussure places his plan for a general semiology under the jurisdiction of psychology: "Everything in language is basically psychological including its material and mechanical manifestations, such as sound changes; and since linguistics provides social psychology with

4. *The Works of Aristotle,* ed. W. D. Ross, vol. 1, *De Interpretatione,* trans. E. M. Edghill (Oxford: Clarendon Press, 1928), 16a.

such valuable data, is it not part and parcel of this discipline?"[5] "A *science that studies the life of signs within society is conceivable;* it would be a part of social psychology, and consequently of general psychology; I shall call it *semiology* (from the Greek *sēmeion,* 'sign'). Semiology would show what constitutes signs, and what laws govern them. Since the science does not yet exist, no one can say what it will be; but it has a right to existence, a place staked out in advance. Linguistics is only a part of the general science of semiology; the laws discovered by semiology will be applicable to linguistics, and the latter will circumscribe a well defined area within the mass of anthropological facts. To determine the exact place of semiology is the task of the psychologist."[6]

Let us deposit the following as a touchstone: significantly, it is the same linguist or glossematician, Hjelmslev, who, while acknowledging the importance of the Saussurean heritage, put into question, as noncritical presuppositions of Saussurian science, *both* the primacy granted to psychology and the privilege granted to the sonorous or phonic "substance of expression." The primacy and the privilege go together, as we shall verify in Hegel's speculative semiology.

In it, the sign is understood according to the structure and movement of the *Aufhebung,* by means of which the spirit, elevating itself above the nature in which it was submerged, at once suppresses and retains nature, sublimating nature into itself, accomplishing itself as internal freedom, and thereby presenting itself to itself for itself, *as such.* The science of this "as such," "*psychology* accordingly studies the faculties or general modes of mental [spiritual] activity *qua* mental—mental vision, ideation, remembering, etc., desires, etc." (sec. 440, p. 179). As in the *Peri Psukhēs* (432ab), Hegel on several occasions rejects any real separation between the alleged "faculties" of the soul (sec. 445). Instead of substantially separating faculties and psychic structures, then, one must determine their mediations, articulations, and joinings, which constitute the unity of an organized and oriented movement. Now it is remarkable that the theory of the sign, which essentially consists of an interpretation of speech and writing, is put forth in two long *Remarks,* remarks much longer than the paragraphs to which they are affixed, in the subchapter "Imagination" (*Die Einbildungskraft,* secs. 445–60).

Semiology, then, is a part of the theory of the imagination, and more precisely, as we shall specify, of a phantasiology or a fantastics.

What is imagination?

Representation (*Vorstellung*) is remembered-interiorized (*erinnerte*) intuition. It properly belongs to intelligence (*Intelligenz*), whose action is to interiorize sensible immediacy in order "itself to pose itself as *having an intuition of itself* (*sich* in sich selbst anschauend *zu setzen*)." Sensible immediacy remaining unilaterally subjective, the movement of intelligence must, by *Aufhebung,* lift and

5. Ferdinand de Saussure, *Course in General Linguistics,* trans. Wade Baskin (New York: McGraw-Hill, 1966), pp. 6–7.
6. Ibid., p. 16.

conserve this interiority in order "to be in itself in an externality of its own" (sec. 451, p. 202). In this movement of representation, intelligence *recalls itself* to itself in becoming objective. *Erinnerung*, thus, is decisive here. By means of *Erinnerung* the content of sensible intuition becomes an image, freeing itself from immediacy and singularity in order to permit the passage to conceptuality. The image thus interiorized in memory (*erinnert*) is no longer *there*, no longer existent or present, but preserved in an unconscious dwelling, conserved without consciousness (*bewusstlos, aufbewahrt*). Intelligence keeps these images in reserve, submerged at the bottom of a very dark shelter, like the water in a nightlike or unconscious pit (*nächtliche Schacht, bewusstlose Schacht*), or rather like a precious vein at the bottom of the mine. "But intelligence is not only consciousness and actual existence, but *qua* intelligence is the subject and potentiality of its own specializations. The image when thus kept in mind [*erinnert*] is no longer existent, but stored up *out of consciousness*" (sec. 453, p. 204).

A path, which we will follow, leads from this night pit, silent as death and resonating with all the powers of the voice which it holds in reserve, to a pyramid brought back from the Egyptian desert which soon will be raised over the sober and abstract weave of the Hegelian text, there composing the stature and status of the sign. And there, the natural source and the historical construction both, though differently, remain silent. That the path, following the ontotheological route, still remains circular, and that the pyramid becomes once again the pit that it always will have been—such is the enigma. We will have to ask if this enigma is to be sought out, like truth speaking by itself from the bottom of a well, or if it is to be deciphered, like an unverifiable inscription left behind on the facade of a monument.

Once in possession of this pit, this reservoir (*Vorrat*), intelligence then can draw from it, can bring to light, produce, "give forth its property (*Eigentum*), and dispense with external intuition for its existence in it. This synthesis of the internal image with the recollected existence (*erinnerten Dasein*) is *representation* proper (*die eigentliche* Vorstellung): by this synthesis the internal now has the qualification of being able to be presented before intelligence (*vor die Intelligenz* gestellt *werden zu konnen*) and to have its existence in it" (sec. 454, p. 205). The image no longer belongs to "the simple night."[7]

7. In a work in preparation on Hegel's family and on sexual difference in the dialectical speculative economy, we will bring to light the organization and displacement of this chain which reassembles the values of night, sepulcher, and divine—familial—feminine law as the law of singularity—and does so around the pit and the pyramid. A citation as a touchstone: "But if the universal thus easily knocks off the very tip of the pyramid (*die reine Spitze seiner Pyramide*) and, indeed, carries off the victory over the rebellious principle of pure individuality, viz., the Family, it has thereby merely entered on a conflict with the divine law, a conflict of self-conscious Spirit with what is unconscious. For the latter is the other essential power, and is therefore not destroyed, but merely wronged (*beleidigt*) by the conscious Spirit. But it has only the bloodless shade to help it in actually carrying out *its* law in face of the power and authority of that other, publicly manifest law. Being the law of weakness and darkness it therefore at first succumbs to the powerful law of the upper world, for the power of the former is effective in the underworld, not on earth." Hegel, *Phenomenology of Spirit*, trans. A. V. Miller (Oxford: Clarendon Press, 1977), p. 286. [The work in preparation has since appeared: *Glas.*]

Hegel names this first process *"reproductive imagination"* (*reproduktive Einbild-ungskraft*). The "provenance" of images is here the "proper interiority of the ego" which from now on keeps them in its power. Thus disposing of a reserve of images, intelligence operates by subsumption, and itself finds itself repro-duced, recalled, interiorized. On the basis of this idealizing mastery, it produces itself as fantasy, as symbolizing, allegorizing, poeticizing (*dichtende*) imagination. But this is only reproductive imagination, since all these formations (*Gebilde*) remain syntheses working on an intuitive, receptive given that is passively received from the exterior, that is proffered in an encounter. Work operates on a found (*gefundene*) or given (*gegebene*) content of intuition. Thus, this imagination does not produce, does not imagine, does not form its own *Gebilde*. Apparently and paradoxically, then, it is exactly insofar as this *Einbildungskraft* does not forge its own *Gebilde*, insofar as it receives the content of that which it seems to form, and does not produce *sponte sua* a thing or an existence, that it still remains closed in on itself. The self-identity of intelligence has found itself once again, but has done so in a subjective unilaterality, in the passivity of impression.

This limit is surpassed in *productive* imagination: self-intuition, the immediate relation to oneself such as it was formed in reproductive imagination, then becomes a *being*; it is exteriorized, produced in the world as a thing. This singular thing is the *sign;* it is engendered by a fantastic production, by an imagination that shows signs of itself, making the sign (*Zeichen machende Phantasie*) as always, emerge from itself in itself. "In creative imagination (*Phantasie*) intelligence has been so far perfected (*vollendet*) as to need no aids for intuition (*Selbstanschauung*). Its self-sprung ideas have pictorial existence. This pictorial creation of its intuitive spontaneity is subjective—still lacks the side of existence. But as the creation unites the internal idea with the vehicle of materialization, intelligence has therein *implicitly* returned both to identical self-relation and to immediacy. As reason, its first start was to appropriate (*anzueignen*) the immediate datum in itself (sec. 445, sec. 435), i.e. to universalize it; and now its action as reason (sec. 438) is from the present point directed toward giving the character of an existent to what in it has been perfected to concrete auto-intuition. In other words, it aims at making itself be (*Sein*), and be a fact (*Sache*). Acting on this view, it is self-uttering (*ist sie sich äussernd*), intuition-producing (Anschauung *produzier-end*): the imagination which creates signs (*Zeichen machende Phantasie*)" (sec. 457, pp. 210–11).

Let us note, first of all, that the most creative production of the sign is reduced, here, to a simple exteriorization, that is to an *expression:* the placing outside of an interior content, along with everything that this highly classical motif com-mands. And yet, inversely, this fantastic production does nothing less than *produce intuitions*. This statement might appear scandalous or unintelligible. In effect, it implies the spontaneous production of that which is to be seen by that which itself is thus able to see and to receive. But if this motif (the unity of concept and intuition, of spontaneity and receptivity, etc.) is the Hegelian motif *par excellence*, for once it bears no implicit criticism of Kant. Which is not fortuitous, and is in accord with the entire system of relationships between Hegel and Kant. In effect, it is a question here of the imagination, that is, of that agency in which all the Kantian oppositions regularly criticized by Hegel are confused or negated. Here we are in that zone—let us indicate it under the heading of the "Critique of Judgment"—where the debate with Kant resembles most an explication and least a break. But it is also for convenience that here we are opposing the development to the displacement. We would also have to reconsider this pair of concepts.

In any event, it remains that the productive imagination—the fundamental concept of the Hegelian aesthetics—has a site and a status analogous to those of the transcendental imagination. Because it is also a kind of natural art—"an art concealed in the depths of the human soul," a "productive imagination,"[8] Kant says too. But above all because the transcendental schematism of imagination, the intermediary between sensibility and understanding, the "third term" homogenous with the category and the phenomenon, carries along with it the contradictory predicates of receptive passivity and productive spontaneity. Finally, the movement of the transcendental imagination is the movement of temporalization:[9] Hegel also recognizes an essential link between the imagination productive of signs and time. Soon we will ask *what* time *signifies*, how it signifies, how it constitutes the process of signification.

Production *and* intuition, the concept of the sign thus will be the place where all contradictory characteristics intersect. All oppositions of concepts are reassembled, summarized and swallowed up within it. All contradictions seem to be resolved in it, but simultaneously that which is announced beneath the same sign seems irreducible or inaccessible to any formal opposition of concepts; being *both* interior and exterior, spontaneous and receptive, intelligible and sensible, the same and the other, etc., the sign is none of these, *neither* this *nor* that, etc.

8. "This schematism of our understanding, in its application to appearances and their mere form, is an art concealed in the depths of the human soul, whose real modes of activity (*Handgriffe*) nature is hardly likely ever to allow us to discover and have open to our gaze. This much only we can assert: the *image* is a product of the empirical faculty of productive imagination [*produktiven Einbildungskraft*: Smith follows Vaihinger and proposes *reproduktiven* for *produktiven*, Note 1; (in the *Aesthetics* Hegel recommends that one distinguish between *Phantasie* and passive imagination (*Einbildungskraft*): "Fantasy is productive (*schaffend*), pt. 3, C 1 a)]; the *schema* of sensible concepts, such as of figures in space, is a product and, as it were, a monogram, of pure *a priori* imagination." Kant, *Critique of Pure Reason*, trans. Norman Kemp Smith (New York: St. Martin's Press, 1965), p. 183.
9. "The pure image of all magnitudes (*quantorum*) for outer sense is space; that of all objects of the senses in general is time. But the pure *schema* of magnitude (*quantitatis*), as a concept of the understanding, is *number*, a representation which comprises the successive addition of homogeneous units. Number is therefore simply the unity of the synthesis of the manifold of a homogeneous intuition in general, a unity due to my generating time itself in the apprehension of the intuition" (ibid., pp. 183–84, chapter on "The Schematism of the Pure Concepts of Understanding").

Is this contradiction dialecticity itself? Is dialectics the resolution of the sign in the horizon of the nonsign, of the presence beyond the sign? The question of the sign soon would come to be confused with the question "what is dialectics?" or, better, with the question: can one examine dialectics and the sign in the form of the "what is"?

Let us cover over this horizon in order to come back to it along the detour of our text.

Immediately after naming the *imagination which creates signs,* Hegel states the fantastic unity of opposites constituted in semiopoetics. The latter is a *Mittelpunkt:* both a central point on which all the rays of opposites converge, a middle point, a middle in the sense of element, of *milieu,* and also the medium point, the site where opposites pass one into the other. "Productive imagination is the *Mittelpunkt* in which the universal and Being, one's own (*das Eigene*) and what is picked up (*Gefundensein*), internal and external, are completely welded into one (*volkommen in Eins geschaffen sind*)" (sec. 457, p. 211).

Thus characterized, the operation of the sign could extend its field infinitely. Nevertheless, Hegel restricts its province by including it immediately in the movement and structure of a dialectics that comprehends it. The moment of the sign is to be put on account, in provisional reserve. This is the limit of abstract *formality.* The semiotic moment remains formal in the extent to which the content and truth of meaning escape it, in the extent to which it remains inferior, anterior and exterior to them. Taken by itself, the sign is maintained only *in sight* of truth. "The creations of imagination are on all hands recognized as such combinations of the mind's own and inward with the matter of intuition; what further and more definite aspects they have is a matter for other departments. For the moment this internal studio (*innere Werkstätte*) of intelligence is only to be looked at in these abstract aspects. Imagination, when regarded as the agency of this unification, is reason, but only a nominal reason, because the matter or theme (*Gehalt*) it embodies is to imagination *qua* imagination a matter of indifference; whilst reason *qua* reason also insists upon the truth (*Wahrheit*) of its content (*Inhalt*)" (sec. 457, p. 211).

First we must insist upon the progress of a semiology which, despite the limit assigned to the so-called formality of the sign, ceases to make of the latter a waste product or an empirical accident. Like imagination, it on the contrary becomes a moment, however abstract, of the development of rationality in sight of the truth. It belongs, as we will see further on, to the work of the negative.

Having emphatically underlined this, we must ask, nevertheless, why truth (presence of the being, here in the form of presence adequate to itself) is announced as absence in the sign. Why is the metaphysical concept of truth in solidarity with a concept of the sign, and with a concept of the sign determined as a lack of full truth? And if one considers Hegelianism as the ultimate reassembling of metaphysics, why does it necessarily determine the sign as a progression with its sight set on truth? *With its sight set:* conceived in its destination on the basis of the truth toward which it is oriented, but also *with sight set on truth*, as one says in order to mark the distance, the lack and the remainder in the process of navigation; *with sight set* still further as a means of manifestation as concerns truth. The light, the brilliance of the appearing which permits vision, is the common source of *phantasia* and of the *phainesthai*..

Why is the relationship between sign and truth thus? This "why" can no longer be understood as a "What does this signify?" And even less as a "What does this mean?" Formulated this way, the questions would be stated naively, presupposing or anticipating an answer. Here we are reaching a limit at which the question "What does signification signify?" "What does meaning mean?" loses all pertinence. Hence we must posit our questions both at the point and in the form in which signification no longer signifies, meaning means nothing; not because they are absurd within their system, that is, within metaphysics, but because the very question would have brought us to the external border of its closure, supposing that such an operation is simple, and simply possible, within our language; and supposing that we know clearly what the inside of a system and a language are. *"Why?"* then no longer marks, here, a question about the "sight-set-on-what" (for what reason?), about the *telos* or *eskhaton* of the movement of signification; nor a question about an origin, a "why?" as a "because of what?" "on the basis of what?" etc. *"Why?"* therefore is the still metaphysical name of the question which we are elaborating here, the question about the metaphysical system which links the sign to the concept, to truth, to presence, to archeology, to teleology, etc.

Hegelian Semiology

The sign unites an "independent representation" and an "intuition," in other words, a concept (signified) and a sensory perception (of a signifier). But Hegel must immediately recognize a kind of separation, a disjointing which, by dislocating the "intuition," opens the space and play of signification. There is no longer in the signifying unity, in the welding of representation and intuition, simply a relationship between two terms. Intuition, here, already is no longer an intuition like any other. Doubtless, as in every intuition, a being is given, a thing is presented and is to be received in its simple presence. For example, says Hegel, the color of a cockade. It is there, immediately visible, indubitable. But insofar as it is united to *Vorstellung* (to a representation), this presence becomes representation, a representation (in the sense of representing) of a representation (in the general sense of conceptual ideality). Put in the place of something other, it becomes *etwas anderes vorstellend:* here *Vorstellen* and *represent* release and reassemble all their meanings at once.

What does this strange "intuition" represent? The signifier thus presented to intuition is the signifier of what? What does it represent or signify?

Hegel evidently defines it as an ideality, in opposition to the corporality of an intuitive signifier. This ideality is that of a *Bedeutung*. This word is usually translated as "signification." Having attempted, in commenting elsewhere upon the *Logical Researches*,[10] to interpret it as the content of a *meaning*, I would like to demonstrate here that such an interpretation is also valid for the Hegelian text. Such an extension is regulated by an internal and essential metaphysical necessity.

Hegel accords to the content of this meaning, this *Bedeutung*, the name and rank of *soul* (*Seele*). Of course it is a soul deposited in a body, in the body of the signifier, in the sensory flesh of intuition. The sign, as the unity of the signifying body and the signified ideality, becomes a kind of incarnation. Therefore the opposition of soul and body, and analogically the opposition of the intelligible and the sensory, condition the difference between the signified and the signifier, between the signifying intention (*bedeuten*), which is an animating activity, and the inert body of the signifier. This will remain true for Saussure; and also for Husserl, who sees the body of the sign as animated by the intention of signification, just as a body (*Körper*) when inhabited by *Geist* becomes a proper body (*Leib*). Husserl says of the living word that it is a *geistige Leiblichkeit*, a spiritual flesh.

Hegel knew that this proper and animated body of the signifier was also a *tomb*. The association *sōma/sēma* is also at work in this semiology, which is in no way surprising.[11] The tomb is the life of the body as the sign of death, the body as the other of the soul, the other of the animate psyche, of the living breath. But the tomb also shelters, maintains in reserve, capitalizes on life by marking that life continues elsewhere. The family crypt: *oikēsis*.[12] It consecrates the disappearance of life by attesting to the perseverance of life. Thus, the tomb also shelters life from death. It *warns* the soul of possible death, warns (of) death of the soul, turns away (from) death. This double warning function belongs to the funerary monument. The body of the sign thus becomes the monument in which the soul will be enclosed, preserved, maintained, kept in maintenance, present,

---

10. TN. See Derrida, *Speech and Phenomena*, for this argument.

11. P. Hochart—my thanks to him here—since then has directed my attention to the following passage from the *Cratylus*, a passage less frequently cited and more interesting for us than the celebrated text of the *Gorgias* (493a) on the couple *sōma/sēma*. "Socrates: You mean 'body' (*sōma*)?—Hermogenes: Yes.—Soc.: I think this admits of many explanations, if a little, even very little, change is made; for some say it is the *tomb* (*sēma*) of the soul, their notion being that the soul is buried in present life; and again, because by its means the soul gives any signs which it gives (*sēmainei ha an sēmainēi nē psukhēi*), it is for this also properly called 'sign' (*sēma*). But I think it most likely that the Orphic poets gave this name, with the Idea that the soul is undergoing punishment for something; they think it has the body for an enclosure to keep it safe, like a prison, and this is, as the name itself denotes, the safe (*sōma*, prison) for the soul until the penalty is paid, and not even a letter needs to be changed." Plato, *Collected Works in Twelve Volumes*, vol. 4 (Cambridge: Harvard University Press, 1926), p. 63.

12. TN. See above, "La différance," note 2, on *oikēsis*.

signified. At the heart of this monument the soul keeps itself alive, but it needs the monument only to the extent that it is exposed—to death—in its living relation to its own body. It was indeed necessary for death to be at work—the *Phenomenology of the Spirit* describes the work of death—for a monument to come to retain and protect the life of the soul by signifying it.

The sign—the monument-of-life-in-death, the monument-of-death-in-life, the sepulcher of a soul or of an embalmed proper body, the height conserving in its depths the hegemony of the soul, resisting time, the hard text of stones covered with inscription—is the *pyramid*.

Hegel, then, uses the word *pyramid* to designate the sign. The pyramid becomes the semaphor of the sign, the signifier of signification. Which is not an indifferent fact. Notably as concerns the Egyptian connotation: further on, the Egyptian hieroglyphic will furnish the example of that which resists the movement of dialectics, history and logos. Is this contradictory?

First, let us assist at the erection of the pyramid.

"In this unity (initiated by intelligence) of an *independent representation* (*selbständiger Vorstellung*) with an intuition, the matter of the latter is, in the first instance, something accepted (*ein Aufgenommenes*), something immediate or given (for example, the color of the cockade, etc.). But in the fusion of the two elements, the intuition does not count positively or as representing itself, but as representative of *something else*" (sec. 458, p. 212).

Thus we have, for once, a kind of intuition of absence, or more precisely the sighting of an absence through a full intuition.

"It [this intuition] is an image, which has received [*in sich empfangen hat:* has received, welcomed, conceived, as a woman would conceive by receiving; and what is conceived here is indeed a concept] as its soul and meaning an *independent* mental representation, its *signification* (*Bedeutung*). This intuition is the *Sign*" (sec. 458, p. 213).

There follows one of the two *Remarks* which contain the entire theory of the sign (which will not prevent Hegel, later, from cirticizing those who grant semiology only the site and status of an appendix). "The sign is some immediate intuition, representing a totally different import from what naturally belongs to it (*die einen ganz anderen Inhalt vorstellt, als den sie für sich hat*" (ibid.). *Vorstellen,* which is generally translated as "to represent," whether in the vaguest sense of intellectual or psychic representation, or in the sense of the representation of an *object* that is put forth to be seen, here also marks the representative detour, the recourse to what represents, to what is put in the place of the other, the delegate of and reference to the other. Here, an intuition is mandated to represent, in its proper content, an *entirely other* content. "The sign is some immediate intuition, representing a totally different import from what naturally belongs to it; it is the *pyramid* [Hegel's emphasis] into which a foreign soul (*eine fremde Seele*) has been conveyed [transposed, transplanted, translated: *versetzt; versetzten* is also to place on deposit; *im Leihause versetzten:* to place in the pawn-

83

shop], and where it is conserved (*aufbewahrt:* consigned, stored, put in storage)" (ibid.).

This situating of the pyramid has fixed several essential characteristics of the sign.

First of all what can be called, without abuse or anachronism, the *arbitrariness* of the sign, the absence of any natural relation of resemblance, participation or analogy between the signified and the signifier, that is, here, between the representation (*Bedeutung*) and the intuition, or further between what is represented and the representative of representation by signs. Hegel emphasizes this heterogeneity, the condition for the arbitrariness of the sign, twice.

1. The soul consigned to the pyramid is *foreign* (*fremd*). If it is transposed, transplanted into the monument like an immigrant, it is that it is not made of the stone of the signifier; neither in its origin nor its destination does it belong to the matter of the intuitive given. This heterogeneity amounts to the irreducibility of the soul and the body, of the intelligible and the sensory, of the concept or signified ideality on the one hand, and of the signifying body on the other, that is, in different senses, the irreducibility of two *representations* (*Vorstellungen*).

2. This is why the immediate intuition of the signifier *represents an entirely other content* (*einen ganz anderen Inhalt*) than that which it has for itself, entirely other than that whose full presence refers only to itself.

This relationship of absolute alterity distinguishes the sign from the symbol. The continuity of a mimetic or analogical participation can always be seen between the symbol and the symbolized. "The *sign* is different from the *symbol:* for in the symbol the original characters (in essence and conception) of the visible object are more or less identical with the import which it bears as symbol; whereas in the sign, strictly so-called, the natural attributes of the intuition, and the connotation of which it is a sign, have nothing to do with one another" (ibid.).

The motif of the arbitrariness of the sign, the distinction between sign and symbol, is clarified at length in the "Introduction" to the section of the *Aesthetics* devoted to "Symbolic Art." There, Hegel specifies the "purely arbitrary linkage" (*ganz willkürliche Verknüpfung*) which constitutes the sign itself, and above all the linguistic sign. "Therefore it is a different thing when a sign is to be a *symbol*. The lion, for example, is taken as a symbol of magnanimity, the fox of cunning, the circle of eternity, the triangle of Trinity. But the lion and the fox do possess in themselves the very qualities whose significance (*Bedeutung*) they are supposed to express. Similarly the circle does not exhibit the endlessness or the capricious limitation of a straight or other line, which does not return into itself, a limitation likewise appropriate enough for some *limited* space of time; and the triangle as a *whole* has the same *number* of sides and angles as that appearing in the idea of God when the determinations which religion apprehends in God are liable to numeration.

"Therefore in these sorts of symbol the sensuously present things (*sinnlichen vorhandenen Existenzen*) have already in their own existence (*Dasein*) that meaning (*Bedeutung*), for the representation (*Darstellung*) and expression of which they are used; and taken in this wider sense, the symbol is no purely arbitrary sign, but a sign which in its externality comprises in itself at the same time the content of the idea (*Vorstellung*) which it brings into appearance. Yet nevertheless it is not to bring *itself* before our minds as the concrete individual thing, but in itself only that universal quality of meaning [which it signifies]."[13]

In the following chapter, "Unconscious Symbolism," there is a section devoted to the Pyramid—this time, if we may still put it thus, in the proper sense of the word. If the Egyptian pyramid, in the *Encyclopedia*, is the symbol or sign of the sign, in the *Aesthetics* it is studied for itself, that is, as a symbol right from the outset. The Egyptians went further than the Hindus in the concept of the relations between the natural and the spiritual: they thought the immortality of the soul, the independence of the spirit, and the form of its duration beyond natural death. This is marked in their funerary practices. "The immortality of the soul lies very close to the freedom of the spirit, because [the conception of immortality implies that] the self comprehends itself as withdrawn from the naturalness of existence and as resting on itself; but this self-knowledge is the principle of freedom. Now of course this is not to say that the Egyptians had completely reached the conception of the free spirit, and in examining this faith of theirs we must not think of our manner of conceiving the immortality of the soul; but still they did already have the insight to take good account, both externally and in their ideas, of the body in its existence separated from life . . .

"If we ask further for a symbolical art-form to express this idea, we have to look for it in the chief structures built by the Egyptians. Here we have before us a double architecture, one above ground, the other subterranean: labyrinth under the soil, magnificent vast excavations, passages half a mile long, chambers adorned with hieroglyphics, everything worked out with the maximum of care; then above ground there are built in addition those amazing constructions amongst which the *Pyramids* are to be counted the chief" (*Aesth.* I, pp. 355–56). After an initial description, Hegel extracts what he sees as the concept of the pyramid: we will compare this text with that of the *Encyclopedia*. "In this way the Pyramids put before our eyes the simple prototype of symbolical art itself; they are prodigious crystals which conceal in themselves an inner meaning (*ein Inneres*) and, as external shapes produced by art, they so envelop that meaning that it is obvious that they are there for this inner meaning separated from pure nature and only in relation to this meaning. But this realm of death and the invisible, which here constitutes the meaning, possesses only one side, and that a formal one, of the true content of art, namely that of being removed from

13. TN. Hegel, *Aesthetics*, trans. T. M. Knox (Oxford: Oxford University Press, 1975), vol. 1, pp. 304–5. Further references to the *Aesthetics* are to this edition (abbreviated as *Aesth.*).

immediate existence; and so this realm is primarily only Hades, not yet a life (*Lebendigkeit*) which, even if liberated from the sensuous as such, is still nevertheless at the same time self-existent and therefore in itself free and living spirit. On this account the shape (*Gestalt*) for such an inner meaning still remains just an external form (*Form*) and veil for the definite content of that meaning. The Pyramids are such an external environment in which an inner meaning rests concealed" (*Aesth.* I, p. 356).

This requisite discontinuity between the signified and the signifier coincides with the systemic necessity that includes semiology in a psychology. It will be recalled, in effect, that psychology—in the Hegelian sense—is the science of the spirit determining itself in itself, as a subject for itself. This is the moment at which "all [spirit] now has to do is to realize the notion of its freedom" (*Encyclopedia*, sec. 440, p. 179). This is why it was indispensable, above, to assert the architectonic articulation between psychology and semiology. This allows us better to comprehend the meaning of arbitrariness: the production of arbitrary signs manifests the freedom of the spirit. And there is more manifest freedom in the production of the sign than in the production of the symbol. In the sign spirit is more independent and closer to itself. In the symbol, conversely, it is a bit more exiled into nature. "Intelligence therefore gives proof of wider choice (*Willkur*) and ampler authority (*Herrschaft*) in the use of intuitions when it treats them as designatory (*als bezeichnend*) rather than as symbolical (*als symbolisierend*)" (*Enc.* sec. 458, p. 213).[14]

According to the framework of this teleology, the semiotic instance, just defined as abstract rationality, also helps impel the manifestation of freedom. Hence its essential place in the development of psychology and logic. Hegel marks this place accessorily, in the middle of the Remark added as a long appendix to the short paragraph that defines the sign. The pyramid had emerged in this space and along the detour of this digression: "In logic and psychology, signs and language are usually foisted in somewhere as an appendix (*Anhang:* supplement,

14. Hegel already inherited this opposition of sign and symbol and the teleology which systematically orients it. This could be easily demonstrated on the basis of each of the concepts that enter into play here. But after Hegel the same opposition and the same teleology maintain their authority. For example in the *Course in General Linguistics.* In the first chapter of the first part in the section entitled: "Principle I: The Arbitrary Nature of the Sign" one may read: "Signs that are wholly arbitrary realize better than the others the ideal of the semiological process; that is why language, the most complex and universal of all systems of expression, is also the most characteristic; in this sense linguistics can become the master-pattern for all branches of semiology although language is only one particular semiological system." [We will soon find the same proposition in Hegel, at the moment when he grants preeminence to the linguistic sign, to speech and the name.] "The word *symbol* has been used to designate the linguistic sign, or more specifically, what is here called the signifier. Principle I in particular weighs against the use of this term. One characteristic of the symbol is that it is never wholly arbitrary; it is not empty, for there is the rudiment of a natural bond between the signifier and the signified. The symbol of justice, a pair of scales, could not be replaced by just another symbol, such as a chariot" (*Course*, p. 68).

codicil), without any trouble being taken to display their necessity and systematic place in the economy of intelligence. The right place for the sign is that just given" (ibid.).

This activity, which consists in animating the intuitive (spatial and temporal) content, of breathing a "soul," a "signification," into it, produces the sign by *Erinnerung*—memory and interiorization. We will now examine this relationship between a certain movement of idealizing interiorization and the process of temporalization. In the production of signs, memory and imagination (that is, time, in this context) are the same interiorization of the spirit relating itself to itself in the pure intuition of itself, and therefore in its freedom, and bringing this intuition of itself to exterior existence.

Which calls for two comments.

1. Appearing in the *Encyclopedia* under the heading of imagination, the theory of signs is immediately followed by the chapter on memory. In the *Philosophical Propedeutics* the same semiological content is inscribed under the rubric of memory.[15]

2. Memory, the production of signs, is also thought itself. In a transitional remark between the chapter devoted to memory and the chapter devoted to thought, Hegel recalls that the "German language has etymologically assigned memory (*Gedächtnis*), of which it has become a foregone conclusion to speak contemptuously, the high position of direct kindred with thought (*Gedanke*)" (*Enc.*, sec. 464, p. 223).

---

15. In the "Philosophical Encyclopedia" of the *Propedeutics* (first section of the "Science of Spirit," chapter on representation, subchapter on memory) we find again the following definitions: "1. *The sign in general.* Representation having been liberated from present external reality and rendered subjective, this reality and the internal representation are situated one facing the other, as two distinct things. An external reality becomes a *sign* when it is *arbitrarily associated* with a representation which does not correspond to it, and which is even distinct from it in its content, such that this reality must be its representation or *signification*" (sec. 155). "*Creative* Memory therefore produces the association between intuition and representation, but a *free* association in which the preceding relationship, in which representation reposed upon intuition, finds itself inversed. In the association as effected by creative memory, the present sensuous reality has no value in itself and for itself, but its sole value is that conferred upon it by spirit" (sec. 156). "*Language.* The highest work of creative memory is language, which is on the one hand verbal and on the other handwritten. Creative memory, or *mnēmosynē*, being the source of language, it can be a question of another source only as far as what concerns the discovery of determined signs. (sec. 158). Language is the disappearance of the sensuous world in its immediate presence, the suppression of this world, henceforth transformed into a presence which is a call apt to awaken an echo in every essence capable of representation" (sec. 159). *Philosophische Propädeutik*, in *Sämtliche Werke*, vol. 3 (Stuttgart: Frommans Verlag), pp. 209–10.

Relever[16]—What Talking Means

The site of semiology has been circumscribed. It would not be feasible, now, to exhaust its contents. Let us merely attempt, in an initial probe, to verify, through an analysis of content, the motif described by the architecture. In this way, let us ask what this semiology signifies, what it means. In putting the question in this form, we are already submitting to the profound schemas of the metaphysics of the sign, the sign which not only "means," but essentially represents itself as a theory of *bedeuten* (meaning) which is from the outset regulated by the *telos* of speech. As much later in Saussure, spoken language here is the "model" of the sign, and linguistics is the model of a semiology of which it still remains a part.

The heart of the thesis is quickly stated: the privilege or excellence of the linguistic system—that is, the phonic system—as concerns any other semiotic system. Therefore, the privilege of speech over writing and of phonetic writing over every other system of inscription, particularly over hieroglyphic or ideographic writing, but equally over mathematical writing, over all formal symbols, algebras, pasigraphies and other projects of the Leibnizian sort—phonetic writing's privilege over everything which has no need, as Leibniz said, "to refer to the voice" or to the word (*vox*).

Thus formulated, the thesis is familiar. Here we wish not so much to recall it as to reformulate it, and in doing so to reconstitute its configuration, to mark the ways in which the authority of the voice is essentially coordinated with the entire Hegelian system, with its archeology, its teleology, its eschatology, with the will to parousia and all the fundamental concepts of speculative dialectics, notably those of negativity and of *Aufhebung*.

The process of the sign is an *Aufhebung*. Thus: "The intuition—in its natural phase a something given (*ein Gegebenes*) and given in space (*ein Räumliches*)—acquires, when employed as a sign, the peculiar characteristic of existing only as *aufgehobene* [that is, both lifted and suppressed, let us say, henceforth, *relevé*, combining the senses in which one can be both raised in one's functions and relieved of them, replaced in a kind of promotion, by that which follows and relays or relieves one. In this sense, the sign is the *relève* of sensory-spatial intuition.] Such is the negativity of intelligence" (sec. 459, p. 213).

16. TN. See above, "La différance," note 23, and "Ousia and Grammē," note 15, for the (non-)translation of *relève*. Here, Derrida is also playing on the "ordinary" sense of *relever*, meaning "to point out." He will come to demonstrate that to point out (*relever*) what talking means is to point out that it means *relever* (*aufheben*). We shall follow Derrida's use of the tenses of *relever*; the reader is reminded that *relever* is the infinitive, *relève* the third person present singular (and also the substantive), *relevé* the past participle, and *relevant* the present participle. Occasionally we shall use "relifts" as a shorthand to prevent confusion between the substantive and the third person present singular. See also note 15 above.

Intelligence, then, is the name of the power which produces a sign by negating the sensory spatiality of intuition. It is the *relève* of spatial intuition. Now, as Hegel shows elsewhere,[17] the *relève* (*Aufhebung*) of space is time. The latter is the truth of what it negates—space—in a movement of *relève*. Here, the truth or teleological essence of the sign as the *relève* of sensory-spatial intuition will be the sign as time, the sign in the element of temporalization. This is what the rest of the paragraph confirms: "Such is the negativity of intelligence; and thus the truer phase of the intuition used as a sign is existence in *time* (*ein Dasein in der Zeit*)."

Dasein in der Zeit, presence or existence in time: this formulation of a mode of intuition must be thought in relation to the formulation which says of time that it is the *Dasein* of the concept.

Why is *Dasein* in time the *truer* form (*wahrhaftere Gestalt*) of intuition such as it may be *relevé* in the sign? Because time is the *relève*—that is, in Hegelian terms, the truth, the essence (*Wesen*) as Being-past (*Gewesenheit*)—of space. Time is the true, essential, past space, space as it will have been thought, that is, *relevé*. *What space will have meant is time.*

It follows, as concerns the sign, that the content of the sensory intuition (the signifier) must erase itself, must vanish before *Bedeutung,* before the signified ideality, all the while conserving itself and conserving *Bedeutung;* and it is only in time, or rather *as* time itself that this *relève* can find its passageway.

Now, what is the signifying substance (what the glossematicians call the "substance of expression") most proper to be produced as time itself? It is *sound,* sound *relevé* from its naturalness and linked to spirit's relation to itself, the psyche as a subject for itself and affecting itself by itself, to wit, *animated* sound, phonic sound, the voice (*Ton*).

Hegel immediately and rigorously draws this conclusion: "Thus the truer phase of the intuition used as a sign is existence in *time* (but its existence vanishes in the moment of being [*Verschwinden des Daseins indem es ist*]) and if we consider the rest of its external psychic quality, its *institution* [a Being-posited: *Gesetzsein*] by intelligence, but an institution growing out of its (anthropological) own naturalness. This institution of the natural is the vocal note (*Ton*), where the inward idea manifests itself in adequate utterance (full utterance: *erfüllte Äusserung*)" (sec. 459, p. 214).

On the one hand, the voice unites the anthropological naturalness of the natural sound to the psychic-semiotic ideality; therefore it articulates the philosophy of spirit with the philosophy of nature; and in the philosophy of spirit its concept is therefore the hinge between anthropology and psychology. Between these two sciences, as we know, is inscribed the phenomenology of spirit, or the science of the experience of consciousness.

17. See for example *Enc.*, secs. 254–60 (*Philosophy of Nature*), and above, "Ousia and Grammē."

On the other hand, this phonic relationship between the sensory and the intelligible, the real and the ideal, etc., is determined here as an expressive relationship between an inside and an outside. The language of sound, speech, which carries the inside to the outside, does not simply abandon it there, as does writing. Conserving the inside in itself as it is in the act of emitting it to the outside, speech is par excellence that which confers existence, presence (*Dasein*), upon the interior representation, making the concept (the signified) exist. But, by the same token, insofar as it interiorizes and temporalizes *Dasein*, the given of sensory-spatial intuition, language lifts existence itself, "relifts" (*relève*) it in its truth, producing thereby a kind of promotion of presence. It makes sensory existence pass into representative or intellectual existence, the existence of the concept. Such a transition is precisely the moment of articulation which transforms sound into voice and noise into language: "The vocal note [the phonic sound: *der Ton*] which receives further articulation to express specific ideas—speech (*die Rede*), and its system, language (*die Sprache*)—gives to sensations, intuitions, conceptions, a second and higher existence than they naturally possess—invests them with the right of existence in the *realm of representation (des Vorstellens)*" (ibid.).

In the passage which concerns us, Hegel is interested in language "only in the special aspect of a product of intelligence for manifesting its ideas in an external medium." He does not undertake the study of language itself, if it can be put thus. He has defined the order of general semiology, its place in psychology, and then the site of linguistics within a semiology whose teleological model is linguistics nevertheless. The *Encyclopedia* goes no further than systematics or architectonics. It does not fill the field whose limits and topography it marks. However the lineaments of a linguistics are indicated. For example, this linguistics will have to submit to the distinction between the formal (grammatical) element and the material (lexicological) element. Such an analysis dissolves the discourse on linguistics, undoes it between its *before* and its *after*.

Lexicology, the science of the material of language, in effect refers us to a discipline *already* treated before psychology: anthropology. And, within anthropology, to psychophysiology. Before appearing to itself as such, ideality is announced in nature, spirit hides itself outside itself in sensory matter; and it does so according to modes and degrees, according to a specific becoming and hierarchy. It is within this teleology that the decisive concept of *physical ideality* is to be understood. Ideality in general, in Hegelian terms, is "the *negation* of the real, but a negation where the real is put past, virtually retained (*virtualiter erhalten*), although it does not *exist*" (sec. 403, p. 92). Since the sign is the negativity which "relifts" (*relève*) sensory intuition into the ideality of language, it must be hewn from a sensory matter which in some way is given to it, offering a predisposed nonresistance to the work of idealization.[18] The idealizing and

18. "The spirit must first withdraw into itself from nature, lift itself above it, and overcome it, before it can prevail in it without hindrance as in an element which cannot withstand it (*widerstandslos*), and transform it into a positive existence (*Dasein*) of its own freedom" (*Aesthetics* I, p. 443).

relevant negativity which works within the sign has always already begun to disturb sensory matter in general. But since sensory matter is differentiated, it forms hierarchies of types and regions according to their power of ideality. Among other consequences it follows from this that one may consider the concept of physical ideality as a kind of teleological anticipation, or inversely that one may recognize in the concept and value of ideality in general a "metaphor." Such a displacement—which would summarize the entire itinerary of metaphysics—also would repeat the "history" of a certain organization of functions that philosophy has called "meaning." The equivalence of these two readings is also an effect of the Hegelian circle: the sensualist or materialist reduction and the idealist teleology following, in opposite directions, the same line. The line that we have just named, as a provisional convenience, "metaphor."

What Hegel calls physical ideality, then, is shared by two regions of the sensory: sensibility to light and sensibility to sound. They are analyzed in the *Encyclopedia* and the *Aesthetics*.

Whether it is a question of light or of sound, the semiological analysis of signifying matters and of sensory intuitions sends us from psychology to anthropology (psychophysiology) and, in the last analysis, from physiology to physics.[19] This is the inverse path of the teleology and the movement of negativity, according to which the idea is reappropriated to itself as spirit in *relevant* (itself from) nature, its Being-other, in which it was negated and lost, all the while announcing itself within it. Now, at the opening of the "Physics," light is posited as a first manifestation, even if a still abstract and empty manifestation, the undifferentiated identity of the first qualified matter. It is by means of light, the neutral and abstract element of appearing, the pure milieu of phenomenality in general, that nature first relates itself to itself. Nature, in light, manifests *itself*, sees *itself*, lets itself be seen and itself sees itself. In this first reflexive articulation, the opening of ideality is by the same token the opening of subjectivity, of nature's relationship to itself: "Light . . . is . . . the earliest ideality, the original

19. Hegel distinguishes between the *organization* of the five senses, a *natural* organization whose concepts are to be fixed by the philosophy of nature, and the *functioning* of these senses, in conformity with their concept, for spiritual ends, for example in art. "Now the senses, because they are *senses*, i.e. related to the material world, to things outside one another and inherently diverse, are themselves different; touch, smell, taste, hearing, and sight. To prove the inner necessity of this ensemble and its articulation is not our business here: it is a matter for the philosophy of nature where I have discussed it. Our problem is restricted to examining whether all these senses—or, if not all, then which of them—are capable by their nature of being organs for the apprehension of works of art. In this matter we have already excluded touch, taste, and smell" (*Aesth.* II, p. 621). In such a hierarchy of the arts, poetry necessarily has the highest place. It is the most *relevant* art, the "total art." Time and sound, now united to conceptual representation (which was not the case for musical interiority) and to the objectivity of language, are the modes of interiority and belong to the concept of poetry. Therefore, this concept requires that poetry be *spoken* and not *read*, because "print, on the other hand, transforms this animation (*Beseelung*) into a mere visibility, which taken by itself is a matter of indifference and has no longer any connection with the spiritual meaning" (ibid., p. 1036).

self of nature. With light, nature begins for the first time to become subjective" (*Aesth.* II, p. 808).

Correlatively, sight is an *ideal* sense, more ideal, by definition and as its name indicates, than touch or taste. One can also say that sight *gives its sense* to theory. It suspends desire, lets things be, reserves or forbids their consummation.[20] The visible has in common with the sign, Hegel tells us, that it cannot be eaten.

However, if sight is ideal, *hearing is even more so.* It "relifts" (*relève*) sight. Despite the ideality of light and vision, the objects perceived by the eye, for example plastic works of art, persist beyond the perception of their sensory, exterior, stubborn existence; they resist the *Aufhebung*, and in and of themselves cannot be absolutely *relevé* by temporal interiority. They hold back the work of dialectics. This being the case for plastic works of art, it certainly will be so for writing as such. But not for music and speech. Hearing is the most sublime sense: "Hearing . . . like sight, is one of the theoretical and not practical senses, and it is still more ideal than sight. For the peaceful and undesiring (*begierdlose*) contemplation of works of art lets them remain in peace and independently as they are, and there is no wish to consume or destroy them; yet what it apprehends is not something inherently posited ideally, but on the contrary something persisting in its visible existence. The ear, on the contrary, without itself turning to a practical (*praktisch*) relation to objects, listens to the result of the inner vibration (*inneren Erzitterns*) of the body through which what comes before us is no longer the peaceful and material shape, but the first and more ideal breath of the soul (*Seelenhaftigkeit*). Further, since the negativity into which the vibrating material (*schwingende Material*) enters here is on one side the *relève* (*Aufheben*) of the spatial situation, a *relève relevé* again by the reaction of the body, therefore the expression of this double negation, i.e. sound (*Ton*), is an externality which in its coming-to-be is annihilated again by its very existence, and it vanishes of itself. Owing to this double negation of externality, implicit in the principle of sound, inner subjectivity corresponds to it because the resounding (*Klingen*),

20. The Hegelian theory of desire is the theory of the contradiction between theory and desire. Theory is the death of desire, death in desire, if not the desire *of* death. The entire introduction to the *Aesthetics* demonstrates this contradiction between desire (*Begierde*), which pushes toward consummation, and "theoretical interest," which lets things be in their freedom. In the extent to which art "is situated between pure sensuousness and pure thought," and to which "in art the sensuous is spiritualized (*vergeistigt*)" and the spirit "sensualized (*versinnlicht*)," art itself in a privileged way is addressed "to the two theoretical senses of sight and hearing" (*Aesth.* II, p. 622). Touch is concerned only with the resistance of sensuous and material individuality as such; taste dissociates and consumes the object; while smell lets it evaporate. "Sight, on the other hand, has a purely theoretical relation to objects (*Gegenständen*) by means of light, this as it were nonmaterial matter. This for its part lets objects persist freely and independently; it makes them shine and appear (*scheinen und erscheinen*) but, unlike air and fire, it does not consume them in practice whether unnoticeably or openly. To vision, void of desire (*begierdelose Sehen*), everything is presented which exists materially in space as something outside everything else (*Aussereinander*), but which, because it remains undisturbed in its integrity, is manifest only in its shape and color" (ibid.).

which in and by itself is something more ideal than independently really sub-sistent corporeality, gives up this more ideal existence also, and therefore be-comes a mode of expression adequate to the inner life" (*Aesthetics*, II, p. 890).[21] There is constant reference to the concept of vibration, of trembling (*Erzittern, schwingende Zittern*). In the *Philosophy of Nature* it is at the center of the physics of sound (*Klang*); and there, as always, it marks the passage, through the op-eration of negativity, of space into time, of the material into the ideal passing through "abstract materiality" (*abstrakte Materialität*).[22] This teleological concept of sound as the movement of idealization, the *Aufhebung* of natural exteriority, the *relève* of the visible into the audible, is, along with the entire philosophy of nature, the fundamental presupposition of the Hegelian interpretation of lan-

21. Elsewhere: "The other theoretical sense is *hearing*. Here the opposite comes into view. Instead of shape, colour, etc., hearing has to do with sound (*Ton*), with the vibration of a body; here there is no process of dissolution, like that required by smell; there is merely a trembling (*Erzittern*) of the object (*Gegenständes*) which is left uninjured thereby. This ideal movement in which simple subjectivity, as it were the soul of the body, is expressed by its sound, is apprehended by the ear just as theoretically as the eye appre-hends colour or shape; and in this way the inner side of objects is made apprehensible by the inner life" (*Aesth.* II, p. 622).

This hierarchical classification combines two criteria: objectivity and interiority, which are only apparently opposed, since idealization has as its meaning (from Plato to Husserl) the simultaneous confirmation of objectivity and interiority one by the other. Ideal objec-tivity maintains its identity with itself, its integrity and its resistance all the more in no longer depending upon an empirical sensuous exteriority. Here, the combination of the two criteria permits the elimination of touch (which is concerned only with a material exteriority: masterable objectivity), taste (a consummation which dissolves the object in the interiority), and smell (which permits the object to dissociate itself into evaporation) from the theoretical domain. Sight is imperfectly theoretical and ideal (it lets the objectivity of the object be, but cannot interiorize its sensuous and spatial opaqueness). According to a metaphor well coordinated with the entire system of metaphysics, only hearing, which preserves both objectivity *and* interiority, can be called fully ideal and theoretical. Therefore in its eminence it is designated by optical language (*idea, theōria*), which permits us to go back to the analysis of this metaphorical system. We will attempt this elsewhere. Here, let us insert the following passage from the "Rat Man" in order to mark, with a dotted line, several references and several intentions: "And here I should like to raise the general question whether the atrophy of the sense of smell (which was an inevitable result of man's assumption of an erect posture) and the consequent organic repression of his pleasure in smell may not have had a considerable share in the origin of his susceptibility to nervous disease. This would afford us some explanation of why, with the advance of civilization, it is precisely the sexual life that must fall a victim to repression. For we have long known the intimate connection between the sexual instinct and the function of the olfactory organ." Freud: *The Standard Edition of the Complete Psychological Works*, vol. 10 (London: Hogarth Press, 1955), p. 248. Hegel again: "But the *objet d'art* should be con-templated in its independent objectivity on its own account; true, it is there for our apprehension but only in a theoretical and intellectual way, not in a practical one, and it has no relation to desire or the will. As for smell, it cannot be an organ of artistic enjoyment either, because things are only available to smell in so far as they are in process and their aroma is dissipated through the air and its practical influence" (*Aesth.* II, p. 622).

22. These propositions are explicated at length in sections 299–302 of the *Encyclopedia* ("Philosophy of Nature," sec. 2, Physics). See also the *Philosophy of Spirit, Enc.*, sec. 401.

guage, notably of the so-called material part of language, lexicology. This pre-supposition forms a specific system that organizes not only the relations of the Hegelian philosophy of nature to the physics of its time and to the totality of the Hegelian teleology, but also its articulation with the more general system and more ample chain of logocentrism.

If lexicology led us back to physics, grammar (the formal element of discourse) projects us, by anticipation, toward the study of intellect and its articulation into categories. In effect, the *Encyclopedia* undertakes this further on: "As to the *formal element*, again it is the work of analytic intellect which informs language with its categories: it is this logical instinct which gives rise to grammar. The study of languages still in their original (*ursprünglich*) state, which we have first really begun to make acquaintance with in modern times, has shown on this point that they contain a very elaborate grammar and express distinctions which are lost or have been largely obliterated in the languages of more civilized nations. It seems as if the language of the most civilized nations has the most imperfect grammar, and that the same language has a more perfect grammar when the nation is in a more uncivilized state than when it reaches a higher civilization. (Cf. W. von Humboldt's *Essay on the Dual*)" (sec. 459, p. 215; cf. also *Reason in History.*)

This *relevant*, spiritual, and ideal excellence of the phonic makes every spatial language—and in general all spacing—remain *inferior* and *exterior*. Writing, according to an extension that transforms our notion of it, may be considered as an example or as the concept of this spacing. In the linguistic part of the semiology, Hegel can make the gesture he cautioned against when it was a question of general semiology: he reduces the question of writing to the rank of an accessory question, treated in an appendix, as a digression, and, in a certain sense of the word, as a supplement. As we know, this was also Plato's gesture, and Rousseau's, as it will also be Saussure's, to cite only specific nuclei in a process and a system. After defining vocal language (*Tonsprache*) explicitly as the original (*ursprüngliche*) language, Hegel writes: "We may touch, only in passing, upon written language (*Schriftsprache*)—a further development [supplementary: *weitere Fortbildung*] in the *particular* sphere of language which borrows the help of an externally practical activity. It is from the province of immediate spatial intuition to which written language proceeds that it takes and produces the signs (Sect. 454)" (sec. 459, p. 215).[23]

23. Writing, the "practical exterior activity" which "comes to the aid" of spoken language. This classical motif carries along with it the condemnation of all mnemotechniques, all language machines, all the supplementary repetitions which cause the life of the spirit, living speech, to emerge from its interior. Such a condemnation paraphrases Plato, including even the necessary ambivalence of memory (*mnēmē/hupomnēsis*)—living memory on the one hand, memory aid on the other (*Phaedrus*). Here we must convey a *Remark* from the *Encyclopedia*: "Given the name lion, we need neither the actual vision of the animal, nor its image even: the name alone, if we *understand* it, is the unimaged simple representation (*bildlose einfache Vorstellung*). We *think* in names. The recent attempts—already, as they deserved, forgotten—to rehabilitate the Mnemonic of the ancients, consist

It is not possible, here, to elaborate all the consequences of such an interpretation of the supplement of writing, its original place in Hegelian logic, and its articulation with the entire traditional and systematic chain of metaphysics. Schematically and programmatically, let us simply give the headings of the theses that ought to be examined.

A. The Teleological Hierarchy of Writings

At the peak of this hierarchy is phonetic writing of the alphabetic type: "Alphabetic writing is on all accounts the more intelligent" (sec. 459, p. 216). To the extent that it respects, translates, or transcribes the voice, that is, idealization, the movement of the spirit relating itself to its own interiority and hearing itself speak, phonetic writing is the most historic element of culture, the element most open to the infinite development of tradition. At least in the principle of its functioning: "What has been said shows the inestimable and not sufficiently appreciated educational value of learning to read and write an alphabetic character. It leads the mind from the sensibly concrete image to attend to the more formal structure of the vocal word and its abstract elements, and contributes much to give stability and independence to the inward realm of mental life" (sec. 459, p. 218).

History—which according to Hegel is always the history of the spirit—the development of the concept as logos, and the ontotheological unfolding of parousia, etc. are not obstructed by alphabetic writing. On the contrary, since it erases its own spacing better than any other, alphabetic writing remains the highest and more *relevant* mediation. Such a teleological appreciation of alphabetic writing constitutes a system and structurally governs the following two consequences:

a. Beyond the *fact* of alphabetical writing, Hegel here is calling upon a teleological ideal. In effect, as Hegel recognizes, in passing, certainly, but quite clearly, there is not and there cannot be a purely phonetic writing. The alphabetic system, such as we practice it, is not and cannot be purely phonetic. Writing can never be totally inhabited by the voice. The nonphonetic functions, if you will, the operative silences of alphabetic writing, are not factual accidents or

---

in transforming names into images, and thus again deposing memory to the level of imagination. The place of the power of memory is taken by a permanent tableau (*Tableau*) of a series of images, fixed in the imagination, to which is then attached the series of ideas forming the composition to be learned by rote (*auswendig*). Considering the heterogeneity between the import of these ideas and those permanent images, and the speed with which the attachment has to be made, the attachment cannot be made otherwise than by shallow, silly, and utterly accidental links" (*Enc.*, sec. 462, p. 220). This exteriority of the "by rote" is confronted by living, spiritual memory, in which everything proceeds from the inside. All these developments are governed by the opposition *Auswendig/Inwendig* and by that of *Entäusserung* and *Erinnerung* in the name. See also the important sections 463–64. On the critique of the *tableau* (*Tabelle*) which masks the "living essence of the thing" and proceeds from "dead understanding," see the Preface to the *Phenomenology of the Mind*, trans. A. V. Miller (Oxford: Clarendon Press, 1977), p. 37.

waste products one might hope to reduce (punctuation, figure, spacing). The *fact* of which we have just spoken is not only an empirical fact, it is the example of an essential law that irreducibly limits the achievement of a teleological ideal. In effect, Hegel concedes this in a parenthetic remark that he closes very quickly, and that we must underline: "Leibniz's practical mind (*Verstand*) misled him to exaggerate the advantages which a complete written language, formed on the hieroglyphic method (*and hieroglyphics are used even where there is alphabetic writing, as in our signs for the numbers, the planets the chemical elements, etc.*), would have as a universal language for the intercourse of nations and especially of scholars" (sec. 459, p. 215).

b. The linguistics implied by all these propositions is a *linguistics of the word,* and singularly of the *name.* The word, and the name, which with its categorem is the word par excellence, functions in this linguistics as the simple, irreducible and complete element that bears the unity of sound and sense in the voice. Thanks to the name, we may do without both the image and sensory existence. "We *think* in names" (sec. 462, p. 220). Today we know that the word no longer has the linguistic rank that had almost always been accorded to it. It is a relative unity, made to stand out between larger or smaller unities.[24] The irreducible privilege of the name is the keystone of the Hegelian philosophy of language. "Alphabetic writing is on all accounts the more intelligent: in it the *word*—the mode, peculiar to the intellect, of uttering its ideas most worthily (*eigentümliche würdigste Art*)—is brought to consciousness and made an object of reflection . . . Thus, alphabetic writing retains at the same time the advantage of vocal language, that the ideas have names strictly so called (*eigentliche Namen*); the name is the simple (*einfache*) sign for the exact idea, i.e., the *simple* (*eigentliche, d.h. einfache*) plain idea, not decomposed into its features and compounded out of them. Hieroglyphics, instead of springing from the direct analysis of sensible signs, like alphabetic writing, arise from an antecedent analysis of ideas. Thus a theory readily arises that all ideas may be reduced to their elements, or simple logical terms, so that from the elementary signs chosen to express these (as, in the case of the Chinese *Koua,* the simple straight stroke, and the stroke broken into two parts) a hieroglyphic system would be generated by their composition. This feature of hieroglyphic—the analytical designations of ideas—which misled Leibniz to regard it as preferable to alphabetic writing is rather in antagonism with the fundamental desideratum of language—the name" (sec. 459, pp. 216–17; see also the three following paragraphs).

B. The Critique of Pasigraphy:
The Prose of Understanding

Projects for a universal writing of a nonphonetic type seem to be marked by the abusive pretensions and insufficiencies of all the formalisms denounced by

24. See, notably, Martinet "Le mot" in *Diogène,* no. 51 (1965). On the function of the name in the Hegelian philosophy of language, see in particular the Jena texts recently translated and presented by G. Planty-Bonjour, entitled *La première philosophie de l'esprit* (Paris: Presses Universitaires de France, 1969), chap. 2.

Hegel. The indictment is directed precisely against the risks of dislocating the word and the name. The principal defendant is obviously Leibniz—his intelligence and his naïveté, his speculative naïveté which impelled him to place his confidence in intelligence, that is, in a formalizing understanding bearing death. But before Leibniz, before the mathematicism which inspires the projects of a universal characteristic, Hegel incriminates what he considers as the great historical models.

a. *Thoth*—The *Egyptian model* first. Above all, Hegel reproaches this model for remaining too "symbolic," in the precise sense we gave to this notion above. Although hieroglyphics do bear elements of phonetic writing, and thus of arbitrary signs (in this respect Hegel refers to Champollion's discoveries),[25] they remain too tied to the sensory representation of the thing. Their naturalness

25. "Of the representations (*Darstellungen*) which Egyptian Antiquity presents us with, one figure must be especially noticed, *viz.* the *Sphinx*—in itself a riddle—an ambiguous form, half brute, half human. The Sphinx may be regarded as a symbol of the Egyptian Spirit. The human head looking out from the brute body, exhibits Spirit as it begins to emerge from the merely Natural—to tear itself loose therefrom and already to look more freely around it; without, however, entirely freeing itself from the fetters Nature had imposed. The innumerable edifices of the Egyptians are half below the ground, and half rise above it into the air. The whole land is divided into a kingdom of life and a kingdom of death. The colossal statue of *Memnon* resounds (*erklingt*) at the first glance of the young morning Sun; though it is not yet the free light of Spirit with which it vibrates (*ertönt*). Written language is still a hieroglyphic; and its basis is only the sensuous image, not the letter itself . . . In recent times attention has especially been recalled to them and after many efforts something at least of the hieroglyphic writing has been deciphered. The celebrated Englishman, *Thomas Young*, first suggested a method of discovery, and called attention to the fact that there are small surfaces separated from the other hieroglyphics, and in which a Greek translation is perceptible . . . It was found at a later date, that a great part of the hieroglyphics are phonetic, that is, express sounds. Thus the figure of an eye denotes first the eye itself, but secondly the first letter of the Egyptian word that means 'eye' . . . The celebrated *Champollion* (the younger), first called attention to the fact that the phonetic hieroglyphs are intermingled with those which mark conceptions (*Vorstellungen*); and thus classified the hieroglyphs and established settled principles for deciphering them." *The Philosophy of History*, trans. J. Sibree (New York: Colonial Press, 1900), pp. 199–200. All further references are to this edition. Thus, unceasingly, Hegel's laborious, violent, rigid effort to inscribe and articulate into the ordered becoming of the freedom of spirit what he interprets, precisely, as the labor of the negative, as the spirit at work, patiently reappropriating its freedom: here, the petroglyph, the symbol, and the enigma simultaneously mark the stage overcome and the necessary halt, process and resistance within the *Aufhebung*: "It [the Egyptian Spirit] is, as we have seen, symbolizing Spirit; and as such, it endeavors to master these symbolizations, and to present them clearly before the mind. The more enigmatical and obscure it is to itself, so much the more does it feel the impulse to labor to deliver itself from its imprisonment, and to gain a clear objective view of itself. It is the distinguishing feature of the Egyptian Spirit, that it stands before us as this mighty taskmaster (*Werkmeister*). It is not splendor, amusement, pleasure, or the like that it seeks. The force which urges it is the impulse of self-comprehension; and it has no other material or ground to work on, in order to teach itself what it is—to realize itself for itself—than this working out (*Hinarbeiten*) its thoughts in stone; and what it engraves (*hineinschreibt*) on the stone are its enigmas—these hieroglyphs. They are of two kinds—hieroglyphs *proper*, designed rather to express language, and having reference to subjective conception; and a class of hieroglyphs of a different kind, viz. those enormous masses of architecture and sculpture, with which Egypt is covered" (ibid., pp. 214–15).

holds back the spirit, encumbers it, compelling the spirit to an effort of mechanical memory, making it wander in an infinite polysemia. A poor model for science and philosophy. *"Hieroglyphic* language is a designation of objects which has no relation to the sonorous sign.—The idea of a written philosophical and universal language, dreamed of by so many minds, comes up against the immense conglomeration of signs that would have to be elaborated and learned."[26] The naturalness of hieroglyphs, the fact that spirit has only partially manifested itself, or rather heard itself speak, in them, is quite precisely marked by a certain absence of the voice, notably in the art forms privileged by Egyptian culture. Under the heading of "Unconscious Symbolism" Hegel writes: "Similarly the hieroglyphic script of the Egyptians is also largely symbolic, since *either* it tries to make us acquainted with the meanings by sketching actual objects which display (*darstellen*) not themselves, but a universal related to them, *or*, more commonly still, in its so-called phonetic element this script indicates the individual letters by illustrating an object the initial letter of which has in speech the same sound as that which is to be expressed" (*Aesth.* I, p. 357). Next, invoking the example of the colossi, which according to legend emitted sounds under the influence of the dew and the first rays of the sun, Hegel believes he can see in them that spirit is only beginning to liberate itself and to recognize itself as such: "But taken as symbols, the meaning to be ascribed to these colossi is that they do not have the spiritual soul freely in themselves and therefore, instead of being able to draw animation (*Belebung*) from within, from what bears proportion and beauty in itself, they require for it light from without which alone liberates the note of the soul from them. The human voice, on the other hand, resounds out of one's own feeling and one's own spirit without any external impulse, just as the height of art in general consists in making the inner give shape to itself out of its own being. But the inner life of the human form is still dumb (*stumm*) in Egypt and in its animation (*Beseelung*) it is only a natural factor that is kept in view" (*Aesth.* I, p. 358).[27]

The naturalness of the hieroglyphic symbol is the condition for its polysemia. For a polysemia which in Hegel's view does not have the merit of the regulated ambivalence of certainly naturally speculative words of the German language. Here, the obscure instability of meaning has to do with spirit's not having clearly

26. *Philosophische Propädeutik*, sec. 161, p. 211.
27. Elsewhere, quite struck by the colonnades, pylons, pillars (*Säule, Pylone, Pfeiler*), and by the forests of columns (*ganzen Wäldern von Säulen, Säulenwald*, etc.), Hegel compares the Egyptian temples to a book. The "symbols of general significations" are there manifested by "writings" and by "graven images." The forms and figures of the temple therefore replace books, supplement them (*die Stelle der Bücher vertreten*). "Here and there Memnons lean against the sloping walls which also form galleries and are bedecked all over with hieroglyphics or enormous pictures in stone so that they appeared to the French scholars who saw them recently as if they were printed in calico. They can be regarded like the pages of a book (*Bücherblatter*)" (*Aesthetics* II, p. 645).

and freely returned to itself. Certainly nature has begun to animate itself, and itself to relate to itself, itself to examine itself, is in motion enough to signal and to symbolize with itself. But spirit does not come back to itself in this, does not yet recognize itself. The materiality of the signifier, it could be said, functions by itself as "unconscious symbolism." "Now owing to this alternating symbolism (*Wechselsymbolik*), the symbol in Egypt is at the same time an ensemble of symbols, so that what at one time appears as meaning (*Bedeutung*) is also used again as a symbol of a related sphere. In a symbolism which confusedly intertwines (*durcheinanderschlingt*) meaning and shape, presages a variety of things in fact or alludes to them, and therefore already comes close to that inner subjectivity which alone can develop itself in many directions, the associations are ambiguous (*vieldeutig*) and this is the virtue of these productions, although their explanation is of course made difficult owing to this ambiguity" (*Aesth.* I, p. 360).

This polysemia is so essential, belongs so necessarily to the structure of the hieroglyph, that the difficulty of deciphering has nothing to do with our situation or lack of contemporaneity. Hegel specifies, rather, that it had to limit the reading of the Egyptians themselves. Hence the transition from Egypt to Greece is the deciphering and deconstitution of the hieroglyph, of the hieroglyph's properly symbolic structure such as it itself is symbolized in the figure of the Sphinx. Greece is the answer of Oedipus, which Hegel interprets as the discourse and operation of consciousness itself. "The works of Egyptian art in their mysterious symbolism are therefore riddles; the objective riddle *par excellence*. As a symbol for this proper meaning of the Egyptian spirit we may mention the Sphinx. It is, as it were, the symbol of the symbolic itself . . . It is in this sense that the Sphinx in the Greek myth, which we ourselves may interpret again symbolically, appears as a monster asking a riddle" (*Aesth.* I, p. 360). With his answer, Oedipus destroys the Sphinx. "The Sphinx propounded the well-known conundrum: What is it that in the morning goes on four legs, at mid-day on two, and in the evening on three? Oedipus found the simple answer: a man, and he tumbled the Sphinx from the rock. The explanation of the symbol lies in the absolute meaning, in the spirit, just as the famous Greek inscription calls to man: Know thyself. The light of consciousness is the clarity which makes its concrete content shine clearly through the shape belonging and appropriate to itself, and its existence reveals itself alone" (*Aesth.* I, p. 361).

With the answer to the riddle, Oedipus's words, the discourse of consciousness, *man* destroys, dissipates, or tumbles the petroglyph. And corresponding to the stature of the Sphinx, the animality of spirit asleep in the stony sign, the mediation between matter and man, the duplicity of the intermediary, is the figure of Thoth, the god of writing. The place Hegel assigns to this demigod (a secondary god, inferior to the god of thought, the animal servant of the great god, man's animal, god's man, etc.) in no way upsets the staging of the *Phae*-

drus.[28] There too we must articulate the systematic chains in their differentiated amplitude. And ask why Hegel, here, reads the Egyptian mythemes as does Plato: "As an important element in the conception Osiris, *Anubis* (*Thoth*)—the Egyptian Hermes—must be specially noticed. In human activity and invention, and in the economy of legislation, the Spiritual, as such, is embodied; and becomes in this form—which is itself determinate and limited—an object of consciousness. Here we have the Spiritual, not as one infinite, independent sovereignty over nature, but as a particular existence, side by side with the powers of Nature—characterized also by intrinsic particularity. And thus the Egyptians had also specific divinities, conceived as spiritual activities and forces; but partly *intrinsically* limited—partly so, as contemplated under natural symbols.

"The Egyptian Hermes is celebrated as exhibiting the spiritual side of their theism. According to Jamblichus, the Egyptian priests immemorially prefixed to all their inventions the name Hermes: Erastosthenes, therefore, called his book, which treated of the entire science of Egypt—'Hermes.' Anubis is called the friend and companion of Osiris. To him is ascribed the invention of writing, and of science generally—of grammar, astronomy, mensuration, music and medicine. It was he who first divided the day into twelve hours: he was moreover the first lawgiver, the first instructor in religious observances and objects, and in gymnastics and orchestics, and it was he who discovered the olive. But, notwithstanding all these spiritual attributes, this divinity is something quite other than the God of Thought. Only particular human arts and inventions are associated with him. Not only so; but he entirely falls back into involvement in existence, and is degraded under physical symbols" (*Philosophy of History*, p. 210).

b. *The tortoise.* Hegel apprehends the *Chinese model* of writing in a circle. To describe it, let us simply link together three propositions. They mark the three predicates between which Chinese writing necessarily goes round in circles: *immobilism* (or slowness), *exteriority* (or superficiality), *naturality* (or animality). All of this is inscribed on the carapace of a tortoise. Three citations:

1. *Immobilism.* "With the Empire of China History has to begin, for it is the oldest, as far as history gives us any information, and its *principle* has such substantiality, that for the empire in question it is at once the oldest and the newest. Early do we see China advancing to the condition in which it is found at this day, for as the contrast between objective existence and subjective freedom of movement in it, is still wanting, every change is excluded, and the fixedness of character which recurs perpetually takes the place of what we should call the truly historical" (*Philosophy of History*, p. 116).

2. *Exteriority.* This immediately follows the preceding in order *to exclude* from history that which nevertheless is defined as the *origin* of history, and which *itself* has inspired the historian more than anything else: "China and India lie,

---

28. TN. On the *Phaedrus* and Thoth, see "Plato's Pharmacy," in Derrida, *Dissemination.*

as it were, still outside the world's History, as the mere presupposition of elements whose combination must be waited for to constitute their vital progress.
The unity of substantiality and subjective freedom so entirely excludes the distinction and contrast of the two elements, that by this very fact, substance cannot
arrive at reflection on itself—at subjectivity. The substantial in its moral aspect
(*Sittliches*), rules therefore, not as the moral disposition (*Gesinnung*) of the Subject, but as the despotism of the Sovereign. No people has a so strictly continuous
series of writers of History as the Chinese" (*Philosophy of History*, p. 116). And
history being confused with the history of philosophy: "The Eastern form must
therefore be excluded from the History of Philosophy, but still, upon the whole,
I will take some notice of it. I have touched on this elsewhere, for some time
ago we for the first time reached a position to judge of it . . . Philosophy proper
commences in the West."[29]

3. *Naturality*. On the carapace of the tortoise we may read an (almost) im-
mobility, (almost) exteriority, (almost) naturality: "Counting is a poor procedure.
It is also often a question of the Chinese philosophy of Fo-Hi, which rests upon
certain lines drawn, it is said, from the carapace of tortoises. According to the
Chinese, the characters of their writing, as well as their philosophy, are founded
upon these lines. One immediately sees that their philosophy has not gone very
far; one finds expressed in it only the most abstract ideas and oppositions. The
two fundamental figures are a horizontal line and an equally long and broken
line; the first figure is named Yang and the second Yin; these are the same
fundamental determinations found in Pythagoras: unity, duality. These figures
are highly honored by the Chinese as the principles of all things; these are the
first determinations, it is true, and consequently the most superficial. They are
united to form 4, then 8, and finally 64 figures."[30]

29. TN. *Lectures on the History of Philosophy*, vol. 1, trans. E. S. Haldane and Frances H.
Simpson (New York: Humanities Press, 1974), p. 99. All further references are to this
edition. It should be noted that this translation is based on Michelet's edition of the
Lectures. Derrida cites Gibelin's translation, *Leçons sur l'histoire de la philosophie* (Paris: Gallimard, 1954), which is based on the more authoritative Hoffmeister edition. There are
serious discrepancies between the two editions: for example, the passage on the tortoise
cited in the next paragraph does not appear in the Haldane translation. Wherever these
discrepancies arise, I will provide the reference to the Gibelin translation, since the only
German text at my disposition is the questionable Michelet. My thanks to Jacques Derrida
for his help here.
30. [Gibelin, p. 190] The guiding intent here is still the critique of arithmetic or geometric
formalism. To the concrete expression of the living concept Hegel opposes the abstraction
of the number and the line. From this point of view the metaphor of the *circle* itself is
disqualified. Elsewhere, among the lengthy developments devoted to the Y-King and to
the Tao To King, in the *Philosophy of History* as much as in the *History of Philosophy*: "The
Chinese have also taken up their attention with abstract thoughts and with pure categories.
The old book Y-King, or the Book of Principles, serves as the foundation for such; it
contains the wisdom of the Chinese, and its origin is attributed to Fo-Hi. That which is
there by him related passes into what is quite mythological, fabulous and even senseless.
The main point in it is the ascription to him of the discovery of a table with certain signs

The Chinese model, which fascinated Leibniz and led him astray, as Hegel takes every opportunity to recall, nevertheless marks a progress over the Egyptian hieroglyph. A progress in formalizing abstraction, a detachment as concerns the sensuous and the natural symbol. But this progress, which corresponds to the moment of abstract understanding, never recovers what it loses: the speculative concreteness of Western speech finds then that the process of idealization has even "relifted" (*relevé*) its sensuous exteriority. Whence the analogy between the structure of Chinese writing and the structures of formal understanding in Western philosophy circumscribed by Hegel, in particular a certain authority of the mathematical model over philosophy: "It must certainly be considered that pure thoughts are brought to consciousness, but in this case we make no advance, merely remaining stationary so far as they are concerned. The concrete is not conceived of speculatively, but is simply taken from ordinary ideas, inasmuch as it is expressed in accordance with their forms of representation and of perception" (*History of Philosophy*, pp. 121–22).

Following the classical framework of the Hegelian critique, Chinese culture and writing are reproached simultaneously for their empiricism (naturalism, historicism) and their formalism (mathematizing abstraction).[31]

A typical movement of the Hegelian text: speculative dialectics sets on its course a sometimes quite precise piece of historical information, but without precautions. A certain number of very determined effects result from this, and in the very form of that which Hegel elsewhere criticizes: the juxtaposition of an empirical content with a henceforth abstract form, an exterior form superimposed on that which it should organize. This is manifest particularly in unnoticed contradictions, contradictions without concepts and not reducible to the speculative movement of contradiction.

The propositions concerning Chinese writing and grammar are a symptomatic example of this. In this sense, Chinese grammar is insufficiently developed, which Hegel does not add to its credit. Compared to Western grammars, Chinese syntax is in a state of stagnant primitiveness, paralyzing the movement of science. Hegel, then, contradicts himself twice, though there is no dialectical negation of negation; it is rather a denegation, a disavowal. In effect, above we noticed the following two motifs: (1) the development and differentiation of

---

or figures (Ho-tu) which he saw on the back of a horse-dragon as it rose out of the river. (Other figures [Lo-Chou] were borrowed from the back of a tortoise and combined with the signs of Fo-Hi.) This table contains parallel lines above one another, which have a symbolical signification; and the Chinese say that these lines are the foundation of their characters as also of their philosophy" (*History of Philosophy*, p. 121; translation modified).

31. "The Chinese have remained with the abstract, and when they arrive at the concrete one finds, on the theoretical side, an exterior connection of objects of the sensory kind; one finds no order, no profound intuition, and the rest is morals. The concrete in which the beginning is pursued consists of morals, of the art of government, of history, etc., but this concrete is not of a philosophical order. In China, in Chinese religion and philosophy, we encounter a particularly perfect prose of understanding" (Gibelin, pp. 252–53).

grammar are in an inverse relation to the spiritual culture and advancement of a language; (2) the "Chinese" moment of culture is a moment of formal under- standing, of mathematical abstraction, etc.; now, in opposition to its material or lexicological function, the formal or grammatical foundation of a language pro- ceeds from the understanding.

Entangling himself in these incoherences, Hegel always ends by incriminating some relation of speech to writing. In China this relation is not what it should have been. "Though in one aspect the sciences appear thus pre-eminently ho- nored and fostered, there are wanting to them on the other side that free ground (*Boden*) of subjectivity, and that properly scientific interest, which make them a truly theoretical occupation of the mind. A free, ideal, spiritual kingdom has here no place. What may be called scientific is of a merely empirical nature, and is made absolutely subservient to the Useful on behalf of the State—its require- ments and those of individuals. The nature of their Written Language is at the outset a great hindrance to the development of the sciences. Rather, conversely, because a true scientific interest does not exist, the Chinese have acquired no better instrument for representing (*Darstellen*) and imparting thought. They have, as is well known, beside a Spoken Language, a *Written Language*; which does not express, as ours does, individual sounds—does not present the spoken words to the eye, but represents (*Vorstellen*) the ideas themselves by signs. This appears at first sight a great advantage, and has gained the suffrages of many great men—among others, of Leibniz. In reality, it is anything but such" (*Phi- losophy of History*, pp. 134–35).

The demonstration which follows alleges the great number of signs to learn (80,000 to 90,000). But as concerns the nefarious influence of writing on spoken language, the demonstration also develops a preceding argument that appears to be difficult to reconcile with the demonstration itself. (The Chinese language is both too differentiated and insufficiently differentiated, too accentuated and insufficiently articulated; the circulation of values posited by Rousseau in the *Essay on the Origin of Languages* is reversed *and* confirmed.)[32] Moreover, how is this argument to be reconciled with Hegel's praise, elaborated elsewhere, for a certain regulated polysemia (regulated, it is true by the speculative dialectics providentially accorded to the natural genius of the German language)?[33] The

32. TN. For the analysis of Rousseau's *Essay on the Origin of Languages*, see *Of Gram- matology*.

33. It is true that there is no place in speculative dialectics for a fixed opposition between natural language and formal (or universal) language. The process of language, as we will show elsewhere, is its denaturalization. Every language, to the extent that it is a language— if we may put it thus—is universal. [TN. The "kettle logic" referred to in the next sentence refers to Freud's illustration of dream "logic" by the responses of the man who returns his neighbor's kettle in damaged condition: 1. The kettle I am returning is new. 2. The holes were already in it when you lent it to me. 3. You never lent me a kettle. Derrida often compares the "kettle logic" to the philosophical treatment of writing. See "Plato's Pharmacy," in *Dissemination*. The passage on the "kettle logic" is in *The Interpretation of Dreams*, Standard Edition, vol. 4, p. 120.]

paradigm for this indictment remains the "kettle logic" (Freud), and the motivated accumulation of mutually incompatible arguments. Let us read the text. "For if we consider in the first place, the effect of such a mode of writing on the Spoken Language, we shall find this among the Chinese very imperfect, on account of that separation. For our Spoken Language is matured to distinctness chiefly through the necessity of finding signs for each single sound, which latter, by reading, we learn to express distinctly. The Chinese, to whom such a means of orthoepic development is wanting, do not mature the modifications of sounds in their language to distinct articulations capable of being represented by letters and syllables. Their Spoken Language consists of an inconsiderable number of monosyllabic words, which are used with more than one signification. The sole methods of denoting distinctions of meaning are the connection, the accent, and the pronunciation—quicker or slower, softer or louder. The ears of the Chinese have become very sensible to such distinctions. Thus I find that the word *Po* has eleven different meanings according to the tone: denoting 'glass'—'to boil'—'to winnow wheat'—'to cleave asunder'—'to water'—'to prepare'—'an old woman'—'a slave'—'a liberal man'—'a wise person'—'a little' " (*Philosophy of History*, p. 135).[34] The discourse of the Chinese, then, entangles itself in the dissemination of meanings and accents. Their writing, no longer reflecting or reassembling living language, paralyzes itself far from the concept, in the cold space of formal abstraction, that is in *space*. In sum, Hegel reproaches the Chinese for *speaking* too much when they speak, and for *writing* too much when they write.

Such a procedure is at least consequent with the system which links the logos to alphabetical writing, as soon as alphabetical writing is taken as an absolute model. Speculative dialectics permits itself to be separated neither from logos nor, simultaneously, from the logos which never thinks or presents itself except in its historical complicity with the voice and phonetic writing. The grammar of the logos thus being confused with the system of metaphysics, Hegel may write, in the course of a long elaboration on the *Tao To King*: "According to Abel Rémusat, Tao means to the Chinese 'Way, means of communication from one place to another,' and then reason, substance, principle. All of this condensed to the metaphorical, metaphysical sense signifies way in general . . . Tao, thus, is the 'original reason, the *nous* (intelligence) which has brought forth the world and governs it as spirit governs the body.' Abel Rémusat says that taken at its best this might be expressed by the Greek in *logos*. However, this remains quite confused. The Chinese language, due to its grammatical structure, creates many difficulties; notably, these objects are difficult to exhibit because of their inherently abstract and undetermined nature. Von Humboldt recently showed, in a letter to Abel Remusat, how undetermined the grammatical construction was (G. von Humboldt, Letter to M. Abel Remusat On the Nature of the Grammatical

34. The same argument can be found in sec. 459 of the *Encyclopedia*.

Forms . . . of the Chinese Language)" (Gibelin, pp. 248–49). Further on: "The Chinese language has no case inflection, the words merely standing in proximity. Thus determinations remain indeterminate" (*Lectures on the History of Philosophy,* p. 125, translation modified).

c. *To write and to calculate: the machine.* In assigning the limits of so-called universal writing, that is, a mute writing, released from the voice and from every natural language, Hegel also criticizes the pretensions of mathematical symbolism and of arithmetic, the operations of formal understanding. The silence of this writing and the space of calculation would interrupt the movement of the *Aufhebung,* or in any case would resist the interiorization of the past (*Erinnerung*), the *relevant* idealization, the history of the spirit, the reappropriation of the logos in self-presence and infinite parousia. If the passage through mathematical abstraction, through formal understanding, spacing, exteriority and death (see the preface to the *Phenomenology of Spirit*) is a necessary passage (the work of the negative, the shedding of the sensory, pedagogical asceticism, purification of thought),[35] this necessity becomes perversion and regression as soon as it is taken as a *philosophical model.*

This is the attitude inaugurated by Pythagoras. And when Leibniz seems to permit himself to be impressed by the Chinese characteristic, he is only rejoining the Pythagorian tradition. About the Y-King: ". . . the philosophy of the Chinese appears therefore to proceed from the same fundamental ideas as that of Pythagoras" (*Philosophy of History,* p. 136). "As we know, Pythagoras represented (*dargestellt*) rational relationships (or philosophemata) by numbers; and more recently, too, numbers and forms of their relations, such as powers and so on, have been employed in philosophy for the purpose of regulating thoughts or expressing them."[36]

Number, or equally, that which can do without any phonetic notation, is absolutely foreign to the concept such as Hegel understands it. More precisely, it is *contrary* to the concept. In and of itself it is certainly indispensable to conceptual movement. "We saw that number is the absolute determinateness of quantity, and its element is the difference (*Unterschied*) which has become indifferent (*gleichgültig*)—an implicit determinateness which at the same time is posited as wholly external. Arithmetic is an analytic science because all the combinations and differences which occur in its subject matter are not intrinsic to it but are effected on it in a wholly external manner. It does not have a concrete subject matter possessing inner, intrinsic, relations which, as at first concealed, as not given in our immediate acquaintance with them, have first to be elicited by the efforts of cognition. Not only does it not contain the Notion [concept] and therefore no problem for speculative thought, but it is the antithesis of the Notion. Because of the indifference of the factors in combination to the com-

---

35. This traditional motif (which, once again, is rigorously Platonic) is at the center of the greater Logic [TN. i.e. *The Science of Logic*], notably in the chapter on *Quantum.*
36. *Hegel's Science of Logic,* p. 212.

bination itself in which there is no necessity, thought is engaged here in an activity which is at the same time the extreme externalization (*äusserste Entäusserung*) of itself, a violent (*gewaltsame*) activity in which it is forced to move in a realm of thoughtlessness (*Gedanklosigkeit*) and to combine elements which are incapable of any necessary relationships. The subject matter is the abstract thought of *externality* itself.

"As this *thought* of externality, number is at the same time the abstraction of the manifoldness of sense, of which it has retained nothing but the abstract determination of externality itself. In number, therefore, sense is brought closest to thought: number is the *pure thought* of thought's own externalization" (*Logic*, pp. 212–13, translation modified).

In arithmetic calculation, then, thought would come face to face with its other. An other that thought itself certainly would have occasioned, and that thought would have opposed to itself with its sights set on reappropriatinig (it to) itself. In order for such a movement not to flounder in regression or in dialectical immobilization, this opposition in its turn would have to permit itself to be interiorized, summarized, *relevé*. Thought is this *relève*. Conversely, if this moment of nonthought was constituted as an ideal model, if this other of thought, calculation, became the ultimate finality, then paralysis would become regression. Philosophy would fall back into childhood. The philosophers fascinated by this "perverted mathematical formalism" are dreaming of a "puerile incapacity" (*Logic*, p. 214). To what are these philosophers blind? Not only to the fact that philosophy must not import into itself the language of another science, and even less let itself be governed by that language,[37] but above all to the fact that the exteriority of arithmetic abstraction remains *sensory*. It has certainly shed all empirical, sensory diversity, is pure of all determined, sensory content; but as "this thought of externality . . . it has retained nothing but the abstract determination of externality itself" (*Logic*, p. 213). As pure sensuousness, ideal sensuousness, formal sensuousness, unsensuous sensuousness, its relation to natural sensuousness is analogous to the relation of the sign to the symbol, in which "the truth is dimmed (*getrübt*) and veiled (*verhüllt*) by the sensuous element" (*Logic*, p. 215). In this sense, the sign *is* (the *relevant* truth of the) symbol, the essence (to have been *relevé*) of the symbol, the symbol past (*gewesen*). The one and the other in turn must be thought (*relevé*) by the living concept, by the language without language, the language become the thing itself, the interior voice murmuring in the greatest proximity to the spirit the identity of the name (and) of Being.

The preface to the *Phenomenology of the Spirit* had posited the equivalence of understanding, formality, the mathematical, the negative, exteriority, and death. It had also posited the necessity of their work, which must be looked at in the

---

37. Philosophy's recourse to the logical formations of other sciences, and not simply to *Logic*, is qualified as an "expedient" (*Notbehalf*) due to "philosophical incapacity" (*Hegel's Science of Logic*, p. 216).

face.[38] Now, calculation, the machine, and mute writing belong to the same system of equivalences, and their work poses the same problem: at the moment when meaning is lost, when thought is opposed to its other, when spirit is absent from itself, is the result of the operation certain? And if the *relève* of alienation is not a calculable certitude, can one still speak of alienation and still produce statements in the system of speculative dialectics? Or in dialectics, whose essence is encapsulated by this system, in general? If the investment in death cannot be integrally amortized (even in the case of a profit, of an excess of revenue), can one still speak of a work of the negative? What might be a "negative" that could not be *relevé*? And which, in sum, as negative, but without appearing as such, without *presenting* itself, that is, without working in the service of meaning, would work? but would work, then, as pure loss?

Quite simply, a machine, perhaps, and one which would function. A machine defined in its pure functioning, and not in its final utility, its meaning, its result, its work.

If we consider the machine along with the entire system of equivalences just recalled, we may risk the following proposition: what Hegel, the *relevant* interpreter of the entire history of philosophy, *could never think* is a machine that would work. That would work without, to this extent, being governed by an order of reappropriation. Such a functioning would be unthinkable in that it inscribes within itself an effect of pure loss. It would be unthinkable as a non-thought that no thought could *relever*, could constitute as its proper opposite, as *its* other. Doubtless philosophy would see in this a nonfunctioning, a non-work; and thereby philosophy would miss that which, in such a machine, works. By itself. Outside.

Of course, this entire logic, this syntax, these propositions, these concepts, these names, this language of Hegel's—and, up to a certain point, this very language—are engaged in the *system of this unpower,* this structural incapacity to think without *relève.* To confirm this, it suffices to make oneself understood within this system. For example, to name machine a machine, functioning a functioning, work a work, etc. Or even simply to ask *why* one has never been able to think this, to seek its causes, reasons, origins, foundations, conditions of possibility, etc. Or even to seek other names. For example, an other name for the "sign," which, no more than the pit or the pyramid, cannot completely do without the machine.

Would it suffice then silently to set some apparatus in place? No. We must still machinate its presentation. For example, through the reading proposed here, now, of the following Hegelian statement, whose severe irony belongs, unwittingly, to a very old procedure.

"Calculation (*Rechnen*) being so much an external and therefore mechanical business, it has been possible to construct machines (*Maschinen*) which perform

38. See pages 21 and 26–36 (in the Miller translation).

107

arithmetical operations with complete accuracy. A knowledge of just this one fact about the nature of calculation is sufficient for an appraisal of the idea of making calculation the principal means for educating the mind and stretching it on the rack in order to perfect it as a machine" (*Logic*, pp. 216–17).

That is, a system of constraints which (itself) regularly repeats the "living," "thinking," "speaking" protest against repetition; in operating to some extent everywhere, for example, this system acts upon the following which is no longer simply included in metaphysics, and even less in Hegelianism: "The time of thinking . . . is different from the time of calculation (*Rechnens*) that pulls our thinking in all directions. Today the computer (*Denkmaschine*) calculates thousands of relationships in one second. Despite their technical uses, they are inessential (*wesenlos*)."[39]

Nor does it suffice to overturn the hierarchy, or to reverse the direction of the current, to attribute an "essentiality" to technology and to the configuration of its equivalents, in order to change the machinery, the system or the terrain.

39. Martin Heidegger, *Identity and Difference*, trans. Joan Stambaugh (New York: Harper and Row, 1969), p. 41. This text, which however belongs to one of the most efficient interrogations of Hegelian thought, would have to be made to communicate with the phonological motifs of Heideggerian discourse that we have already pointed out and that we will make more specific elsewhere. See "The Ends of Man," below [and "Ousia and Grammē" above].

The Ends of Man

First published in French in *Marges de la philosophie* (1972), this lecture was given in New York in October 1968 at an international colloquium. The theme proposed was "Philosophy and Anthropology."

"Now, I say, man and, in general, every rational being exists as an end in himself and not merely as a means to be arbitrarily used by this or that will. In all his actions, whether they are directed to himself or to other rational beings, he must always be regarded at the same time as an end . . ."

Kant, *Foundations of the Metaphysics of Morals*[1]

"Ontology . . . has merely enabled us to determine the ultimate ends of human reality, its fundamental possibilities, and the value which haunts it."

Jean-Paul Sartre, *Being and Nothingness*[2]

"As the archeology of our thought easily shows, man is an invention of recent date. And one perhaps nearing its end."

Michel Foucault, *The Order of Things*[3]

Every philosophical colloquium necessarily has a political significance. And not only due to that which has always linked the essence of the philosophical to the essence of the political. Essential and general, this political import nevertheless burdens the a priori link between philosophy and politics, aggravates it in a way, and also determines it when the philosophical colloquium is announced as an international colloquium. Such is the case here.

The possibility of an international philosophical colloquium can be examined infinitely, along many pathways, and at multiple levels of generality. In its greatest extension, to which I will return in a moment, such a possibility implies that contrary to the essence of philosophy—such as it has always represented itself at least—philosophical nationalities have been formed. At a given moment, in a given historical, political, and economic context, these national groups have judged it possible and necessary to organize international encounters, to present

1. In *The Critique of Practical Reason and Other Writings on Moral Philosophy*, trans. Lewis White Beck (Chicago: University of Chicago Press, 1949), p. 86. Further references are to this edition.
2. Trans. Hazel Barnes (New York: Pocket Books, 1966), p. 784.
3. (*Les mots et les choses*) (London: Tavistock Publications, 1970), p. 387.

111

themselves, or to be represented in such encounters by their national identity (such, at least, as it is assumed by the organizers of the colloquium), and to determine in such encounters their proper difference, or to establish relations between their respective differences. Such an establishment of relations can be practiced, if at all, only in the extent to which national philosophical identities are assumed, whether they are defined in the order of doctrinal content, the order of a certain philosophical "style," or quite simply the order of language, that is, the unity of the academic institution, along with everything implied by language and institution. But the establishing of relations between differences is also the promised complicity of a common element: the colloquium can take place only in a medium, or rather in the representation that all the participants must make of a certain transparent ether, which here would be none other than what is called the universality of philosophical discourse. With these words I am designating less a fact than a project, which is linked by its essence, (and we should say by essence itself, by the thought of Being and of truth), to a certain group of languages and "cultures." For something must happen or must have happened to the diaphanous purity of this element.

How else are we to understand that international colloquia—which aim to repair, to surmount, to erase, or simply to relate national philosophical differences one to another—seem possible and necesary? Conversely, and above all, how are we to understand that something like an international philosophical encounter is an extremely rare thing in the world? The philosopher knows, and today can say to himself, that this extremely recent and unexpected thing, which was unimaginable a century ago, becomes a frequent phenomenon—of a disconcerting facility, I even would say—in certain societies, but is of a no less remarkable rarity in the greater part of the world. On the one hand, as far as thought—which perhaps is repulsed by this haste and volubility—is concerned, what is disquieting has to do more with the fever for colloquia and the multiplication of organized or improvised exchanges. On the other hand, it remains no less the case that the societies, languages, cultures, and political or national organizations with which no exchange in the form of an international philosophical colloquium is possible are of considerable number and extent. Nor must we hasten to interpret this impossibility. Essentially, it does not have to do with a prohibition overtly deriving from politico-ideological jurisdiction. For when this prohibition exists, there is every chance that this issue already has become meaningful within the occidental orb of metaphysics or philosophy, that it already has been formulated in political concepts drawn from the metaphysical reserve, and that the *possibility* of such a colloquium henceforth is apparent. Without this no overt prohibition could be articulated. Also, speaking of the noncolloquium, I was not alluding to some ideologico-political barrier which would sector, with borders or curtains, an already philosophical field. I was thinking, first of all, of all those places—cultural, linguistic, political, etc.—where the organization of a philosophical colloquium simply would have no meaning, where it would be no more meaningful to instigate it than to prohibit it. If I permit myself to recall this obvious fact, it is because a colloquium which has chosen *anthropos*, the discourse on anthropos, philosophical anthropology, as its theme, must feel bearing down on its borders the insistent weight of this difference, which is of an entirely other order than that of the internal or intra-philosophical differences of opinion which could be freely exchanged here. Beyond these borders, what I will call the philosophical *mirage* would consist as much in perceiving philosophy—a more or less constituted and adult philosophy—as in perceiving the desert. For this other space is neither philosophical nor desert-like, that is, barren. If I recall this obvious fact, it is also for another reason: the anxious and busy multiplication of colloquia in the West is doubtless an effect of that difference which I just said bears down, with a mute, growing and menacing pressure, on the enclosure of Western collocution. The latter doubtless makes an effort to interiorize this difference, to master it, if we may put it thus, by affecting itself with it. The interest in the universality of the anthropos is doubtless a sign of this effort.

Now I would like to specify, still as a preamble, but in another direction, what appears to be one of the general political implications of our colloquium. While refraining from any precipitous appreciation of this fact, simply rendering it for all to reflect upon, I will indicate here what links the possibility of an international philosophical colloquium with the form of democracy. I am indeed saying with the *form*, and with the form of *democracy.*

Here, *democracy* must be the *form* of the political organization of society. This means at least that:

1. The national philosophical identity accommodates a nonidentity, does not exclude a relative diversity and the coming into language of this diversity, eventually as a minority. It goes without saying that the philosophers present here no more identify with each other in their thought (why else would they be several?) than they are mandated by some unanimous national discourse. As for the fact that the totality of this diversity might be exhaustively represented—this can only remain problematical, and in part depends upon the discourses to be proffered here.

2. No more than they identify with each other, the philosophers present here do not assume the official policies of their countries. Let me be permitted to speak in my own name here. Moreover, I will do so only insofar as the problem before me refers in truth to an essential generality; and it is in the form of this generality that I wish to state it. When I was invited to this meeting, my hesitation could end only when I was assured that I could bear witness here, now, to my agreement, and to a certain point my solidarity with those, in this country, who were fighting against what was then their country's official policy in certain parts of the world, notably in Vietnam. It is evident that such a gesture—and the fact that I am authorized to make it—signifies that those who are welcoming my discourse do not identify with the policies of their country

any more than I do, and do not feel justified in assuming those policies, at least insofar as they are participating in this colloquium.

And yet it would be naive or purposely blind to let oneself be reassured by the image or appearance of such a freedom. It would be illusory to believe that political innocence has been restored, and evil complicities undone, when opposition to them can be expressed in the country itself, not only through the voices of its own citizens but also those of foreign citizens, and that hencefoth diversities, i.e. oppositions, may freely and discursively relate to one another. That a declaration of opposition to some official policy is authorized, and authorized by the authorities, also means, precisely to that extent, that the declaration does not upset the given order, is not *bothersome*. This last expression, "bothersome," may be taken in all its senses. This is what I wished to recall, in order to begin, by speaking of the *form of democracy* as the political milieu of every international philosophical colloquium. And this is also why I proposed to place the accent on *form* no less than on *democracy*. Such, in its most general and schematic principle, is the question which put itself to me during the preparations for this encounter, from the invitation and the deliberations that followed, up to acceptance, and then to the writing of this text, which I date quite precisely from the month of April 1968: it will be recalled that these were the weeks of the opening of the Vietnam peace talks and of the assassination of Martin Luther King. A bit later, when I was typing this text, the universities of Paris were invaded by the forces of order—and for the first time at the demand of a rector—and then reoccupied by the students in the upheaval you are familiar with. This historical and political horizon would call for a long analysis. I have simply found it necessary to mark, date, and make known to you the historical circumstances in which I prepared this communication. These circumstances appear to me to belong, by all rights, to the field and the problematic of our colloquium.

Humanism or Metaphysics

Thus the transition will be made quite naturally between the preamble and the theme of this communication, as it was imposed upon me, rather than as I chose it.

Where is France, as concerns man?

The question "of man" is being asked in very current fashion in France, along highly significant lines, and in an original historico-philosophical structure. What I will call "France," then, on the basis of several indices and for the time of this exposition, will be the nonempirical site of a movement, a structure and an articulation of the question "of man." Following this is would be possible, and doubtless necessary—but then only—rigorously to relate this site with every other instance defining something like "France."

Where then is France, as concerns man?

114

After the war, under the name of Christian or atheist existentialism, and in conjunction with a fundamentally Christian personalism, the thought that dominated France presented itself essentially as humanist. Even if one does not wish to summarize Sartre's thought under the slogan "existentialism is a humanism," it must be recognized that in *Being and Nothingness, The Sketch of a Theory of the Emotions*, etc., the major concept, the theme of the last analysis, the irreducible horizon and origin is what was then called "human-reality." As is well known, this is a translation of Heideggerian *Dasein*. A monstrous translation in many respects, but so much the more significant. That this translation proposed by Corbin was adopted at the time, and that by means of Sartre's authority it reigned, gives us much to think about the reading or the nonreading of Heidegger during this period, and about what was at stake in reading or not reading him in this way.

Certainly the notion of "human-reality" translated the project of thinking the meaning of man, the humanity of man, on a new basis, if you will. If the neutral and undetermined notion of "human reality" was substituted for the notion of man, with all its metaphysical heritage and the substantialist motif or temptation inscribed in it, it was also in order to suspend all the presuppositions which had always constituted the concept of the unity of man. Thus, it was also a reaction against a certain intellectualist or spiritualist humanism which had dominated French philosophy (Brunschvig, Alain, Bergson, etc.). And this neutralization of every metaphysical or speculative thesis as concerns the unity of the anthropos could be considered in some respects as the faithful inheritance of Husserl's transcendental phenomenology and of the fundamental ontology in *Sein und Zeit* (the only partially known work of Heidegger's at the time, along with *What Is Metaphysics?* and *Kant and the Problem of Metaphysics*). And yet, despite this alleged neutralization of metaphysical presuppositions,[4] it must be recognized that the unity of man is never examined in and of itself. Not only is existentialism a humanism, but the ground and horizon of what Sartre then called his "phenomenological ontology" (the subtitle of *Being and Nothingness*) remains the unity of human-reality. To the extent that it describes the structures of human-reality,

---

4. The humanism which marks Sartre's philosophical discourse in its depths, however, is very surely and very ironically taken apart in *Nausea*: in the caricature of the Autodidact, for example, the same figure reassembles the theological project of absolute knowledge and the humanist ethic, in the form of the encyclopedic epistemophilia which leads the Autodidact to undertake the reading of the world library (which is really the Western library, and definitely the municipal library) in alphabetical order by author's name, and in areas where he is able to love Man ("There is an aim, sir, there is an aim . . . there are men . . . one must love them, one must love them") in the representation of men, preferably young men. It is in the dialogue with the Autodidact that Roquentin levels the worst charges against humanism, against all humanist styles; and at the moment when nausea is slowly rising in him, he says to himself, for example, "I don't want to be integrated, I don't want my good red blood to go and fatten this lymphatic beast: I will not be fool enough to call myself 'anti-humanist.' I *am not* a humanist, that's all there is to it." *Nausea*, trans. Lloyd Alexander (New York: New Directions, 1959), p. 160.

phenomenological ontology is a philosophical anthropology. Whatever the breaks marked by this Hegelian-Husserlian-Heideggerian anthropology as concerns the classical anthropologies, there is an uninterrupted metaphysical familiarity with that which, so naturally, links the *we* of the philosopher to "we men," to the *we* in the horizon of humanity. Although the theme of history is quite present in the discourse of the period, there is little practice of the history of concepts. For example, the history of the concept of man is never examined. Everything occurs as if the sign "man" had no origin, no historical, cultural, or linguistic limit. At the end of *Being and Nothingness,* when Sartre in programmatic fashion asks the question of the unity of Being (which in this context means the totality of beings), and when he confers upon this question the rubric "metaphysical" in order to distinguish it from phenomenological ontology which described the essential specificity of regions, it goes without saying that this metaphysical unity of Being, as the totality of the in-itself and the for-itself, is precisely the unity of human-reality in its project. Being in-itself and Being for-itself were *of Being;* and this totality of beings, in which they were effected, itself was linked up to itself, relating and appearing to itself, by means of the essential project of human-reality.[5] What was named in this way, in an allegedly neutral and undetermined way, was nothing other than the metaphysical unity of man and God, the relation of man to God, the project of becoming God as the project constituting human-reality. Atheism changes nothing in this fundamental structure. The example of the Sartrean project remarkably verifies Heidegger's proposition according to which "every humanism remains metaphysical," metaphysics being the other name of ontotheology.

Thus defined, humanism or anthropologism, during this period, was the common ground of Christian or atheist existentialisms, of the philosophy of values (spiritualist or not), of personalisms of the right or the left, of Marxism

5. "Each human reality is at the same time a direct project to metamorphose its own For-itself in an In-itself-For-itself and a project of the appropriation of the world as a totality of being-in-itself, in the form of a fundamental quality. Every human reality is a passion in that it projects losing itself so as to found being and by the same stroke to constitute the In-itself which escapes contingency by being its own foundation, the *Ens causa sui,* which religions call God. Thus the passion of man is the reverse of that of Christ, for man loses himself as man in order that God may be born. But the idea of God is contradictory and we lose ourselves in vain. Man is a useless passion." *Being and Nothingness,* trans. Hazel Barnes (New York: Pocket Books, 1966), p. 784. This synthetic unity is determined as *lack:* lack of totality in beings, lack *of* God that is soon transformed into a lack *in* God. Human-reality is a *failed* God: "Also the *ens causa sui* remains as the *lacked . . .*" (p. 789). ". . . the for-itself determines its being as *a lack . . .*" (p. 795). As concerns the meaning of the Being of this totality of beings, as concerns the history of this concept of negativity as a relationship to God, the meaning and origin of the concept of (human) reality, and the reality of the real, no questions are asked. In this respect, what is true of *Being and Nothingness* is even more so of the *Critique of Dialectical Reason.* The concept of *lack,* linked to the non-self identity of the subject (as consciousness) and to the desire and agency of the Other in the dialectic of the master and the slave, was then beginning to dominate the French ideological scene.

in the classical style. And if one takes one's bearings from the terrain of political ideologies, anthropologism was the unperceived and uncontested common ground of Marxism and of Social-Democratic or Christian-Democratic discourse. This profound concordance was authorized, in its philosophical expression, by the *anthropologistic* readings of Hegel (interest in the *Phenomenology of Spirit* as it was read by Kojève), of Marx (the privilege accorded the *Manuscripts of 1844*), of Husserl (whose descriptive and regional work is emphasized, but whose transcendental questions are ignored), and of Heidegger, whose projects for a philosophical anthropology or an existential analytic only were known or retained (*Sein und Zeit*). Of course, here I am picking out the dominant traits of a period. The period itself is not exhausted by these dominant traits. Nor can one say in absolutely rigorous fashion that this period started after the war, and even less that it is over today. Nevertheless, I believe that the empiricism of this cross-section is justifiable here only insofar as it permits the reading of a *dominant* motif and insofar as it takes its authority from indices which are unarguable for anyone approaching such a period. Further, the cross-section is provisional, and in an instant we will reinscribe this sequence in the time and space of a larger totality.

In order to mark in boldface the traits that opposed this period to the following one, the one in which we are, and which too is probably undergoing a mutation, we must recall that during the decade that followed the war we did not yet see the reign of the all-powerful motif of what we call today, more and more, and even exclusively, the "so-called *human* sciences," the expression itself marking a certain distance, but a still respectful distance. On the contrary, the current questioning of humanism is contemporary with the dominating and spellbinding extension of the "human sciences" within the philosophical field.

The *Relève* of Humanism

The anthropologistic reading of Hegel, Husserl, and Heidegger was a mistake in one entire respect, perhaps the most serious mistake. And it is this reading which furnished the best conceptual resources to postwar French thought.

First of all, the *Phenomenology of Spirit,* which had only been read for a short time in France, does not have to do with something one might simply call man. As the science of the experience of consciousness, the science of the structures of the phenomenality of the spirit itself relating to itself, it is rigorously distinguished from anthropology. In the *Encyclopedia,* the section entitled *Phenomenology of Spirit* comes after the *Anthropology,* and quite explicitly exceeds its limits. What is true of the *Phenomenology* is a fortiori true of the system of the *Logic.*

Similarly, in the second place, the critique of anthropologism was one of the inaugural motifs of Husserl's transcendental phenomenology. This is an explicit critique, and it calls anthropologism by its name from the *Prologomena to Pure*

117

Logic on.[6] Later this critique will have as its target not only empirical anthropologism, but also transcendental anthropologism.[7] The transcendental structures described after the phenomenological reduction are not those of the intrawordly being called "man." Nor are they essentially linked to man's society, culture, language, or even to his "soul" or "psyche." Just as, according to Husserl, one may imagine a consciousness without soul (*seelenlos*),[8] similarly— and a fortiori—one may imagine a consciousness without man.

Therefore it is astonishing and highly significant that at the moment when the authority of Husserlian thought was asserted and then established in postwar France, even becoming a kind of philosophical mode, the critique of anthropologism remained totally unnoticed, or in any event without effect. One of the most paradoxical pathways of this motivated misconstruing passes through a reductive reading of Heidegger. Because one has interpreted the analytic of Dasein in strictly anthropological terms, occasionally one limits or criticizes Husserl on the basis of Heidegger, dropping all the aspects of phenomenology that do not serve anthropological description. This pathway is quite paradoxical because it follows the itinerary of a reading of Heidegger that was also Husserl's. In effect, Husserl precipitously interpreted *Sein und Zeit* as an anthropologistic deviation from transcendental phenomenology.[9]

In the third place, immediate following the war and after the appearance of *Being and Nothingness*, Heidegger, in his *Letter on Humanism*, recalled—for all those who did not yet know, and who had not even taken into account the very first sections of *Sein und Zeit*—that anthropology and humanism were not the milieu of his thought and the horizon of his questions. The "destruction" of metaphysics or of classical ontology was even directed against humanism.[10] After the tide of humanism and anthropologism that had covered French philosophy, one might have thought that the antihumanist and antianthropologist ebb that followed, and in which we are now, would rediscover the heritage of the systems of thought that had been disfigured, or in which rather, the figure of man too quickly had been discerned.

Nothing of the sort has happened, and it is the significance of such a phenomenon that I now wish to examine. The critique of humanism and anthro-

6. Chapter 7, "Psychologism as Sceptical Relativism," sec. 39, "Anthropologism in Sigwart's Logic," sec. 40, "Anthropologism in Erdmann's Logic."

7. *Ideas I,* see e.g. secs. 49 and 54.

8. Ibid.

9. See the Afterword to *Ideas,* and the marginal notes in the copy of *Sein und Zeit* (Husserl Archives, Louvain).

10. "Every humanism is either grounded in a metaphysics or is itself made to be the ground of one. Every determination of the essence of man that already presupposes an interpretation of being without asking about the truth of Being, whether knowingly or not, is metaphysical. The result is that what is peculiar to all metaphysics, specifically with respect to the way the essence of man is determined, is that it is 'humanistic.' Accordingly, every humanism remains metaphysical." "Letter on Humanism," in *Basic Writings*, ed. David Farrell Krell (New York: Harper and Row, 1977), p. 202.

pologism, which is one of the dominant and guiding motifs of current French thought, far from seeking its sources or warranties in the Hegelian, Husserlian, or Heideggerian critiques of the same humanism or the same anthropologism, on the contrary seem, by means of a gesture sometimes more implicit than systematically articulated, to *amalgamate* Hegel, Husserl, and—in a more diffuse and ambiguous fashion—Heidegger with the old metaphysical humanism. I am purposely using the word "amalgam" which in its usage unites references to alchemy, which is the primary one here, with a strategic or tactical reference to the domain of political ideology.

Before attempting to interpret this phenomenon of paradoxical demeanor, we must take several precautions. First of all, this amalgam does not exclude that some progress has been made in France in the reading of Hegel, Husserl, or Heidegger, nor that this progress has led to requestioning the humanist insistence. But this progress and requestioning do not occupy center stage, and this must be significant. Conversely and symmetrically, among those who do practice the amalgamation, the schemas of the anthropologistic misinterpretation from Sartre's time are still at work, and occasionally it is these very schemas which govern the rejection of Hegel, Husserl, and Heidegger into the shadows of humanist metaphysics. Very often, *in fact*, those who denounce humanism at the same time as metaphysics have remained at the stage of this "first reading" of Hegel, Husserl, and Heidegger, and one could locate more than one sign of this in numerous recent texts. Which leads us to think that in certain respects, and at least to this extent, we are still on the same shore.

But no matter, as concerns the question I would like to ask, that such and such an author has read such and such a text poorly, or simply not at all, or that he remains, as concerns systems of thought he believes he has surpassed or overturned, in a state of great ingenuousness. This is why we shall not concern ourselves here with any given author's name or with the title of any given work. What must hold our interest, beyond the justifications which, as a matter of fact, are most often insufficient, is the kind of profound justification, whose necessity is subterranean, which makes the Hegelian, Husserlian, and Heideggerian critiques or *de-limitations* of metaphysical humanism appear to belong to the very sphere of that which they criticize or de-limit. In a word, whether this has been made explicit or not, and whether it has been articulated or not (and more than one index leads us to believe that it has not), what authorizes us today to consider as essentially *anthropic* or anthropocentric everything in metaphysics, or at the limits of metaphysics, that believed itself to be a critique or delimitation of anthropologism? What is the *relève* of man in the thought of Hegel, Husserl, and Heidegger?

The Near End of Man

Let us reconsider, first of all, within the order of Hegelian discourse, which still holds together the language of our era by so many threads, the relations between

The Ends of Man

anthropology on the one hand and phenomenology and logic on the other.[11] Once the confusion of a purely anthropological reading of the *Phenomenology of Spirit* has been rigorously avoided, it must be recognized that according to Hegel the relations between anthropology and phenomenology are not simply external ones. The Hegelian concepts of truth, negativity, and *Aufhebung*, with all their results, prevent this from being so. In the third part of the *Encyclopedia* which treats the "Philosophy of Spirit," the first section ("Philosophy of Spirit") inscribes the *Phenomenology of Spirit* between the "Anthropology" and the "Psychology." The *Phenomenology of Spirit* succeeds the Anthropology and precedes the Psychology. The Anthropology treats the spirit—which is the "truth of nature"—as soul or as natural-spirit (*Seele* or *Naturgeist*). The development of the soul, such as it is retraced by the anthropology, passes through the natural soul (*natürliche Seele*), through the sensible soul (*fühlende Seele*), and through the real or effective soul (*wirkliche Seele*). This development accomplishes and completes itself, and then opens onto consciousness. The last section of the Anthropology[12] defines the general form of consciousness, the very one from which the *Phenomenology of Spirit* will depart, in the first chapter on "Sensuous Certitude."[13] Consciousness, i.e. the phenomenological, therefore, is the *truth* of the soul, that is, precisely the truth of that which was the object of the anthropology. Consciousness is the truth of man, phenomenology is the truth of anthropology. "Truth," here, must be understood in a rigorously Hegelian sense. In this Hegelian sense, the metaphysical essence of truth, the truth of the truth, is achieved. Truth is here the presence or presentation of essence as *Gewesenheit*, of *Wesen* as having-been. Consciousness is the truth of man to the extent that

11. Without neglecting the complexity of the relations between the *Logic* and the *Phenomenology of Spirit*, the question we are asking authorizes us to consider them *together* at the point of opening where Absolute Knowledge articulates them one with the other.
12. "The actual soul with its sensation and its concrete self-feeling turned into habit, has implicitly realised the 'ideality' of its qualities; in this externality it has recollected and inwardized (*erinnert*) itself, and is infinite self-relation. This free universality thus made explicit shows the soul awaking to the higher stage of the ego, or abstract universality, in so far as it is *for* the abstract universality. In this way it gains the position of thinker and subject—specially a subject of the judgment in which the ego excludes from itself the sum total of its merely natural features as an object, a world external to it—but with such respect to that object that in it it is immediately reflected into itself. Thus soul rises to become *Consciousness*. (Die wirkliche Seele in der *Gewohnheit* des Empfindens und ihres *konkreten* Selbst gefühlt ist an sich die für sich seiende *Idealität* ihrer Bestimmtheiten, in ihrer Äusserlichkeit *erinnert* in sich und unendliche Beziehung an sich. Die Fürsichsein der freien Allgemeinheit ist das höhere Erwachen der Seele zum *Ich*, der abstrakten Allgemeinheit, insofern sie für die abstrakte Allgemeinheit ist, welche so *Denken* und *Subjekt* für sich und zwar bestimmt Subjekt seines Urteils ist, in welchem es die natürliche Totalität seiner Bestimmungen als ein Objekt, eine ihm *äussere* Welt, von sich ausschliesst und sich darauf bezieht, so dass es in derselben unmittelbar in sich reflektiert ist, das *Bewusstsein*.)" *Philosophy of Mind*, trans. William Wallace (Oxford: Oxford University Press, 1971), sec. 412, p. 151.
13. That is, objectivity in general, the relation of an "I" in general with a being-object in general.

120

man appears to himself in consciousness in his Being-past, in his to-have-been, in his past surpassed and conserved, retained, interiorized (*erinnert*) and *relevé*. *Aufheben* is *relever*, in the sense in which *relever* can combine to relieve, to displace, to elevate, to replace and to promote, in one and the same movement.[14] Consciousness is the *Aufhebung* of the soul or of man, phenomenology is the *relève* of anthropology. It is *no longer*, but it is *still* a science of man. In this sense, all the structures described by the phenomenology of spirit—like everything which articulates them with the Logic—are the structures of that which has *relevé* man. In them, man remains in relief. His essence rests in *Phenomenology*. This equivocal relationship of *relief* doubtless marks the end of man, man past, but by the same token it also marks the achievement of man, the appropriation of his essence. *It is the end of finite man* [*C'est la fin de l'homme fini*]. The end of the finitude of man, the unity of the finite and the infinite, the finite as the surpassing of the self—these essential themes of Hegel's are to be recognized at the end of the Anthropology when consciousness is finally designated as the "infinite relationship to self." The *relève* or *relevance* of man is his *telos* or *eskhaton*. The unity of these two *ends* of man, the unity of his death, his completion, his accomplishment, is enveloped in the Greek thinking of *telos*, in the discourse on *telos*, which is also a discourse on *eidos*, on *ousia*, and on *alētheia*. Such a discourse, in Hegel as in the entirety of metaphysics, indissociably coordinates teleology with an eschatology, a theology, and an ontology. *The thinking of the end of man, therefore, is always already prescribed in metaphysics, in the thinking of the truth of man*. What is difficult to think today is an end of man which would not be organized by a dialectics of truth and negativity, an end of man which would not be a teleology in the first person plural. The *we*, which articulates natural and philosophical consciousness with each other in the *Phenomenology of Spirit*, assures the proximity to itself of the fixed and central being for which this circular reappropriation is produced. The *we* is the unity of absolute knowledge and anthropology, of God and man, of onto-theo-teleology and humanism. "*Being*" and language—the group of languages—that the *we* governs or opens: such is the name of that which assures the transition between metaphysics and humanism via the *we*.[15]

14. TN. This passage should be read in conjunction with the discussion of *relève* in "La différance," note 23, "Ousia and Grammē," note 15, and "The Pit and the Pyramid," note 16, above.

15. We could verify the necessity of the framework of this ambiguity or *relevance*, which is accomplished in Hegelian metaphysics and persists wherever metaphysics—that is, our language—maintains its authority, not only in our immediate vicinity, but already in all pre-Hegelian systems. In Kant, the figure of finitude organizes the capacity to know from the very emergence of the anthropological limit.

A. *On the one hand*, it is precisely when Kant wishes to think something like the *end*, the pure *end*, the *end* in itself, that he must criticize anthropologism, in the *Metaphysics of Morals*. One cannot deduce the principles of morality on the basis of a knowledge of the nature of a particular being named *man*: "But a completely isolated metaphysics of morals, mixed with no anthropology, no theology, no physics or hyperphysics, and even less with

We have just perceived the necessity which links the thinking of the *phainesthai* to the thinking of the *telos*. The teleology which governs Husserl's transcendental phenomenology can be read in the same opening. Despite the critique of anthropologism, "humanity," here, is still the name of the being to which the transcendental *telos*—determined as Idea (in the Kantian sense) or even as Reason—is announced. It is man as *animal rationale* who, in his most classical metaphysical determination, designates the site of teleological reason's unfolding, that is, history. For Husserl as for Hegel, reason is history, and there is no history but of reason. The latter "functions in every man, the *animal rationale*, no matter how primitive he is . . ." Every kind of humanity and human sociality has "a

occult qualities (which might be called hypophysical), is not only an indispensable substrate of all theoretically sound and definite knowledge of duties; it is also a desideratum of the highest importance to the actual fulfilment of its precepts" ("Foundations of the Metaphysics of Morals," in *The Critique of Practical Reason* . . . , p. 70). "Furthermore, it is evident that it is not only of the greatest necessity in a theoretical point of view when it is a question of speculation but also of the utmost practical importance to derive the concepts and laws of morals from pure reason and to present them pure and unmixed, and to determine the scope of this entire practical but pure rational knowledge (the entire faculty of pure practical reason) without making the principles depend upon the particular nature of human reason, as speculative philosophy may permit and even sometimes find necessary. But since moral laws should hold for every rational being as such, the principles must be derived from the universal concept of a rational being generally. In this manner all morals, which need anthropology for their application to men, must be completely developed first as pure philosophy, i.e. metaphysics, independently of anthropology" (ibid., p. 71). "With a view to attaining this, it is extremely important to remember that we must not let ourselves think that the reality of this principle can be derived from the *particular constitution of human nature (aus der besondern Eigenschaft der menschlichen Natur)*. For duty is practical unconditional necessity of action; it must, therefore, hold for all rational beings (to which alone an imperative can apply), and *only for that reason* can it be a law for all human wills" (ibid., p. 83). We see in these three passages that what is always of the "greatest importance" (*von der höchsten Wichtigkeit . . . von der grössten praktischen Wichtigkeit . . . von der äussersten Wichtigkeit*) is to determine the end in itself (as an unconditioned principle of morality), independently of any anthropological givens. One cannot think the purity of the end on the basis of man.
B. But, *on the other hand*, and inversely, man's specificity, man's essence as a rational being, as the rational animal (*zōon logon ekhon*), announces itself to itself only on the basis of thinking the end in itself; it announces itself to itself *as* the end in itself; that is, equally, as an infinite end, since the thinking of the unconditioned is also the thinking which raises itself above experience, that is, above finitude. Thus is explained the fact that despite the critique of anthropologism, of which we have just given a few indices, man is the *only example*, the only case of a rational being that can ever be cited at the very moment when by all rights one distinguishes the universal concept of a rational being from the concept of the human being. It is through the offices of this *fact* that anthropology regains all its contested authority. This is the point at which the philosopher says "we," and at which in Kant's discourse "rational being" and "humanity" are always associated by the conjunction "and" or *vel*. For example "Now, I say, man *and in general (und überhaupt)* every rational being, *exists* as an end in himself, and not merely as a means" (*Foundations* . . . , p. 86). [Note that this phrase is from the passage that serves as the first epigraph to this text. The deconstruction of the end and of man takes place on the *margins* of philosophy: in titles and footnotes.] "This principle of humanity and of every rational creature as an end in itself" (ibid., pp. 88–89).

root in the essential structure of what is generally human, through which a teleological reason running throughout all historicity announces itself. With this is revealed a set of problems in its own right related to the totality of history and to the full meaning which ultimately gives it its unity."[16] Transcendental phenomenology is in this sense the ultimate achievement of the teleology of reason that traverses humanity.[17] Thus, under the jurisdiction of the founding concepts of metaphysics, which Husserl revives and restores (if necessary affecting them with phenomenological brackets or indices), the critique of empirical anthropologism is only the affirmation of a transcendental humanism. And, among these metaphysical concepts which form the essential resource of Husserl's discourse, the concept of *end* or of *telos* plays a decisive role. It could be shown that at each stage of phenomenology, and notably each time that a recourse to the "Idea in the Kantian sense" is necessary, the infinity of the *telos*, the infinity of the end regulates phenomenology's capabilities. The end of man (as a factual anthropological limit) is announced to thought from the vantage of the end of man (as a determined opening or the infinity of a *telos*). Man is that which is in relation to his end, in the fundamentally equivocal sense of the word. Since always. The transcendental end can appear to itself and be unfolded only on the condition of mortality, of a relation to finitude as the origin of ideality. The name of man has always been inscribed in metaphysics between these two ends. It has meaning only in this eschato-teleological situation.

Reading Us

The "we," which in one way or another always has had to refer to itself in the language of metaphysics and in philosophical discourse, arises out of this situation. To conclude, what about this *we* in the text which better than any other has given us to read the essential, historical complicity of metaphysics and humanism in all their forms? What about this *we*, then, in Heidegger's text?

This is the most difficult question, and we will only begin to consider it. We are not going to emprison all of Heidegger's text in a closure that this text has delimited better than any other. That which links humanism and metaphysics as ontotheology became legible as such in *Sein und Zeit*, the *Letter on Humanism*, and the later texts. Referring to this acquisition, attempting to take it into account, I would like to begin to sketch out the forms of the hold which the "humanity" of man and the thinking of Being, a certain humanism and the truth of Being,

16. "The Origin of Geometry," in *The Crisis of European Sciences and Transcendental Phenomenology*, trans. David Carr (Evanston: Northwestern University Press, 1970), p. 378.

17. In a brief fragment from 1934 (*Stufen der Geschichtlichkeit. Erste Geschichtlichkeit*, Beilage XXVI, in *Die Krisis der europäischen Wissenschaften und die transzendentale Phänomenologie* [The Hague: Martinus Nijhoff,1954], pp. 502–3) Husserl distinguishes between three levels and three stages of historicity: culture and tradition as human sociality in general; European culture and the theoretical project (science and philosophy); "the conversion of philosophy into phenomenology."

maintain on one another. Naturally, it will not be a question of the falsification which, in opposition to Heidegger's most explicit warnings, consists in making this hold into a mastery or an ontic relationship in general. What will preoccupy us here will concern, rather, a more subtle, hidden, stubborn privilege, which, as in the case of Hegel or Husserl, leads us back to the position of the *we* in discourse. Once one has given up positing the *we* in the metaphysical dimension of *"we men,"* once one has given up charging the *we men* with the metaphysical determinations of the proper of man (*zōon logon ekhon,* etc.), it remains that man—and I would even say, in a sense that will become clear in a moment, the *proper of man*—the thinking of the proper of man is inseparable from the question or the truth of Being. This occurs along the Heideggerian pathways by means of what we may call a kind of magnetic attraction.

Here, I can only indicate the general rubric and several effects of this magnetization. In the effort to disclose it at the continuous depth at which it operates, the distinction between given periods of Heidegger's thought, between the texts before and after the so-called *Kehre*, has less pertinence than ever. For, on the one hand, the existential analytic had already overflowed the horizon of a philosophical anthropology: *Dasein* is not simply the man of metaphysics. On the other hand, conversely, in the *Letter on Humanism* and beyond, the attraction of the "proper of man" will not cease to direct all the itineraries of thought. At least this is what I would like to suggest, and I will regroup the effects or indices of this magnetic attraction beneath the general concept of *proximity.* It is in the play of a certain proximity, proximity to oneself and proximity to Being, that we will see constituted, against metaphysical humanism and anthropologism, another insistence of man, one which relays, relieves, supplements that which it destroys, along pathways on which we are, from which we have hardly emerged—perhaps—and which remain to be examined.

What about this proximity? First, let us open *Sein und Zeit* at the point at which the question of Being is asked in its "formal structure" (sec. 2). Our "vague average" understanding of the words "Being" or "is" finds itself acknowledged as a Fact (*Faktum*): "Inquiry (*Suchen*), as a kind of seeking, must be guided beforehand by what is sought. So the meaning of Being must already be available to *us* in some say. As we have intimated, *we always already* conduct our activities in an understanding of Being. Out of this understanding arise both the explicit question of the meaning of Being and the tendency that leads us toward its conception. We do not *know* what 'Being' means. But even if we ask, 'What is "Being"?', *we* keep within an understanding of the 'is,' though *we* are unable to fix conceptually what that 'is' signifies. We do not even know the horizon in terms of which that meaning is to be grasped and fixed. *But this vague average understanding of Being is still a Fact.*"[18] I have italicized the *we (us)* and the

18. TN. *Being and Time,* trans. John Macquarrie and Edward Robinson (New York: Harper and Row, 1962), p. 25.

always already. They are determined, then, in correspondence with this under-standing of "Being" or of the "is." In the absence of every other determination or presupposition, the "we" *at least* is what is open to such an understanding, what is always already accessible to it, and the means by which such a factum can be recognized as such. It automatically follows, then, that this *we*—however simple, discreet, and erased it might be—inscribes the so-called formal structure of the question of Being within the horizon of metaphysics, and more widely within the Indo-European linguistic milieu, to the possibility of which the origin of metaphysics is essentially linked. It is within these limits that the factum can be understood and accredited; and it is within these determined, and therefore material, limits that the factum can uphold the so-called formality of the question. It remains that the meaning of these "limits" is given to us only on the basis of the question of the meaning of Being. Let us not pretend, for example, to know what "Indo-European linguistic milieu" means.

This "formal structure of the question of Being" having been asked by Hei-degger, the issue then, as is well known, is to acknowledge the exemplary being (*exemplarische Seiende*) which will constitute the privileged text for a reading of the meaning of Being. And I recall that according to Heidegger the formal structure of the question, of any question, must be composed of three instances: the *Gefragte,* that which is asked about, here the meaning of Being; the *Erfragte,* that which is to be found out insofar as it is properly targeted by a question, the meaning of Being as what is questioned; finally the *Befragte,* that which is in-terrogated, the being that will be interrogated, to which will be put the question of the meaning of Being. The issue then is to choose or to recognize this ex-emplary *interrogated* being with one's sights set on the meaning of Being: "In *which* entities is the meaning of Being to be discerned (*abgelesen*)? From which entities is the disclosure of Being to take its departure? Is the starting-point optional, or does some particular entity have priority (*Vorrang*) when we come to work out the question of Being? Which entity shall we take for our example, and in what sense does it have priority?"[19]

What will dictate the answer to this question? In what milieu of evidentiality, of certitude, or at least of understanding must it be unfolded? Even before claiming the phenomenological method (sec. 7), at least in a "provisional con-cept," as the method for the elaboration of the question of Being, the determi-nation of the exemplary being is in principle "phenomenological." It is governed by phenomenology's principle of principles, the principle of presence and of presence in self-presence, such as it is manifested to the being and in the being that *we* are. It is this self-presence, this absolute proximity of the (questioning) being to itself, this familiarity with itself of the being ready to understand Being, that intervenes in the determination of the *factum,* and which motivates the

19. TN. Ibid., p. 26. Note that Macquarrie and Robinson translate *Seiend* (which we give as "being," as do most of the recent Heidegger translations) as "entity."

choice of the exemplary being, of the text, the good text for the hermeneutic of the meaning of Being. It is the proximity to itself of the questioning being which leads it to be chosen as the privileged interrogated being. The proximity to itself of the inquirer authorizes the identity of the inquirer and the interrogated. We who are close to ourselves, *we* interrogate *ourselves* about the meaning of Being. Let us read this protocol of reading: "If the question about Being is to be explicitly formulated and carried through in such a manner as to be completely transparent to itself, then any treatment of it in line with the elucidations we have given requires us to explain how Being is to be looked at, how its meaning is to be understood and conceptually grasped; it requires us to prepare the way for choosing the right entity for our example, and to work out the genuine way of access to it. Looking at something, understanding and conceiving it, choosing access to it—all these ways of behaving are constitutive of our inquiry, and therefore are modes of Being for those particular entities which we, the inquirers, are ourselves *(eines bestimmten Seienden, des Seienden, das wir, die Fragenden, je selbst sind)*. Thus to work out the question of Being adequately, we must make an entity—the inquirer—transparent in his own Being. The very asking of this question *(das Fragen dieser Frage)* is an entity's mode of *Being;* and as such it gets its essential character from what is inquired about *(gefragt)*—namely, Being. *This entity which each of us is himself* and which includes inquiring as one of the possibilities of its Being, we shall denote by the term *'Dasein' (fassen wir terminologisch als Dasein)*. If we are to formulate our question explicitly and transparently, we must first give a proper explication of an entity (Dasein) with regard to its Being."[20]

Doubtless this proximity, this identity or self-presence of the "entity that we are"—of the inquirer and of the interrogated—does not have the form of subjective consciousness, as in transcendental phenomenology. Doubtless too, this proximity is still prior to what the metaphysical predicate "human" might name. The *Da-* of *Dasein* can be determined as a coming presence only on the basis of a rereading of the question of Being which summons it up. Nevertheless, the process of disengaging or of elaborating the question of Being, as a question of the *meaning* of Being, is defined as a *making explicit* or as an interpretation that makes explicit. The reading of the text *Dasein* is a hermeneutics of unveiling or of development (see sec. 7). If one looks closely, it is the phenomenological opposition "implicit/explicit" that permits Heidegger to reject the objection of the vicious circle, the circle that consists of first determining a being in its Being, and then of posing the question of Being on the basis of this ontological predetermination (p. 27). This style of a reading which makes explicit, practices a continual bringing to light, something which resembles, at least, a coming into consciousness, without break, displacement, or change of terrain. Moreover, just as Dasein—the being which *we ourselves are*—serves as an exemplary text,

20. TN. Ibid., pp. 26–27. Further references are to this edition.

a good "lesson" for making explicit the meaning of Being, so the name of man remains the link or the paleonymic guiding thread which ties the analytic of Dasein to the totality of metaphysics' traditional discourse. Whence the strange status of such sentences or parentheses as: "As ways in which man behaves, sciences have the manner of Being which this entity—man himself—possesses. This entity we denote by the term *'Dasein'* (*Dieses Seiende fassen wir terminologisch als Dasein*)" (p. 32). Or again: "The problematic of Greek ontology, like that of any other, must take its clues from Dasein itself. In both ordinary and philosophical usage, Dasein, man's Being (*das Dasein, d.h. das sein des Menschen*), is 'defined' (*umgrenzt*) as the *zōon logon ekhon*—as that living thing whose Being is essentially determined by the potentiality for discourse (*Redenkonnen*)" (p. 47). Similarly, a "complete ontology of Dasein" is posited as the prerequisite condition for a "'philosophical' anthropology" (p. 38). We can see then that Dasein, though *not* man, is nevertheless *nothing other* than man. It is, as we shall see, a repetition of the essence of man permitting a return to what is before the metaphysical concepts of *humanitas*. The subtlety and equivocality of this gesture, then, are what appear to have authorized all the anthropologistic deformations in the reading of *Sein und Zeit*, notably in France.

The value of proximity, that is, of presence in general, therefore decides the essential orientation of this analytic of Dasein. The motif of proximity surely finds itself caught in an opposition which henceforth will unceasingly regulate Heidegger's discourse. The fifth section of *Sein und Zeit* in effect seems not to contradict but to limit and contain what was already gained, to wit that the Dasein "which we are" constitutes the exemplary being for the hermeneutic of the meaning of Being by virtue of its proximity to itself, of our proximity to ourselves, our proximity to the being that we are. At this point Heidegger marks that this proximity is *ontic*. Ontologically, that is, as concerns the Being of that being which we are, the distance, on the contrary, is as great as possible. "Ontically, of course, Dasein is not only close to us—even that which is closest: we *are* it, each of us, we ourselves. In spite of this, or rather for just this reason, it is ontologically that which is farthest."[21]

The analytic of Dasein, as well as the thinking which, beyond the *Kehre*, will pursue the question of Being, will maintain itself in the space which separates and relates to one another such a proximity and such a distance. The *Da* of *Dasein* and the *Da* of *Sein* will signify as much the near as the far. Beyond the common closure of humanism and metaphysics, Heidegger's thought will be

21. "In demonstrating that Dasein is ontico-ontologically prior, we may have misled the reader into supposing that this entity must also be what is given as ontico-ontologically primary (*primär*), not only in the sense that it can itself be grasped 'immediately,' but also in that the kind of Being which it possesses is presented just as 'immediately.' Ontically, of course, Dasein is not only close to us—even that which is closest: we *are* it, each of us, we ourselves. In spite of this, or rather for just this reason, it is ontologically that which is farthest . . . Dasein is ontically 'closest' (*am nächsten*) to itself and ontologically farthest; but pre-ontologically it is surely not a stranger (*nicht fremd*)" (pp. 36–37).

guided by the motif of Being as presence—understood in a more originary sense than it is in the metaphysical and ontic determinations of presence or of presence as the present—and by the motif of the proximity of Being to the essence of man. Everything transpires as if one had to reduce the ontological distance acknowledged in *Sein und Zeit* and to state the proximity of Being to the essence of man.

To support this last proposition, several indicative references to the *Letter on Humanism*. I will not insist upon the major and well-known theme of this text: the unity of metaphysics and humanism.[22] Any questioning of humanism that does not first catch up with the archeological radicalness of the questions sketched by Heidegger, and does not make use of the information he provides concerning the genesis of the concept and the value man (the reedition of the Greek *paideia* in Roman culture, the Christianizing of the Latin *humanitas*, the rebirth of Hellenism in the fourteenth and eighteenth centuries, etc.), any metahumanist position that does not place itself within the opening of these questions remains historically regional, periodic, and peripheral, juridically secondary and dependent, whatever interest and necessity it might retain as such.

It remains that the thinking of Being, the thinking of the truth of Being, in the name of which Heidegger de-limits humanism and metaphysics, remains as thinking *of* man. Man and the name of man are not displaced in the question of Being such as it is put to metaphysics. Even less do they disappear. On the contrary, at issue is a kind of reevaluation or revalorization of the essence and dignity of man. What is threatened in the extension of metaphysics and technology—and we know the essential necessity that leads Heidegger to associate them one to another—is the essence of man, which here would have to be thought before and beyond its metaphysical determinations. "The widely and rapidly spreading devastation of language not only undermines aesthetic and moral responsibility in every use of language; it arises from a threat to the essence of humanity (*Gefährdung des Wesens des Menschen*)."[23] "Only thus does the overcoming of homelessless (*Überwindung der Heimatlosigkeit*) begin from Being, a homelessness in which not only man but the essence of man (*das Wesen der Menschen*) stumbles aimlessly about."[24] Therefore, this essence will have to be reinstated. "But if man is to find his way once again into the nearness of

22. "Every humanism is either grounded in a metaphysics or is itself made to be the ground of one. Every determination of the essence of man that already presupposes an interpretation of being without asking about the truth of Being, whether knowingly or not, is metaphysical. The result is that what is peculiar to all metaphysics, specifically with respect to the way the essence of man is determined, is that it is 'humanistic.' Accordingly, every humanism remains metaphysical. In defining the humanity of man humanism not only does not ask about the relation of Being to the essence of man; because of its metaphysical origin humanism even impedes the question by neither recognizing nor understanding it." "Letter on Humanism," in *Basic Writings*, ed. Krell, p. 202.
23. Ibid., p. 198.
24. Ibid., p. 218.

Being (*in die Nähe des Seins*) he must first learn to exist in the nameless (*im Namenlosen*). In the same way he must first recognize the seductions of the public realm as well as the impotence of the private. Before he speaks (*bevor er spricht*) man must first let himself be claimed again (*wieder ansprechen*) by Being, taking the risk that under this claim (Anspruch) he will seldom have much to say. Only thus will the preciousness of its essence be once more bestowed upon the word (*dem Wort*), and upon man a home (*Behausung*) for dwelling in the truth of Being. But in the claim (*Anspruch*) upon man, in the attempt to make man ready for this claim, is there not implied a concern about man? Where else does 'care' tend but in the direction of bringing man back to his essence (*den Menschen wieder in sein Wesen zurückzubringen*)? What else does that in turn betoken but that man (*homo*) becomes human (*humanus*)? Thus *humanitas* really does remain the concern of such thinking. For this is humanism: meditating and caring (*Sinnen und Sorgen*) that man be human and not inhumane (*unmenschlich*), 'inhuman,' that is, outside his essence. But in what does the humanity of man consist? It lies in his essence."[25]

Once the thinking of essence is removed from the opposition *essentia/existentia*, the proposition according to which " 'man ek-sists' is not an answer to the question of whether man actually is or not; rather, it responds to the question concerning man's 'essence' (*Wesen*)."[26]

25. Ibid., pp. 199–200. In the same sense, one could cite many other passages of the *Letter*. Thus, for example, "But we must be clear on this point, that when we do this we abandon man to the essential realm of *animalitas* even if we do not equate him with beasts but attribute a specific difference to him. In principle we are still thinking of *homo animalis*— even when *anima* is posited as *animus sive mens*, and this in turn is later posited as subject, person or spirit. Such positing is the manner of metaphysics. But then the essence of man is too little (*zu gering*) heeded and not thought in its origin, the essential provenance that is always the essential future for historical mankind (*geschichtliche Menschentum*). Metaphysics thinks of man on the basis of *animalitas* and does not think in the direction of his *humanitas*.

"Metaphysics closes itself to the simple essential fact that man essentially occurs only in his essence (*in seinem Wesen west*) where he is claimed (*angesprochen*) by Being. Only from that claim 'has' he found that wherein his essence dwells. Only from this dwelling 'has' he 'language' as the home that preserves the ecstatic for his essence. Such standing in the lighting of Being (*Lichtung des Seins*) I call the ek-sistence of man. This way of Being is proper (*eignet*) only to man. Ek-sistence so understood is not only the ground of the possibility of reason, *ratio*, but is also that in which the essence of man preserves (*wahrt*) the source that determines him.

"Ek-sistence can be said only of the essence of man, that is, only of the human 'to be.' For as far as our experience shows, only man is admitted to the destiny of ek-sistence (*in das Geschick der Eksistence*)." "Letter," pp. 203–4.

The motif of the *proper (eigen, eigentlich)* and the several modes of *to propriate* (particularly *Ereignen* and *Ereignis*), both of which thematically dominate the question of the truth of Being in *Zeit und Sein*, has long been at work in Heidegger's thought. In the "Letter on Humanism" in particular. The themes of the *house* and of the *proper* are regularly brought together: as we will attempt to show later, the value of *oikos* (and of *oikēsis*) plays a decisive, if hidden, role in the semantic chain that interests us here. [See above, "La différance," note 2, on *Oikos* and *Oikēsis*.]

26. "Letter," p. 207.

The restoration of the essence is also the restoration of a dignity and a proximity: the co-responding dignity of Being and man, the proximity of Being and man. "What still today remains to be said could perhaps become an impetus (*Anstoss*) for guiding the essence of man to the point where it thoughtfully (*denkend*) attends to that dimension of the truth of Being which thoroughly governs it. But even this could take place only to the honor of Being and for the benefit of Dasein which man eksistingly sustains (*nur dem Sein zur Würde und dem Da-sein zugunsten geschehen, das der Mensch eksistierend aussteht*); not, however, for the sake of man so that civilization and culture through man's doings might be vindicated."[27]

The ontological distance from *Dasein* to what *Dasein* is as ek-sistence and to the *Da* of *Sein*, the distance that first was given as ontic proximity, must be reduced by the thinking of the truth of Being. Whence, in Heidegger's discourse, the dominance of an entire metaphorics of proximity, of simple and immediate presence, a metaphorics associating the proximity of Being with the values of neighboring, shelter, house, service, guard, voice, and listening. As goes without saying, this is not an insignificant rhetoric; on the basis of both this metaphorics and the thinking of the ontico-ontological difference, one could even make explicit an entire theory of metaphoricity in general.[28] Several examples of this language, so surely connoted by its inscription in a certain landscape: "But if man is to find his way once again into the nearness of Being (*in die Nähe des Seins*), he must first learn to exist in the nameless." "The statement 'The "substance" of man is eksistence' says nothing else but that the way that man in his proper essence (*in seinem eigenen Wesen*) becomes present to Being (*zum Sein anwest*) is ecstatic inherence in the truth of Being. Through this determination of the essence of man the humanistic interpretations of man as *animal rationale*, as 'person,' as spiritual-ensouled-bodily being, are not declared false and thrust aside. Rather, the sole implication is that the highest determinations of the essence of man in humanism still do not realize the proper dignity of man (*die eigentliche Würde des Menschen*). To that extent the thinking in *Being and Time* is against humanism. But this opposition does not mean that such thinking aligns itself against the humane and advocates the inhuman, that it promotes the inhumane and deprecates the dignity of man. Humanism is opposed because it does not set the *humanitas* of man high enough."[29] " 'Being'—that is not God and not a cosmic ground. Being is farther than all beings and is yet nearer (*näher*) to man than every being, be it a rock, a beast, a work of art, a machine, be it angel or God. Being is the nearest (*Das Sein ist das Nächste*). Yet the near remains farthest from man. Man at first clings always and only to beings."[30] "Because man as the one who ek-sists comes to stand in this relation that Being destines

27. Ibid., p. 209.
28. See below, "White Mythology."
29. "Letter," pp. 209–10.
30. Ibid., pp. 210–11.

(*schickt*) for itself, in that he ecstatically sustains it, that is, in care takes it upon himself, he at first fails to recognize the nearest (*das Nächste*) and attaches himself to the next nearest (*das Übernächste*). He even thinks that this is the nearest. But nearer than the nearest and at the same time for ordinary thinking farther than the farthest is *nearness* itself: the truth of Being."[31] "The one thing (*das Einzige*) thinking would like to attain and for the first time tries to articulate in *Being and Time* is something simple (*etwas Einfaches*). As such, Being remains mysterious, the simple (*schlicht*) nearness of an unobtrusive governance. The nearness occurs essentially as language itself."[32] "But man is not only a living creature who possesses language along with other capacities. Rather, language is the house of Being in which man ek-sists by dwelling, in that he belongs to the truth of Being, guarding it (*hütend gehört*)."[33]

This proximity is not ontic proximity, and one must take into account the properly ontological repetition of this thinking of the near and the far.[34] It remains that Being, which is nothing, is not a being, cannot be said, cannot say itself, except in the ontic metaphor. And the choice of one or another group of metaphors is necessarily significant. It is within a metaphorical insistence, then, that the interpretation of the meaning of Being is produced. And if Heidegger has radically deconstructed the domination of metaphysics by the *present*, he has done so in order to lead us to think the presence of the present. But the thinking of this presence can only metaphorize, by means of a profound necessity from which one cannot simply decide to escape, the language that it deconstructs.[35]

31. Ibid., pp. 211–12.

32. Ibid., p. 212.

33. Ibid., p. 213.

34. "The 'Introduction' to *Being and Time* says simply and clearly, even in italics, 'Being is the *transcendens* pure and simple (*das Transcendens schlechthin*).' Just as the openness of spatial nearness seen from the perspective of a particular thing exceeds all things near and far, so is Being essentially broader than all beings, because it is the lighting (*Lichtung*) itself. For all that, Being is thought on the basis of beings, a consequence of the approach—at first unavoidable—within a metaphysics that is still dominant." "Letter," p. 216.

35. Several examples of the predominance granted to the value of ontological proximity: "This destiny comes to pass as the lighting of Being (*Lichtung des Seins*), as which it is. The lighting grants nearness to Being. In this nearness, in the lighting of the *Da*, man dwells as the ek-sisting one without yet being able properly to experience and take over this dwelling. In the lecture on Hölderlin's elegy 'Homecoming' (1943) this nearness 'of' Being, which the *Da* of Dasein is, is thought on the basis of *Being and Time* . . . it is called the 'homeland' " (ibid., p. 217). "The homeland of this historical dwelling is nearness to Being" (ibid., p. 218). "In his essential unfolding within the history of Being, man is the being whose Being as ek-sistence consists in his dwelling in the nearness of Being (*in der Nähe des Seins wohnt*). Man is the neighbor of Being (*Nachbar des Seins*)" (ibid., p. 222). " 'Ek-sistence,' in fundamental contrast to every *existentia* and '*existence*,' is ecstatic dwelling in the nearness of Being" (ibid.). "Or should thinking, by means of open resistance to 'humanism,' risk a shock that could for the first time cause perplexity concerning the *humanitas* of *homo humanus* and its basis? In this way it could awaken a reflection (*Besinnung*)—if the world-historical moment did not itself already compel such a reflec-

The Ends of Man

Thus, the prevalence granted to the *phenomenological* metaphor, to all the varieties of *phainesthai*, of shining, lighting, clearing, *Lichtung*, etc., opens onto the
space of presence and the presence of space, understood within the opposition
of the near and the far—just as the acknowledged privilege not only of language,
but of spoken language (voice, listening, etc.), is in consonance with the motif
of presence as self-presence.[36] The near and the far are thought here, conse-

tion—that thinks not only about man but also about the 'nature' of man, not only about
his nature but even more primordially about the dimension in which the essence of man,
determined by Being itself is at home" (ibid., p. 225). "Thinking does not overcome
metaphysics by climbing still higher, surmounting it, transcending it somehow or other;
thinking overcomes metaphysics by climbing back down into the nearness of nearest (*in
die Nähe des Nächsten*)" (ibid., p. 231).
To destroy the privilege of the present-now (*Gegenwart*) always leads back, on the Heideggerian pathway, to a presence (*Anwesen, Anwesenheit*) that none of the three modes of
the present (present-present, past-present, future-present) can exhaust or terminate, but
which, on the contrary, provides their playing space, on the basis of a fourfold whose
thinking entirely informs what is at stake in our question. The fourfold can be maintained
or lost, risked or reappropriated—an alternative always suspended over its "own proper"
abysm—never winning except by losing (itself). It is the text of dissemination.
Now this presence of the fourfold, in turn, is thought, in *On Time and Being* notably,
according to the opening of propriation as the nearness of the near, proximation, approximation. Here we will refer to the analysis of the four-dimensionality of time and of
its play. "True time is four-dimensional . . . For this reason we call the first, original,
literally incipient extending (*Reichen*) in which the unity of true (*eigentlichen*) time consists
'nearing nearness,' 'nearhood' (*Nahheit*), an early word still used by Kant. But it brings
future, past and present near to one another by distancing them." *On Time and Being*,
trans. Joan Stambaugh (New York: Harper and Row, 1972), p. 15. "In the sending of the
destiny of Being (*Im Schicken des Geschickes von Sein*), in the extending (*Reichen*) of time,
there becomes manifest a dedication (*Zueignen*), a delivering over (*Übereignen*) into what
is their own (*in ihr Eigenes*), namely of Being as presence (*Anwesenheit*) and of time as the
realm of the open. What determines both, time and Being, in their own, that is in their
belonging together, we shall call: *Ereignis*, or event of Appropriation" (ibid., p. 19). "What
the name 'event of Appropriation' (*Ereignis*) names can no longer be represented by means
of the current meaning of the word; for in that meaning 'event of Appropriation' is
understood in the sense of occurrence and happening—not in terms of Appropriating
(*Eignen*) as the extending and sending which opens and preserves" (ibid., p. 20).
The facility, and also the necessity, of the transition from the near to the proper will
have been noticed. The Latin medium of this transition (*prope, proprius*) is lost in other
languages, for example in German.
36. On the topic of what unites the values of self-presence and spoken language, I
permit myself to refer to *Of Grammatology* and *Speech and Phenomena*. Implicitly or explicitly,
the valorization of spoken language is constant and massive in Heidegger. I will study it
elsewhere in and of itself. Having reached a certain point in the analysis, it is necessary
to measure the extent of this valorization rigorously: if it covers almost the entirety of
Heidegger's text (in that it leads all the metaphysical determinations of the *present* or of
being back to the matrix of Being as presence, *Anwesenheit*), it is also erased at the point
at which is announced the question of a *Wesen* that would not even be an *Anwesen*. (On
this subject, see "Ousia and Grammē," above.) Thus is explained, for example, the disqualification of literature, which is opposed to thinking and to *Dichtung*, and also to an
artisan- and "peasant"-like practice of the letter: "In written form thinking easily loses its
flexibility . . . On the other hand, written composition exerts a wholesome pressure toward
deliberate linguistic formulation" ("Letter," p. 195). "The truth of Being . . . would thus

quently, before the opposition of space and time, according to the opening of a spacing which *belongs* neither to time nor to space, and which dislocates, while producing it, any presence of the present. Therefore, if "Being is farther than all beings and is yet nearer to man than every being," if "Being is the nearest," then one must be able to say that Being is *what is near* to man, and that man is *what is near* to Being. The near is the proper; the proper is the nearest (*prope, proprius*). Man is the proper of Being, which right near to him whispers in his ear; Being is the proper of man, such is the truth that speaks, such is the proposition which gives the *there* of the truth of Being and the truth of man. This proposition of the *proper,* certainly, is not to be taken in a metaphysical sense: the proper of man, here, is not an essential attribute, the predicate of a substance, a characteristic among others, however fundamental, of a being, object or subject, called man. No more can one speak in this sense of man as the proper of Being. Propriety, the co-propriety of Being and man, is proximity as inseparability. But it is indeed as inseparability that the relations between being (substance, or *res*) and its essential predicate were thought in metaphysics *afterward.* Since this co-propriety of man and of Being, such as it is thought in Heidegger's discourse, is not ontic, does not relate two "beings" one to the other but rather, within language, relates the *meaning* of Being and the *meaning* of man. The proper of man, his *Eigenheit,* his "authenticity," is to be related to the meaning of Being; he is to hear and to question (*fragen*) it in ek-sistence, to stand straight in the proximity of its light: "Das Stehen in der Lichtung des Seins nenne ich die Ek-sistenz des Menschen. Nur dem Menschen eignet diese Art zu sein" ("Such standing in the lighting of Being I call the ek-sistence of man. This way of Being is proper only to man").[37]

Is not this security of the near what is trembling today, that is, the co-belonging and co-propriety of the name of man and the name of Being, such as this co-propriety inhabits, and is inhabited by, the language of the West, such as it is buried in its *oikonomia,* such as it is inscribed and forgotten according to the history of metaphysics, and such as it is awakened also by the destruction of ontotheology? But this trembling—which can only come from a certain outside—was already requisite within the very structure that it solicits.[38] Its margin was

be more easily weaned from mere supposing and opining and directed to the now rare handicraft of writing" (ibid., p. 223). "What is needed in the present world crisis is less philosophy, but more attentiveness in thinking; less literature, but more cultivation of the letter" (ibid., p. 242). "We must liberate *Dichtung* from literature" (text published in *Revue de poésie,* Paris, 1967).

37. Elsewhere ("La parole soufflée," in *Writing and Difference,* and in *Of Grammatology*) I have attempted to indicate the passage between the near, the "proper" and the *erection* of the "standing upright."

38. TN. Derrida is using "to solicit" in its etymological sense here, as he often does elsewhere. "To solicit" derives from the Latin *sollus,* whole, and *ciere,* to move, and thus has the sense of "to make the whole move." The reference to *oikonomia* and burial in the preceding sentence is explained in "La différance," note 2, above.

marked in its own (*propre*) body. In the thinking and the language of Being, the end of man has been prescribed since always, and this prescription has never done anything but modulate the equivocality of the *end*, in the play of *telos* and death. In the reading of this play, one may take the following sequence in all its senses: the end of man is the thinking of Being, man is the end of the thinking of Being, the end of man is the end of the thinking of Being. Man, since always, is his proper end, that is, the end of his proper. Being, since always, is its proper end, that is, the end of its proper.

To conclude I would like to reassemble, under several very general rubrics, the signs which appear, in accordance with the anonymous necessity that interests me here, to mark the effects of the total trembling as concerns what I have called, for convenience, and with the necessary quotation marks or precautions, "France" or French thought.

1. *The reduction of meaning.* The attention given to system and structure, in its most original and strongest aspects, that is, those aspects which do not immediately fall back into cultural or journalistic gossip, or, in the best of cases, into the purest "structuralist" tradition of metaphysics—such an attention, which is rare, consists neither (a) in restoring the classical motif of the system, which can always be shown to be ordered by *telos*, *alētheia*, and *ousia*, all of which are values reassembled in the concepts of essence or of *meaning;* nor (b) in erasing or destroying meaning. Rather, it is a question of determining the possibility of *meaning* on the basis of a "formal" organization which in itself has no meaning, which does not mean that it is either the non-sense or the anguishing absurdity which haunt metaphysical humanism. Now, if one considers that the critique of anthropologism in the last great metaphysical systems (Hegel and Husserl, notably) was executed in the name of truth and meaning, if one considers that these "phenomenologies"—which were metaphysical systems—had as their essential motif a *reduction to meaning* (which is *literally* a Husserlian proposition), then one can conceive that the reduction *of* meaning—that is, of the signified—first takes the form of a critique of phenomenology. Moreover, if one considers that the Heideggerian destruction of metaphysical humanism is produced initially on the basis of a *hermeneutical* question on the *meaning* or the *truth* of Being, then one also conceives that the reduction of meaning operates by means of a kind of break with a thinking of Being which has all the characteristics of a *relève (Aufhebung)* of humanism.

2. *The strategic bet.* A radical trembling can only come from the *outside*. Therefore, the trembling of which I speak derives no more than any other from some spontaneous decision or philosophical thought after some internal maturation of its history. This trembling is played out in the violent relationship of the whole of the West to its other, whether a "linguistic" relationship (where very quickly the question of the limits of everything leading back to the question of

the meaning of Being arises), or ethnological, economic, political, military, relationships, etc. Which does not mean, moreover, that military or economic violence is not in structural solidarity with "linguistic" violence. But the "logic" of every relation to the outside is very complex and surprising. It is precisely the force and the efficiency of the system that regularly change transgressions into "false exits." Taking into account these effects of the system, one has nothing, from the inside where "we are," but the choice between two strategies:

a. To attempt an exit and a deconstruction without changing terrain, by repeating what is implicit in the founding concepts and the original problematic, by using against the edifice the instruments or stones available in the house, that is, equally, in language. Here, one risks ceaselessly confirming, consolidating, *relifting* (*relever*), at an always more certain depth, that which one allegedly deconstructs. The continuous process of making explicit, moving toward an opening, risks sinking into the autism of the closure.

b. To decide to change terrain, in a discontinuous and irruptive fashion, by brutally placing oneself outside, and by affirming an absolute break and difference. Without mentioning all the other forms of *trompe-l'oeil* perspective in which such a displacement can be caught, thereby inhabiting more naively and more strictly than ever the inside one declares one has deserted, the simple practice of language ceaselessly reinstates the new terrain on the oldest ground. The effects of such a reinstatement or of such a blindness could be shown in numerous precise instances.

It goes without saying that these effects do not suffice to annul the necessity for a "change of terrain." It also goes without saying that the choice between these two forms of deconstruction cannot be simple and unique. A new writing must weave and interlace these two motifs of deconstruction. Which amounts to saying that one must speak several languages and produce several texts at once. I would like to point out especially that the style of the first deconstruction is mostly that of the Heideggerian questions, and the other is mostly the one which dominates France today. I am purposely speaking in terms of a dominant style: because there are also breaks and changes of terrain in texts of the Heideggerian type; because the "change of terrain" is far from upsetting the entire French landscape to which I am referring; because what we need, perhaps, as Nietzsche said, is a change of "style"; and if there is style, Nietzsche reminded us, it must be *plural*.

3. *The difference between the superior man and the superman.* Beneath this rubric is signaled both the increasingly insistent and increasingly rigorous recourse to Nietzsche in France, and the division that is announced, perhaps, between two *relèves* of man. We know how, at the end of *Zarathustra*, at the moment of the "sign," when *das Zeichen kommt*, Nietzsche distinguishes, in the greatest proximity, in a strange resemblance and an ultimate complicity, at the eve of the last separation, of the great Noontime, between the superior man (*höhere Mensch*) and the superman (*Übermensch*). The first is abandoned to his distress in a last

movement of pity. The latter—who is not the last man—awakens and leaves, without turning back to what he leaves behind him. He burns his text and erases the traces of his steps. His laughter then will burst out, directed toward a return which no longer will have the form of the metaphysical repetition of humanism, nor, doubtless, "beyond" metaphysics, the form of a memorial or a guarding of the meaning of Being, the form of the house and of the truth of Being. He will dance, outside the house, the *aktive Vergesslichkeit*, the "active forgetting" and the cruel (*grausam*) feast of which the *Genealogy of Morals* speaks. No doubt that Nietzsche called for an active forgetting of Being: it would not have the metaphysical form imputed to it by Heidegger.

Must one read Nietzsche, with Heidegger, as the last of the great metaphysicians? Or, on the contrary, are we to take the question of the truth of Being as the last sleeping shudder of the superior man? Are we to understand the eve as the guard mounted around the house or as the awakening to the day that is coming, at whose eve we are? Is there an economy of the eve?

Perhaps we are between these two eves, which are also two ends of man. But who, we?

May 12, 1968

The Linguistic Circle
of Geneva

A lecture given at the colloquium on Jean-Jacques Rousseau, 3–4 February 1968, in London. Originally published in the *Revue internationale de philosophie*, 1967/4, no. 82, under the title "La linguistique de Rousseau."

Linguists are becoming more and more interested in the genealogy of linguistics. And in reconstituting the history or prehistory of their science, they are discovering numerous ancestors, sometimes with a certain astonished recognition. Interest in the origin of linguistics is awakened when the problems of the origin of language cease to be proscribed (as they had been from the end of the nineteenth century), and when a certain geneticism—or a certain generativism—comes back into its own. One could show that this is not a chance encounter. This historical activity is no longer elaborated solely on the margins of scientific practice, and its results are already being felt. In particular, we are no longer at the stage of the prejudice according to which linguistics as a science was born of a single "epistemological break"—a concept, called Bachelardian, much used or abused today—and of a break occurring in our immediate vicinity. We no longer think, as does Grammont, that "everything prior to the nineteenth century, which is not yet linguistics, can be expedited in several lines."[1] Noam Chomsky, in an article announcing his *Cartesian Linguistics*, which presents in its major lines the concept of "generative grammar," states: "My aim here is not to justify the interest of this investigation, nor to describe summarily its procedure, but instead to underline that *by a curious detour* it takes us back to a tradition of ancient thought, rather than constituting a new departure or a radical innovation in the domain of linguistics and psychology."[2]

If we were to set ourselves down in the space of this "curious detour," we could not help encountering the "linguistics" of Rousseau. We would have to ask ourselves, then, in what ways Rousseau's reflections on the sign, on language, on the origin of languages, on the relations between speech and writing, etc., announce (but what does "announce" mean here?) what we are so often tempted to consider as the very modernity of linguistic science, that is, modernity *as* linguistic science, since so many other "human sciences" refer to linguistics as their titular model. And we are all the more encouraged to practice this detour in that Chomsky's major references, in the *Cartesian Linguistics*, are to the *Logic* and *General and Reasoned Grammar* of Port-Royal, works that Rousseau knew well and that were held in high esteem by him.[3] For example, on several occasions Rousseau cites Duclos's commentary on the *General and Reasoned Grammar*. The *Essay on the Origin of Languages* even closes with one of these citations. Thus Rousseau acknowledges his debt.

1. Cited by Chomsky in *Cartesian Linguistics* (New York: Harper and Row, 1966), p. 1. See also ibid., note 1.

2. "De quelques constantes de la théorie linguistique," in *Diogène*, no. 51 (1965). My italics. See also *Current Issues in Linguistic Theory* (The Hague: Mouton, 1964), pp. 15ff. There is an analogous gesture in Jakobson, who refers not only to Peirce and, as does Chomsky, to Humboldt, but also to John of Salisbury, to the Stoics, and to Plato's *Cratylus*. See "A la recherche de l'essence du langage, *Diogène*, no. 51 (1965).

3. "I began with some book of philosophy, like the Port-Royal *Logic*, Locke's *Essay*, Malebranche, Leibniz, Descartes, etc." *Confessions*, in *Oeuvres complètes* (Paris: Gallimard, Editions de la Pleiade, 1959), vol. 1, p. 237.

There is only one allusion to Rousseau himself in the *Cartesian Linguistics*, in a note which on the one hand compares him to Humboldt, and which on the other, while referring only to the most general propositions of the second *Discourse*, presents him as strictly Cartesian, at least as concerns the concepts of animality and humanity. Although one might, in a certain sense, speak of Rousseau's fundamental Cartesianism in this regard, it seems that a more important and original place must be reserved for him in such a history of philosophy and linguistics. It is in this sense, under the heading of a very preliminary schema, that I am venturing the following propositions here.

One is authorized to speak of a linguistics of Rousseau only on two conditions and in two senses:

1. On the condition and in the sense of a systematic formulation, one that defines the project of a theoretical science of language, in its method, its object, and its rigorously proper field. This might be accomplished by means of a gesture that for convenience' sake could be called an "epistemological break," there being no assurance that the stated intention to "break" has such an effect, nor that the so-called break is ever a—unique—datum in a work or an author. This first condition and first sense should always be implied by what we will entitle the *opening of the field*, it being understood that such an opening also amounts to a *delimitation* of the field.

2. On the condition and in the sense of what Chomsky calls the "constants of linguistic theory": in that the system of fundamental concepts, the exigencies and norms that govern the linguistics called modern, such as it is entitled and represented in its scientificity as in its modernity, is already at work, and discernible as such, in Rousseau's enterprise, in its very text. Which, moreover, would not only be (and doubtless would not at all be) to interpret this text as the happy anticipation of a thinker who is to have predicted and preformed modern linguistics. On the contrary, is this not a question of a very general ground of possibilities, a ground on which might be raised all kinds of subordinate cross-sections and secondary periodizations? Is it not a question of both Rousseau's project and modern linguistics belonging in common to a determined and finite system of conceptual possibilities, to a common language, to a reserve of oppositions of signs (signifiers/concepts) which first of all is none other than the most ancient fund of Western metaphysics? The latter is articulated, in its diverse epochs, according to schemas of implication that are not as easily mastered as is sometimes believed: whence the illusions of the break, the mirages of the new, the confusion or crushing of layers, the artifice of extractions and cross-sections, the archeological lure. The *closure of concepts:* such would be the title that we might propose for this second condition and this second sense.

These two conditions seem to be fulfilled; and in these two senses it seems that one may legitimately speak of a linguistics of Rousseau. Here we can delineate it only through several indices.

The Opening of the Field

Rousseau states and wants, or in any cases states that he wants, to break with every supernatural explication of the origin and functioning of language. If the theological hypothesis is not simply set aside, it never intervenes in its own name, de jure, in Rousseau's explication and description. This rupture is signified in at least two texts and at two points: in the second *Discourse* and in the *Essay on the Origin of Languages.*

Referring to Condillac, to whom he recognizes he owes a great deal, Rousseau clearly expresses his disagreement as concerns the procedure followed in the *Essay on the Origin of Human Knowledge.* Condillac, in effect, *seems* to take a constituted society, created by God, as given at the very moment when he asks the question of language, the question of the genesis and system of language, of the relations between natural and instituted signs, etc. Now Rousseau wants to account for the very emergence of convention, that is, in his own words, to account simultaneously for society and language on the basis of a "pure state of nature." So he must put between parentheses everything that Condillac takes as given, and in effect this is what he allegedly does.

The concept of *nature,* therefore, bears the burden of scientificity here, as much in the requirement of a natural (nonsupernatural) explanation, as in the ultimate reference to a purely (presocial, prehistoric, prelinguistic, etc.) natural state. The field of the analysis, the genealogical regression, the explanation of functioning, are all opened as such in the demand for neutrality. We do not mean that Rousseau *himself* opened this field and this demand. We simply wish to recognize the signs that show him caught in this opening whose history and system remain to be constituted. The difficulty of the task and the theoretical or methodological innovations called for are such that to point out signs can only attribute, assign, and situate these signs as touchstones.

Before even asking whether natural naturality and originality are not still theological functions in Rousseau's discourse—and in general in every discourse—let us make specific the criticism addressed to Condillac. It could be shown—but this is not our aim here—that Condillac's procedure is not so far removed in its principles from Rousseau's, and that the theological reference easily accommodates a concern for natural explanation: "Adam and Eve did not owe to experience the exercise of the operations of their soul, and, emerging from the hands of God, by means of this extraordinary help, they were capable of reflection and of communicating their thoughts to each other. But I suppose that, some time after the deluge, two children, one of each sex, had been lost in the general desolation, before knowing the use of any sign. I am authorized to do so because of the fact I have reported. Who knows if a people does not exist somewhere that owes its origin only to such an event? Permit me to make this supposition; the question is to know how this growing nation fashioned for

141

itself a language."[4] Further on, at the end of a note: "If I suppose two children in the necessity of imagining even the very first signs of language, it is because I have believed that it is not sufficient for a philosopher to say that a thing has been accomplished by extraordinary means; but that it was his duty to explain how it *could have* been done by natural means."[5] I italicize the conditional tense, which supports the entire scientificity of the argument.

Thus, Condillac renounces neither a natural explanation nor the conjunction of the questions of the origin of languages and the origin of societies. Theological certitude is accommodated to a natural explanation according to a very classical framework in which the concepts of nature, experience, creation, and fall are strictly inseparable. (The most remarkable example of such a "system" is doubtless that of Malebranche, which I am recalling here only because of its well-known influence on Rousseau.) Here, the event of the flood, whose analog will be found in Rousseau, liberates the functioning of the natural explanation.

This does not prevent Rousseau from taking his leave from Condillac precisely at the point at which he reproaches Condillac for taking as given that which is to be explained, that is, "a kind of already established society among the inventors of language." Rousseau reproaches Condillac less for rejecting every model of natural explanation—that would be untrue—than for not radicalizing his concept of nature: Condillac would not have descended to a pure state of nature to analyze the emergence of language: "Permit me for a moment to consider all the confusions of the origin of Languages. I could content myself with citing or repeating here all of Abbé de Condillac's investigations into this matter, which fully confirm my feeling, and which, perhaps, gave me my first ideas. But given the manner in which this Philosopher resolves the difficulties he creates for himself on the origin of institutionalized signs, that is, a kind of already established society among the inventors of language, I believe that in referring to his reflections I must add to them my own."[6]

Thus Condillac seems to have committed what Rousseau a little further on calls "the fault of those who, reasoning on the State of Nature, transport into it ideas taken from Society."

The properly scientific concern, therefore, is indicated by the decision to refer only to purely natural cuases. Such is the motif on which the *Essay on the Origin of Languages*[7] opens, from its very first paragraph: "In order to tell, it is necessary to go back to some principle that belongs to the locality itself and antedates its customs, for speech, being the first social institution, owes its form to natural

4. Condillac, *Essai sur l'origine des connaisances humaines* (Paris: Galilée, 1973), p. 193.
5. Ibid., note 1.
6. *Discours sur l'origine de l'inégalité* (second *Discours*), in *Oeuvres complètes*, vol. 3 (1964), p. 146. On all the problems of language in Rousseau, I refer most notably to the very valuable notes of Jean Starobinski in this edition, and of course to the other works on Rousseau by this author, particularly *La transparence et l'obstacle* (Paris: Plon, 1964).
7. Translated by John H. Moran (New York: Frederick Ungar, 1966). All further references to the *Essay* are to this edition.

causes alone" (p. 5). Now, without even entering into the content of the natural genealogy of language that Rousseau proposes, let us note that the so-called "epistemological break" paradoxically corresponds to a kind of break in the field of natural causality. If "speech," "the first social institution, owes its form to natural causes alone,"[8] then the latter, themselves acting as a force of break with nature, *naturally* inaugurate an order radically *heterogeneous* to the natural order. The two—apparently contradictory—conditions for the constitution of a scientific field and object, here language, would thus be fulfilled: a natural, a continuously natural causality, and a break designating the irreducible autonomy and originality of a domain. The question of the origin is in itself suspended, in that it no longer calls for a continuous, real, and natural description, being but the index of an internal structural description.

Certainly all this is neither without difficulty nor without a certain apparent incoherence, for which Rousseau often has been reproached. And it has been that much easier to make this reproach because Rousseau himself on several occasions seems to renounce the natural explanation and to admit a kind of violent—catastrophic—interruption into the concatenation of natural causality. An arbitrary interruption, an interruption of the arbitrary, the decision which permits only the arbitrary and the conventional to be instituted. One comes back to the necessity of this question wherever the conceptuality organized around the opposition nature/arbitrary is accredited. Before defining the necessity both of the break and the at least apparent failure, before underlining the scientific and heuristic motivation that accommodates its opposite here, let us briefly recall its well known points of apparition.

1. After attempting, by means of a fiction, a derivation of languages on the basis of a primitive dispersion in the state of pure nature, on the basis of the biological nucleus uniting mother and child, Rousseau has to step back and suppose "this first difficulty overcome": "Notice again that the Child having all his needs to explain, and consequently more things to say to the Mother than the Mother to the Child, it is he who must bear the burden of invention, and that the language he employs must in great part be his own handiwork; which

---

8. Attention must be paid to the word "form": natural causes must produce the variety of forms *of* speech as the variety *of* languages. The *Essay* accounts for this by means of physics, geography, and climatology. This distinction between speech itself and languages underlies the notion of form at the beginning of the *Essay*: "Speech distinguishes man among the animals; language distinguishes nations from each other; one does not know where a man comes from until he has spoken. Out of usage and necessity, each learns the language of his own country. But what determines that this language is that of his country and not that of another? In order to tell, it is necessary to go back to some principle that belongs to the locality itself and antedates its customs, for speech, being the first social instituiton, owes its form to natural causes alone" (p. 5). But the text that follows perhaps permits an extension of the variety of forms beyond the diversity of oral languages to include the multiplicity of "substances of expressions," the means of communication. These natural means are the senses, and each sense has its language. See below, "The Closure of Concepts."

multiplies Languages by as many individuals as there are to speak them, to which the wandering and vagabond life, which leaves no idiom the time to become consistent, contributes further still; for to say that the Mother dictates to the child words which he will have to use to ask her for such and such a thing well demonstrates how already formed Languages are taught, but teaches us nothing about how they are formed. *Let us suppose this first difficulty overcome: For a moment let us step across the immense space there had to be between the pure state of Nature and the need for Languages; and supposing them necessary, let us seek out how they might have begun to be established. A new difficulty, worse still than the preceding one; for if men had need of speech in order to learn to think, they had even greater need of knowing how to think in order to find the art of speech . . ."* (my italics).[9]

2. And later, when he has taken as given, by means of a *supposition*, both the "immense space there had to be between the pure state of Nature and the need for Languages," and the solution of the circle that demands speech before thought and thought before speech, Rousseau must yet again, *a third time*, recoil before a *third difficulty*; he must even feign giving up on a natural explanation in order to refer back to the hypothesis of divine institution. It is true that in the interval between the supposition and the apparent resignation he will have proposed an entire theory of language: a functional, systematic, and structural theory, whose elaboration is occasioned by the pretext of a genetic question, a fictitious problematic of the origin.

Rousseau's formulation of his apparent resignation, at the point of the third difficulty in the *Discourse* ("As for myself, frightened by the mounting difficulties, and convinced of the almost demonstrable impossibility that Languages could have been born and established by purely human means, I leave to whoever would like to undertake it the discussion of this difficult problem: which was more necessary, an already bound Society, for the institution of Languages, or already invented languages, for the establishment of Society"),[10] is to be juxtaposed with the following formulation from the *Essay*, in which Rousseau, confronted by the necessity of acknowledging an unforeseen and inexplicable irruption at the origin of languages (transition from the inarticulate cry to articulation and convention), cites Father Lamy's theological hypothesis without criticizing it, although without assuming it, simply in order to illustrate the difficulty of natural explanation: "In all tongues, the liveliest exclamations are inarticulate. Cries and groans are simple sounds. Mutes, which is to say the deaf, can make only inarticulate sounds. Father Lamy thinks that if God had not taught men to speak, they would never have learned by themselves."[11]

9. Second *Discours*, p. 147.
10. Ibid., p. 151.
11. *Essay*, p. 14. On Father Lamy, I refer to Geneviève Rodin-Lewis's study, "Un théoricien du langage au XVIIᵉ siècle, Bernard Lamy," *Le français moderne*, January 1968, pp. 19–50. In the *Confessions*, Rousseau recalls all that he owes to Father Lamy: "one of my favorite Authors, whose works I still reread with pleasure" (p. 238). Further on: "The

The three difficulties have the same form: the circle in which tradition (or transmission) and language, thought and language, society and language, each precede the other, postulate and produce each other reciprocally. But these apparent, and apparently avowed, confusions have a reverse side for which in a way they pay the price. The circle, as a vicious circle, a logical circle, by the same token constitutes the rigorously limited, closed, and original autonomy of a field. If there is no entry into the circle, if it is closed, if one is always already set down within it, if it has always already begun to carry us along in its movement, no matter where it is entered, it is because the circle forms a perfectly underivable figure and does so by means of a continuous causality, something other than itself. It has been posited decisively by an absolute, and absolutely irruptive, initiative, making it simultaneously open and closed. Society, language, convention, history, etc., together with all the possibilities that go along with them, form a system, an organized totality which, in its orginality, can be the object of a theory. Beyond its negative and sterilizing effects, beyond the question which it seems incapable of answering logically, the "logical circle" positively delimits an epistemological circle, a field whose objects will be specific. The condition for the study of this field as such is that the genetic and factual derivation be interrupted. Ideal genealogy or structural description: such is Rousseau's project. Let us cite this text once more: "Let us begin by setting aside all the facts, for they do not touch upon the question. The Investigations one may enter into on this subject must not be taken as historical truths, but only as hypothetical and conditional reasoning; more apt to enlighten the Nature of things than to show their veritable origin, and similar to the Investigations made every day by our Physicians concerning the formation of the World."[12]

3. This is what accounts for the absolutely unforeseeeable intervention, in the *Essay*, of the "slight movement" of a finger which produces the birth of society and languages. Since the system of the state of Nature could not depart *from itself*, could not itself depart from itself (*Discourse*, p. 162), could not spontaneously interrupt itself, some perfectly exterior causality had to come to provoke—*arbitrarily*—this departure, which is none other, precisely, than the *possibility of the*

---

taste that I had for him [M. Salomon] extended to the subjects of which he treated, and I began to seek out books which could help me better to understand him. Those which mixed devoutness with the sciences suited me best; such, particularly, were those of the Oratoire and of Port-Royal. I set myself to reading them, or rather to devouring them. Of these, one fell into my hands by Father Lamy, entitled *Entretiens sur les sciences*. It was a kind of introduction to the knowledge of the books on this topic. I read and reread it a hundred times; I resolved to make it my guide" (p. 232). One might pick out more than one correspondence between the two theories of language, notably as concerns the relations between speech and writing. In Father Lamy's *Rhetoric* one may read: "Words on paper are like a dead body laid out on the ground. In the mouth of whoever proffers them they are efficacious; on paper they are without life, incapable of producing the same effects." And "a written discourse is dead," "the tone, gestures, and air of the face of the speaker support his words" (cited by Rodin-Lewis, p. 27).

12. *Discours*, pp. 132–33.

arbitrary. But this arbitrary and exterior causality will also have to act along natural or quasi-natural lines. The causality of the break will have to be both natural and exterior to the state of pure Nature, and most notably to the state of nature, the state of the earth that corresponds to the state of nature. Only a *terrestrial revolution*, or rather the catastrophe of terrestrial revolution, could furnish the model for this causality. This is the center of the essay: "Supposing eternal spring on the earth; supposing plenty of water, livestock, and pasture, and supposing that men, as they leave the hands of nature, were once spread out in the midst of all that, I cannot imagine how they would ever be induced to give up their primitive liberty, abandoning the isolated pastoral life so fitted to their natural indolence, to impose upon themselves unnecessarily the labors and the inevitable misery of a social mode of life. He who willed man to be social, by the touch of a finger shifted the globe's axis into line with the axis of the universe. I see such a slight movement changing the face of the earth and deciding the vocation of mankind: in the distance I hear the joyous cries of a naive multitude; I see the building of castles and cities; I see men leaving their homes, gathering to devour each other, and turning the rest of the world into a hideous desert: fitting monument to social union and the usefulness of the arts" (pp. 38–39).[13]

This fiction has the advantage of sketching out a model that explicates *nature's departure from itself*; this departure is simultaneously absolutely natural and absolutely artificial; it must simultaneously respect and violate natural legality. Nature *itself inverts itself*, which it can only do on the basis of a point absolutely exterior to itself, that is, on the basis of a force simultaneously void and infinite. By the same token, this model respects the heterogeneity of the two orders or the two moments (nature and society, nonlanguage and language, etc.), and coordinates the continuous with the discontinuous according to what we have analyzed elsewhere under the rubric of *supplementarity*.[14] For the absolute irruption, the unforeseen revolution which made possible language, institutions, articulation, the arbitrary, etc., however, has done nothing but develop the *virtualities* already present in the state of pure nature. As is said in the second *Discourse*, "*Perfectibility*, the social virtues, and the other faculties that Natural man had received in abundance, could never have been developed by themselves . . . ; they needed for this the fortuitous concourse of several foreign causes which could never be born, and without which he would have remained eternally in his primitive condition."[15]

The notion of virtuality, therefore, assures a cohering and joining function between the two discontinuous orders, as between the two temporalities—imperceptible progression and definitive break—which scan the passage from na-

13. See also the fragment on *L'influence des climats sur la civilisation* (*Oeuvres complètes*, vol. 3, p. 531) and *De la grammatologie* (Paris: Editions de Minuit, 1967), pp. 360ff.
14. Ibid. *L'influence*, ibid., and *De la grammatologie*, ibid.
15. *Discours*, p. 162.

ture to society.[16] But despite the concepts of pure nature and of virtuality, and even if the original movement of the finger can still supplement the theological hypothesis, even if divine Providence is called upon elsewhere, it remains that Rousseau, at a certain surface of his discourse, can by all rights allege to do without any supernatural explanation, and, putting all history and all factual chronology between parentheses, can propose a structural order of the origin and function of language. In doing so, even while respecting the original order of language and society, he correlates this order, and systematically maintains this correlation, with the order of nature, primarily with the geological or geographical order of his nature. Thereby the typology of languages, in the *Essay*, will conform to a general topology, and "local difference" will be taken into account in the origin of languages (chap. 8). Corresponding to the opposition south/north is the opposition of languages of passion to languages of need, which are distinguished by the predominance granted to accentuation in the one and articulation in the other, to the vowel in one and to the consonant in the other, to metaphor in one and to exactness and correctness in the other. The latter—the languages of the north—lend themselves more easily to writing; the former naturally reject it. Thus we have a series of correlations. At the pole of the origin, at the point of greatest proximity to the birth of language, there is the chain origin-life-south-summer-heat-passion-accentuation-vowel-metaphor-song, etc. At the other pole, to the extent that one departs from the origin: decadence-illness-death-north-winter-cold-reason-articulation-consonant-correctness-prose-writing. But, by a strange motion, the more one departs from the origin, the more one tends to come back to what precedes it, to a nature which *has not yet* awakened to speech and to everything that is born along with speech. And, between the two polar series, regulated relations of supplementarity: the second series is added to the first in order to be *substituted* for it, but, in supplementing a lack in the first series, also to *add* something new, an addition, an *accident*, an excess that *should not have* overtaken the first series. In doing this, the second series will hollow out a new lack or will enlarge the original lack, which will call for a new supplement, etc. The same logic is at work in the historic and systematic classification of writings: corresponding to the three states of man in society (savage, barbaric, or policed peoples) are three types of writings (pictographic, ideographic, phonetic).[17] But, although writing has a

16. While marking the absolute break which—de jure and structually—must separate nature and language or society, Rousseau alludes "to the inconceivable pains and infinite time that the first invention of Language must have cost" (*Discours*, p. 146), to the "almost imperceptible progress of the beginnings"; "for the more that events were slow to succeed one another, the quicker they are to describe" (p. 167).

17. "These three ways of writing correspond almost exactly to the three different stages according to which one can consider men gathered into a nation. The depicting of objects is appropriate to a savage people; signs of words and of propositions to a barbaric people; and the alphabet to civilized (*policés*) peoples" (*Essay*, p. 17). "To the preceding division there correspond the three conditions of man considered in relation to society. The savage is a hunter, the barbarian is a herdman, and civil man is a tiller of the soil" (p. 38).

regular relation to the state of language ("Another way of comparing languages and determining their relative antiquity is to consider their script," *Essay,* chap. 5, p. 16), its system forms an independent totality in its internal organization and in its principle: "The art of writing does not at all depend upon that of speaking. It derives from needs of a different kind which develop earlier or later according to circumstances entirely independent of the duration of the people" (p. 19).

Reduced to their most impoverished, most general, most principial framework, such would be the motifs of an opening of the linguistic field. Did Rousseau *himself* and *himself alone* execute this opening, or is he already taken up and included in it? The question has not yet been elaborated fully enough, the terms are still too naive, the alternative is still too restricted for us to be tempted to offer an answer. No problematic, no methodology today seems to us to be capable of pitting itself effectively against the difficulties effectively announced in these questions. Thus, without great risk, and still in the form of a touchstone, we will say that despite the massive borrowings, despite the complicated geography of sources, despite the passive situation in a milieu, what can be discerned empirically under the rubric of the "work of Jean-Jacques Rousseau" yields a reading of a relatively original and relatively systematic effort to delimit the field of a linguistic science. Today, the poverty of these propositions will be more easily accepted, perhaps, if one thinks of the imprudent, that is foolish, statements from which they protect us, at least provisionally.

Of course, it is not a matter of comparing the content of the linguistic knowledge discovered in a given field with the content of modern linguistic knowledge. But the disproportion that would make such a comparison derisory is a disproportion of content: it is massively reduced when theoretical intentions, lineaments, and fundamental concepts are in question.

The Closure of Concepts

It is tempting now to invert the procedure of verification and to bring to light, on the basis of certain exemplary projects in modern linguistics, the thread which leads back to Rousseau. Here we can only single out Saussurian linguistics and semiology, taking our justification both from the fact that this is the base of all the modern theories and from the self-evidence or number of the analogies it holds in store.

1. Rousseau and Saussure grant an ethical and metaphysical privilege to the voice. Both posit the inferiority and exteriority of writing in relation to the "internal system of language" (Saussure), and this gesture, whose consequences extend over the entirety of their discourses, is expressed in formulations whose literal resemblance is occasionally surprising. Thus:

148

Saussure: "Language and writing are two distinct systems of signs; the second exists for the sole purpose of representing the first."[18]

Rousseau: "Languages are made to be spoken, writing serves only as a supplement of speech . . . writing is only the representative of speech."[19]

Saussure: "Whoever says that a certain letter must be pronounced in a certain way is mistaking the written image of a sound for the sound itself . . . To attribute this oddity [*bizarrerie*] to an exceptional pronunciation is also misleading" (p. 30).

Rousseau: "Writing is only the representation of speech; it is odd [*bizarre*] that more care is taken to determine the image than the object."[20]

And one could continue to proliferate citations in order to show that both fear the effects of writing on speech, and thus condemn these effects from a moral point of view. All of Rousseau's invective against a writing which "alters" and "enervates" language, obstructing liberty and life (*Essay,* chaps. 5 and 20), find their echo in Saussure's warnings: "The linguisitic object is not both the written and the spoken forms of words; the spoken forms alone constitute the object" (pp. 23–24). "Writing obscures language; it is not a guise for language but a disguise" (p. 30). The bond between writing and language is "fictitious," "superficial," and yet "writing acquires primary importance," and thus "the natural sequence is reversed" (p. 25). Writing is therefore a "trap," and its actions are "vicious" and "tyrannial" (today we would say *despotic*); its misdeeds are monstrosities, "teratological cases" that linguistics "should put . . . into a special compartment for observation" (p. 32). Finally, both Rousseau and Saussure consider nonphonetic writing—for example, a universal characteristic of the Leibnizian type—as evil itself.[21]

2. Both make linguistics a part of general semiology, the latter itself being only a branch of the social psychology which grows out of general psychology and general anthropology.

Saussure: "*A science that studies the life of signs within society* is conceivable; it should be a part of social psychology and consequently of general psychology; I shall call it *semiology* (from the Greek *sēmeion,* 'sign'). Semiology should show what constitutes signs, what laws govern them. Since the science does not yet exist, no one can say what it would be; but it has a right to existence, a place staked out in advance. Linguistics is only a part of the general science of semiology; the laws discovered by semiology will be applicable to linguistics, and the latter will circumscribe a well-defined area within the mass of anthropological facts. To determine the exact place of semiology is the task of the psychologist" (p. 16).

18. *Course in General Linguistics,* trans. Wade Baskin (New York: McGraw-Hill, 1959), p. 23. All further references are to this edition.
19. Fragment on *Prononciation (Oeuvres complètes,* vol. 2, pp. 1249–52).
20. Ibid.
21. See *De la grammatologie,* pp. 57 and 429.

From the very first chapter of the *Essay on the Origin of Languages* ("On the Various Means of Communicating Our Thoughts"), Rousseau also proposes a general theory of signs ordered according to the regions of sensibility that furnish the various signifying substances. This general semiology is part of a general sociology and anthropology. Speech is the "first social institution," and thus can be studied only by studying the origin and general structure of society, from within a general theory of the forms and substances of signification. This theory is inseparable from a psychology of the passions. For "the first invention of speech is due not to need but passion" (p. 11). "As soon as one man was recognized by another as a sentient, thinking being similar to himself, the desire or need to communicate his feelings and thoughts made him seek the means to do so. Such means can be derived only from the senses, the only instruments through which one man can act upon another. Hence the institution of sensate signs for the expression of thought. The inventors of language did not proceed rationally in this way; rather their instinct suggested the consequence to them. Generally, the means by which we can act on the senses of others are restricted to two: that is, movement and voice. The action of movement is immediate through touching, or mediate through gesture. The first can function only within arm's length, while the other extends as far as the visual ray. Thus vision and hearing are the only passive organs of language among dispersed individuals" (chap. 1, pp. 5–6). There follows a confrontation of the language of gesture and the language of voice; although both are "natural," they are unequally dependent upon convention. From this point of view, Rousseau certainly can vaunt the merits of mute signs, which are more natural and more immediately eloquent. But, in linking society to passion and convention, he grants a privilege to speech within the general system of signs; and consequently to linguistics within semiology. This is the third point of a possible comparison of principles or program.

3. The privilege of speech is linked, in particular, in Saussure as in Rousseau, to the institutionalized, conventional, arbitrary character of the sign. The verbal sign is more arbitrary, Rousseau and Saussure think, than other signs:

Saussure: "Signs that are wholly arbitrary realize better than the others the ideal of the semiological process; that is why language, the most complex and universal of all systems of expression, is also the most characteristic; in this sense linguistics can become the master-pattern for all branches of semiology although language is only one particular semiological system" (p. 67).

Rousseau: "Although the language of gesture and spoken language are equally natural, still the first is easier and depends less upon conventions" (chap. 1, p. 6). And, on the other hand, only linguistics is an anthropological, social and psychological science, because "conventional language is characteristic of man alone" (p. 10), and because the origin of speech is in passion and not need ("It seems then that need dictated the first gestures, while the passions stimulated the first words," chap. 2, p. 11). This explains the fact that language is originally metaphorical (chap. 3). The originality of the linguistic field has to do with the break from natural need, a break which simultaneously initiates passion, convention, and speech.

4. For the same reason, and as Saussure will do later, Rousseau rejects any pertinence of the physiological point of view in the explication of language. The physiology of the phonic organs is not an intrinsic part of the discipline of linguistics. With the same organs, with no assignable physiological or anatomic difference, men speak and animals do not.

Saussure: "The question of the vocal apparatus obviously takes a secondary place in the problem of speech" (p. 10).

Rousseau: "Conventional language is characteristic of man alone. That is why man makes progress, whether for good or ill, and animals do not. That single distinction would seem to be far-reaching. It is said to be explicable by organic differences. I would be curious to witness this explanation" (p. 10). (There are other analogous texts due to the topicality and sharpness of the debate over this question at the time when Rousseau was editing the *Dictionnaire de Musique.* Most notably, see the article "Voice," and Dodart's critique, cited by Duclos, under "Declamation of the Ancients.")

5. If animals do not speak, it is because they do not articulate. The possibility of human language, its emergence from animal calls, what makes possible the functioning of conventional language, is therefore *articulation*. The word and the concept of articulation play a central role in the *Essay*, despite the dream of a natural language, a language of unarticulated song, modeled after the neuma. In the *Course*, immediately after noting that the "question of the vocal apparatus obviously takes a secondary place in the problem of speech," Saussure continues: "One definition of *articulated speech* might confirm that conclusion. In Latin, *articulus* means a member, part, or subdivision of a sequence; applied to speech, articulation designates either the subdivision of a spoken chain into syllables or the subdivision of the chain of meanings into significant units; *gegliederte Sprache* is used in the second sense in German. Using the second definition, we can say that what is natural to mankind is not oral speech but the faculty of constructing a language, i.e. a system of distinct signs corresponding to distinct ideas" (p. 10).

One could push the inventory of analogies a long way, far beyond the pro-grammatic and principial generalities. Since their interweaving is systematic, one may say a priori that no locus of the two discourses absolutely escapes it. For example, it suffuces to accredit absolutely, here and there, the oppositions nature/convention, nature/arbitrary, animal/human, or the concepts of sign (sig-nifier/signified), or of representation (representer/represented) for the totality of the discourse to be affected systematically. The effects of such an opposition— which we know goes back further than Plato—can occasion an infinite analysis from which no element of the text escapes. By all rights this analysis is assumed by any question, however legitimate and necessary, concerning the specificity of the effects of the same opposition in different texts. But the classical criteria of these differences ("language," "period," "author," "title and unity of the work," etc.) are even more derivative, and today have become profoundly problematical.

Within the system of the same fundamental conceptuality, (fundamental, for example, at the point at which the opposition of *physis* to its others—*nomos, technē*—which opened the entire series of oppositions nature/law, nature/convention, nature/art, nature/society, nature/freedom, nature/history, nature/mind, nature/culture, etc., has governed, throughout the "history" of its modifications, the entire thinking and language of the philosophy of science up to the twentieth century), the play of structural implications, and the mobility and complication of sedimentary layers are complex enough, and unlinear enough, for the same constraint to occasion surprising transformations, partial exchanges, subtle discrepancies, turnings backward, etc. Thus, for example, one may legitimately criticize certain elements of the Saussurian project only to rediscover pre-Saussurian motifs; or even criticize Saussure on the basis of Saussure or even on the basis of Rousseau. This does not prevent everything from "holding together" in a certain way within "Saussure's" discourse and in the kinship that links him to "Rousseau." Put simply, this unity of the totality must be differentiated otherwise than is usually done, if this play is to be accounted for. It is only on this condition, for example, that one is able to explain the presence in "Rousseau's" text of motifs that are indispensable to the linguists who, despite their debt to Saussure in this regard, are no less critical of his phonologism and psychologism (Hjelmslev)[22] or of his taxinomism (Chomsky).[23] It is by attending to the subtlety of these displacements that one may detect the conceptual premises of glossematics and of the theory of generative grammar in the second *Discourse* and in the *Essay on the Origin of Languages*. One very quickly can see at work, beneath other names, the combined oppositions of the notions of "substance" and "form," of "content" and "expressions," and each of the two former applied alternately, as in glossematics, to each of the two latter. And how can we not give credit to Rousseau for everything accredited to "Cartesian linguistics"? Did not he who "began" with the *Port-Royal Logic* associate, from the very beginning, the theme of the creativity of language with the theme of a structural genesis of general grammaticality?[24]

22. "La stratification du langage," in *Essais linguistiques* (*Travaux du cercle linguistique de Copenhague*, XII, 1959), p. 56; and *Prolégomènes à une theorie du langage* (1943), trans. Canger (Paris: Editions de Minuit, 1971).

23. For example, see *Current Issues in Linguistic Theory*, 1964, pp. 23ff.

24. For example, in the First Part of the second *Discours*, when Rousseau describes the order in which is produced the "Division of the Discourse into its constitutive parts," that is, the origin of the distinction between subject and attribute, verb and noun, on the basis of a primitive indifferentiation ("They gave to each word the sense of an entire proposition" . . . "substantives at first were but so many proper names," "the infinitive—the present of the infinite—was the only tense of the verbs, and as for adjectives, the notion of them could only have developed with great difficulty, because every adjective is an abstract word, and abstractions are painful Operations of the mind," etc.; p. 149). Again, as goes without saying, this is the description of an order rather than of a history, although the latter distinction is no longer pertinent in a logic of supplementarity.

Once more, we are not concerned with comparing the content of doctrines, the wealth of positive knowledge; we are concerned, rather, with discerning the repetition or permanence, at a profound level of discourse, of certain fundamental schemes and of certain directive concepts. And then, on this basis, of formulating questions. Questions, doubtless, about the possibility of given "anticipations," that some might ingenuously judge "astonishing." But questions too about a certain closure of concepts; about the metaphysics in linguistics, or, as you will, about the linguistics in metaphysics.

Form and Meaning:
A Note on the Phenomenology of Language

Originally published in the *Revue internationale de philosophie*, 1967/3, no. 81.

—*To gar ikhnos tou amorphou morphē.*
Plotinus[1]

Phenomenology's critique of the state of metaphysics was aimed only at its restoration. Phenomenology ascertained this state in order to reawaken metaphysics to the essence of its task, the authentic originality of its design. In its final pages, the *Cartesian Meditations* remind us of this: as opposed to "adventurous" speculation, to "naive" and "degenerate" metaphysics, we must turn back to the critical project of "first philosophy." If certain metaphysical systems awaken suspicion, and even if the entirety of metaphysics is de facto "suspended" by phenomenology, the latter does not exclude "metaphysics in general."[2]

The concept of *form* could serve as a thread to be followed in phenomenology's elaboration of a purifying critique. Even if the word "form" translates several Greek words in a highly equivocal fashion, nevertheless one may rest assured that these words all refer to fundamental concepts of metaphysics. In reinscribing the Greek words (*eidos, morphē,* etc.) into phenomenological language, in playing on the differences between Greek, Latin, and German, Husserl certainly wished to deliver these concepts from the latter-day metaphysical interpretations that had overtaken them, accusing these interpretations of having deposited, in the word itself, the entire burden of an invisible sedimentation.[3] But Husserl always does so in order to reconstitute (and, if need be, against the *founders,* against Plato and Aristotle), an *original* sense that *began by* being perverted immediately upon its inscription into tradition. Whether it is a question of determining *eidos* in opposition to "Platonism," or form (*Form*) (in the problematic of formal logic and ontology) or *morphē* (in the problematic of its transcendental constitution and in its relation with *hylē*) in opposition to Aristotle, the force, vigilance, and efficacy of the critique remain intrametaphysical by means of all their resources. How could it be otherwise? As soon as we utilize the concept of form—even if to criticize *an other* concept of form—we inevitably have recourse to the self-evidence of a kernel of meaning. And the medium of this self-evidence can be nothing other than the language of metaphysics. In this language we know what "form" means, how the possibility of its variations is regulated, what its limit is, and in what field all imaginable objections to it are to be maintained. The

---

1. TN. See above, "Ousia and Grammē," note 40, and note 16 below, for more on this citation from Plotinus. The reader would do well to consult these notes again after finishing this essay in order to understand Derrida's choice of epigraph here.

2. TN. Trans. Dorian Cairns (The Hague: Martinus Nijhoff, 1960).

3. See the Introduction to *Ideas: General Introduction to Pure Phenomenology,* trans. W. R. Boyce Gibson (New York: Humanities Press, 1969). All further references are to this edition.

system of oppositions in which something like form, the formality of form, can be thought, is a finite system. Moreover, it does not suffice to say that "form" has a *meaning* for us, a center of self-evidence, or that its *essence* as such is given for us: in truth, this concept cannot be, and never could be, dissociated from the concept of appearing, of meaning, of self-evidence, of essence. Only a form is *self-evident*, only a form has or is an *essence*, only a form *presents itself* as such. This is an assured point, a point that no interpretation of Platonic or Aristotelian conceptuality can displace. All the concepts by means of which *eidos* or *morphē* have been translated or determined refer to the theme of *presence in general*. Form is presence itself. Formality is whatever aspect of the thing in general presents itself, lets itself be seen, gives itself to be thought. That metaphysical thought—and consequently phenomenology—is a thought of Being as form, that in metaphysics thought thinks itself as a thought of form, and of the formality of form, is nothing but what is necessary; a last sign of this can be seen in the fact that Husserl determines the *living present (lebendige Gegenwart)* as the ultimate, universal, absolute *form* of transcendental experience in general.

Although the privilege of *theōria*, in phenomenology, is not as simple as has sometimes been said, and although the classical theoretisms are profoundly put back into question in phenomenology, the metaphysical domination of the concept of form is bound to occasion some submission to sight. This submission always would be a submission of *sense* to sight, of sense to the sense-of-vision, since sense in general is the very concept of every phenomenological field. One could elaborate the implications of such a *placing-on-view*. One might do so in numerous directions, and based upon the most apparently diverse places of the phenomenological problematic and text: for example, by showing how this placing on view and this concept of form permit one to circulate between the project of formal ontology, the description of time or of intersubjectivity, the latent theory of the work of art, etc.

But, if sense is not discourse, their relationship, as concerns this *placing on view*, doubtless merits some particular attention. Thus have we chosen to narrow our angle here, and to approach a text concerning the status of language in *Ideas*. Between the determination of this status, the privilege of the formal, and the predominance of the theoretical, a certain circulation is organized into a system. And yet coherence, here, seems to be worked upon by a certain exterior of the relation to the exterior that is the relation to form. We only wish to point out several signs of both this circularity and this uneasiness in a preliminary way, taking our authority from the assurance that not only does *Ideas* not contradict the *Logical Investigations* on this point—on the contrary, it continuously clarifies the *Investigations*—but also that nothing beyond *Ideas* ever overtly put these analyses into question.

Meaning in the Text

For more than two-thirds of the book, everything occurs as if transcendental experience were silent, inhabited by no language; or rather deserted by *expres-*

sivity as such, since, starting with the *Investigations*, Husserl in effect determined the essence or *telos* of language as *expression (Ausdruck)*. The transcendental description of the fundamental structures of all experience is pursued up to the end of the penultimate "section" without even touching upon the problem of language. The worlds of culture and of science indeed have been evoked, but even if the predicates of culture and of science are unthinkable outside a world of language, Husserl gave himself the right, for methodological reasons, not to consider the "layer" of expression, provisionally putting it between parentheses.

Husserl can give himself this right only by supposing that expressivity constitutes an original and rigorously delimited "stratum" (*Schicht*) of experience. The *Investigations* had proposed an insistent demonstration that acts of expression are original and irreducible; and this remains presupposed in *Ideas*. Thus, at a certain moment of the descriptive itinerary, one may come to consider linguistic expressivity as a circumscribed problem. And at the point at which the problem is approached, one already knows that the "stratum of logos" will be included in the *most general structure* of experience, the structure whose poles or correlations have just been described: the parallel opposition of noesis and noema. Thus, it is already a given that however original, the stratum of the logos would have to be organized according to the parallelism of noesis and noema. The problem of "meaning" (*bedeuten*)[4] is approached in section 124, which is entitled "The Noetic-Noematic Stratum of the 'Logos.' Meaning and Meaning Something (*Bedeuten und Bedeutung*)." The metaphor of the *stratum* (*Schicht*) has two implications. On the one hand, meaning is founded on something other than itself, and this dependence will be confirmed ceaselessly by Husserl's analysis. On the other hand, meaning constitutes a stratum whose unity can be rigorously delimited. Now, if the metaphor of the stratum remains credible throughout this section, it will become suspect in the section's final lines. This suspicion is not purely rhetorical but, rather, translates a profound disquiet as concerns the descriptive fidelity of discourse. If the metaphor of the stratum does not correspond to the structure one seeks to describe, how could it have been used for so long? "For we should not hold too hard by the metaphor of stratification (*Schichtung*); expression is not of the nature of an overlaid varnish (*übergelagerter Lack*) or covering garment; it is a mental formation (*geistige Formung*), which exercises new intentional influences (*Funktionen*) on the intentional substratum (*an der intentionalen Unterschicht*) and experiences from the latter correlative intentional influences"[5] (p. 349).

4. I have attempted to justify this translation in *La voix et le phénomène* (Paris: Presses Universitaires de France, 1967; trans. David Allison as *Speech and Phenomena* [Evanston: Northwestern University Press, 1973]), which refers especially to the first of the *Logical Investigations*. [T.N. It should be recalled throughout this essay that Derrida's translation of *bedeuten* is *vouloir-dire*, which emphasizes the relation of *meaning* to *speech*, to saying (*dire*).]

5. I refer the reader to the invaluable commentary that accompanies Ricoeur's translation of the work into French. Occasionally, for reasons due only to the intentions of the present analysis, I have had to italicize certain German words and to emphasize their metaphorical charge.

This distrust of a metaphor is manifested the moment a new complication of the analysis becomes necessary. Here, I have sought only to indicate that the effort to isolate the logical "stratum" of expression encounters, even *before the difficulties of its theme*, the difficulties of its *enunciation*. The discourse on the *logic* of the discourse is entangled in a play of metaphors. The metaphor of the stratum, as we shall see, is far from being the only one.

It is apparent from the very opening of the analysis that it is a question of tracking down in discourse that which assures the properly logical functioning of discourse; that the essence or *telos* of language here are determined as *logical*; that, as in the *Investigations*, the theory of discourse reduces the considerable mass of whatever is not purely *logical* in language to an *extrinsic value*. A metaphor itself betrays the difficulty of this first reduction; this difficulty is the very one which will call for new formulations and new distinctions at the end of the section. It only will have been deferred and led elsewhere. "Acts of expression, act-strata in the specific 'logical' sense, are interwoven (*verweben sich*) with all the acts hitherto considered, and in their case no less than in the others the parallelism of noesis and noema must be clearly brought out. The prevalent and unavoidable ambiguity of our ways of speaking, which is caused by this parallelism and is everywhere operative where the concomitant circumstances are mentioned, operates also of course when we talk of expression and meaning" (p. 345).

The *interweaving (Verwebung)* of language, the interweaving of that which is purely language in language with the other threads of experience constitutes a cloth. The word *Verwebung* refers to this metaphorical zone. The "strata" are "woven," their intercomplication is such that the warp cannot be distinguished from the woof. If the stratum of the logos were simply *founded*, one could extract it and bring to light its underlying stratum of nonexpressive acts and contents. But since this superstructure acts back upon the *Unterschicht* in an essential and decisive manner, one is indeed obliged, from the very outset of the description, to associate a properly *textual* metaphor with the geological metaphor: for cloth means *text*. *Verweben* here means *texere*. The discursive is related to the nondiscursive, the linguistic "stratum" is intermixed with the prelinguistic "stratum" according to the regulated system of a kind of *text*. We know already—and Husserl acknowledges this—that in fact, at least, the secondary threads are going to act on the primary threads; in what is *spun (ourdir)* in this way, it is precisely the operation of the beginning (*ordiri*) which can no longer be grasped; what is woven as language is that the discursive warp cannot be construed as warp and takes the place of a woof which has not truly preceded it. This texture is all the more inextricable in that it is highly significant: *the nonexpressive threads are not without signification*. In the *Investigations* Husserl had shown that their signification is simply of an *indicative* nature. And in the section that concerns us, he recognizes that the words *bedeuten* and *Bedeutung* can largely overflow the "expressive" field: "We restrict our glance exclusively to the 'meaning-content'

(*Bedeutung*), and 'the act of meaning' (*Bedeuten*). Originally these words relate only to the sphere of speech (*sprachliche Sphäre*), that of 'expression' (*des Ausdrückens*). But it is almost inevitable, and at the same time an important step for knowledge, to extend the meaning of these words, and to modify them suitably so that they may be applied in a certain way to the whole noetico-noematic sphere, to all acts, therefore, whether these are interwoven (*verflochten*) with expressive acts or not" (p. 346).

Faced with this inextricable texture, this interlacing (*Verflechtung*)[6] which seems to defy analysis, the phenomenologist is not discouraged. His patience and scrupulousness must, in principle, undo the tangle. At stake is phenomenology's "principle of principles." If the description does not bring to light an absolutely and simply founding ground of signification, if an intuitive and perceptive ground, a pedestal of silence, does not found discourse in the originally given presence of the thing itself, if the texture of the text, in a word, is irreducible, not only will the phenomenological description have failed but the descriptive "principle" itself will have been put back into quesiton. The stakes of this disentanglement are therefore the phenomenological motif itself.

Mirror Writing

Husserl begins by delimiting the problem, by simplifying or purifying its givens. He then proceeds to a double exclusion, or if you will, to a double reduction, bowing to a necessity whose rightful status was acknowledged in the *Investigations*, and which will never again be put into question. *On the one hand*, the *sensory face* of language, its sensory and nonmaterial face, what might be called the animate "proper body" (*Leib*) of language, is put out of circulation. Since, according to Husserl, expression supposes an intention of meaning (*Bedeutungsintention*), its essential condition is therefore the pure act of animating intention, and not the body to which, in some mysterious fashion, intention unites itself and gives life. It is this enigmatic unity of informing intention and informed matter that Husserl authorizes himself to dissociate from the outset. This is why, *on the other hand*, he defers—forever, it seems—the problem of the unity of the two faces, the problem of the union of soul and body. "Let us start from the familiar distinction between the sensory, the so to speak bodily aspect (*leibliche Seite*) of expression, and its nonsensory 'mental' aspect. There is no need for us to enter more closely into the discussion of the first aspect, nor upon the way of uniting the two aspects, though we clearly have title-headings here indicated for phenomenological problems that are not unimportant" (p. 346).[7]

6. On the sense and importance of the *Verflechtung*, and on the functioning of this concept in the *Investigations*, see "The Reduction of Indication" in *Speech and Phenomena*.

7. In the *Investigations* these precautions had been taken and justified at length. For all that these justifications are demonstrative, of course, they are no less inherent to the interior of traditional metaphysical polarities (soul/body, psychical/physical, living/nonliv-

Having taken this double precaution, we see the contours of the problem more clearly: what are the distinctive traits that essentially separate the expressive stratum from the preexpressive stratum, and how to submit the effects of the one upon the other to an eidetic analysis? This question will receive its full formulation only after a certain progress of the analysis: "how to interpret the 'expressing' of 'what is expressed,' how expressed experiences stand in relation to those that are not expressed, and what changes the latter undergo when expression supervenes; one is then led to the question of their 'intentionality,' of their 'immanent meaning,' of their 'content' (*Materie*) and quality (i.e. the act-character of the thesis), of the distinction of this meaning and these phases of the essence which lie in the pre-expressive from the meaning of the expressing phenomenon itself and its own phases, and so forth. One gathers still in various ways from the writings of the day how little justice is apt to be done to the great problems here indicated in their full and deep-lying significance" (p. 348).

Certainly this problem already had been posed, notably at the beginning of the sixth of the *Logical Investigations*. But here, the path which leads to it is different; and not only for very general reasons (access to an openly transcendental problematic, appeal to the notion of noema, acknowledged generality of the noetico-noematic structure), but particularly because of the distinction, arisen in the interval, between the concepts of *Sinn* and *Bedeutung*. Not that Husserl now accepts this distinction proposed by Frege, one that he had objected to in the *Investigations*.[8] Rather, he simply finds it convenient to reserve the pair *bedeuten-Bedeutung* for the order of expressive meaning (*vouloir-dire*), for discourse itself, and to extend the concept of *sense (Sinn)* to the totality of the noematic face of experience, whether or not it is expressive.[9]

Once the extension of *sense* absolutely overflows the extension of *meaning*, discourse will always have to *draw upon its sense*. In a way, discourse will be able only to *repeat* or to *reproduce* a content of sense which does not await discourse in order to be what it is.[10] If things are thus, discourse will only transport to the

---

ing, intentionality/nonintentionality, form/matter, signified/signifier, intelligible/sensory, ideality/empiricity, etc.). These precautions are encountered particularly in the first of the *Investigations* (which in sum is nothing but a long explication of this issue), in the fifth *Investigation* (chap. 2, sec. 19), and in the sixth (chap. 1, sec. 7). They are confirmed unceasingly in *Formal and Transcendental Logic* and in *The Origin of Geometry*.

8. Sec. 15.

9. Sec. 124, p. 346. It goes without saying that by "discourse itself" we do not mean a discourse actually, physically, proffered, but, following Husserl's indications, the animation of verbal expression by a meaning, by an "intention" that can remain silent without being essentially affected.

10. From this point of view the entire latent aesthetics of phenomenology might be examined, the entire theory of the work of art which is discernible throughout the didactics of examples, whether the problem of the imaginary is being expounded or the status of ideality, the "once-ness" of the work, whose ideal identity can be reproduced infinitely as the *same*. A system and classification of the arts is announced in this description of the relation between archetype and reproductive examples. Can the Husserlian theory of the

exterior a sense that is constituted before it and without it. This is one of the reasons why the essence of logical meaning is determined as expression (*Ausdruck*). Discourse is expressive in its essence, because it consists in transporting to the outside, in *exteriorizing* a content of interior thought. It is never without the *sich äussern* which was spoken of in the first of the *Investigations* (sec. 7).

Thus, we are already in possession of the first distinctive trait of the expressive stratum. If it *proffers* only a constituted sense, physically or not, it is essentially reproductive, that is, *unproductive*. Husserl's analysis is on its way to this definition in its first stage: "The stratum of expression—and this constitutes its peculiarity—apart from the fact that it lends expression to all other intentionalities, is not productive. Or if one prefers: *its productivity, its noematic service, exhausts itself in expressing,* and in the *form of the conceptual* which first comes with the expressing" (pp. 348–49).

This unproductivity of the logos is *embodied,* if we may put it thus, in the Husserlian description. It again permits itself to be *seduced* by two metaphors to which we cannot not pay attention.

The first seems to pass by Husserl unnoticed. It is displaced between a writing and a mirror. Or rather, it says mirror writing. Let us follow its constitution.

In order to set forth the difference between *Sinn* and *Bedeutung,* Husserl recurs to a perceptual example, the silent perception of a "white thing." In a certain way, the statement "this is white" is perfectly independent of the perceptual experience. It is even intelligible for someone who has not had this perception. And the *Investigations* had demonstrated this rigorously. This independence of the expressive value equally implies the independence of the perceptual *sense.* We can make this *sense* explicit: "This process makes no call whatsoever on 'expression,' neither on expression in the sense of verbal sound nor on the like as verbal meaning, and here the latter can also be present independently of the verbal sound (as in the case when this sound is 'forgotten')" (p. 347).

Consequently, the transition to being stated adds nothing to sense, or in any event adds no content of sense; and yet, despite this sterility, or rather because of it, the appearance of expression is rigorously new. Because it only reissues the noematic sense, in a certain way, expression is rigorously novel. To the extent that it neither adds nor in any way deforms, expression can always in principle repeat sense, by providing access to "conceptual form": "If we have '*thought*' or *stated* 'This is white,' a new stratum is there with the rest, and unites

---

ideality of the work of art and of its relations to perception account for the differences between the musical and the plastic work, between the literary and the nonliterary work in general? And, moreover, do the precautions taken by Husserl concerning the originality of the imaginary, even at their most revolutionary, suffice to lift the work of art from an entire metaphysics of art as reproduction, from a *mimetics?* One could show that art, according to Husserl, always refers to perception as to its ultimate resource. And is it not already an aesthetic and metaphysical decision to offer works of art as examples in a theory of the *imaginary?*

with the 'meant as such' in its pure perceptive form. On these lines everything remembered or fancied can, as such, have its meaning made more explicit and expressible (*explizierbar und ausdrückbar*). Whatever is 'meant (*gemeint*) as such,' every meaning (*Meinung*) in the noematic sense (and indeed as noematic nucleus) of any act whatsoever *can be expressed conceptually* (*durch 'Bedeutungen')''* (p. 347).

And then Husserl posits as a universal rule that logical meaning is an act of expression (*Logische Bedeutung ist ein Ausdruck*). Thus, everything must be capable of being said, everything must be capable of attaining the conceptual generality which properly constitutes the logic of the logos. And this not despite but because of the originality of the logical medium of expression: in effect, this originality consists in not having to erase itself as an unproductive transparency facing the passageway of sense.

But this transparency must have some consistency: not only in order to *express*, but primarily in order to let itself be *impressed* by what afterward it will give to be read: "From the noetic standpoint the rubric 'expressing' should indicate a special act-stratum to which all other acts must adjust themselves in their own way, and with which they must blend remarkably in such wise that every noematic act-sense, and consequently the relation to objectivity which lies in it, *stamps itself (sich ausprägt:* impresses, strikes itself) 'conceptually' (*begrifflich*) in the noematic phase of the expressing" (p. 347).

Thus, the preexpressive noema, the prelinguistic sense, must be imprinted in the expressive noema, must find its conceptual mark in the content of meaning. Expression, in order to limit itself to transporting a constituted sense to the exterior, and by the same token to bring this sense to conceptual generality without altering it, in order to express what is already thought (one almost would have to say written), and in order to redouble faithfully—expression then must permit itself to be imprinted by sense at the same time as it expresses sense. The expressive noema must offer itself, and this is the new image of its unproductivity, as a blank page or virgin tablet; or at least as a palimpsest given over to its pure receptivity. Once the inscription of the sense in it renders it legible, the logical order of conceptuality will be constituted as such. It then will offer itself *begrifflich*, in graspable, manipulable, conceivable, conceptual fashion. The order of the concept is inaugurated by expression, but this inauguration is the redoubling of a preexisting conceptuality, since it first will have had to imprint itself on the naked page of meaning. Following the implacable necessity of these two concepts, *production* and *revelation* are united in the impression-expression of discourse. And since Husserl, here, is not considering the verbal order, with all its "entangled" (physical and intentional) complexity, but the still silent intention of meaning (the moment when *Bedeutung* has appeared, which is more than *sense*, but has not yet effectively and physically proffered itself), it must be concluded that sense in general, the noematic sense of every experience, is something which by its nature already must be capable of *imprinting itself* in a meaning, leaving or receiving its formal mark in a *Bedeutung*. Thus, sense already would be a kind of blank and mute writing redoubling itself in meaning.

The originality of the stratum of the *Bedeutung*, therefore, would only be a kind of tabula rasa. The grave problems posed by this metaphor can already be foreseen. In particular, if there is an original history and permanence of concepts—such as they are already and uniquely inscribed in meaning, supposing that meaning can be separated from the history of language and of signifiers—concepts themselves are always older than sense, and in turn constitute a text. Even if, in principle, one could suppose that some textual virginity *in illo tempore* welcomed the first production of sense, *in fact* the systematic order of meaning in some way would have had to impose its sense upon sense, dictating the form of sense, obliging it to imprint itself according to a given rule, syntactic or otherwise. And this "in fact" is not one empirical necessity among others; it cannot be put between parentheses in order to pose transcendental questions of rightfulness, since the status of meaning cannot be fixed without simultaneously determining the status of sense. The placing of this "fact" between parentheses is a decision concerning the status of sense in general in its relations to discourse. *This gesture does not come out of phenomenology, but opens it noncritically.* And although Husserl never afterward put this juridical "anteriority" of sense in relation to meaning (of *Sinn* in relation to *bedeuten*) back into question, it is difficult to see how it can be reconciled with his future thematic, for example that of *The Origin of Geometry*. This thematic is *simultaneously*, and quite precisely, the one which we are following at the moment *and* that of a sedimented history of *bedeuten*. And even if one considers only egological history, how is the perpetual restoration of meaning in its virginity to be thought?

However, the scriptural analogy does not hold Husserl's attention here. Another metaphor demands it.

The milieu that receives the imprint would be neutral. Husserl has just evoked conceptual *Ausprägung*. He then determines the neutrality of the milieu as that of a medium without its own color, without a determined opaqueness, without power to refract. But this neutrality, then, is less that of transparency than that of specular reflection: "A peculiar intentional instrument lies before us which essentially possesses the outstanding characteristic of reflecting back as from a mirror (*widerzuspiegeln*) every other intentionality according to its form and content, of copying (*abzubilden*) it whilst colouring it in its own way, and thereby of working into (*einzubilden*) it its own form of 'conceptuality' " (pp. 347–48).

A double effect of the milieu, a double relation of logos to sense: on the one hand, a pure and simple *reflection*, a *reflection* that respects what it accepts, and refers, *de-picts*, sense as such, in its proper original colors, re-presenting it in person. This is language as *Abbildung* (copy, portrait, figuration, representation). But, on the other hand, this reproduction imposes the blank mark of the concept. It informs meaning with sense, producing a specific nonproduction which, without changing anything in sense, *paints* something in it. The concept has been produced without adding anything to sense. Here one could speak, in a sense, of a conceptual *fiction* and of a kind of *imagination* that picked up the intuition of sense in the generality of the concept. This would be language as *Einbildung*. The two words do not occur fortuitously in Husserl's description: the unproductive production of logic would be original due to this strange concurrence of *Abbildung* and *Einbildung*.

Is this a contradiction? In any event Husserl displays a certain discomfort. And there would be much to think about in Husserl's attribution of the indecision of his description to the accidental metaphoricity of language, to precisely what he calls the *Bildlichkeit* of discourse. It is because discourse occasionally must utilize images, figures, and analogies—which would be as its debris—that logos must be described simultaneously as the unproductivity of the *Abbildung* and as the productivity of the *Einbildung*. If one eliminated the *Bildlichkeit* in descriptive discourse, by the same token one would eliminate the apparent contradiction between *Abbildung* and *Einbildung*. But Husserl does not ask about this nuclear *bilden* in its relations to logos. The passage we were citing above continues this way: "Yet these figures of speech which here thrust themselves upon us, those of mirroring and copying, must be adopted with caution, as the imaginativeness (*Bildlichkeit*: metaphoricity, pictorial representation) which colours their application might easily lead one astray (*irreführen*)" (p. 348). Therefore metaphor is seductive, in every sense of the word. And phenomenological discourse is to resist this seduction.

The Limiting Power of Form

If Husserl suspects all the predicates brought into the milieu of the logos, he never criticizes the concept of the *medium* itself. The expressive stratum is a *medium*, an ether that both accepts sense and is a means to bring it to conceptual form. The word "medium" appears often in the pages that follow. It gives its heading, precisely, to the problem of the history of concepts whose difficulty we just evoked and that we related to the future themes of *The Origin of Geometry*. Here Husserl formulates the very difficulty[11] which will constitute the central theme of *The Origin*: "Problems of exceptional difficulty beset the phenomena which find their place under the headings 'to mean' (*Bedeuten*) and 'meaning' (*Bedeutung*). Since every science, viewed from the side of its theoretical content, of all that constitutes its 'doctrine' (*Lehre*) (theorem, proof, theory), is objectified in a specific 'logical' medium, the medium of expression, it follows that for philosophers and psychologists who are guided by general logical interests the problems of expression and meaning (*Bedeutung*) lie nearest of all, and are also the first, generally speaking, which, so soon as one seeks seriously to reach their

11. This problem was given form in the Introduction to the *Logical Investigations* (sec. 2).

foundations, compel towards phenomenological inquiry into the essential nature of things" (p. 348).

Theory, therefore, is the name of that which can neither dispense with objectification in the medium nor tolerate the slightest deformation in its subjection to the medium. There is no scientific sense (*Sinn*) without meaning (*bedeuten*), but it belongs to the essence of science to demand an unequivocality without shadow, the absolute transparence of discourse. Science would need what it needs (discourse as pure meaning) to be useless: it is only to preserve and to glance at the sense which science confers upon it. Nowhere else can discourse simultaneously be more productive and more unproductive than as an element of theory.

Which indeed confirms—if this unproductive productivity is the *telos* of expression—that logico-scientific discourse has never ceased to function, here, as the model of every possible discourse.

The entire analysis, henceforth, will have to be displaced between two concepts or two values. On the one hand, ideal discourse will have to accomplish an overlapping or a *coincidence (Deckung)* of the nonexpressive stratum of sense and of the expressive stratum of meaning. But, for all the reasons we have already recognized, this overlapping can never be a *confusion*. And the work of clarification, distinction, articulation, etc. must bear upon the two strata as such. The difference between coincidence and confusion leads us back, therefore, to the very opening of our problematical space. But perhaps this formulation permits us to make some progress.

In the best of cases, that of the perfect overlapping of the two strata, there should be a *parallelism*, then. The concept of the parallel would respect at once the perfect correspondence and the nonconfusion of strata. And, following an analogy that ought to be investigated, the concept of the parallel would play as decisive a role here as when Husserl explicitly makes it intervene in order to describe the relation between the purely psychic and the transcendental.

The parallelism of the two strata can be a perfect overlapping only if meaning (if not actual discourse) reproduces the meaning of the underlying stratum *completely*. There is always a certain overlapping of the two strata, for without it the phenomenon of expression would not even occur; but this overlapping may be incomplete: "We must further lay stress on the difference between *complete (vollständigem)* and *incomplete (unvollständigem) expression*. The unity of the expressing and the expressed in the phenomenon is indeed that of a certain overlapping (*Deckung*), but the upper layer need not extend its expressing function over the entire lower layer. Expression is complete when the *stamp of conceptual meaning has been impressed (ausprägt) upon all the synthetic forms and matter (Materien) of the lower layer;* incomplete when this is only partially effected: as when, in regard to a complex process, the arrival of the carriage, perhaps, bringing guests that have been long expected; we call out: the carriage! the guests! This difference of completeness will naturally cut across that of relative clearness and distinctness" (p. 352).

Up to now, one might have believed that the noncompleteness of expression and the nonparallelism of the two layers have the value of a fact or an accident; and that even if such a *fact* occurs often, even if it almost always affects our discourse in its totality, *it does not belong to the essence of expression.* The example Husserl has just cited in effect belongs to the language of daily life, and it may still be assumed that the mission and power of scientific expression consist in mastering these shadows and restituting the completeness of the sense aimed at in expression.

At the risk of compromising an axiom (the unproductive and reflective value of expression), Husserl also brings to light an *essential* noncompletion of expression, an insufficiency that no effort ever will be able to overcome, precisely because it has to do with *conceptual form,* the very formality without which expression would not be what it is. Although Husserl, above, apparently wanted to stress the reflective, reproductive, repetitive nature of expression, its *Abbilden,* thereby neutralizing, in return, its effects, and its marks, its power to deform or refract, that is, its *Einbilden,* now, on the other hand, he stresses an essential displacement of expression that will forever prevent it from reissuing the stratum of sense (*Sinn*): and this difference is nothing less than the difference of the concept. We must read the entire paragraph: "An incompleteness of a totally different kind (*Eine total andere Unvollständigkeit*) from the one just discussed is that which belongs to the essential nature of the expression as such, namely, to its *generality (Allgemeinheit).* 'I would like,' expresses the wish in a general form; the form of command, the command; 'might very well be' the presumption, or the likely as such, and so forth. Every closer determination in the unity of the expression is itself again expressed in general form. It lies in the meaning of the generality which belongs to the essential nature of the expressing function that it would not ever be possible for all the specifications of the expressed to be reflected (*sich reflektieren*) in the expression. The stratum of the meaning function is not, and in principle is not, a sort of duplication (*Reduplikation*) of the lower stratum" (p. 352).

And referring to the entire problematic of complete and incomplete expressions in the *Logical Investigations,* Husserl then mentions the values of the underlying layer which in principle cannot be repeated in expression (the qualities of clarity, of distinction, attentional modifications, etc.).

This impoverishment is the condition for scientific formalization. Unequivocality is furthered in the extent to which the complete repetition of sense in meaning is given up. Therefore, one cannot even say that a factual, accidental, inessential noncompleteness is reduced via a teleology of scientific discourse, or that it is included as a provisional obstacle within the horizon of an infinite task. The *telos* of scientific discourse bears within itself, *as such,* a renunciation of completeness. Here, the difference is not a provisional deficiency of the *epistēmē* as discourse, but is its very resource, the positive condition for its activity and productivity. It is as much the limit of scientific power as it is the power of the scientific limit: the limiting-power of its formality.

Form "Is"—Its Ellipsis

It seems that these propositions concerned, before anything else, the relation between the form of the statement and the content of sense, between the order of meaning and the order of the noema in general. However, they also imply an essential decision concerning the *relation of statements to each other,* within the general system of expressivity. For the relation of expression to sense to be ready to accept the determination we have just sketched out, did not an absolute privilege have to be granted to a certain type of statement? Is there not an essential relation between the value of formality and a certain structure of the sentence? And by the same token, is there not a *facility of transition* between a certain type of noema (or experience of sense) and the order of meaning which in a way would ensure the very possibility of this entire phenomenology of the logos?

With this question we are retracing our first steps: what is the status of the concept of form? How does it inscribe phenomenology within the closure of metaphysics? How does it determine the meaning of Being as presence, that is, as the present? What brings it into secret communication with the delimitation of the meaning of Being which gives us to think Being par excellence in the verbal form of the present and, more narrowly still, in the third person present indicative? What does the complicity of form in general (*eidos, morphē*) and of the "is" (*esti*) give us to think?

Let us reestablish the contact between these questions and Husserl's text at the point at which formal impoverishment has just been acknowledged as an essential rule. The problem of the relation between the different kinds of statement arises quite naturally. Is statement in the form of judgment, "it *is* thus," one kind of statement among others? Is there not some excellence reserved for it in the stratum of expressivity? "We must be clear about all these points if one of the oldest and hardest problems of the sphere of meaning (*Bedeutungssphäre*) is to be solved, a problem which hitherto, precisely because it lacked the requisite phenomenological insight, has remained without solution: the problem, namely, as to *how statement as the expression of judgment is related to the expressions of other acts*" (p. 353).

The answer to such a question had been prepared, and its necessity announced, at a stage of the analysis which did not yet concern the stratum of expression. There it was a question of setting forth, within practical or affective experiences, within acts of esthetic, moral, etc. evaluation, a "doxic" kernel which, while still permitting values to be thought as beings (the wished for as being-wished, the pleasant as being-pleasant, etc. (sec. 114)), constitutes, if we

169

may put it thus, the *logicity* of the preexpressive stratum. It is because this silent stratum always bears within it—or always has the power of restoring—a relation to form, that it can always convert its affective or axiological experience, its relation to what is not being-present, into an experience in the form of being-present (the beautiful as being-present, the desired as being-desired, the dreaded-future as being-dreaded-future, the inaccessible as being-inaccessible, and, finally, the absent as being-absent), and that it offers itself without reserve to the logical discourse watched over by predicative form, that is, by the present indicative of the verb to be.[12] From Husserl's point of view, not only would this not reduce the originality of experiences and of practical, affective, axiological discourses, but also would ensure the possibility of their formalization without limit.[13]

Having ascertained that "every act, as also every act-correlate, harbours explicitly or implicitly a 'logical' factor" (sec. 117, p. 332), Husserl had only to draw the conclusions that concern the expressive recasting of these acts, and to confirm, rather than to discover, the privilege of the *is* or of the predicative statement. The moment he repeats[14] the question in the order of meaning, there

12. Husserl wishes both to respect the novelty or originality of the (practical, affective, axiological) sense added to the kernel of sense in the naked thing (*Sache*) as such, *and*, nevertheless, to bring to light its "founded," superstructural character. "The new sense introduces a *totally new dimension of sense:* with it there is constituted no new determining marks of the mere '*material*' (*Sachen*), but *values of the materials*—qualities of value (*Wertheiten*), or concrete objectified values (*Wertobjektitäten*): beauty and ugliness, goodness and badness; or the object for use, the work of art, the machine, the book, the action, the deed, and so forth . . . Further, the consciousness in respect of this new character is once again a *positional* consciousness: the 'valuable' can be doxically posited as being valuable (*als wert seiend*). The 'state of being' (*seiend*) which belongs to the 'valuable' as *its* characterization can be thought of also as *modalized*, as can every 'state of being' " (sec. 116, p. 327). "We can therefore also say: *Every act, as also every act-correlate, harbours explicitly or implicitly a 'logical' factor (ein Logisches)* . . . It results from all this *that all acts generally— even the acts of feeling and will—are 'objectifying' ('objektivierende') acts, original factors in the 'constituting' of objects,* the necessary sources of different regions of being and of the ontologies that belong therewith . . . Here lies the deepest of the sources for shedding light on the *universality of the logical,* in the last resort that of the predicative judgment (to which we must add the stratum of meaningful expression [*des bedeutungsmässigen Ausdrückens*] which we have not yet subjected to closer study" (sec. 117, pp. 332–33).

13. "But therein in the last resort are grounded those analogies which have at all times been felt to hold between general logic, general theory of value, and ethics, which, when pursued into their farthest depths, lead to the constituting of general *formal* disciplines on lines parallel to the above, formal logic, formal axiology, and the formal theory of practice (*Praktik*)" (sec. 117, p. 330).

14. "We have expressive predications in which a 'thus it is!' (*'So ist es!'*) comes to expression. We have expressive presumptions, questions, doubts, expressive wishes, commands, and so forth. Linguistically we have here forms of sentence whose structure is in part distinctive, while yet they are of ambiguous interpretation: by the side of sentences that embody statements we have sentences embodying questions, presumptions, wishes, commands and so forth. The original debate bore on the issue whether, disregarding the grammatical wording and its historical forms, we had here to do with coordinate types of meaning (*gleichgeordnete Bedeutungsarten*), or whether the case was not rather that all

is already, in fact, a requisite answer. Nor is there any cause for surprise or disappointment. Here, there is something like a rule of discourse or of the text: the question can be inscribed only in the form dictated by the answer that awaits it, namely, that has not awaited it. We have only to ask how the response has prescribed the form of the question: not according to the necessary, conscious, and calculated anticipation of one who conducts a systematic exposition, but, as it were, behind his back. For example, we may ask, here, to what extent the reference to the expressive stratum, before even becoming a theme, has secretly carried out analyses of the preexpressive stratum, and permitted a kernel of logical sense to be discovered in it, in the universal and allegedly silent form of being-present.

And we may ask if some irreducible complicity, between Being as being-present in the form of meaning (*bedeuten*) and Being as being-present in the so-called preexpressive form of sense (*Sinn*), has not been operative, welding the strata to each other, as well as permitting them both to be related one to the other and to be articulated within this entire problematic. Is this not the site of the decision for all the problems we have discerned thus far?[15] Does not the idea of an expressive language become problematic on the basis of this question? And, along with it, does not the possibility of a distinction between the stratum of sense and the stratum of meaning also become problematic? Above all, can the relations between the two strata be thought in the category of expression? To say, in effect, that the description of the infrastructure (of sense) has been guided secretly by the superstructural possibility of meaning, is not to contest, against Husserl, the duality of the strata and the unity of a certain transition

---

these sentences, so far as their meaning is concerned, are not in truth sentences that state. If the latter, then all act-constructions, such, for instance, as those of the sphere of feeling, which in themselves are not acts of judgment, can achieve 'expression' only in a round-about way (*Umweg*) through the mediation of an act of judging which is grounded in them" (sec. 127, p. 353).

15. Even though the answer has prescribed the form of the question, or, if you will, itself has been prescribed in it, its thematic articulation is not simply redundant. It engages new concepts and encounters new difficulties, for example, at the end of Section 127, when it is a question of the *direct* or *indirect* expressions of sense, and of the status of the periphrastic detour (*Umweg*). Let us locate several points of orientation in this paragraph: "*Is the medium for the expressing of meaning, this unique medium of the Logos, specifically doxic?* . . . This would not of course exclude the possibility of there being various ways of expressing such experiences, those of feeling, for instance. A single one of these would be the *direct* [*schlicht:* our italics] plain expression of the experience (or of its noema, in the case of the correlative meaning of the term 'expression') through the *immediate* [our italics] adjustment of an articulated expression to the articulated experience of feeling whereby doxic and doxic tally together. Thus it would have been the *doxic* form dwelling in respect of all its component aspects within the experience of feeling that made possible the adjustability of the expression, as an exclusively doxothetic (*doxothetischen*) experience, to the experience of feeling . . . To speak more accurately, this *direct* expression, if it would be true and complete, should be applied only to the *doxic nonmodalized* experiences . . . There exist at all times *a number of alternative indirect expressions* involving 'roundabout phrases' (*mit 'Umwegen')" (pp. 354–55).

which relates them one to the other. It is neither to wish to reduce one stratum to the other nor to judge it impossible completely to recast sense in meaning. It is neither to reconstruct the experience (of sense) as a *language*, above all if one takes this to be a *discourse*, a verbal fabric, nor to produce a critique of language on the basis of the ineffable riches of sense. It is simply to ask questions about *another relationship* between what are called, problematically, *sense* and *meaning*.

That is, about the unity of sense and the word in the "is": which in principle could promise the recasting of all language only by having already, teleologically, promised all sense to meaning. And about the relations between the *is* and formality in general: it is within the self-evidence of the (present) *is*, within *self-evidence itself*, that we find proposed all of transcendental phenomenology seen at its most ambitious, proposing both to constitute an absolutely *formal* logic and ontology, and to provide a transcendental description of self *presence* or of original consciousness.

One might think then that the *sense of Being* has been limited by the imposition of the *form* which, in its most overt value and since the origin of philosophy, seems to have assigned to Being, along with the authority of the *is*, the closure of presence, the form-of-presence, presence-in-form, form-presence.[16] One might think, on the other hand, that formality—or formalization—is limited by the sense of Being which, in fact, throughout its entire history, has never been separated from its determination as presence, beneath the excellent surveillance of the *is:* and that henceforth the thinking of form has the power to extend itself beyond the thinking of Being. But that the two limits thus denounced are *the same* may be what Husserl's enterprise illustrates: phenomenology could push to its extreme limit the *formalist demand* and could criticize all previous formalisms only on the basis of a thinking of Being as *self-presence*, on the basis of a transcendental *experience* of pure consciousness.

16. Form (presence, self-evidence) would not be the ultimate recourse, the last analysis to which every possible sign would refer, the *archē* or the *telos*. Or rather, in a perhaps unheard-of fashion, *morphē, archē,* and *telos* still signal. In a sense—or a non-sense—that metaphysics would have excluded from its field, while nevertheless remaining in secret and incessant relation with this sense, form in itself already would be the *trace (ikhnos)* of a certain nonpresence, the vestige of the un-formed, which announces-recalls its other, as did Plotinus, perhaps, for all of metaphysics. The trace would not be the mixture, the transition between form and the amorphous, presence and absence, etc., but that which, by eluding this opposition, makes it possible in the irreducibility of its excess. Henceforth, the closure of metaphysics, the closure that the audaciousness of the *Enneads* seems to indicate by transgressing it, would not occur *around* a homogenous and continuous field of metaphysics. Rather, it would fissure the structure and history of metaphysics, *organically* inscribing and systematically *articulating* the traces of the *before* and the *after* both from within and without metaphysics. Thereby proposing an infinite, and infinitely surprising, reading. An irreducible rupture and excess can always be produced within an era, at a certain point of its text (for example, in the "Platonic" fabric of "Plotinism"). Already in Plato's text, no doubt.

Thus, one probably does not have to choose between two lines of thought. Rather, one has to meditate upon the circularity which makes them pass into one another indefinitely. And also, by rigorously repeating this *circle* in its proper historical possibility, perhaps to let some *elliptical* displacement be produced in the difference of repetition: a deficient displacement, doubtless, but deficient in a way that is not yet—or is no longer—absence, negativity, non-Being, lack, silence. Neither matter nor form, nothing that could be recast by some philosopheme, that is, by some dialectics, in whatever sense dialectics may be determined. An ellipsis both of meaning and of form: neither full speech nor a perfect circle. More and less, neither more nor less. Perhaps an entirely other question.

The Supplement
of Copula:
Philosophy
before Linguistics

Originally published in *Langages,* 24 December 1971.

If, on the basis of the naively accepted opposition between language and speech, language and discourse, we attempted to elaborate a theory of *philosophical* discourse, it would be difficult to circumvent the classical question: is philosophical discourse governed—to what extent and according to what modalities—by the constraints of language? In other words, if we consider the history of philosophy as one great discourse, a powerful discursive chain, is not that history immersed in a reserve of language, the systematic reserve of a lexicology, a grammar, a set of signs and values? And once this is so, is not the history of philosophy limited by the resources and the organization of that reserve?

How to determine this language of philosophy? Is it a "natural language," or a family of natural languages (Greek, Latin, Germanic, Indo-European, etc.)? Is it rather a formal code elaborated on the basis of these natural languages? These questions have an old history, doubtless going back to the origin of philosophy itself. But they cannot be reelaborated without displacing the pairs of concepts which constitute philosophy. These pairs, for example natural language/formal language, language/speech, etc. having been produced by philosophical discourse, belong to the field which they are to dominate; which, without stripping them of all authority, makes them incapable of mastering the relation of philosophical "discourse" to its constraints.

Moreover, at a given moment these questions, which long remained special and virtual ones, become dominant and obsessing. This is certainly not insignificant as concerns the "historical" relation of philosophy to its proper limit and to the singular form of this closure. This singularity is manifested regularly along the lines of the following *turn:* whoever alleges that philosophical discourse belongs to the closure of a language must still proceed within this language and with the oppositions it furnishes. According to a law that can be formalized, philosophy always reappropriates for itself the discourse that de-limits it.

Finally, although the question about these linguistic constraints has a certain philosophical permanence, the form in which we are advancing the question today has doubtless been constituted within a very particular and very complex historico-theoretical configuration. This configuration is bound to numerous fields of criticism but above all remains inseparable from the development of historical linguistics in the nineteenth century. In reminding the philosopher that he remains enclosed in a language, Nietzsche was surely more violent and more explicit than anyone else, but he was also exploiting a possibility that had been coming to the surface almost everywhere for a half century, even if most often reappropriated by philosophical interest. In this situation, Nietzschean discourse, no more than any other, could not simply escape the law of reappropriation. For example, Nietzsche determines as liberation (or liberty of thought) the movement which finally would free us from the language and grammar that until now have governed the philosophical order. Quite traditionally, he thus comes to define the law of language or of the signifier as a "slavery" from which one must be freed, and, at the most critical or "overturning" moment of his enterprise, he remains a philosopher, shall we say, *provisionally:* "Logic is only slavery within the bonds of language (*die Sklaverei in den Banden der Sprache*). Language, however, has within it an illogical element, metaphor. Its primary force operates (*bewirkt*) an identification of the nonidentical (*Gleichsetzen des Ungleichen*); it is therefore an operation of the imagination (*Wirkung der Phantasie*). The existence of concepts, forms, etc. rests thereupon."[1] This movement is repeated regularly, and primarily when Nietzsche analyzes the philosophical illusion of "truth": compliance with an order of signs which one has forgotten to be "arbitrary" (*willkürlich*). Has not philosophy always recalled the arbitrariness of the sign in order to posit the contingent and superficial exteriority of language to thought, the secondariness of the sign in relation to the idea, etc.? With an entirely other aim, Nietzsche must resort to an analogous argument: "Only by means of forgetfulness (*Vergesslichkeit*) can man ever arrive at imagining that he possesses 'truth' in that degree just indicated. If he does not mean to content himself with truth in the shape of tautology, that is, with empty husks, he will always obtain illusions instead of truth. What is a word? The expression of a nerve-stimulus in sounds. But to infer a cause outside us from the nerve-stimulus is already the result of a wrong and unjustifiable application of the proposition of causality. How should we dare, if truth with the genesis of language, if the point of view of certainty with the designations, had alone been decisive; how indeed should we dare to say: the stone is hard; as if 'hard' was known as otherwise; and not merely as an entirely subjective stimulus! We divide things according to gender; we designate the tree as masculine, the plant as feminine: what arbitrary metaphors (*welche willkürlichen Ubertragungen*)! How far flown beyond the canon of certainty."[2] There follows the example of the "serpent" and an interpretation of metaphor as the very structure or condition of possibility of all language and of every concept.

Let us note here as a touchstone that the diagnosed illusion bears upon the value of the "is," which has as its function to transform a "subjective excitation" into an objective judgment, into a pretension to truth. A grammatical function? A lexicological function? This is a question that will be determined later.

The example of the stone or the serpent illustrated a semantic or lexicological arbitrariness. But Nietzsche most often incriminates grammar or syntax. With their very structure, the latter would support the entire metaphysical edifice: "Our oldest metaphysical fund is the one that we will be rid of last, supposing that we ever succeed in getting rid of it—the fund that has incorporated itself into language and into grammatical categories and has made itself indispensable to the point that it seems that we should cease to think if we renounced this metaphysics. Philosophers are precisely those who have the greatest difficulty

---

1. *Le livre du philosophe, études théoretiques (Das Philosophenbuch, Theoretische Studien)*, bilingual ed., trans. A. K. Marietti (Paris: Aubier-Flammarion, 1969), p. 207.
2. "On Truth and Falsity in their Ultramoral Sense," in *The Complete Works of Friedrich Nietzsche* (London: Oscar Levy, 1911), vol. 2, p. 177.

in liberating themselves from the belief that fundamental concepts and categories of reason by their nature belong to the realm of metaphysical certainties; they always believe in reason as in a piece of the metaphysical world itself, this backward belief always reappears in them as an all-powerful regression."[3]

At a given moment, then, Nietzsche has to appeal to philosophical schemes, (for example, the arbitrariness of the sign, or the emancipation of thought as concerns a language), in his critical operation against metaphysics. This is not an incoherence for which a *logical* solution is to be sought, but a textual strategy and stratification that must be analyzed in *practice*. One could also do so by following Heidegger's path, for he too came to grips with analogous difficulties. These are explicitly formulated in the *Letter on Humanism:* "Metaphysics, which very early on in the form of Occidental 'logic' and 'grammar' seized control of the interpretation of language. We today can only begin to descry what is concealed in that occurrence. The liberation of language from grammar into a more original essential framework is reserved for thought and poetic creation."[4] And elsewhere, recalling that *Sein und Zeit* remained incomplete: "Here everything is reversed. The section in question was held back because thinking failed in the adequate saying of this turning and did not succeed with the help of the language of metaphysics."[5]

Rhapsodies

Rather than follow this immense problematic onto the high seas, so to speak, perhaps it would be better, given the demands and limits of this essay, to take our point of departure from the propositions of a modern linguist. We know that Benveniste, in "Categories of Thought and Language,"[6] analyzed the limiting constraints which the Greek language imposed upon the system of Aristotelian categories.

Benveniste's propositions are part of a stratified ensemble; nor does he restrict himself to the text which directly states the thesis of the ensemble. We will have to take this into account when the time comes. Moreover, this thesis already has encountered objections of the philosophical type;[7] together the thesis and the objections form a debate which in its development will be invaluable for us.

3. *La volonté de puissance,* trans. G. Bianquis (Paris: Gallimard, 1947), vol. 1, p. 65. [As Creech and Harari note in their translation of this essay, this 1886 fragment does not appear in any of the English translations of *The Will to Power.*]
4. Heidegger, "Letter on Humanism," trans. Frank Capuzzi, in *Basic Writings,* ed. David Farrell Krell (New York: Harper and Row, 1977), p. 194.
5. Ibid., p. 208.
6. In Benveniste, *Problems in General Linguistics,* trans. Mary E. Meek (Coral Gables: University of Miami Press, 1971). All further references are to this edition.
7. See Pierre Aubenque, "Aristote et le langage, note annexe sur les catégories d'Aristote. A propos d'un article de M. Benveniste," *Annales de la faculté des Lettres d'Aix* 43 (1965); and J. Vuillemin, *De la logique à la théologie, Cinq études sur Aristote* (Paris: Flammarion, 1967), pp. 75ff.

First, the thesis: "Now it seems to us—and we shall try to show—that these distinctions are primarily categories of language and that, in fact, Aristotle, reasoning in the absolute, is simply identifying certain fundamental categories of the language in which he thought" (p. 57).

What are the presuppositions of this thesis? Benveniste starts from a certain number of generally acknowledged—at least since Saussure—characteristics of language. In the first place, "the reality of language" is "unconscious," which resembles Saussure's propositions concerning the fact that "language is not a function of the speaking subject." We will not pause to consider this premise, which raises more than one difficulty, however, and not only because of its empirical form. ("In their diversity, these uses [of language] have, however, two characteristics in common. One is that the reality of language, as a general rule, remains unconscious"; p. 55.) What does "reality of language" mean here? What is the status of "reality" in the phrase "reality of language"? Why only "as a general rule"? Is it or is it not an essential predicate of the so-called reality to remain unconscious? The difficulty of distinguishing conscious from unconscious is at its most obscure when the issue is one of language or of the use of language. And the difficulty is not attenuated, quite to the contrary, when the unconscious risks becoming an indistinct consciousness ("The reality of language, as a general rule, remains unconscious; except when language is especially studied for itself, we have no more than a very faint and fleeting awareness of the operations which we accomplish in order to talk"; p. 55), or when the activity of linguistics, in its relation to language, is determined as a coming to, or an increase of, consciousness. These questions are raised neither to emphasize what are doubtless secondary links in Benveniste's demonstration, nor to object to his discourse, but merely to indicate an example of the aporias that appear to engage anyone who takes on the task of defining the constraints which limit philosophical discourse; for it is from the latter that the noncritical notions which are applied to its delimitation must be borrowed. The notions of system, form, content, which serve to define the characteristics of language, equally could have given us pause ("Now this language has a configuration in all its parts and as a totality. It is in addition organized as an arrangement of distinct and distinguishing 'signs,' capable themselves of being broken down into interior units or of being grouped into complex units. This great structure, which includes substructures of several levels, gives its *form* to the content of thought"; p. 55). The notion of a linguistic *system*, even if opposed to the notions of logical system, or system of categories, and even if one attempted to reduce the latter to the former, would never have been possible outside the history (and) of the concepts of metaphysics as theory, *epistēmē*, etc. Whatever the displacements, breaks, and secondary discontinuities of every kind, (and they surely have to be taken very strictly into account), this filiation has never been absolutely interrupted. Benveniste acknowledges this elsewhere:[8] and here he acknowledges that he must

8. *Problems*, p. 18: "Everyone knows that western linguistics originated in Greek philosophy. This appears from all the evidence. Our linguistic terminology is made up in large part of Greek terms adopted directly or through their Latin translations."

immediately criticize as metaphor or "image" a great classical opposition, inherited from philosophy, but that nevertheless was at the center of the passage we just cited: "To speak of the container and the contents is to simplify. The image should not delude us. Strictly speaking, thought is not matter to which language lends form, since at no time could this 'container' be imagined as empty of its 'contents,' nor the 'contents' as independent of their 'container' " (p. 56). Precautions of this kind could be taken for each concept; we are using these examples only to remark upon the necessity proper to the structure of a discourse or a project, not at all to the initiative of an author.

Here we take our leave from the propedeutic opening of Benveniste's text and come to the major problem. It is put this way:

"And so the question becomes the following: while granting absolutely that thought cannot be grasped except as formed and made a reality in language, have we any means to recognize in thought such characteristics as would belong to it alone and owe nothing to linguistic expression? We can describe language by itself. It would be necessary in the same way to apprehend thought directly. If it were possible to define thought by features belonging to it exclusively, it would be seen at once how it accommodates itself to language and what the nature of their relationship is.

"It might be convenient to approach the problem by way of 'categories,' which appear as intermediaries. They present different aspects, depending on whether they are categories of thought or language. This difference might shed light on their respective natures. For example, we immediately perceive that thought can freely specify its categories and invent new ones, while linguistic categories, as attributes of a system which each speaker receives and maintains, are not modifiable according to each person's whim. We also see this other difference: that thought can claim to set up universal categories but that linguistic categories are always categories of a particular language. At first sight, this would confirm the preeminent and independent position of thought with regard to language.

"We cannot, however, as so many authors have done, simply pose the question in such general terms. We must enter into a concrete historical situation and study the categories of a specific thought and a specific language. Only on this condition will we avoid arbitrary stands and speculative solutions. Now, we are fortunate to have at our disposal data which one would say were ready for our examination, already worked out and stated objectively within a well-known system: Aristotle's categories. In the examination of these categories, we may dispense with philosophical technicalities. We will consider them simply as an inventory of properties which a Greek thinker thought could be predicated of a subject and, consequently, as the list of a priori concepts which, according to him, organize experience. It is a document of great value for our purpose" (pp. 56–57).

Thus defined, this problematic appears to encompass at least three presuppositions. They all concern a certain "historicity" of concepts.

1. Recourse has been necessary—even if provisionally, and under the heading of a point of departure which could be criticized later—to the difference or opposition between language and thought. ("We can describe language by itself. It would be necessary in the same way to apprehend thought directly. If it were possible to define thought by features belonging to it exclusively, it would be seen at once how it accommodates itself to language and what the nature of their relationship is.") Doubtless, Benveniste starts from this separation only in order to reduce it afterward, in order to resolve the characteristics which allegedly belong exclusively to thought into structures of language. But throughout the analysis no question is asked about the origin and possibility of that initial distinction, about what has made the presumption, at least, of this noncoincidence historically possible, in other words the question about the very opening of the problem. What, at least in the structure of language (since everything there is given: "We can describe language by itself"), has opened this dehiscence and has determined it as the difference between thought and language?

2. Thus, in the second paragraph cited, we are dealing with an eventual or alleged opposition of "categories of thought" and "categories of language." What is not examined at any time is the common category of the category, the *categoriality in general* on the basis of which the categories of language and the categories of thought may be dissociated. The concept or category of the category systematically comes into play in the history of philosophy and of science (in Aristotle's *Organon* and *Categories*) at the point where the opposition of language to thought is impossible, or has only a very derivative sense. Although Aristotle certainly did not reduce thought to language in the sense intended here by Benveniste, he did attempt to take the analysis back to the site of the emergence, that is to the common root, of the language/thought couple. This site is the site of "Being." Aristotle's categories are simultaneously of language and of thought: of language in that they are determined as answers to the question of knowing how Being *is said (legetai);* but also, how *Being* is said, how is said what is, in that it is, such as it is: a question of thought, thought itself, the word "thought" which Benveniste uses as if its signification and its history went without saying, in any case never having meant anything outside its relation to Being, its relation to the truth of Being such as it is and in that it is (said). "Thought"—that which lives under this name in the West—could never emerge or announce itself except on the basis of a certain configuration of *noein, legein einai* and of the strange sameness of *noein* and *einai* spoken of in Parmenides' poem.[9] Now, without going further in this direction, we must at least emphasize that at the moment when Aristotle sets categories, and the category of category, in place (the inaugural gesture for the very idea of logic, that is, for the science of science, and

9. TN. On *noein* and *legein* see above, "Ousia and Grammē," note 5. Derrida is also referring to another fragment from Parmenides here: *to gar auto noein estin te kai einai,* which Heidegger gives as: "For the same perceiving (thinking) as well as being." See *Identity and Difference,* trans. Joan Stambaugh (New York: Harper and Row, 1974), p. 27.

then for any determined science, rational grammar, linguistic system, etc.), he intends to answer a question which does not admit, on the site where it is posed, the distinction between language and thought. The category is one of the ways for "Being" to say itself or to signify itself, that is, to open language to its exterior, to what is in that it is or such as it is, to truth. "Being" is given in language, precisely, as that which opens language to nonlanguage, beyond what would be only the ("subjective," "empirical," in the anachronistic sense of these words) interior of a language. It is evident—and Benveniste formulates this explicitly—that to reduce the categories of thought to categories of language is to affirm that a language's pretentions to "thought," that is, to truth, universality, the ontological, are unjustifiable. But as it happens, the category of the category is but a systematic setting in place of the pretension to an exterior of language, making it both language and thought because language is examined at the site where the signification "Being" is produced.

Among the several presentations of the categories, the most complete list is probably the one cited by Benveniste (*Categories,* chap. 4, l, b 25). But the text of the *Metaphysics* (E 2 1026 a 33), which also proposes a list of the categories, precedes this list with a kind of principial definition. The categories answer the question of knowing in what ways Being is said, since it is said *pollakōs,* in many ways: "The science which studies this will be prior to physics, and will be primary philosophy and universal in this sense, that it is primary. And it will be the province of this science to study Being *qua* Being (*kai peri tou ontos hēi on, tautēs an eiē theōrēsai*); what it is (*ti esti*), and what the attributes are which belong to it *qua* Being (*kai ta huparkhonta hēi on*). But since the simple term 'being' (*to haplōs legomenon: Haplōs:* simply, frankly, in a word, without detour) is used in various senses (*pollakōs legetai*), of which we saw that one was *accidental (kata sumbebēkos),* and another true (*ōs alēthes*), not-being being used in the sense of false (*kai to mē on ōs to pseudos*); and since besides these there are the categories (*ta skhēmata tēs katēgorias*), e.g. the 'what' (*ti*), quality (*poion*), quantity (*poson*), place (*pou*), time (*pote*), and any other similar meanings (*ei ti allo sēmainei ton tropon touton*)."[10]

Thus, Aristotle knows that he is examining the *ways of saying*[11] being in that it is *pollakōs legomenon.* The categories are the figures (*skhēmata*) according to which the "simple term" being is said in that it is said in several ways, through several tropes. The system of the categories is the system of being's turns of

10. *Metaphysics,* trans. Hugh Tredenick (Cambridge: Harvard University Press, 1933), chap. 6 (2 1026 a 33), p. 299.
11. This is what Aubenque recalls ("Aristote et le langage," p. 104): "Thus it is a fact of language—the equivocality of Being—that Aristotle overtly has in mind and that he attempts to regulate, or as we have said, 'to administer' with a procedure that is itself 'linguistic': the distinction of the multiple significations of the contested word. Conversely, Aristotle nowhere presents the categories as properties of things or as laws of thought. Therefore, one cannot impute to Aristotle an alleged 'unconsciousness' of the relations between his ontology and language."

phrase. It brings the problematic of the analogy of Being, its equivocalness or unequivocalness, into communication with the problematic of the metaphor in general. Aristotle explicitly links these problematics in affirming that the best metaphor coordinates itself to the analogy of proportionality. Which would suffice to prove that the question of metaphor is no more to be asked in the margins of metaphysics than metaphorical style and the use of figures is an accessory embellishment or secondary auxiliary of philosophical discourse.

Therefore, the word category cannot be used as if it had no history. And it is difficult to oppose the category of language and the category of thought as if the idea of category in general (and the idea of the category of language in particular, a notion never criticized by Benveniste) were in some way natural. Is it not necessary, first of all, to ask where it comes from? Is it not necessary to take into account the fact that it was produced on the very terrain where the simple opposition of language and thought was put into question? To know what a category is, what a language is, a theory of language as system, a science of language in general, etc.: none of this would have been possible without the emergence of a value of the category in general, a value whose principal effect was to make problematical the simple face-to-face of two entities that would be known as language and thought. When Benveniste recalls that there is no simple relationship of exteriority between the "container" and the "contained," language and thought, etc., and when he directs this proposition against Aristotle, to what extent does he bow to the fact that the proposition remains within Aristotle's province, at least to the extent that the function of "Being," such as it operates as a representation of the opening of language and thought onto one another, has not been examined in a radically new way?

3. This historical precipitousness is signaled in other ways. The problem having been put thus, Benveniste in effect comes to think that in order to study this *general* problem, "we are fortunate enough to have at our disposal data which one would say were ready for our examination . . . a document of great value for our examination," namely, Aristotle's text on the *Categories*. Everything happens, thus, as if the general problem had nothing specifically Aristotelian about it, as if it were not essentially linked to the history indicated by the name of Aristotle or of his "heritage." Everything happens as if the same problem could have been formulated in the same terms in the absence of any reference to Aristotelian discourse, which, then, would furnish but a happy random example, a very convenient illustration that we would have had the luck to encounter in our library. Then, using the conventional style of the paraphrase to announce the "document of great value for our examination," the linguist has transposed its terms—as if this were of no consequence—into an anachronistic, and singularly Kantian, conceptuality, to the point of the following kinds of approximations, to which we will have to return: "In the examination of these categories, we may dispense with philosophical [technicalities]. We will consider them simply as an inventory of *properties* which a Greek thinker thought could be *predicated*

of a subject and, consequently, as the list of *a priori concepts* which, according to him, organize *experience*. It is a document of great value for our purpose" (p. 57; my italics).

We are in the preamble. The question is asked, but the content of the answer has not yet been elaborated. Thus:

"Let us recall at first the fundamental text, which gives the most complete list of these properties, ten in all (*Categories*, IV):

"Each expression when it is not part of a combination means: the *substance*, or *how much*, or *of what kind*, or *relating to what*, or *where*, or *when*, or *to be in a position*, or *to be in a condition*, or *to do*, or *to undergo*. 'Substance,' for example, 'man,' 'horse';—'how much,' for example, 'two cubits,' 'three cubits'; 'of what kind,' for example, 'white,' 'educated';—'relating to what,' for example, 'double,' 'half,' 'larger';—'where,' for example, 'at the Lyceum,' 'at the market';—'when,' for example, 'today,' 'last year';—'to be in a position,' for example, 'he is lying down,' 'he is seated'; 'to be in a condition,' for example, 'he is shod,' 'he is armed';—'to do,' for example, 'he cuts,' 'he burns';—'to undergo,' for example, 'he is cut,' 'he is burned.'

"Aristotle thus posits the totality of predications that may be made about a being, and he aims to define the logical status of each one of them. Now it seems to us—and we shall try to show—that these distinctions are primarily categories of language and that, in fact, Aristotle, reasoning in the absolute, is simply identifying certain fundamental categories of the language in which he thought. Even a cursory look at the statement of the categories and the examples that illustrate them will easily verify this interpretation, which apparently has not been proposed before. Let us consider the ten terms in order" (p. 57).

"This interpretation, which *apparently* has not been proposed before": prudence was imperative indeed. Aristotle has often been reproached with overlooking the origin of the categories, with having assembled them using an empirical procedure (as Benveniste also will say, and we shall come back to this: "Unconsciously he took as a criterion the empirical necessity of a distinct *expression* for each of his predications"; p. 61), and even with having been content to reflect the grammatical structures of the Greek language. Among all those who have accused Aristotle of empirically formulating what Leibniz called *eine Musterrolle* (a rosterlike catalogue of paradigms), we must first recall Kant. And we must cite a classical text which precisely foreshadows Benveniste's propositions, providing him with his vocabulary if not his concepts. In this text we are concerned not with language or with grammar, only with an *empirical* survey of categories: but categories such as they *present themselves;* and where, then, could they present themselves if not in language? The text is taken from the presentation of the table of categories in the *Analytic of Concepts:*

"In this manner there arise precisely the same number of pure concepts of the understanding which apply *a priori* to objects of intuition in general, as, in the preceding table, there have been found to be logical functions in all possible judgments. For these functions specify the understanding completely, and yield an exhaustive inventory of its powers. These concepts we shall, with Aristotle, call *categories*, for our primary purpose is the same as his, although widely diverging from it in manner of execution.

"Table of Categories . . .

"This then is the list of all original pure concepts of synthesis that the understanding contains within itself *a priori*. Indeed, it is because it contains these concepts that it is called pure understanding; for by them alone can it *understand* anything in the manifold of intuition, that is, think an object of intuition. This division is developed systematically from a common principle, namely, the faculty of judgment (which is the same as the faculty of thought). It has not arisen rhapsodically, as the result of a haphazard search after pure concepts, the complete enumeration of which, as based on induction only, could never be guaranteed. Nor could we, if this were our procedure, discover why just these concepts, and no others, have their seat in the pure understanding. It was an enterprise worthy of an acute thinker like Aristotle to make search for these fundamental concepts. But as he did so on no principle, he merely picked them up as they came his way, and at first procured ten of them, which he called *categories* (predicaments). Afterwards he believed that he had discovered five others, which he added under the name of post-predicaments. But his table still remained defective."[12]

This charge of empiricism is also made by Hegel,[13] Prantl, Hamelin, etc. We are not recalling this fact primarily to indicate that Benveniste elaborates his problematic on the basis of motifs whose history remains hidden for him. The issue is rather this: as there have been several attempts, since Aristotle, to constitute tables of categories which were not the effect or empirical reflection of language, should not the linguist's demonstration have been focused on these attempts? Without such a focus, one acts as if nothing had happened since Aristotle, which is not unthinkable, but demands to be proven, and the task would not be easy. For in this case one also would have to prove, for example, that the Kantian categories are effects of language. At the very least, this problematic would be complicated, and would compel, without prejudicing the results, an entire transformation of the concepts of language and thought utilized by Benveniste. When Kant proposes a system of categories governed by the "faculty of judgment," which is the same as the "faculty of thought," is grammar still the guiding thread of the investigation? This is by no means excluded; but what kind of historical labyrinth are we drawn into then? What kind of entan-

12. Kant, *Critique of Pure Reason*, trans. Norman Kemp Smith (New York: St. Martin's Press, 1965), pp. 113–14.
13. "Er stellte sie so neben einander" (He juxtaposed them.) Cited from the *Lectures on the History of Philosophy* in Bönitz, *Über die Kategorien des Aristoteles* (1853; Darmstaedt: Reed, 1957), p. 38.

glement of linguistic and philosophical structures would have to be taken into account? In effect, the relation of the Kantian categories to language is mediated by an entire philosophical stratification (viz., the entire heritage of Aristotle, which is to say, many things), and by an entire set of linguistic displacements whose complexity is easily glimpsed. The enormousness of this task does not reduce its necessity. This is why, above all, we are not trying to gainsay the question asked by Benveniste, quite the contrary; we are, rather, attempting to analyze certain of its presuppositions, and perhaps to pursue, however minimally, its elaboration.

Not only has Aristotle's empiricism been delineated, or allegedly so, but quite precisely, and of long date, his categories have been recognized as productions of language. The most precise and systematic attempt here was Trendelenburg's (1846).[14] As Aubenque[15] also recalls, Benveniste has an immediate predecessor, whom at times he even seems to paraphrase, in the person of Brunschvicg. In his *Les Ages de l'intelligence* (1939), Brunschvicg also accused Aristotle of taking "the universe of discourse" for "the universe of reason," believing that thereby he could unmask "the entirely verbal character of his ontology," "and doubtless of every ontology," for "Being as Being is the kind of word that cannot be more than a word."[16] "He [Aristotle] seeks knowledge of things only in sensory perception . . . and in language, or, more accurately, in the language that he spoke, whose particularities he *unconsciously* [my italics] elevates into the necessary and universal conditions of thought."[17] Which means, as Brunschvicg says elsewhere citing Serrus, that Aristotle would only have "made explicit a certain spontaneous metaphysics of the Greek language." Aubenque further cites a thesis of Rougier's: "Bergson said that Aristotle's metaphysics is the spontaneous metaphysics of the human mind: it would be more correct to say that it is the spontaneous metaphysics of the Indo-European languages, and of the Greek language in particular."[18]

Cassirer, who has never been cited in this debate, is surely Benveniste's most remarkable and immediate predecessor. In "The Influence of Language on the Development of Thought in the Natural Sciences," he also recalls the previous attempts, notably Trendelenburg's: "When Aristotle, in his analyses of the theory of categories, follows language and commits himself to its guidance, there is nothing to discuss about his procedure, from a modern point of view. But we would demand that he carefully distinguish between the 'universal' and the 'particular,' and that he not make of certain determinations, which find their

14. Cited by Vuillemin, *De la logique*, p. 75, and by Aubenque, "Aristote et le langage," p. 103. On the interpretation of Trendelenburg, and on the debate to which it gave rise, see Bönitz, *Über die Kategorien*, pp. 37ff.
15. "Aristote et le langage," pp. 87–88.
16. Brunschvicg, *Les Ages de l'intelligence* (Paris: Alcan, 1939), p. 65.
17. Ibid., p. 68.
18. Aubenque, "Pseudo-problèmes soulevés et résolus par la logique d'Aristote," in *Actes du Congrès international scientifique* (Paris, 1935).

legitimacy and *raison d'être* in a certain language or in certain groups of languages, characteristics of language and thought in general. If we consider this as historians, it is true that we understand how and why this condition could not possibly have been met by Aristotle. He did not yet have any possibility of comparison and sure delimitation. He could not think outside the Greek language, or against it, but only in it and with it."[19]

And, after a long reference to the works of von Humboldt, Cassirer continues: "As concerns Aristotle, it has long been recognized that the particular categories he distinguishes in Being are in strict relationship with the categories of language and grammar. Aristotle's theory of categories proposes to describe and determine Being in the extent to which Being is made explicit, and in a way is analyzed, in the different forms of statement. But every statement first requires a *subject* to which it can be attached, a thing about which one states a predicate. Therefore the category of Being is placed at the summit of the theory of categories. This Being (*ousia*) is defined by Aristotle in a sense that is both ontological and linguistic . . . Thus, the unity of *physis* and *logos* appears in Aristotle's system not accidentally, but necessarily."[20]

This brief reminder intends merely to suggest that Benveniste's interpretation had been "proposed" more than once before, and that its "verification" at the very least calls for rather "long commentaries." Certain philosophers are often criticized, justifiably, for extracting given scientific propositions from their contexts, or from the work that produced them, and for then imprudently manipulating these propositions for nonscientific ends. But is the text of philosophy any more immediately accessible and open? Can one part of a "document" that we might be "fortunate to have at our disposal" simply be extracted? It is a mistake to believe in the immediate and ahistorical legibility of a philosophical argument, just as it is a mistake to believe that without a prerequisite and highly complex elaboration one may submit a metaphysical text to any grid of scientific deciphering, be it linguistic, psychoanalytic, or other. One of the first precautions must concern the way the concepts that often constitute this "scientific" grid belong to metaphysics. Here, for example, none of the concepts utilized by Benveniste could have seen day, including that of linguistics as a science and the very notion of language, without a certain small "document" on the categories. Philosophy is not only *before* linguistics as one might find oneself *facing* a new science, a new way of seeing or a new object; it is also *before* linguistics, preceding linguistics by virtue of all the concepts philosophy still provides it, for better or for worse; and it sometimes intervenes in the most critical, and occasionally in the most dogmatic, least scientific, operations of the linguist. Naturally if there is a noncritical precipitousness by the philosopher to manip-

19. TN. Cassirer's article first appeared in a shorter version in the *Journal of Philosophy* 39, no. 12. Derrida cites the expanded French version which appeared in *Journal de Psychologie normale et pathologique* 39, no. 2, p. 136.
20. Ibid., pp. 137–39.

ulate scientific propositions whose actual production eludes him, and if, inversely, there is a haste on the part of the scientist in his approach to the philosophical text, the laurels go to the rhapsodists who disqualify the parts of a philosophical text whose mechanics are unknown to them, using a scientific alibi on which they have never set foot or hand.

Transference

Transcription, transposition, projection of the categories of language into the categories of thought: this is how Benveniste defines Aristotle's *unconscious* operation, and, inversely, the symmetrical decoding which he consciously sets himself to undertake: "The ten categories can now be transcribed in linguistic terms. Each of them is given by its designation and followed by its equivalent: *ousia* ('substance'), substantive; *poion, poson* ('what kind, in what number'), adjectives derived from pronouns like the Latin *qualis* and *quantus; pros ti* ('relating to what'), comparative adjective; *pou* ('where'), *pote* ('when'), adverbs of place and time; *keisthai* ('to be placed'), middle voice; *ekhein* ('to be in a state'), the perfect; *poiein* ('to do'), active voice; *paskhein* ('to undergo'), passive voice" (p. 60).

Thus, the linguist *transcribes* in terms of language what the philosopher previously, "unconsciously" *transposed,* or *projected* from language into terms of thought:

"We have thus an answer to the question raised in the beginning which had led us to this analysis. We asked ourselves what was the nature of the relationship between categories of thought and categories of language. No matter how much validity Aristotle's categories have as categories of thought, they turn out to be transposed from categories of language. It is what one can *say* which delimits and organizes what one can think. Language provides the fundamental configuration of the properties of things as recognized by the mind. This table of predication informs us above all about the class structure of a particular language.

"It follows that what Aristotle gave us as a table of general and permanent conditions is only a conceptual projection of a given linguistic state" (p. 61).

Transcription, here, does not amount to a *translation,* that is to an *intra-linguistic* movement assuring the transport of a signified from one language to another, from one system of signifiers to another. Thus, one cannot call translation the passage from a categorial (nonlinguistic) structure said to be of "thought," to a linguistic categorial structure said to be of "language." The sense of "transcription," therefore, refers back to what is called "transposition" or "projection" further on. The linguist's transcription seems to move in the opposite direction, bringing back into language what allegedly escaped it by means of transposition and projection.

What about this strange transference? How could it have been produced? Along the lines of what necessity? Benveniste recognizes this unique correspondence that one hesitates, for obvious reasons, to call *homology;* but he examines neither the status of the operation, nor the conditions of what lures one into it, nor the space or medium in which projection, and then transcription are produced: for example, the field of categoriality in general. In order to avoid this "philosophical technicality," which he sets aside at the outset, he certainly does not ask himself by means of what aberration the names of the categories of thought came to be given to (what were but) the names of categories of language. (A double recourse, then, to homonymy and synonymy: Aristotle has given the same name to different things, thought and language, and different names, thought and language, to what is fundamentally the same thing, language. How can the same name be given to distinguishable concepts and things? How can different names be given to identical concepts and things? This question, we will note in passing, is also explicitly asked by Aristotle. Precisely in the *Organon,* at the opening of the text on the *Categories.* And when the question concerns its own element, that is, language in general, it takes on a totally singular form. Among many other things, it assumes it possible to arrive at some clarity concerning what language and thought might *be* or *mean,* this alternative already concentrating and reflecting the entire problem.)

Throughout Benveniste's analysis, only a single sentence seems to be given as an explanation and to have some relation to these last questions: "Unconsciously he [Aristotle] took as a criterion the empirical necessity of a distinct *expression* for each of his predications" (p. 61).

What does "empirical" mean here? Taken literally, this explanation would suppose that Aristotle, having at his disposition, moreover, and outside of language, predicates, or *conceivable* classes of predicates, and faced with the *empirical* necessity of expressing these contents (the word *expression* is underlined by Benveniste), confused the distinction of predicates and the distinction of expressions. He is alleged to have taken the chain of expressing unities for the chain of expressed unities. "Unconsciously" and without wanting to, he has thus taken the "class of forms," such as the system of language offers it, for the system of the expressed or the expressible. (And supposing, moreover, that this is so, is there not in the practice of a language, in the belonging to a language, a structural necessity for this "unconscious" to be produced, such that what is pointed out in Aristotle would be but the confirmation of the general law of unconsciousness that is recalled in the preamble?)

We must insist upon the adjective "empirical." Although grammatically, "empirical" qualifies "necessity," it may find itself being deported by means of the word "necessity"—both as concerns its construction, and the elements of the phrase which depend upon it—in the direction of the word "expression" or "distinct expression" ("empirical necessity of a distinct expression"). These two possibilities open two hypotheses.

In the first hypothesis, the most likely one, it is the *necessity* to express (each of the predicates) that remains empirical. Empirical, then, is not only the situation within a language in general, and then within a natural language, but also the tie between the structure of a predicate thought outside of language and its "expression" in language. Language in general and natural language then become, following the most traditional motif, the contingent exteriority of thought and of conceivable and signifiable meaning. A distinction can still be made, of course, between logos (or language in general) and a specific natural language in order to assert that the empirical necessity no longer concerns the tie of thought and language in general, but the tie of a universal logos, in a way, and of a natural language. Although not identical, these two possibilities are in the strictest analogy. They both amount to positing language as the empirical shell of meaning in general, of essential, universal, etc. thought or language.[21] In this first hypothesis, Benveniste himself can only repeat the operation he imputes to Aristotle: to distinguish *saying* from *thinking* (these are his words), and to consider that there is only an empirical relation between them. The only difference: Aristotle would maintain the distinction in order to remain within it, believing that he is concerned with thinking where it is only a question of saying; Benveniste would maintain the distinction in order to demonstrate that by substitution articulations of language have been taken for articulations of thought.

This first reading of "empirical necessity of a distinct expression" finds itself confirmed in several propositions of the same text, notably in its conclusions: "Surely it is not by chance that modern epistemology does not try to set up a table of categories. It is more productive to conceive of the mind as a virtuality than as a framework, as a dynamism than as a structure. It is a fact that, to satisfy the requirements of scientific methods, thought everywhere adopts the same procedures in whatever language it chooses to describe experience. In this sense, it becomes independent, not of language, but of particular linguistic structures. Chinese thought may well have invented categories as specific as the *tao*, the *yin*, and the *yang*; it is nonetheless able to assimilate the concepts of dialectical materialism or quantum mechanics without the structure of the Chinese language proving a hindrance. No type of language can by itself alone foster or hamper the activity of the mind. The advance of thought is linked much more closely to the capacities of man, to general conditions of culture, and to the organization of society than to the particular nature of a language. But the possibility of thought is linked to the faculty of speech, for language is a structure informed with signification, and to think is to manipulate the signs of language" (pp. 63–64).

Since they are certainly inseparable from language in general, the "advance of thought" and the "activity of the mind" cannot be linked essentially to a particular language. Which amounts to acknowledging that there can be "contents" of thought without any essential link to the "forms" of a particular lan-

21. In the extent to which this essentially metaphysical presupposition *also* remains at work in Benveniste's text, it is no longer paradoxical that the *philosophical* objections that his project already has encountered are fundamentally of the same type.

guage. Under these conditions, neither Aristotle, nor any of the philosophers who have attempted to constitute a table of categories of thought principially independent of the categories of language, appear to have been wrong in principle. Thought is not language, or *a* language, Benveniste seems to admit here. But Aristotle deluded himself *in practice:* because he believed in a *table*, and especially because, through unconsciousness and empiricism, he confused what he should have distinguished.

We are still with the first hypothesis. Is it not strange to qualify as empirical the necessity of an expression, the necessity to bring the conceivable to statement in a given language? In the last analysis, the value of empiricity has never been related to anything but the variability of sensory and individual givens, and by extension to every passivity or activity without concept; for example, to cite Leibniz, to "a simple practice without theory."[22] Now, if anyone ever has been able to concede that there was any pure empiricity in the practice of language, this could only be so, finally, as concerns the sensory and singular event of a material (phonic or graphic) signifier; even supposing that such a pure, nonrepeatable event, escaping every formal generality, ever intervenes in linguistic or semiotic practice. Above all, how can one affirm the empiricity of the movement which leads to signifying in general and to signifying within a language, and that does so with recourse to an organization of forms, a distribution of classes, etc.? Finally, on the basis of what system, and also from whence historically, do we receive and understand—before even positing the empiricity of signification—the signification of empiricity? On this matter no analysis will either circumvent or exclude the tribunal of Aristotelianism. This does not imply that Aristotle is the author or origin of the concept of empiricity, even if the opposition of the empirical and the theoretical (the a priori, the scientific, the objective, the systematic, etc.) in one way or another envelops Aristotle's metaphysics. Even if such a concept is not fixed once and for all in an "origin," one cannot comprehend the history and system of its mutations or transformations without taking into account the general code of metaphysics, and within this code, the decisive mark of Aristotelianism. In *Die Zeit des Weltbildes*[23] (1938), Heidegger notes that "it is Aristotle who was the first to understand what *empeiria* signified." If one wished to use the word "empirical" in a sense totally foreign to Aristotle's, or to its sense in the history of philosophy, one explicitly would have to undertake the labor of this transformation. Nothing in Benveniste's text signals or announces such a displacement.

But then, it will be said, one cannot even employ in passing a small word as innocent as *empirical*, a word everyone understands ordinarily, in a demonstration that aims further and higher. I would be tempted to answer thus: given what is at stake in this demonstration, and given its strategically decisive char-

22. In Leibniz, *Discourse on Metaphysics, Correspondence with Arnauld and Monadology,* trans. George Montgomery (LaSalle, Ill.: Open Court Publishing Co., 1968), sec. 28.
23. French translation in *Chemins qui mènent nulle part* (Paris: Gallimard, 1957).

acter, if certain terms, at secondary sites of the itinerary, could be advanced without infinite precautions, it would certainly not be this one, for in fact it bears the entire weight of the critical argument.

Second hypothesis: "empirical necessity" determines less the "expression" than, more indirectly, the expression in that it is "distinct for each of its predications." This being the case, Aristotle did not only, or essentially, accede to the so-called empirical necessity of *expressing* predicates; rather, in acceding to it, in establishing the list of classes, he proceeded in empirical fashion. Not only the project but its formation, the procedures of its practice, remained empirical.

Here the argument would be very weak. On the one hand it would amount to the most traditional philosophical objection; on the other hand, it would contradict what is most convincing and most novel in Benveniste's analysis. As Vuillemin quite correctly has emphasized,[24] this analysis demonstrates in effect that (1) the table of categories is systematic and not rhapsodic; (2) by operating a *selection* in the categories of language, the table is no longer their simple carbon copy or empirical reflection.

The Transcendental and Language

We have not yet come to the major area of the problem. This is displayed fully when Benveniste proposes that the "remark can be elaborated further." We are

24. Vuillemin, *De la logique*, pp. 76–77. A long citation is necessary. "This demonstration [Benveniste's] possesses a double merit.

"First, it brings to notice the organization of the table of categories, which had always been reproached for its rhapsodic character. The first six categories all refer to nominal forms, the four last to verbal forms. Within this division, with the exception of one case, the enumeration proceeds by opposition of pairs. The category of the substantives seems to be the exception to this rule; but this category itself is found to be subdivided into proper nouns (primary substances) and common nouns (secondary substances). The adjectives *poson* and *poion* correspond (*hosos/hoios, tosos/toios*), as do the adverbs *pou* and *pote* (*hou/hote, tou/tote*). The *pros ti*, which is presented alone, only expresses the fundamental property of Greek adjectives, that of providing a comparative. As for the four verbal forms, if *poiein* and *paskhein* (to do/to undergo) visibly constitute an opposition corresponding to that of the active and the passive, *keisthai* (to be in a position) and *ekhein* (to be in a condition) equally form a pair, when they are interpreted as categories of language: 'There are, indeed, various relationships, both formal and functional between the Greek perfect and the middle voice, which as inherited from Indo-European, formed a complex system; for example, an active perfect, *gegona* goes with middle present, *gignomai*' (Benveniste, p. 60).

"In the second place, it is concluded that Aristotle, believing that he is classing notions, in reality has classed categories of language, such that the particularities of the Greek language have dominated the fate in philosophy in the West.

"This second conclusion, however, goes beyond what the argument has demonstrated. In effect, it cannot legitimately be concluded from the fact that a philosophy borrows from the oppositions of a language the concepts and oppositions recognized as fundamental for thought not only that the language proposes its suggestions to thought, but also that it is impossible to think that which is not expressed in this language; moreover, it cannot legitimately be concluded that the table of the categories of thought reflects that of the

in the final pages, at the moment when the general propositions seem fulfilled and the demonstration made: "This table of predications informs us above all about the class structure of a particular language. It follows that what Aristotle gave us as a table of general and permanent conditions is only a conceptual projection of a given linguistic state. This remark can be elaborated further. Beyond the Aristotelian terms, above that categorization, there is the notion of 'being' which envelops everything. Without being a predicate itself, 'being' is the condition of all predicates. All the varieties of 'being-such,' of 'state,' all the possible views of 'time,' etc., depend on the notion of 'being.' Now here again, this concept reflects a very specific linguistic quality" (p. 61).

We can ascertain the thrust of this kind of postscript. It does much more than "elaborate further" a remark. We are finally touching upon the possibility of the field of categories, the very opening of the Aristotelian project: the constitution of a table of the figures of predication which provides the turns of phrase for the "simple term 'being' " which is "used in various senses." This time, we are no longer dealing with one category or, at least, one category among others[25]

---

categories of language. To go this far, it would have been necessary to show that the arrangement of categories borrowed from language is also the *complete* arrangement of categories as concerns language. In the opposite case, there will be a selection, and if the philosopher chooses from the linguistic categories, it is just because his choice is no longer dictated uniquely by the consideration of language. Now this is indeed what happens, since no one could allege that the structure of the categories of the Greek language is exhaustively laid out in Aristotle's arrangement.

"In fact, Aristotle's table follows a logical articulation which, at the same time, possesses an ontological bearing."

The two principal arguments (systematicity and selection), to which it is difficult not to subscribe, nevertheless are elaborated here on a terrain which seems to us to be highly problematical. For example: does philosophy *"borrow"* from language? And what does *borrow* mean here? Can one borrow "from the oppositions of a language the concepts and oppositions recognized as fundamental for thought" as one borrows a tool? A tool whose value, moreover, has been recognized by thought? How is one to understand that "language proposes its suggestions to thought"? The formula is taken up again, and assumed to a greater extent, elsewhere: "Morphology and syntax thus reunited indeed constitute a language, but this philosophical language separates itself as much as necessary from the suggestions primally imposed by the Greek language" (p. 225). The general presupposition of this discourse seems to be the—symmetrical—opposite of that which supports Benveniste's analyses (or at least when the latter proceeds as a linguist and not as a philosopher of the "activity of the mind" and of the "vitality of thought"): the contents of thought are essentially, principially, and structurally independent of language, despite the "borrowings" and "suggestions." As it is stated, the "logical" and the "ontological" have no intrinsic link with the linguistic. The specular symmetry of the present theses, their profound resemblance in an in(de)terminable opposition, from the outset and by itself would invite a reelaboration of the problem; a reelaboration in which one would not in advance take as given, and as if it went without saying, with a feeling of familiarity, mastery, and "knowledge," the access to the "essence" of "thought" and of "language," to their opposition or identity. This is only one example.

25. This point being ascertained (and it suffices for what concerns us here), we cannot become engaged in the complexity of its context. Analysis and references may be found in Aubenque's *Le Problème de l'être chez Aristote*, notably pp. 171ff. "As can be seen, essence

in the system; it can no longer be a matter of "projecting" or "transcribing" one determined category into another, that is, of proceeding more or less empirically. The elaboration of the remark leaps forward: in one move it goes beyond the field designated in the title and in the initial formulation of the problem. What Benveniste very quickly calls the "notion of 'being' " is no longer one category that is simply homogeneous with all the others: it is the transcategorial condition of the categories. Benveniste recognizes this: "Beyond the Aristotelian terms, above that categorization, there is the notion of 'being' which envelops everything. Without being a predicate itself, 'being' is the condition of all predicates" (p. 61). We must read this reminder within the immense vein which flows from the *Sophist* (which Benveniste's phrase reminds us of, almost literally: "Many forms differing from one another but included in one greater form, and again . . . one form evolved by the union of many wholes and of many forms entirely apart and separate"),[26] through Aristotle's affirmation that Being is not a genre, through the affirmation found in the *Critique of Pure Reason* (" '*Being*' is obviously not a real predicate; that is, not a concept of something which could be added to the concept of a thing. It is merely the positing of a thing, or of certain determinations, as existing in themselves."),[27] and through the questions asked by Heidegger, notably in "Kant's Thesis on Being" (*Kants These über das Sein*).

"Being," therefore, is not on the table. Nor is it elsewhere. The linguist or the logician who wishes to establish a rule of transliteration or correspondence between categories of language and categories of thought will never encounter something he might simply call "Being."

What Benveniste discovers then, by virtue of this further "elaboration," is the absolutely unique relationship between the transcendental and language. Here we are taking the word "transcendental" in its most rigorous accepted sense, in its most avowed "technicalness," precisely as it was fixed in the course of the development of the Aristotelian problematic of the categories, including whatever remains beyond the categories. Transcendental means transcategorial. Literally: "that which *transcends* every genre." (Despite the contextual differences, this definition of a word undoubtedly invented by the Chancellor Philip, 1128, also suits the Kantian and Husserlian concepts of the transcendental.)

What about the transcendental value of "Being" as concerns language? Such is the question now.

---

itself is presented here as a predicate, even though it is defined elsewhere as that which is always subject and never predicate (*Prior Analytics* 1, 27, 43 a 25; *Physics* 1, 7, 190 a 34; *Metaphysics* Z, 3, 1028 a 36). But essence, which in effect is the subject of every conceivable attribute, secondarily can be attributed to itself, and it is in this sense that it is a category, that is, one of the figures of predication, one of the possible meanings of the copula." See also pp. 190ff.

26. TN. Plato, *The Sophist*, trans. Harold North Fowler (Cambridge: Harvard University Press, 1921), 253d (p. 401).

27. *Critique*, p. 504.

In order to assert that "Being" is fundamentally rooted in a very specific natural language, Benveniste emphasizes that all languages do not dispose of the verb "to be": "Greek not only possesses a verb 'to be' (which is by no means a necessity in every language), but it makes very peculiar uses of this verb" (p. 61). This singularity is described in a paragraph that we must read, in order to indicate several problematic focal points: "It [Greek] gave it [the verb 'to be'] a logical function, that of the copula (Aristotle himself had remarked earlier that in that function the verb did not actually signify anything, that it operated simply as a synthesis), and consequently, this verb received a larger extension than any other whatever. In addition, 'to be' could become, thanks to the article, a nominal notion, treated as a thing; it gave rise to varieties, for example its present participle, which itself had been made a substantive, and in several kinds (*to on; hoi ontes; ta onta*); it could serve as a predicate itself, as in the locution *to ti ēn einai* designating the conceptual essence of a thing, not to mention the astonishing diversity of particular predicates with which it could be construed, by means of case forms and prepositions . . . Listing this abundance of uses would be endless; but they really are facts of language, of syntax, and of derivation. Let us emphasize this, because it is in a linguistic situation thus characterized that the whole Greek metaphysics of 'being' was able to come into existence and develop—the magnificent images of the poem of Parmenides as well as the dialectic of the *Sophist*. The language did not, of course, give direction to the metaphysical definition of 'being'—each Greek thinker has his own—but it made it possible to set up 'being' as an objectifiable notion which philosophical thought could handle, analyze, and define just as any other concept" (pp. 61–62).

1. If "to be," at least as a copula, does "not actually signify anything," because it unfolds its extension to infinity, then it is no longer linked to the determined form of a word, or rather, of a name (a name in the Aristotelian sense, which includes nouns and verbs), that is to the unity of a *phōnē sēmantike*[28] armed with a content of meaning. Is it not, then, an impossible or contradictory operation to define the copula's presence in one language and its *absence* in another? We will come back to this.

2. How can one be sure that these "are facts of language, of syntax, and of derivation"? As yet no definition of language, nor of the self-immanence of the system of language in general, has been given. What about this immanence, this inclusion *within* language of a structure or an operation whose effect—whose linguistic effect, if you like—is to open language onto its exterior, to articulate the linguistic with the nonlinguistic? And does so, in the case of "to be," and everything resulting from it, *by definition* and *par excellence?*

3. How can one qualify as "images" (a very derivative philosophical name, charged with history) the pathways, crossroads, bifurcation, palintrope, sphere, veil, axis, wheel, sun, moon, etc., of Parmenides' poem, that is, to keep to this

28. See "White Mythology," below.

one characteristic, of a text which in positing a certain sameness of "to think" and "to be" has *remarked* opening within language, the opening to the presence of Being, to truth, the opening onto that which always has *represented an infraction* into language's closure on itself?[29]

4. "The language did not, of course, give direction to the metaphysical definition of 'being'—each Greek thinker has his own." How can one reconcile this statement with all the statements which reduce the categories of thought to the categories of language? What does "give direction" mean in this case? Would the "metaphysical definition of 'being' " now be completely free as concerns language? If the linguistic constraint has not weighed down upon "the metaphysical definition of 'being' " (a highly obscure notion), on what has it borne? On a formal function without semantic content? But if so, how can this be reserved exclusively for the Greek grammar or lexicology? A moment ago we noted that this problem still awaits us. Finally, if language has so little given "direction" to the "metaphysical definition" of " 'being' " that "each Greek thinker has his own," what then has language governed in philosophy? Where then is the lure which has tricked the philosopher into taking language for thought? And can one say (but what does one say in this case?) that "each Greek thinker has his own"? Never has the constraint of language been so loose. And what about the inheritors of "Greek metaphysics" who have thought-spoken-written in Latin or Germanic? None of this comes close to demonstrating the absence of linguistic constraints on philosophy, but it surely demonstrates the necessity of reelaborating the current concept of linguistic constraint. The obscurity and contradictions are condensed when Benveniste uses the notions of "predisposition" and "vocation," just as Vuillemin spoke of "borrowings" and "suggestions": "All we wish to show here is that the linguistic structure of Greek predisposed the notion of 'being' to a philosophical vocation" (p. 63).

5. Finally, if, as is true, "without being a predicate itself, 'being' is the condition of all predicates," then it is no longer possible to believe that "philosophical thought could handle, analyze, and define [it] just as any other concept" (p. 62).

In order to "elaborate further this remark," one should not only enlarge the domain of the demonstration, but also overturn the structure of the ground thus far gained. Without the transcategoriality of "to be," which "envelops everything," the transition between categories of language and categories of thought would not have been possible, either in one sense or the other, for Aristotle or for Benveniste.

---

29. TN. In what follows the reader should keep in mind that in Greek, German, and French infinitives can be used as substantives, while they cannot in English. Thus the point in Parmenides' poem is the sameness of "the 'to think' " (*noein, denken, penser*) and "the 'to be' " (*einai, sein, être*).

The Remainder as Supplement:
On the Third Person Singular of the
Present Indicative of the Verb "To Be"

These difficulties propagate their effects; they mark the counterproof proposed by Benveniste. If Greek metaphysics, with its pretensions to truth, universality, etc., depends upon a particular linguistic fact which has gone unnoticed by philosophers, then the examination of a different language should confirm the demonstration.

"That this is primarily a matter of language will be better realized if the behavior of this same notion in a different language is considered. It is best to choose a language of an entirely different type to compare with the Greek, because it is precisely in the internal organization of their categories that linguistic types differ the most. Let us only state that what we are comparing here are facts of linguistic expression, not conceptual developments.

"In the Ewe language (spoken in Togo), which we have chosen for this contrast, the notion of 'to be,' or what we shall designate as such, is divided among several verbs" (p. 62).

Let us note immediately that this analysis, (which strangely proposes to keep to "facts of linguistic expression" without considering "conceptual developments"), is not at all concerned with the pure and simple *absence* of the verb "to be," as one might have thought—"Greek not only possesses a verb 'to be' (which is by no means a necessity in every language)"—but rather another distribution, another division of this function "among several verbs." Now, in the Indo-European languages as well, the "ontological" function is not entrusted to a single verb or to a single verbal form.[30]

The analysis of the Ewe language will consist of locating, in a language without the "verb 'to be,' " a multiplicity of analogous functions otherwise distributed. What resources of translation are put to work here? Benveniste asks this question himself; but in disqualifying his own description as "a bit contrived," he does not wonder how such a contrivance is possible and why it is not totally absurd or inoperative:

"This description of the state of things in Ewe is a bit contrived. It is made from the standpoint of *our* language and not, as it should have been, within the framework of the language itself. Within the morphology or syntax of Ewe, nothing brings these five verbs into relationship with one another. It is in connection with our own linguistic usages that we discover something common to them. But that is precisely the advantage of this 'egocentric' comparison: it throws light on ourselves; it shows us, among that variety of uses of 'to be' in Greek, a phenomenon peculiar to the Indo-European languages which is not at

---

30. Benveniste recalls this himself, p. 63. See also Heidegger, "On the Grammar and Etymology of the Word 'Being,' " in *An Introduction to Metaphysics*, trans. Ralph Mannheim (New York: Anchor Books, 1961), pp. 42ff. All further citations are to this edition.

all a universal situation or a necessary condition. Of course the Greek thinkers in their turn acted upon the language, enriched the meanings, and created new forms. It is indeed from philosophical reflection on 'being' that the abstract substantive derived from *einai* arose; we see it being created in the course of history: at first as *essia* in Dorian Pythagorism and in Plato, then as *ousia*, which won out. All we wish to show here is that the linguistic structure of Greek predisposed the notion of 'being' to a philosophical vocation. By comparison, the Ewe language offers us only a narrow notion and particularized uses. We cannot say what place 'being' holds in Ewe metaphysics, but a priori, the notion must be articulated in a completely different way" (p. 63).

Is there a "metaphysics" outside the Indo-European organization of the function "to be"? This is not in the least an ethnocentric question. It does not amount to envisaging that other languages might be *deprived* of the surpassing mission of philosophy and metaphysics but, on the contrary, avoids projecting outside the West very determined forms of "history" and "culture."

So we should ask how the absence of the (unique) verbal function of "to be" in any given language is to be read. Is such an absence possible and how is it to be interpreted? This is not the absence of a word from a lexicon; in the first place because the function "to be" is conveyed by several words in the Indo-European languages. No more is it the absence of a determined semantic content, of a simple signified, since "to be" signifies nothing determinable; thus, it is even less the absence of a thing that could be referred to.

The question has been asked by Heidegger: "Let us suppose that this indeterminate meaning of Being does not exist and that we also do not understand what this meaning means. What then? Would there merely be a noun and a verb less in our language? No. *There would be no language at all.* No being *as such* would disclose itself in words, it would no longer be possible to invoke it and speak about it in words. For to speak of a being as such includes: to understand it in advance as a being, that is, to understand its Being. Assuming that we did not understand Being at all, assuming that the word 'Being' did not even have its vaporous meaning, there would not be a single word."[31]

If there were an ethnocentrism of Heideggerian thought, it would never be simplistic enough to refuse to call language (at least in a sense not derived from the philosophical tradition) every non-Western system of signification; these pronouncements must have another aim. If we recall that elsewhere Heidegger distinguishes the sense of "Being" from the word "Being" and the concept of "Being," this amounts to saying that it is no longer the presence in a langue of the word or (signified) concept "Being" or "to be" that he makes into the condition for the Being-language of language, but an entirely other possibility which remains to be defined. The very concept of "ethnocentrism" would pro-

31. TN. I have consistently modified Mannheim's translation to conform with the general practice of using being and Being for *seiend* and *Sein*.

vide us with no critical assurance for as long as the elaboration of this other possibility remains incomplete.

In order to approach this possibility—and as we cannot systematically examine all of Heidegger's text here—let us come back to Benveniste. But this time let us consider another essay than the one we have been concerned with until now: "The Linguistic Functions of 'To Be' and 'To Have,' "[32] published two years later. This essay's point of departure is precisely the absence, or, to use Benveniste's word, the fact that the verb "to be" is "missing" not only in certain non-Indo-European languages, but especially in certain typical operations of "our" languages.[33] "The study of sentences with the verb 'to be' is obscured by the difficulty, indeed the impossibility, of setting up a satisfactory definition of the nature and functions of the verb 'to be.' First of all, is 'to be' a verb? If it is one, why is it so often missing? And if it is not, how does it happen that it has taken on the status and forms of a verb while remaining what is called a 'substantive-verb'?" (p. 163).

Benveniste then offers as evidence what he calls a "contradiction." To us, this also seems to be a contradiction between Benveniste's two texts, or at least between the affirmation that the verb "to be" does not belong to every language and the affirmation that the *equivalence* of verb-phrases "to be" is a universal phenomenon. Thus, it is this substitutive equivalence that concentrates within it the entire difficulty: "The fact that there is a 'nominal sentence' characterized by the absence of the verb and that this is a universal phenomenon seems to contradict the fact, also very widespread, that it has a sentence with the verb 'to be' as its equivalent. The data seem to elude analysis, and the whole problem is still so poorly worked out that one finds no firm ground to stand on. The cause for this is probably that one reasons, implicitly at least, as if the verb 'to be' were a logical and chronological continuation of a stage of language which did not have such a verb. But this linear reasoning collides at all points with the contradictions of linguistic reality without, however, satisfying any theoretical necessity" (p. 163).

One cannot but subscribe to this last proposition. But does it not invalidate certain affirmations of the text on the categories? How is one to conceive now that *all* languages dispose of an equivalent of sentences with the verb "to be"?

1. The function of the "copula" or of the "grammatical mark of identity" is absolutely distinct from the "full-fledged" use of the verb "to be." "*The two have coexisted* and will always be able to coexist since they are completely different. But in many languages they have merged" (p. 163). Consequently, "when one speaks of the verb 'to be,' it is necessary to state specifically if it is a matter of the grammatical notion or the lexical. Without this distinction, the problem is insoluble and cannot even be stated clearly" (pp. 163–64).

32. Also in *Problems in General Linguistics.*
33. From this point of view one could study the rarefaction of "to be" and "is" in Mallarmé's language. See "The Double Session," in *Dissemination.*

But Benveniste demonstrates the universality of the grammatical function of the copula with an abundance of examples. This function is found in every language that does not possess the verb "to be" in its lexical presence.

2. In all languages, a certain function comes to supplement the lexical "absence" of the verb "to be." In truth, this supplementarity makes good an absence only for those who, like ourselves, practice a language in which the two functions—grammatical and lexical—have "merged" (at least to a certain extent), along with all the fundamental "historical" consequences this entails. Is not what we perceive, outside the West, as a supplement of absence or as vicariousness in fact an original possibility which comes to be added to the lexical function of the verb "to be"—and thus equally well does without it, indeed even dispensing with any reference to it? And does so even within Indo-European?

The most general form of this supplement of copula is the nominal sentence: "Here the most generally found expression does not require any verb. This is the 'nominal sentence' as it appears today in Russian or Hungarian, for example, in which a zero morpheme, the pause, assures the conjunction of the terms and asserts that they are identical, no matter what the modality of this assertion may be: a formal equation ('Rome is the capital of Italy'), class inclusion ('the dog is a mammal'), or class membership ('Pierre is French'), etc.

"What matters is to see clearly that there is no connection, either by nature or by necessity, between the verbal notion of 'to exist, really to be there' and the function of the 'copula.' One need not ask how it happens that the verb 'to be' can be lacking or omitted. This is to reason in reverse. The real question should be the opposite: how is it that there is a verb 'to be' which gives verbal expression and lexical consistency to a logical relationship in an assertive utterance?" (p. 164).

Thus it happens that the lexical absence is "supplemented" only by absence period, the grammatical function of "to be" then being fulfilled by the blank of a spacing, by a somehow erased punctuation, by a *pause:* an oral interruption, that is, an arrest of the voice (is this then an *oral phenomenon?*), that no *graphic* sign, in the usual sense of the word, no written plenitude could come to mark. The absence of "to be," the absence of this singular lexeme, is absence itself. In general, is not the semantic value of *absence* dependent on the lexical-semantic value of "to be"? It is within the horizon of this question that we would have to analyze what Benveniste again calls a "supplementary feature," that is, a feature that is only "probable," that neither *exists in* nor *consists of* anything but a certain suspension: "As is known, ancient Semitic did not have a verb 'to be.' It sufficed to juxtapose the nominal terms of the utterance in order to get a nominal sentence with the supplementary feature—probable, although not graphemically represented—of a pause between the terms. The example of Russian and Hungarian and other languages gives this pause the value of an element in the utterance; it is actually the sign of the predication. It is probable that wherever the structure of a language permits the construction of a predicative utterance by the juxtaposition of two nominal forms in a free order, one should grant that a pause separates them" (p. 165).

3. Another very common form of this supplement of copula is syntactic play with the pronoun, for example repeating it at the end of a proposition: *man yas man*, "I am young" (I young I), *san yas san*, "you are young," in certain Oriental dialects, for example Altaic: *ol bay ol*, "he is rich" (he rich he). "This syntactic assigning of the pronoun to the function of a copula is a phenomenon whose general significance must be emphasized" (p. 166).

Henceforth, the process of objectification leads to a constant privileging of the third person singular. The hidden relationship between such a privilege and the law of the supplement of copula unfolds a problem that linguistics and ontology *as such* cannot but designate from afar, primarily because in principle they are subject, as *science* and as *philosophy*, to the authority of the *is* whose possibility is to be examined. Let us illustrate this with a simple juxtaposition.

Here we must consult another essay by Benveniste, "The Nominal Sentence":[34] "Since the memorable article (*Mémoires de la Société Linguistique de Paris*, 14) in which A. Meillet defined the situation of the nominal sentence in Indo-European, thus giving it its first linguistic status, several studies relating in particular to the ancient Indo-European languages have contributed to the historical description of this type of utterance. Briefly characterized, the nominal sentence consists of a predicate nominative, without a verb or copula, and it is considered the normal expression in Indo-European where a possible verbal form would have been the *third person of the present indicative of 'to be.'* These definitions have been widely used, even outside the domain of Indo-European, but without leading to a parallel study of the conditions that made this linguistic situation possible. The theory of this highly peculiar syntactic phenomenon has not by any means kept pace with the gradual realization of how widespread it is.

"This type of sentence is not limited to one family or to certain families of languages. Those in which it has been noticed are only the first of a list that can now be considerably lengthened. The nominal sentence is encountered not only in Indo-European, in Semitic, in Finno-Ugric, and in Bantu, but also in the most diverse languages: Sumerian, Egyptian, Caucasian, Altaic, Dravidian, Indonesian, Siberian, Amerindian, etc. . . . . To what necessity is the nominal sentence bound for it to be produced in similar ways by so many different languages, and how does it happen—the question will seem strange but the strangeness is in the facts—that the verb of existence, out of all other verbs, has this privilege of being present in an utterance in which it does not appear? As soon as one probes further into the problem, one is forced to envisage the relationships of the verb and noun as a whole, and then the particular nature of the verb 'to be' " (pp. 131–32).

34. Also in *Problems in General Linguistics*.

This emphasis on the third person singular of the present indicative of the verb "to be" seems also to have left its mark on the history of the languages in which "to be" bore a lexical presence. In this case the function of the copula governed the interpretation of the meaning of "to be" invisibly, in having always somehow worked it from within.

Heidegger: "We understand the verbal substantive '*Being*' through the infinitive, which in turn is related to the 'is' and its diversity that we have described. The definite and particular verb form 'is,' the *third person singular of the present indicative*, has here a pre-eminent rank. We understand 'Being' not in regard to the 'thou art,' 'you are,' 'I am,' or 'they would be,' though all of these, just as much as 'is,' represent verbal inflections of 'to be.' 'To be' is for us the infinitive of 'is.' And involuntarily, almost as though nothing else were possible, we explain the infinitive 'to be' to ourselves through the 'is.'

"Accordingly, 'Being' has the meaning indicated above, recalling the Greek view of the essence of Being (*Wesen des Seins*) hence a determinateness which has not just dropped on us accidentally from somewhere but has dominated our historical Being-there (*geschichtliches Dasein*)" (p. 77).

However eternally troubled and worked upon from within, the fusion of the grammatical and lexical functions of "to be" certainly bears an essential relation to the history of metaphysics and to everything coordinated to this history in the West.

There is a strong, indeed barely repressible, temptation to consider the growing predominance of the formal function of the copula as a process of falling, an abstraction, degradation, or emptying of the semantic plenitude of the lexeme "to be" and of all lexemes which, likewise, have let themselves dwindle or be replaced. Is not to examine this "history," (but the word "history" belongs to this process of meaning), as the history of meaning, and to ask the "question of Being" as the question of the "meaning of Being" (Heidegger), to limit the destruction of classical ontology to a reappropriation of the semantic plenitude of "Being," a reactivation of the lost origin, etc.? Is it not to constitute the supplement of copula as a historical accident, even if one considers it to be structurally necessary? Is it not to suspect a kind of original fall in the copula, with all that such a perspective would imply?

Finally, why does the horizon of meaning dominate the question of the linguist as well as the question of the philosophical thinker? What desire impels both the one and the other, as what they are, to proceed analogically toward a superlapsarian agency, something before the supplement of copula? That their procedures and horizons remain analogous in this respect, one sees in the following:

"The entire range of the inflections of the verb 'to be' (*sein*) is determined by three different stems.

"The first two stems to be named are Indo-European and also occur in the Greek and Latin words for 'Being.'

"1. The oldest, the actual radical word is *es*, Sanskrit *asus*, life, the living, that which from out of itself stands and which moves and rests in itself . . . It is noteworthy that the *'is'* (*ist*) has maintained itself in all Indo-European languages from the very start (Greek—*estin*, Latin—*est*, German—*ist*).

"2. The other Indo-European radical is *bhu*, *bheu*. To it belong the Greek *phuō*, to emerge, to be powerful, of itself to come to stand and remain standing. Up until now this *bhu* has been interpreted according to the usual superficial view of *physis* and *phuein* . . .

"3. The third stem occurs only in the inflection of the Germanic verb *'sein'*: this is *wes*; Sanskrit: *vasami*; Germanic: *wesan*, to dwell, to sojourn . . . The substantive *'Wesen'* did not originally mean 'whatness,' quiddity, but enduring as presence (*Gegenwart*), pre-sence (*An-wesen*) and ab-sence (*Ab-wesen*). The *sens* in the Latin *prae-sens* and *ab-sens* has been lost . . . From the three stems we derive the three initial concrete meanings: to live, to emerge, to linger or endure. These are established by linguistics which also establishes that these initial meanings are extinct today, that only an 'abstract' meaning 'to be' has been preserved . . .

"8. Can the meaning of Being, which on the basis of a purely logical, grammatical interpretation strikes us as 'abstract' and hence derived, be inherently whole and fundamental?

"9. *Can this be shown through language if we take a sufficiently basic view of it?* . . . 'Being' remains barely a sound to us, a *threadbare (vernutzter)* appellation. If nothing more is left to us, *we must seek at least* to grasp *this last vestige (Rest) of a possession.* Therefore we ask 'How does it stand with the *word* Being?'

"We have answered this question in two ways which have led us into the grammar and the etymology of the word. Let us sum up the results of this twofold discussion of the word 'Being.'

"1. Grammatical investigation of the word form shows that in the infinitive the definite meanings of the word no longer make themselves felt; they are *effaced (verwischt)*. Substantivization completely stabilizes and objectifies this *effacement*. The word becomes a name for something indeterminate.

"2. Etymological investigation of the word's meaning has shown that in respect to meaning what we have called by the name of 'Being' is a *levelling (ausgleichende) mixture* of three different radical meanings. None of these reaches up independently to determine the meaning of the word. *Mixture (Vermischung)* and *effacement (Verwischung)* go hand in hand"[35] (pp. 58–61; slightly modified).

Benveniste: "It remains to complete these suggestions by examining the situation of the verb 'to be' with respect to the nominal sentence. We must insist upon the necessity for rejecting every implication of a lexical 'to be' in the analysis of the nominal sentence, and of reforming the habits of translation

35. I have italicized *threadbare, this last vestige of a possession, effaced, effacement, levelling mixture, mixture, effacement.* [The importance of these underlinings is one of the topics of the next essay, "White Mythology."]

imposed by the different structure of modern Western languages. One can start a strict interpretation of the nominal sentence only by freeing oneself from that servitude and by recognizing the verb *esti* in Indo-European as a verb just like the others. It is such, not only in that it bears all the morphological marks of its class and that it serves the same syntactic function but because it must have had a definite lexical meaning before *falling*—at the end of a long historical development—to the rank of 'copula.' It is no longer possible to attain this meaning directly, but the fact that *bhu*, 'to put forth, to grow,' furnished part of the forms of *es* gives an inkling of it. In any case, even in interpreting it as 'to exist, to have real substance' (cf. the sense of 'truth' attached to the adjectives *sannr* in Old Icelandic, *sons* in Latin, and *satya* in Sanskrit), one has defined it sufficiently by its function as an intransitive capable of being used either absolutely or accompanied by an appositive adjective; so that *esti* used absolutely or *esti* with the adjective functions like a great number of intransitive verbs in this double position (such as seem, appear, grow, remain, lie, spring, fall, etc.) . . . *We must restore its full force and its authentic function to the verb 'to be'* in order to measure the distance between a nominal assertion and an assertion with 'to be' "[36] (p. 138).

Perhaps this will appear (if, at least, it were entrusted to appearing in whatever way) from a site that is waiting not so much for a name as for an inscription of its elaboration. This site could in no way be an ontology, a regional science, or anything else which submits to this hierarchy. For the hierarchy itself, in effect, can coordinate the particular sciences with the regional ontologies, and then with fundamental ontology, only by presupposing that which (*is*) comes into question here.

What about the *word*? And then, what about the opposition of the lexical (the semantic, the etymological) and the grammatical which dominates these discourses without being examined for itself? Where and how was this opposition constituted? Why does the *is* still give its form to all these questions? What about the relationship between truth, (the) meaning (of Being), and the third person singular of the present indicative of the verb "to be"? What is it to *remain* or not to *remain*? What remains in a supplement of copula?

If it were still a question, here, of a word to say, it would surely not be for philosophy or linguistics as such to say it.

36. I have italicized *falling* and *restore its full force and its authentic function to the verb 'to be.'*

White Mythology:
Metaphor in the Text
of Philosophy

Originally published in *Poétique* 5 (1971).

Exergue[1]

From philosophy, rhetoric. That is, here, to make from a volume, approximately, more or less, a flower, to extract a flower, to mount it, or rather to have it mount itself, bring itself to light—and turning away, as if from itself, come round again, such a flower engraves—learning to cultivate, by means of a lapidary's reckoning, patience . . .

Metaphor *in* the text of philosophy. Certain that we understand each word of this phrase, rushing to understand—to inscribe—a figure in the volume capable of philosophy, we might prepare to treat a particular question: is there metaphor in the text of philosophy? in what form? to what extent? is it essential? accidental? etc. Our certainty soon vanishes: metaphor seems to involve the usage of philosophical language in its entirety, nothing less than the usage of so-called natural language *in* philosophical discourse, that is, the usage of natural language *as* philosophical language.

In sum, the question demands a book: of philosophy, of the *usage* or of the good usage of philosophy. And it is in our interest that the involvement promises more than it gives. Thus we will content ourselves with a chapter, and for usage we will substitute—subtitle—*usure*.[2] And first we will be interested in a certain *usure* of metaphorical force in philosophical exchange. *Usure* does not overtake a tropic energy otherwise destined to remain intact; on the contrary, it constitutes the very history and structure of the philosophical metaphor.

How can we make this *sensible*[3] except by metaphor? which is here the word *usure*. In effect, there is no access to the usure of a linguistic phenomenon without giving it some figurative representation. What could be the *properly named usure* of a word, a statement, a meaning, a text?

1. TN. *Exergue* derives from the Greek *ex-ergon*, literally "outside the work." In French and English it has a specifically numismatic sense, referring to the space on a coin or medal reserved for an inscription. In French it also has the sense of an epigraph, of something "outside the work." This combination of meanings—the coin, the inscription, the space, the epigraph, the "outside"—disseminates (in the "technical" sense understood by Derrida) its effects over this entire section of "White Mythology." See also note 2 below.

2. TN. *Usure* in French means both usury, the acquisition of too much interest, and using up, deterioration through usage. The *exergue,* then, is to explain why the subtitle of "White Mythology" is an economic term that inscribes an irreducible effect of both profit and loss. Thus, the preceding sentences noted that it is in our *interest* ("profitable") that involvement with metaphor *promises more than it gives,* i.e. is not profitable, leads to loss. For Derrida, the "general economy" is the one that shows how metaphysics's eternal attempt to *profit* from its ventures is based upon an irreducible *loss,* an "expenditure without reserve" without which there could be no idea of profit. Thus, this essay inscribes the concept of metaphor in the general economy. On all these questions see "From Restricted to General Economy," in *Writing and Difference.*

3. TN. As always Derrida is playing on the double meaning of *sensible* here, i.e. that which is related to the senses and that which is nonsensory, meaningful in an "abstract" way. Throughout this essay I have inflected the translation of *sensible,* often giving it as *sensory.*

Let us take all the risk of unearthing an example (and merely an example, as a frequent type), of this metaphor of (the) *usure* (of metaphor), the ruining of the figure, in *The Garden of Epicurus*. As the exergue to this chapter, let us remark, the metaphor borrowed from Anatole France—the philosophical *usure* of this figure—also, by chance, describes the active erosion of an exergue.

Almost at the end of the *Garden of Epicurus*[4] a short dialogue between Aristos and Polyphilos is subtitled "or the language of metaphysics." The two interlocutors are exchanging views, indeed, on the sensory figure which is sheltered and used (up), to the point of appearing imperceptible, in every metaphysical concept. Abstract notions always hide a sensory figure. And the history of metaphysical language is said to be confused with the erasure of the efficacity of the sensory figure and the *usure* of its effigy. The word itself is not pronounced, but one may decipher the double import of *usure:* erasure by rubbing, exhaustion, crumbling away, certainly; but also the supplementary product of a capital, the exchange which far from losing the original investment would fructify its initial wealth, would increase its return in the form of revenue, additional interest, linguistic surplus value, the two histories of the meaning of the word remaining indistinguishable. "Polyphilos: It was just a reverie. I was thinking how the Metaphysicians, when they make a language for themselves, are like [image, comparison, a figure in order to signify figuration] knife-grinders, who instead of knives and scissors, should put medals and coins to the grindstone to efface the exergue, the value and the head. When they have worked away till nothing is visible in their crown-pieces, neither King Edward, the Emperor William, nor the Republic, they say: 'These pieces have nothing either English, German or French about them; we have freed them from all limits of time and space; they are not worth five shillings any more; they are of an inestimable value, and their exchange value is extended indefinitely.' They are right in speaking thus. By this needy knife-grinder's activity words are changed from a physical to a metaphysical acceptation. It is obvious that they lose in the process; what they gain by it is not so immediately apparent" (pp. 194–95).

The issue here is not to capitalize on this reverie but to watch the configuration of our problem, along with its theoretical and historical conditions, take shape by means of the logic implicit in this text. There are at least two limits: (1) Polyphilos seems anxious to save the integrity of capital, or rather, before the accumulation of capital, to save the natural wealth and original virtue of the sensory image, which is deflowered and deteriorated by the history of the concept. Thereby he supposes—and this is a classical motif, a commonplace of the eighteenth century—that a purity of sensory language could have been in circulation at the origin of language, and that the *etymon* of a primitive sense always

4. *The Garden of Epicurus* by Anatole France, trans. Alfred Allinson (New York: Dodd, Mead, 1923). All further references are to this edition. It also contains a kind of reverie on the figures of the alphabet, the original forms of certain letters ("How I discoursed one night with an apparition on the first origins of the alphabet").

remains determinable, however hidden it may be; (2) this etymologism interprets degradation as the passage from the physical to the metaphysical. Thus, he uses a completely philosophical opposition, which also has its own history, and its own metaphorical history, in order to determine what the philosopher might be doing, unwittingly, with metaphors.

The rest of the dialogue confirms this: it examines, precisely, the possibility of restoring or reactivating, beneath the metaphor which simultaneously hides and is hidden, the "original figure" of the coin which has been worn away (*usé*), effaced, and polished in the circulation of the philosophical concept. Should one not always have to speak of the ef-*face*ment of an original figure, if it did not by itself efface itself?

"All these words, whether defaced by usage, or polished smooth, or even coined expressly in view of constructing some intellectual concept, yet allow us to frame some idea to ourselves of what they originally represented. So chemists have reagents whereby they can make the effaced writing of a papyrus or a parchment visible again. It is by these means palimpsests are deciphered.

"If an analogous process were applied to the writings of the metaphysicians, if the primitive and concrete meaning that lurks yet present under the abstract and new interpretations were brought to light, we should come upon some very curious and perhaps instructive ideas" (pp. 201–2).

The primitive meaning, the original, and always sensory and material, figure ("The vocabulary of mankind was framed from sensuous images, and this sensuousness is to be found . . . even in the technical terms concocted by metaphysicians . . . fatal materialism inherent in the vocabulary," p. 201) is not exactly a metaphor. It is a kind of transparent figure, equivalent to a literal meaning (*sens propre*). It becomes a metaphor when philosophical discourse puts it into circulation. Simultaneously the first meaning and the first displacement are then forgotten. The metaphor is no longer noticed, and it is taken for the proper meaning. A double effacement. Philosophy would be this process of metaphorization which gets carried away in and of itself. Constitutionally, philosophical culture will always have been an obliterating one.

And this is an economic rule: in order to reduce the labor of rubbing, metaphysicians prefer to choose the most worn out (*usé*) words from natural language: "they go out of their way to choose for polishing such words as come to them a bit obliterated already. In this way, they save themselves a good half of the labor. Sometimes they are luckier still, and put their hands on words which, by long and universal use, have lost from time immemorial all trace whatever of an effigy" (p. 199). And reciprocally we are unwitting metaphysicians in proportion to the *usure* of our words. Polyphilos cannot avoid the extreme case, although he does not see it as a problem or treat it thematically—the *absolute usure* of a sign. What is this? And is not this loss—that is, this unlimited surplus-value—what the metaphysician systematically prefers, for example in his choice of concepts in the negative, *ab-solute, in-finite, in-tangible, non-Being?* "In three

211

pages of Hegel, taken at random, in his *Phenomenology* [a book quite infrequently cited in the French university of 1900, it appears], out of six and twenty words, the subjects of important sentences, I found nineteen negative terms as against seven affirmatives . . . These *abs* and *ins* and *nons* are more effective than any grindstone in planing down. At a stroke they make the most rugged words smooth and characterless. Sometimes, it is true, they merely twist them round for you and turn them upside down" (pp. 196–97). Beyond the jest, the relation between metaphorization, which takes off on its own, and negative concepts remains to be examined. For in dissolving any finite determination, negative concepts break the tie that binds them to the meaning of any particular being, that is, to the totality of what is. Thereby they suspend their apparent metaphoricity. (Later we will give a better definition of the problem of negativity, when we can recognize the connivance between the Hegelian *relève*[5]—the *Aufhebung*, which is also the unity of loss and profit—and the philosophical concept of metaphor.) "Such is the general practice, so far as I have observed, of the metaphysicians—more correctly, the *Metataphysicians;* for it is another remarkable fact to add to the rest that your science itself has a negative name, one taken from the order in which the treatises of Aristotle were arranged, and that strictly speaking, you give yourselves the title: Those who come after the *Physicians*. I understand of course that you regard these, the physical books, as piled atop of each other, so that to come after is really to take place above. All the same, you admit this much, that you are outside of natural phenomena" (pp. 196–97).

Although the metaphysical metaphor has turned everything upside down, and although it has also erased piles of physical discourses, one always should be able to reactivate the primitive inscription and restore the palimpsest. Polyphilos indulges in this game. He extracts from a work which "reviews all systems one by one from the old Eleatics down to the latest Eclectics, and . . . ends up with M. Lachelier," a sentence of particularly abstract and speculative appearance: *"The spirit possesses God in proportion as it participates in the absolute"* (p. 193). Then he undertakes an etymological or philological work which is to reawaken all the sleeping figures. To do this, he concerns himself not with "how much truth the sentence contained," but only with its "verbal form." And after having specified that the words "God," "soul," "absolute," etc., are *symbols* and not *signs*, what is symbolized maintaining a tie of natural affinity with the symbol, and thus authorizing the etymological reactivation, (arbitrariness, thus, as Nietzsche also suggests, being only a degree of the *usure* of the symbolic), Polyphilos presents the results of his chemical operation:

"Wherefore I was on the right road when I investigated the meanings inherent in the words *spirit, God, absolute,* which are symbols and not signs.

" 'The spirit possesses God in proportion as it participates in the absolute.'

5. TN. On *relève*, see above, "La différance," note 23; "Ousia and Grammē," note 15; "The Pit and the Pyramid," note 16; and "The Ends of Man," note 14.

"What is this if not a collection of little symbols, much worn and defaced, I admit, symbols which have lost their original brilliance, and picturesqueness, but which still, by the nature of things, remain symbols? The image is reduced to the schema, but the schema is still the image. And I have been able, without sacrificing fidelity, to substitute one for the other. In this way I have arrived at the following.

" 'The breath is seated on the shining one in the bushel of the part it takes in what is altogether loosed (or subtle),' whence we easily get as a next step: 'He whose breath is a sign of life, man, that is, will find a place (no doubt after the breath has been exhaled) in the divine fire, source and home of life, and this place will be meted out to him according to the virtue that has been given him (by the demons, I imagine) of sending abroad this warm breath, this little invisible soul, across the free expanse (the blue of the sky, most likely).'

"And now observe, the phrase has acquired quite the ring of some fragment of a Vedic hymn, and smacks of ancient Oriental mythology. I cannot answer for having restored this primitive myth in full accordance with the strict laws governing language. But no matter for that. Enough if we are seen to have found symbols and a myth in a sentence that was essentially symbolic and mythical, inasmuch as it was metaphysical.

"I think I have at last made you realize one thing, Aristos, that any expression of an abstract idea can only be an analogy. By an odd fate, the very metaphysicians who think to escape the world of appearances are constrained to live perpetually in allegory. A sorry lot of poets, they dim the colours of the ancient fables, and are themselves but gatherers of fables. They produce white mythology" (pp. 213–14 [translation modified; the last sentence reads: "Their output is mythology, an anemic mythology"]).

A formula—brief, condensed, economical, almost mute—has been deployed in an interminably explicative discourse, displaying itself like a pedagogue, with the derisive effect always produced by the prolix and gesticulating translation of an oriental ideogram. Parody of the translator, naiveté of the metaphysician or of the pitiful peripatetic who does not recognize his own figure and does not know where it has marched him to.

Metaphysics—the white mythology which reassembles and reflects the culture of the West: the white man takes his own mythology, Indo-European mythology, his own *logos*, that is, the *mythos* of his idiom, for the universal form of that he must still wish to call Reason. Which does not go uncontested. Aristos (*Ariste*), the defender of metaphysics (a typographical error will have imprinted in the title *Artiste*), finishes by *leaving*, determined to break off dialogue with a cheater: "I leave unconvinced. If only you had reasoned by the rules, I could have rebutted your arguments quite easily" (p. 215).

White mythology—metaphysics has erased within itself the fabulous scene that has produced it, the scene that nevertheless remains active and stirring, inscribed in white ink, an invisible design covered over in the palimpsest.

This dissymmetrical—false—dialogue does not deserve its position as exergue only because it is striking; or because in striking reason no less than the imagination, it engraves our problem in a theatrical effigy. There are other justifications. Very schematically:

1. Polyphilos' propositions seem to belong to a configuration whose historical and theoretical distribution, whose limits, interior divisions, and gaps remain to be interpreted. Guided by the question of rhetoric, such an interpretation would require examination of the texts of Renan[6] and Nietzsche[7] (who both, as philologists, recalled what they considered to be the metaphorical origin of concepts, and most notably of the concept which seems to support literal, proper meaning, the propriety of the proper, Being), as well as those of Freud,[8] Bergson,[9] and Lenin,[10] all of whom, in their attentiveness to metaphorical activity in theoretical or philosophical discourse, proposed or practiced the multiplication of antagonistic metaphors in order better to control or neutralize their effect. The efflorescence of historical linguistics in the nineteenth century does not suffice to explain the interest in the metaphorical sedimentation of concepts. And it goes without saying that the configuration of the motifs has no linear chronological or historical limit. The names we have just associated show this clearly, and the cleavages to be defined or maintained, moreover, occur within discourses

6. See e.g. *De l'origine du langage* (1848), in *Oeuvres complètes*, vol. 8, chap. 5.
7. See, for example, "Philosophy During the Tragic Age of the Greeks," in *Early Greek Philosophy*, trans. Maximilian Mugge (New York: Russell and Russell, 1964).
8. See e.g. Breuer's and Freud's texts in the *Studies in Hysteria* (*Standard Edition* II, 227–28, 288–90); or further, *Jokes and Their Relation to the Unconscious* (*SE* VIII, 210–11); *Beyond the Pleasure Principle* (*SE* XVIII, end of chap. 6); *Introductory Lectures on Psycho-Analysis* (*SE* XVI, 295; on the metaphor of the antichamber); *The Question of Lay Analysis* (*SE* XX, 187–88). Moreover, concerning the intervention of rhetorical schemes in psychoanalytic discourse, naturally I refer to Lacan's *Ecrits* (Paris: Seuil, 1966; see the "Index raisonné des concepts majeurs," by J. A. Miller); to Benveniste, "Remarks on the Function of Language in Freudian Discovery," in *Problems in General Linguistics*, trans. Mary E. Meek (Coral Gables: University of Miami Press, 1971); and to Jakobson, "Two Aspects of Language and Two Types of Aphasic Disturbance," in Roman Jakobson and Morris Halle, *Fundamentals of Language* (The Hague: Mouton, 1956).
9. See e.g. "Introduction à la métaphysique," in *La pensée et le mouvant* (Paris: Presses Universitaires de France, 1946), p. 185.
10. In his *Notebooks* (*Collected Works*, vol. 38 [London: Lawrence and Wishart, 1961]) on Hegel's dialectics, Lenin most often defines the relation of Marx to Hegel as an "overturning" (head over heels), but also as a "decapitation" (the Hegelian system minus everything that governs it: the absolute, the Idea, God, etc.), or further as the development of a "germ" or a "seed," and even as the "peeling" which proceeds from the skin to the pit, etc.
On the question of metaphor in the reading of Marx, and in a Marxist problematic in general, see, notably, Louis Althusser, *For Marx*, trans. Ben Brewster (Harmondsworth: Penguin, 1969), part 3, "Contradiction and Overdetermination"; Louis Althusser and Etienne Balibar, *Reading Capital*, trans. Ben Brewster (London, 1970), pp. 24, 121n., 187ff.; Althusser, "Les appareils idéologiques d'Etat," in *La pensée*, no. 151 (June 1970), pp. 7–9; and Jean-Joseph Goux, "Numismatiques" I, II, in *Tel Quel* 35–36.

signed by a single name. A new determination of the unity of bodies of work has to precede or accompany the elaboration of these questions.

2. To read within a concept the hidden history of a metaphor is to privilege *diachrony* at the expense of system, and is also to invest in the *symbolist* conception of language that we have pointed out in passing: no matter how deeply buried, the link of the signifier to the signified has had both to be and to remain a link of natural necessity, of analogical participation, of resemblance. Metaphor has always been defined as the trope of resemblance; not simply as the resemblance between a signifier and a signified but as the resemblance between two signs, one of which designates the other. This is the most general characteristic of metaphor, which is what authorizes us to group under this heading all the so-called *symbolical* or *analogical* figures mentioned by Polyphilos (figure, myth, fable, allegory). In this critique of philosophical language, to take an interest in metaphor—in this particular figure—is therefore also to take a symbolist stand. It is above all to take an interest in the nonsyntactic, nonsystematic pole of language, that is, to take an interest in semantic "depth," in the magnetic attraction of the similar, rather than in positional combinations, which we may call "metonymic" in the sense defined by Jakobson,[11] who indeed emphasizes the affinity between the predominance of the metaphorical, i.e. symbolism (as much, we would say, as a literary school as a linguistic conception)—and romanticism (as more historical, that is, historicist, and more hermeneutical). It goes without saying that far from belonging to this problematic and sharing its presuppositions, the question of metaphor, such as we are repeating it here, on the contrary should delimit them. However, the issue is not, symmetrically, to reaffirm what Polyphilos chooses as his target; it is rather to deconstruct the metaphysical and rhetorical schema at work in his critique, not in order to reject and discard them but to reinscribe them otherwise, and especially in order to begin to identify the historico-problematic terrain on which philosophy systematically has been asked for the metaphorical rubrics of its concepts.

3. The value of *usure* also has to be subjected to interpretation. It seems to have a systematic tie to the metaphorical perspective. It will be rediscovered wherever the theme of metaphor is privileged. And it is also a metaphor that implies a *continuist presupposition:* the history of a metaphor appears essentially not as a displacement with breaks, as reinscriptions in a heterogeneous system, mutations, separations without origin, but rather as a progressive erosion, a regular semantic loss, an uninterrupted exhausting of the primitive meaning: an empirical abstraction without extraction from its own native soil. Not that the enterprise of the authors cited is entirely covered by this presupposition, but, rather, the enterprise recurs to it every time it gives the metaphorical point of view the upper hand. This characteristic—the concept of *usure*—belongs not to a narrow historico-theoretical configuration, but more surely to the concept

---

11. "Two Aspects of Language," in *Fundamentals*, pp. 77–78.

of metaphor itself, and to the long metaphysical sequence that it determines or that determines it. We will be interested in this question as our point of departure.

4. In signifying the metaphorical process, the paradigms of coin, of metal, silver and gold, have imposed themselves with remarkable insistence. Before metaphor—an effect of language—could find its metaphor in an economic effect, a more general analogy had to organize the exchanges between the two "regions." The analogy within language finds itself represented by an analogy between language and something other than itself. But here, that which seems to "represent," to figure, is also that which opens the wider space of a discourse on figuration, and can no longer be contained within a regional or determined science, linguistics or philology.

Inscription on coinage is most often the intersection, the scene of the exchange between the linguistic and the economic. The two types of signifier supplement each other in the problematic of fetishism, as much in Nietzsche as in Marx.[12] And the *Contribution to the Critique of Political Economy* organizes into a system the motifs of *usure*, of "coinage speaking different languages," of the relations between "differences in name" and "differences in shape," of the conversion of coinage into "gold *sans phrase*," and reciprocally of the idealization of gold, which "becomes a symbol of itself and . . . cannot serve as a symbol of itself" ("nothing can be its own symbol," etc.).[13] The reference seems to be economic

12. See e.g. *Capital,* trans. Eden and Cedar Paul (New York: Dutton, 1972), book 1: "For this reason, likewise, the fetishistic character of commodities is comparatively easy to discern . . . Whence did the illusions of the monetary system arise? The mercantilists (the champions of the monetary system) regarded gold and silver, not simply as substances which, when functioning as money, represented a social relation of production, but as substances which were endowed by nature with peculiar social properties . . . If commodities could speak they would say . . . Now let us hear how the economist interprets the mind of the commodity" (pp. 57–58).

13. *A Contribution to the Critique of Political Economy,* trans. N. F. Stone (Chicago, 1904), pp. 139 and 145. We are only recalling these texts. In order to analyze them from the point of view that interests us here (the critique of etymologism, questions about the history and value of the proper—*idion, proprium, eigen*), it would be necessary to account for this fact particularly: Marx, along with several others (Plato, Leibniz, Rousseau, etc.), did not only criticize etymologism as an abuse, or as a kind of nonscientific meandering, the practice of poor etymology. His critique of etymologism chose the *proper* as its example. Here, we cannot cite the entire critique of Destutt de Tracy, who plays on the words *property* and *proper,* as "Stirner" did with *Mein* and *Meinung* (mine, my opinion; Hegel did this too), *Eigentum* and *Eigenheit* (property and individuality). We cite only the following passage, whose target is the reduction of economic science to the play of language, and the reduction of the stratified specificity of concepts to the imaginary unity of an *etymon:* "Above 'Stirner' refuted the communist abolition of private property by first transferring private property into 'having' and then declaring the verb 'to have' an indispensable word, an eternal truth, because even in communist society it could happen that Stirner will 'have' a stomach-ache. In exactly the same way he here bases the impossibility of abolishing private property by transferring it into the concept of property ownership, by exploiting the etymological connection between the words *Eigentum* (property) and *eigen* (proper, own), and declaring the word *eigen* an eternal truth because a stomach-ache will be *eigen* to him. All this theoretical nonsense, which seeks refuge in bad etymology, would be

216

and the metaphor linguistic. That Nietzsche also, at least apparently, inverses the course of the analogy is certainly not insignificant but must not dissimulate the common possibility of both the exchange and the terms: "What then is truth? A mobile army of metaphors, metonymics, anthropomorphisms: in short, a sum of human relations which became poetically and rhetorically intensified, metamorphosed, adorned, and after long usage, seem to a nation fixed, canonic and binding; truths are illusions of which one has forgotten that they *are* illusions; worn out metaphors which have become powerless to affect the senses (*die abgenützt und sinnlich kraftlos geworden sind*), coins which have their obverse (*Bild*) *effaced* and now are no longer of account as coins but merely as metal."[14]

If we were to accept a Saussurean distinction, we would say that here the question of metaphor derives from a theory of *value* and not only from a theory of *signification*. It is at the very moment when Saussure justifies this distinction that he posits a necessary intersection of the synchronic and diachronic axes for all sciences of value, but for these alone. He then elaborates the analogy between economics and linguistics: "that duality [between synchrony and diachony] is already forcing itself upon the economic sciences. Here, in contrast to the other sciences, political economy and economic history constitute two clearly separated disciplines within a single science . . . Proceeding as they have, economists are—without being aware of it—obeying an inner necessity. A similar necessity obliges us to divide linguistics into two parts, each with its own principle. Here as in political economy we are confronted with the notion of *value*; both sciences

---

impossible if the actual private property which the communists want to abolish had not been transformed into the abstract notion of 'property.' This transformation, on the one hand, saves one the trouble of having to say anything, or even merely to know anything about actual private property and, on the other hand, makes it easy to discover a contradiction in communism, since *after* the abolition of (*actual*) property it is, of course, easy to discover still all sorts of things which can be included in the term 'property.' " Karl Marx and Frederick Engels, *The German Ideology*, ed. C. J. Arthur (London: Lawrence and Wishart, 1965), part 2, "The Language of Property," p. 247. This critique—which opens, or leaves open, the questions of the "reality" of the proper, of the "abstraction" and the concept (not the general reality) of the proper—is continued further on, à propos of some remarkable examples: "For example, *propriété*—property (*Eigentum*) and feature (*Eigenschaft*); property—possession (*Eigentum*) and peculiarity (*Eigentümlichkeit*); 'eigen' (one's own)—in the commercial and in the individual sense; *valeur*, value, *Wert* ('worth', 'value'); commerce, *Verkehr* ('intercourse,' 'traffic,' 'commerce'); *échange, exchange, Austausch* ('exchange'), etc., all of which are used both for commercial relations and for features and mutual relations of individuals as such. In the other modern languages this is equally the case. If Saint Max seriously applies himself to exploit this ambiguity, he may easily succeed in making a brilliant series of new economic discoveries, without knowing anything about political economy; for, indeed, his new economic facts, which we shall take note of later, lie wholly within this sphere of synonymy" (ibid., p. 249).

14. Nietzsche, "On Truth and Falsity in their Ultramoral Sense," in *Complete Works of Nietzsche*, ed. D. Levy (London and Edinburgh, 1911), vol. 2, p. 180. This motif of the erasure, of the paling of the image, is also found in the *Traumdeutung* (*SE* IV, 43), but it does not determine the theory of metaphor in unequivocal or unilateral fashion any more in Freud than in Nietzsche.

are concerned with *a system for equating things of different orders*—labour and wages in one, and a signified and a signifier in the other."[15]

In order to define the notion of value, even before it is specified as economic or linguistic value, Saussure describes the general characteristics which will ensure the metaphoric or analogic transition, by similarity or proportionality, from one order to another. And, once again, by analogy, metaphoricity constitutes each of the two orders as much as it does their relationship.

The five-franc piece once more pays the expense of the demonstration:

"We must clear up the issue [of the relation of signification to value] or risk reducing language to a simple naming process . . . To resolve this issue, let us observe from the outset that even outside language all values are apparently governed by the same paradoxical principle. They are always composed:

"1) of a *dissimilar* thing that can be *exchanged* for the thing of which the value is to be determined; and

"2) of *similar* things that can be *compared* with the thing of which the value is to be determined.

"Both factors are necessary for the existence of a value. To determine what a five-franc piece is worth one must therefore know: 1) that it can be exchanged for a fixed quantity of a different thing, e.g., bread; and 2) that it can be compared with a similar value of the same system, e.g. a one-franc piece, or with coins of another system (a dollar, etc.). *In the same way* [my italics] a word can be exchanged for something dissimilar, an idea; besides, it can be compared with something of the same nature, another word. Its value is therefore not fixed so long as one simply states that it can be 'exchanged' for a given concept, i.e. that it has this or that signification: one must also compare it with similar values, with other words that stand in opposition to it. Its content is really fixed only by the concurrence of everything that exists outside it. Being part of a system, it is endowed not only with a signification but also and especially with a value, and this is something quite different."[16]

Value, gold, the eye, the sun, etc., are carried along, as has been long known, in the same tropic movement. Their exchange dominates the field of rhetoric *and* of philosophy. A remark of Saussure's on the next page, therefore, can be viewed from the vantage of Polyphilos' translations (the "seated breath," the "divine fire, source and home of life," etc.). Saussure's remark reminds us that the most natural, most universal, most real, most luminous thing, the apparently most exterior referent, the sun, does not completely escape the general law of metaphoric value as soon as it intervenes (as it always does) in the process of axiological and semantic value: "The value of just any term is accordingly determined by its environment; it is impossible to fix even the value of the signifier

15. Ferdinand de Saussure, *Course in General Linguistics*, trans. Wade Baskin (New York: Philosophical Library, 1959), p. 79.
16. Ibid., pp. 113–14.

'sun' without considering its surroundings: in some languages it is not possible to say 'sit in the *sun.*' "[17]

In the same constellation, but in its own irreducible place, once again we should reread[18] the entirety of Mallarmé's texts on linguistics, aesthetics, and political economy, all that he wrote on the sign *or* [gold], which calculates textual effects that check the oppositions of the literal [*propre*] and the figurative, the metaphoric and the metonymic, figure and ground, the syntactic and the semantic, speech and writing in their classical senses, the more and the less. And does so notably on the page which disseminates its title *or* in the course of "fantasmagoric settings of the sun."[19]

Plus de métaphore[20]

The exergue effaced, how are we to decipher figures of speech, and singularly metaphor, in the philosophic text? This question has never been answered with a systematic treatise, doubtless not an insignificant fact. Here, instead of venturing into the prologomena to some future metaphorics, let us rather attempt to recognize in principle the *condition for the impossibility* of such a project. In its most impoverished, most abstract form, the limit would be the following: metaphor remains, in all its essential characteristics, a classical philosopheme, a metaphysical concept. It is therefore enveloped in the field that a general metaphorology of philosophy would seek to dominate. Metaphor has been issued from a network of philosophemes which themselves correspond to tropes or to figures, and these philosophemes are contemporaneous to or in systematic solidarity with these tropes or figures. This stratum of "tutelary" tropes, the layer of "primary" philosophemes (assuming that the quotation marks will serve as a sufficient precaution here), cannot be dominated. It cannot dominate itself, cannot be dominated by what it itself has engendered, has made to grow on its own soil, supported on its own base. Therefore, it gets "carried away" each time that one of its products—here, the concept of metaphor—attempts in vain to include under its own law the totality of the field to which the product belongs. If one wished to conceive and to class all the metaphorical possibilities of philosophy, one metaphor, at least, always would remain excluded, outside the

17. Ibid., p. 116.
18. I have sketched this reading in "The Double Session," sec. 2, in *Dissemination.*
19. TN. *Or* is one of the prose pieces from *Grands Faits Divers* in Mallarmé, *Oeuvres Complètes* (Paris: Gallimard, 1945), p. 398.
20. TN. The title of this section, "Plus de métaphore," is untranslatable as it means both "more metaphor" and "no more metaphor." See the end of the first paragraph of this section, where Derrida explains how "the extra turn of speech becomes the missing turn of speech." This idea is related to the "general economy" of metaphor explained in notes 1 and 2 above; in this economy "profit" produces "loss": *more* metaphor, the extra turn of speech, becomes *no more* metaphor, the missing turn of speech. What Derrida shows is that this paradox is intrinsic to the concept of metaphor.

system: the metaphor, at the very least, without which the concept of metaphor could not be constructed, or, to syncopate an entire chain of reasoning, the metaphor of metaphor. This extra metaphor, remaining outside the field that it allows to be circumscribed, extracts or abstracts itself from this field, thus substracting itself as a metaphor less. By virtue of what we might entitle, for economical reasons, tropic supplementarity, since the extra turn of speech becomes the missing turn of speech, the taxonomy or history of philosophical metaphors will never make a profit. The state or status of the complement will always be denied to the interminable *dehiscence* of the supplement (if we may be permitted to continue to garden this botanical metaphor). The field is never saturated.

In order to demonstrate this, let us imagine what such a simultaneously historic and systematic sampling of philosophical metaphors might be. First, it would have to be governed by a rigorous concept of metaphor, a concept to be carefully distinguished, within a general tropology, from all the other turns of speech with which metaphor is too often confused. Provisionally, let us take such a definition as granted. One then would have to acknowledge the importation into so-called philosophical discourse of exogenous metaphors, or rather of significations that become metaphorical in being transported out of their own habitat. Thus, one would classify the places they come from: there would be metaphors that are biological, organic, mechanical, technical, economic, historical, mathematical—geometric, topologic, arithmetic—(supposing that in the strict sense there might be mathematical metaphors, a problem to be held in reserve for now). This classification, which supposes an indigenous population and a migration, is usually adopted by those, not numerous, who have studied the metaphorics of a single philosopher or particular body of work.

In classifying metaphors according to their native regions, one would necessarily—and this has indeed happened—have to reduce the "lending" discourses, the discourses of the origin—in opposition to the borrowing discourses—to two major types: those which precisely appear more original in and of themselves,[21] and those whose object has ceased to be original, natural, primitive. The first kind provides metaphors that are physical, animal, and biological, and the second those that are technical, artificial, economic, cultural, social, etc. This derivative opposition, (of *physis* to *tekhnē*, or of *physis* to *nomos*), is at work everywhere. Sometimes the thread of the argument is not stated. It happens that there is an alleged break with tradition. The results are the same. These taxonomical principles do not derive from a particular problem of method. They are governed by the concept of metaphor and by its system (for example, the oppositions of the place of origin, the *etymon*, and the proper, to all their others),

21. Those which primarily are *encountered* in nature demand only to be picked, like flowers. The flower is always youthful, at the greatest proximity to nature and to the morning of life. The rhetoric of the flower, for example in Plato, always has this meaning. See *Symposium* 183e, 196a–b, 203e, 210c; *Republic* 474e, 601b; and *Politics* 273d, 310d, etc.

and for as long as this concept is not solicited[22] the methodological reform remains without impact. For example, in his thesis *Plato's Metaphors* (Rennes, 1945), Pierre Louis announces that he will not follow the model of "genealogical" or migrationist classification. Therefore, he tells us, he will prefer the principle of the internal organization of metaphors to the external criterion of the domain of provenance. The issue is thus to let oneself be governed by the author's intentions, by what he means, by what the play of figures signifies. An all the more legitimate proposition, apparently, in that we are concerned here with a philosophical discourse, or a discourse treated as such: what is important then, as we all know, is the signified content, the meaning, the intention of truth, etc. The requirement that one take into account Platonic thought, its system and its internal articulation, can hardly be contested by anyone attempting to reconstitute the system of Plato's metaphors. But it can quickly be seen that the internal articulation is not that of the metaphors themselves, but that of the "philosophical" ideas, metaphor playing exclusively the role of a pedagogical ornament, no matter how the author might have it. As for the properly philosophical configuration of Platonic thought, it is but an anachronistic projection. Let us consider first the discourse on method: "The traditional method, in this kind of study, consists in grouping images according to the domain from which the author borrows them. At the limit, this method may be suitable when we are concerned with a poet for whom images are but ornaments whose beauty bears witness to an exceptional wealth of imagination. In this case, one is hardly concerned with the profound meaning of the metaphor or the comparison, but rather above all with its original brilliance. Now, Platonic images do not recommend themselves solely for their brilliant qualities. Whoever studies them quickly perceives that they are not simply ornaments, but are all destined to express ideas more aptly than would a long elaboration" (pp. 13–14).

These are simultaneously paradoxical and traditional propositions. Poetic metaphor is rarely considered as an extrinsic ornament, especially in order to oppose it to philosophical metaphor. And it is rarely deduced from this that philosophical metaphor deserves to be studied for itself for just this reason, and that it has no identity of its own except in its exteriority as a signifier. Conversely, this "economist" theory of metaphor destined to spare a "long elaboration,"[23]

22. TN. This is Derrida's familiar use of the word "solicit" in its "etymological" sense, meaning "to shake the whole."
23. Metaphor and other figures of speech, notably comparison, thus would be homogenous, distinguished only by their degree of elaboration. The briefest of the figures of speech, metaphor, also would be the most general one, economizing all the others. This "economist" theory can claim Aristotle as one of its proponents: "The simile (*eikōn:* image) too is a metaphor; the difference is but small (*diapherei gar mikron*). When the poet says of Achilles 'he sprang at them like (*hōs*) a lion,' this is a simile (*eikōn*); when he says 'the lion sprang on them,' this is a metaphor." *Works,* ed. W. D. Ross (Oxford: Oxford University Press, 1924), III, 4, 1406b20–22. All further references to the *Rhetoric* will be to this edition. The same motif reappears in Cicero (*De Oratore* III, 38, 156; 39, 157; *Orator* XXVII 92–94),

and above all a comparison, is as classical as can be. However, Louis allegedly had opposed himself to this tradition. "If we must have a criterion for distinguishing metaphor from comparison, I would say rather that comparison always appears as something external, easily detachable from the work, while metaphor is absolutely indispensable to the meaning of the sentence."[24] The economic procedure of abbreviation, thus, appears to act not upon another figure but directly upon the expression of the "idea," the meaning, with which metaphor this time seems to have an internal and essential link. This is what makes it cease to be an ornament, or at least an "ornament too much." (The thesis bears as its exergue a maxim of Fenelon's: "Every ornament that is only an ornament is too much.") Nothing too much in the precious ornament that is metaphor; and nothing in metaphor overburdens the necessary flowering of the idea, the natural unfolding of meaning. It follows, according to an implacable logic, that metaphor will be more "too much" than ever: identifying itself with its guardian, in custody of the signified idea, metaphor could neither be distinguished from

---

in Quintilian (*Institutio Oratoria* VIII, 6, sec. 4), in Condillac (*De l'art d'écrire* II, 4), and in Hegel: "Between metaphor on one side and simile (*Gleichnis*) on the other we may place the image. For it has such a close affinity with metaphor that it is strictly only a metaphor *in extenso* (*ausführlich*), which therefore now acquires a great resemblance to simile (*Vergleichung*)." *Aesthetics*, trans. T. M. Knox (Oxford: Clarendon Press, 1975), p. 408. All further references to the *Aesthetics* will be to this edition. And it still survives: "Metaphor is an abridged comparison." J. Vendryes, *Language*, trans. Paul Radin (London, 1925), p. 178. It seems that what deserves examination here is less the economic consideration in itself than the mechanical character of the explanations to which it gives rise (abbreviation, homogenous quantity of abridgment, shrinking of time and space, etc.). Moreover, in this case the law of economy is acknowledged in the movement from one constituted figure to another at least implicitly constituted figure, and not in the production itself of the figure. The economy of this production could not be so mechanical and external. Let us say that the extra ornament is never useless, or that the useless can always be put to use. Here, we have neither the time nor the place to comment upon the page from the *Vases communicants* on which Breton analyzes an ornament, attending to the rhetorical equivalents of condensation and displacement, and to their economy: "There is no doubt that I have a 'complex' about ties. I detest this incomprehensible ornament of masculine costume. From time to time I reproach myself for surrendering to such an impoverished custom as knotting each morning before a mirror (I am trying to explain to psychoanalysts) a piece of cloth which by means of an attentive little nothing is to augment the already idiotic expression of a morning jacket. Quite simply, it is disconcerting. I am not unaware, from another point of view, and indeed cannot hide from myself, that just as coin operated machines, the sisters of the dynamometer on which Jarry's Supermale practices victoriously ("Come, Madame"), symbolize sexually—the disappearance of the tokens in the slot— and metonymically—the part for the whole—woman, so the tie, and even if only according to Freud, figures the penis 'not only because (they) are long dependent objects and peculiar to men, but also because they can be chosen according to taste, a liberty which in the case of the object symbolized, is forbidden by nature.' (Freud, *Interpretation of Dreams, SE* V, 356)." *Les vases communicants* (Paris: Cahiers Libres, 1932), pp. 46–47. On the "work of condensation" and "the law of *extreme briefness* which has imprinted upon modern poetry one of its most remarkable characteristics" see also p. 58.

24. Here Louis supports his argument with W. B. Stanford, *Greek Metaphor* (Oxford, 1936), and H. Konrad, *Etude sur la métaphore* (Paris, 1939).

this idea, nor distinguish itself, except by falling back into the status of a su-
perfluous sign, which immediately fades away. Outside of thought, as an effect
of the "imagination," metaphors "are all destined to express ideas more aptly
than would a long elaboration. In these conditions, it has appeared interesting
to me to seek out what these ideas were. And this is what has led me to prefer
another method than the traditional classification, a method that F. Dornseiff
already has used in his study of Pindar's style (*Pindars Stil*, Berlin, 1921). This
method, which consists in grouping metaphors according to the ideas they
express, has the great advantage of making salient the writer's way of thinking,
instead of emphasizing only his imagination. And in exactly specifying the
meaning of each image, this method also allows us to see in a certain dialogue
one dominant metaphor that the author 'weaves' throughout his work. Finally,
the method has the merit of making tangible every change in the use of metaphors, by showing the new images which, from one dialogue to another, may
appear in the expression of the same idea. In a word, it satisfies not only the
need for classification, but also helps to gain a deeper understanding of the role
and value of images" (p. 14).

In order not to treat metaphor as an imaginative or rhetorical ornament, in
order to come back to the internal articulation of philosophical discourse, figures
are reduced to modes of "expression" of the idea. In the best of cases, this could
have given rise to an immanentist structural study, transposing into rhetoric—
but is that theoretically possible?—M. Guéroult's method or, more accurately,
V. Goldschmidt's program in *Le paradigme dans la dialectique platonicienne*.[25] (Citing
the definition of the *paradigm* in the *Politics* 278c, Louis ventures the following
exclamation: "It would suffice to replace *paradeigma* by *metaphora* to obtain a
Platonic definition of metaphor!" p. 5.) But in the present case the methodological
justification is supported by an entire implicit philosophy whose authority is
never examined: metaphor is charged with *expressing an idea*, with placing outside
or representing the content of a thought that naturally would be called "idea,"
as if each of these words or concepts did not have an entire history of its own
(to which Plato is no stranger), and as if an entire metaphorics, or more generally
an entire tropic system, had not left several marks within this history. In this
initial classification, the alleged respect for the Platonic articulations yields the
following headings: two major parts, "Inquiry and Doctrine," and nine chapters:
"Intellectual Activity (Reflection and Creation)," "Dialectics," "Discourse,"
"Man," "The Soul," "Theory of Knowledge," "Morals," "Social Life," "God and
the Universe." So many anachronistic categories and architectonic violations
imposed, under the pretext of fidelity, upon the thought of the philosopher who
recommended respect for the articulations of the living organism, and thus for
those of discourse. That these distinctions could have no meaning outside any

25. Paris: Presses Universitaires de France, 1947. See, notably, chap. 3, "Paradigme et
métaphore," pp. 104–10.

kind of Platonism does not automatically permit them to be applied to the Platonic system. Finally, they have not relieved the author from the task of affixing, as an appendix, a methodical inventory arranged according to the opposition identified above (*physis/nomos, physis/technē*). Headings of the Appendix: "Inventory of Metaphors and Comparisons Classified According to the Domains from which Plato Borrows Them: I. Nature; II. Man; III. Society; IV. Mythological Historical and Literary Reminiscences."

Thus, the criteria for a classification of philosophical metaphors are borrowed from a derivative philosophical discourse. Perhaps this might be legitimate if these figures were governed, consciously and calculatedly, by the identifiable author of a system, or if the issue were to describe a philosophical rhetoric in the service of an autonomous theory constituted before and outside its own language, manipulating its tropes like tools. This is an undoubtedly philosophic, and certainly Platonic, ideal, an ideal that is produced in the separation (and order) between philosophy or dialectics on the one hand and (sophistic) rhetoric on the other, the separation demanded by Plato himself. Directly or not, it is this separation and this hierarchy that we must question here.

The difficulties we have just pointed out are accentuated with respect to the "archaic" tropes which have given the determinations of a "natural" language to the "founding" concepts (*theōria, eidos, logos,* etc.). And the signs (words/ concepts) from which this proposition is made, beginning with those of trope and *arkhē*, already have their own metaphorical charge. They are metaphorical, resisting every meta-metaphorics, the values of concept, foundation, and theory. And let us not insist upon the optic metaphor which opens up every theoretical point of view under the sun. What is fundamental corresponds to the desire for a firm and ultimate ground, a terrain to build on, the earth as the support of an artificial structure. This value has a history, is a history, of which Heidegger has proposed an interpretation.[26] Finally, even if not reducible to this framework, the concept of the concept cannot not retain the gesture of mastery, taking-and-maintaining-in-the-present, comprehending and grasping the thing as an object.

26. Kant, in expounding his theory of hypotyposis, had recourse to the example of the "ground." Hypotyposis can be *schematic* (direct presentation of an intuition to a purely rational concept) or *symbolic* (indirect presentation of an intuition to a purely rational concept). "Hitherto this function has been but little analyzed, worthy as it is of a deeper study. Still this is not the place to dwell upon it In language we have many such indirect presentations (*Darstellungen*) modelled upon an analogy enabling the expression in question to contain, not the proper (*eigentliche*) scheme for the concept, but merely a symbol for reflection. Thus the words *ground (Grund)* (support, *Stütze-*, basis, *Basis-*), to *depend* (to be held up from above), to *flow* from (instead of to follow), *substance* (as Locke puts it: the support of accidents), and numberless others, are not schematic, but rather symbolic hypotyposes, and express concepts without employing a direct intuition for the purpose, but only drawing upon an analogy with one, i.e. transferring the reflection (*mit . . . der Übertragung der Reflexion*) upon an object of intuition to quite a new concept, and one with which perhaps no intuition could ever directly correspond." *The Critique of Judgement,* trans. J. C. Meredith (Oxford: Oxford University Press, 1952), p. 223.

Which holds for the Latin as well as for the Germanic languages. Noticing this fact, Hegel, in passing, defines our problem, or rather determines the problem with an answer indistinguishable from the proposition of his own speculative and dialectical logic:

"Metaphor has its principal application in linguistic expressions which in this connection we may treat under the following aspects:

"a) In the first place, every language already contains a mass of metaphors. They arise from the fact that a word which originally signifies only something sensuous (*nur etwas ganz sinnliches bedeutet*) is carried over (*übertragen wird*) into the spiritual sphere (*auf Geistiges*). *Fassen, begreifen* [to grasp, to apprehend], and many words, to speak generally, which relate to knowing, have in respect of their literal meaning (*eigentliche Bedeutung, sens propre*) a purely sensuous content, which then is lost and exchanged for a spiritual meaning, the original sense being sensuous (*der erste Sinn ist sinnlich*), the second spiritual.

"b) But gradually the metaphorical element in the use (*im Gebrauche*) of such a word disappears and by custom (*durch die Gewohnheit*) the word changes from a metaphorical (*uneigentliche, non propre*) to a literal expression (*eigentlichen Ausdruck, expression propre*), because owing to readiness to grasp in the image only the meaning, image and meaning are no longer distinguished, and the image directly affords only the abstract meaning itself instead of a concrete picture. If, for example, we are to take *begreifen* in a spiritual sense, then it does not occur to us at all to think of a perceptible grasping by the hand. In living languages the difference between actual metaphors (*wirklicher Metaphern*) and words already reduced by usage (*durch die Abnutzung*) to literal expressions (*eigentliche Ausdrücken, expressions propres*) is easily established; whereas in dead languages this is difficult because mere etymology cannot decide the matter in the last resort. The question does not depend on the first origin of a word or on linguistic development generally; on the contrary, the question above all is whether a word which looks entirely pictorial, deceptive, and illustrative has not already, in the life of the language, lost this its first sensuous meaning, and the memory of it, in the course of its use in a spiritual sense and been *relevé (AUFGEHOBEN HATTE)* into a spiritual meaning."[27]

Here, the opposition between actual, effective metaphors and inactive, effaced metaphors corresponds to the value of *usure (Abnützung)*, whose implications we have already discussed. This is an almost constant characteristic in the discourse on philosophical metaphor: there are said to be inactive metaphors, which have no interest at all since the author *did not think of them,* and since the metaphorical effect is to be studied in the field of consciousness. The traditional opposition between living and dead metaphors corresponds to the difference

27. *Aesthetics*, pp. 404–5. [The last phrase has been modified to include the verb *aufheben*, which Derrida of course renders as *relever.*] There are analogous considerations of the figures of prehension in Valéry, in his *Discours aux Chirurgiens,* in *Oeuvres* (Paris: Gallimard, 1957), vol. 1, p. 919. See also below, "Qual Quelle."

between effective and extinct metaphors.[28] Above all, the movement of meta-phorization (origin and then erasure of the metaphor, transition from the proper sensory meaning to the proper spiritual meaning by means of the detour of figures) is nothing other than a movement of idealization. Which is included under the master category of dialectical idealism, to wit, the *relève (Aufhebung)*, that is, the memory *(Erinnerung)* that produces signs, interiorizes them in ele-vating, suppressing, and conserving the sensory exterior. And in order to think and resolve them, this framework sets to work the oppositions nature/spirit, nature/history, or nature/freedom, which are linked by genealogy to the oppo-sition of *physis* to its others, and by the same token to the oppositions sensual/spiritual, sensible/intelligible, sensory/sense *(sinnlich/Sinn)*. Nowhere is this sys-tem as explicit as it is in Hegel. It describes the space of the possibility of metaphysics, and the concept of metaphor thus defined belongs to it.[29]

Let us suppose, provisionally, that these oppositions can be given credence, and that the program of a general metaphorics of philosophy can be entrusted to them. In classifying the (natural) original metaphors, we would quickly have to resort to the mythology of the four elements. This time we would be dealing not with a kind of psychoanalysis of the material imagination applied to a rather indeterminate corpus,[30] but rather with a rhetorical analysis of the philosophical text, supposing that assured criteria were available for identifying this text as such. This would lead to an inevitable intersection of the classification of the native regions of metaphor with a general grid, no longer constituted on the basis of these elementary regions of phenomena (what appears), but on the basis

28. This is central to T. Spoerri's study "La puissance métaphorique de Descartes," *Colloque Philosophique de Royaumont* (Paris: Éditions de Minuit, 1957). See also Perelman and Olbrechts-Tyteca, *Traité de l'argumentation* (Paris: Presses Universitaires de France, 1958).
29. This explains the distrust that the concept of metaphor inspires in Heidegger. In *Der Satz vom Grund* he insists above all on the opposition sensory/nonsensory, an impor-tant, but neither the only, nor the first, nor the most determining characteristic of the value of metaphor. "But here, the following remark will suffice: Since our hearing and seeing are never a simple reception by the senses, it is not any longer suitable to affirm that the interpretation of thought as grasped by hearing *(als Er-hören)* and vision *(Er-blicken)* represent only a metaphor *(Übertragung)*, a transposition into the non-sensory of the so-called sensory. The notion of 'transposition' and of metaphor *(Metapher)* rest on the dis-tinction, not to say the separation, of the sensory and the non-sensory as two domains each subsisting for itself. This kind of separation between the sensory and the non-sensory, between the physical and the non-physical, is a fundamental characteristic of what is called 'metaphysics,' which confers upon Western thought its essential characteristics. Once this distinction of the sensory and the non-sensory is recognized as insufficient, metaphysics loses its rank as authoritative thought. Once this limitation of metaphysics has been seen, the determining conception *(massgebende Vorstellung)* of 'metaphor' collapses by itself. It is particularly determinant for the way in which we represent the Being of language. This is why metaphor is often utilized as an auxiliary means in the interpretation of poetic, or more generally artistic, works. The metaphorical exists only within the borders of metaphysics."
30. TN. The reference is to Bachelard, discussed in the last section of this essay ("*La métaphysique—relève de la métaphore.*")

of the receptive zones, the regions of sensibility. Outside the mathematical text—which it is difficult to conceive as providing metaphors in the strict sense, since it is attached to no determined ontic region and has no empirical sensory content—all the regional discourses, to the extent that they are not purely formal, procure for philosophical discourse metaphorical contents of the sensory type. Thus one does actually speak of visual, auditory, and tactile metaphors, (where the problem of knowledge is in its element), and even, more rarely, which is not insignificant, olfactory[31] or gustatory ones.

But there must be, in correspondence to this empirical aesthetics of sensory contents, as the very condition of its possibility, a transcendental and formal aesthetics of metaphor. It would lead us back to the a priori forms of space and time. In effect, do we not actually speak of temporalizing metaphors, metaphors that call upon the sense of hearing not only, as from Plato to Husserl, according to the musical paradigm, but also as an appeal to listening, to understanding (*entendement*) itself, etc.? Nietzsche relaxes the limits of the metaphorical to such an extent that he attributes a metaphoric capacity to every phonic enunciation: do we not transport into the time of speech that which in itself is heterogeneous to this time?[32] Inversely, is it not frequently said that every metaphoric enunciation spatializes as soon as it gives us something to imagine, to see, or to touch? Bergson is far from alone in being wary of spatial metaphors.

How is this final regression to occur? How is recourse to the final opposition of space and time possible without taking on in depth this traditional philosophical problem? (And it is as concerns both this transcendental aesthetic and the pure, a priori forms of sensibility that the problem of mathematical metaphors would find one of its loci.) How are we to know what the temporalization and spatialization of a meaning, of an ideal object, of an intelligible tenor, are, if we have not clarified what "space" and "time" mean? But how are we to do this

31. "We thought it necessary to begin with the sense of smell, because of all the senses it is the one which appears to contribute least to the knowledge of the human mind." Condillac, *Traité des sensations, Introduction,* in *Oeuvres Philosophiques de Condillac,* ed. Georges Le Roy (Paris: Presses Universitaires de France, 1947), p. 222.

32. Which amounts, strangely enough, to making every signifier a metaphor of the signified, although the classical concept of metaphor designates only the substitution of one signified for another, one signified becoming the signifier of the other. Does not Nietzsche's operation consist, here, in extending to every element of discourse, under the name of metaphor, what classical rhetoric considered, no less strangely, to be a quite particular figure, the *metonymy of the sign?* Du Marsais says that this figure consists in taking "the sign for the thing signified," and it occupies the last place in the list of the five species of metonymy he identified. Fontanier devotes less than a page to it. This is explained by the fact that the sign examined here is a part of the thing signified, and not the very stuff of the figures of discourse. The examples are first those of *symbolic,* nonarbitrary, signs (*scepter*), for the rank of king, *staff* for that of marshal, *hat* for that of cardinal, *sword* for soldier, *robe* for magistrate, "*lance* to signify a *man, and distaff* to indicate a woman: *fief which falls from lance to distaff,* that is a fief which passes from the males to the females." Du Marsais, *Traité des tropes* (Geneva: Slatkine Reprints, 1967), chap. 2, ii.

before knowing what might be a logos or a meaning that in and of themselves spatio-temporalize everything they state? What logos as metaphor might be?

Already the opposition of meaning (the atemporal or nonspatial signified as meaning, as content) to its metaphorical signifier (an opposition that plays itself out within the element of meaning to which metaphor belongs in its entirety)[33] is sedimented—another metaphor—by the entire history of philosophy. Without taking into account that the separation between sense (the signified) and the senses (sensory signifier) is enunciated by means of the same root (*sensus*, *Sinn*). One might admire, as does Hegel, the generousness of this stock, and interpret its secret *relève* speculatively, dialectically; but before utilizing a dialectical concept of metaphor, one must examine the double turn which opened metaphor and dialectics, permitting to be called *sense* that which should be foreign to the senses.

Thus, the general taxonomy of metaphors—so-called philosophical metaphors in particular—would presuppose the solution of important problems, and primarily of problems which constitute the entirety of philosophy in its history. Thus a metaphorology would be derivative as concerns the discourse it allegedly would dominate, whether it does so by taking as its rule the explicit consciousness of the philosopher or the systematic and objective structure of his text, whether it reconstitutes a meaning or deciphers a symptom, whether or not it elaborates an idiomatic metaphorics (proper to a philosopher, a system, or a particular body of work) based on a more general, more constricting, more durable metaphorics. The concept of metaphor, along with all the predicates that permit its ordered extension and comprehension, is a philosopheme.

The consequences of this are double and contradictory. On the one hand it is impossible to dominate philosophical metaphorics as such, *from the exterior*, by using a concept of metaphor which remains a philosophical product. Only philosophy would seem to wield any authority over its own metaphorical productions. But, on the other hand, for the same reason philosophy is deprived of what it provides itself. Its instruments belonging to its field, philosophy is incapable of dominating its general tropology and metaphorics. It could perceive its metaphorics only around a blind spot or central deafness. The concept of metaphor would describe this contour, but it is not even certain that the concept thereby circumscribes an organizing center; and this formal law holds for every philosopheme. And this for two cumulative reasons: (1) The philosopher will never find in this concept anything but what he has put into it, or at least what he believes he has put into it as a philosopher. (2) The constitution of the fundamental oppositions of the metaphorology (*physis/tekhnē*, *physis/nomos*, sensible/intelligible; space/time, signifier/signified, etc.) has occurred by means of the

33. This complex structure leads to many confusions. Some of them may be avoided by means of I. A. Richards's proposed distinction between the metaphorical *tenor* and the metaphorical *vehicle*. Sense, the meaning "must be clearly distinguished from the tenor." *The Philosophy of Rhetoric* (New York: Oxford University Press, 1965), p. 100.

history of a metaphorical language, or rather by means of "tropic" movements which, no longer capable of being called by a philosophical name—i.e. metaphors—nevertheless, and for the same reason, do not make up a "proper" language. It is from beyond the difference between the proper and the nonproper that the effects of propriety and nonpropriety have to be accounted for. By definition, thus, there is no properly philosophical category to qualify a certain number of tropes that have conditioned the so-called "fundamental," "structuring," "original" philosophical oppositions: they are so many "metaphors" that would constitute the rubrics of such a tropology, the words "turn" or "trope" or "metaphor" being no exception to the rule. To permit oneself to overlook this *vigil* of philosophy, one would have to posit that the sense aimed at through these figures is an essence rigorously independent of that which transports it, which is an already philosophical *thesis,* one might even say philosophy's *unique thesis,* the thesis which constitutes the concept of metaphor, the opposition of the proper and the nonproper, of essence and accident, of intuition and discourse, of thought and language, of the intelligible and the sensible.

That is what would be at stake. Supposing that we might reach it (touch it, see it, comprehend it?), this tropic and prephilosophical resource could not have the archeological simplicity of a proper origin, the virginity of a history of beginnings. And we know already that it could derive neither from a *rhetoric* of philosophy nor from a *metaphilosophy* analogous to what Bachelard, in his psychoanalysis of material imagination, called *meta-poetics.* We know this, already, on the basis of the law of supplementarity (between the concept and the field) viewed in its formal necessity. Provisionally, let us take this law for a hypothesis. In attempting to verify it in several "examples," perhaps we might, at the same time, *fill* the concept of metaphor, following its entire tradition, a tradition which is as much philosophical as rhetorical, and might also recognize, at the same time as the rule of its transformations, the limit of its plasticity.

The Ellipsis of the Sun:
Enigmatic, Incomprehensible,
Ungraspable

He may do [the deed], but in ignorance of his relationship, and discover that afterwards, as does
Oedipus in Sophocles. Here the deed
is outside the play (exō tou dramatos).
(Poetics, 1453b29–32)[34]

There should be nothing improbable
(alogon) among the actual incidents
(en tois pragmasin). If it be unavoidable, however, it should be outside
the tragedy, like the improbability in
the Oedipus of Sophocles. (1454b6–8)

A likely impossibility (adunata eikota)
is always preferable to an uncon-
vincing possibility (dunata apithana).
The story (logous) should never be
made up of improbable incidents (ek
merōn alogōn); there should be nothing of the sort in it. If, however, such
incidents are unavoidable, they
should be outside the piece (exō tou
mutheumatos), like the hero's ignorance (to mē eidenai) in Oedipus of the
circumstances of Laius' death . . .
(1460a26–30)

Neither a *rhetoric* of philosophy nor a *metaphilosophy* appear to be pertinent here—
such is the hypothesis. In the first place, why not rhetoric as such?

Each time that a rhetoric defines metaphor, not only is *a* philosophy implied,
but also a conceptual network in which philosophy *itself* has been constituted.
Moreover each thread in this network forms a *turn*, or one might say a metaphor,
if that notion were not too derivative here. What is defined, therefore, is implied
in the defining of the definition.

As goes without saying, no petition is being made here to some homogenous
continuum ceaselessly relating tradition back to itself, the tradition of metaphysics as the tradition of rhetoric. Nevertheless, if we did not begin by attending
to such of the most durable constraints which have been exercised on the basis
of a very long systematic chain, and if we did not take the trouble to delimit the
general functioning and effective limits of this chain, we would run the risk of
taking the most derivative effects for the original characteristics of a historical
subset, a hastily identified configuration, an imaginary or marginal mutation.
By means of an empiricist and impressionistic rush toward alleged differences—
in fact toward cross-sections that are in principle linear and chronological—we
would go from discovery to discovery. A break beneath every step! For example,
we could present as the physiognomy proper to "eighteenth century" rhetoric
a whole set of characteristics, (such as the privilege of the name), inherited,

34. TN. Aristotle, *Poetics*, trans. I. Baywater, in *The Works of Aristotle*, ed. W. D. Ross
(Oxford: Oxford University Press, 1924). All further references to the *Poetics* will be to this
edition.

although not in a direct line, and with all kinds of divisions and inequalities of transformation, from Aristotle or the Middle Ages. Here, we are being led back to the program, still entirely to be elaborated, of a new delimitation of bodies of work and of a new problematic of the signature.

There is a code or a program—a rhetoric, if you will—for every discourse on metaphor: following custom, in the *first place* the Aristotelian definition must be recalled, at least the one in the *Poetics* (1457b). We will not fail to do so. Certainly, Aristotle invented neither the word nor the concept of metaphor. However, he seems to have proposed the first systematic situating of it, which in any event has been retained as such with the most powerful historical effects. It is indispensable to study the terrain on which the Aristotelian definition could have been constructed. But this study would lose all pertinence if it were not preceded, or in any event controlled, by the systematic and internal reconstitution of the text to be reinscribed. Even if partial and preliminary the task is not limited to a commentary on a textual surface. No transparency is granted it. The issue already is one of an active interpretation setting to work an entire system of rules and anticipations.

"Metaphor (*metaphora*) consists in giving (*epiphora*)[35] the thing a name (*onomatos*) that belongs to something else (*allotriou*), the transference being either from genus to species (*apo tou genous epi eidos*), or from species to genus (*apo tou eidous epi to genos*), or from species to species (*apo tou eidous epi eidos*), or on the grounds of analogy (*ē kata to analogon*)" (1457b6–9).

This definition, doubtless the most explicit, the most precise, and in any event the most general,[36] can be analyzed along two lines. It is a philosophical thesis

---

35. TN. Derrida's citation of the Greek terms is particularly important here. The French translation of *epiphora* as *"transport"* preserves a "metaphoric" play on words that is lost in the English rendering "giving." Meta-*phora* and epi-*phora* have the same root, from the Greek *pherein*, to carry, to transport.

36. This generality poses problems which recently have been reactivated in a way, as is well known. We will come back to them in our conclusion. In any event, Aristotle is the first to consider metaphor as the general form of all the figures of words, whether metaphor *includes* them (as in these examples of transport by metonymy or synecdoche), constitutes their *economy* (abridged comparison), or finds its own *best form* in the analogy of proportionality (*Rhetoric* III). Doubtless this generality is proportional to the impoverishment of the determination of metaphor. Aristotle, from early on, was accused or excused for this. "Some Ancients have condemned Aristotle for putting under the name of metaphor the first two, which properly are but synecdoches; but Aristotle spoke in general, and he was writing at a time when there was still no refinement of figures, both in order to distinguish them and in order to give to each the name which would have best explained its nature. Cicero justifies Aristotle sufficiently when he writes in his *De Oratore: Itaque genus hoc Graeci appellant allegoricum, nomine recte, genere melius ille (Aristoteles) qui ista omnia translationes vocat.*" André Dacier, *Introduction à la poétique d'Aristote*, 1733. Hugh Blair: "Aristotle, in his Poetics, uses Metaphor in this extended sense, for any figurative meaning imposed upon a word; as a whole put for the part, or a part for the whole; a species for the genus, or a genus for the species. But it would be unjust to tax this most acute writer with any inaccuracy on this account; the minute subdivisions, and various names of Tropes, being unknown in his days, and the invention of later rhetoricians." *Lectures on Rhetoric and Belles Lettres* XV, "Metaphor."

on metaphor. And it is also a philosophical discourse whose entire surface is worked by a metaphorics.

The philosophical thesis belongs to a system of interpretation joining together *metaphora, mimēsis, logos, physis, phōnē, sēmainein, onoma*. In order to restore the movement of this chain, one must be attentive to the *place* of the discussions on metaphor, as much in the *Poetics* as in book 3 of the *Rhetoric*.[37] The place reserved for metaphor is already significant in itself. In both works, it belongs to a theory of *lexis*. "The Plot and Characters having been discussed, it remains to consider the Diction and Thought (*peri lexeōs kai dianoias*)" (1456a33–34; there is an analogous development at the beginning of book 3 of the *Rhetoric*). Although it has only just been mentioned, "thought" (here, *dianoia*) covers the range of that which is given to language, or of what one is given to think through language, as a cause or an effect or content of language, but not as the act of language itself (statement, diction, elocution, *lexis*). *Dianoia* thus determined is the subject of rhetoric, at least in its first two books. "As for the Thought, we may assume what is said of it in our Art of Rhetoric, as it belongs more properly to that department of inquiry" (1456a34). The difference between *dianoia* and *lexis* is due to the fact that the first is not made manifest by itself. Now, this manifestation, which is the act of speech, constitutes the essence and very operation of tragedy. If there were no difference between *dianoia* and *lexis*, there would be no space for tragedy: "What indeed would be the good (*ergon*) of the speaker (*tou legontos*) if things appeared in the required light even apart from anything he says (*ei phanoito nēi deoi kai mē dia ton logon*)?" (1456b7–8).[38] This difference is

---

37. On the relations between the *Rhetoric* and the *Poetics* on this point, and notably as concerns the notions of *metaphora* and *eikōn*, see Marsh H. McCall, *Ancient Rhetorical Theories of Simile and Comparison* (Cambridge: Harvard University Press, 1969). "Neither work can be proved to precede the other—almost certainly both were revised and supplemented from time to time. The odd absence of *eikōn* from the *Poetics* must be left unresolved." This is not a total absence (see at least 1048b10 and 15).

38. TN. F. C. T. Moore, in the notes to his translation of this essay, contends that Derrida's last two citations from Aristotle (*Poetics* 1456a34 and 1456b7–8) are based on an "incorrect translation" (note 29) and a "conjectural" reading of a "corrupt" text (notes 29 and 30). On the first point, there is no question that while the Budé translation cited by Derrida and the Bywater translation do not correspond word for word, the *entire* sentence (not the fragment of it cited by Moore) does say that the examination of thought (*dianoia*) is the province of rhetoric. On the second point, it is true that Bywater and Budé have different readings of what Budé gives as *dianoia* and translates as "thought." Bywater, whose translation I have adhered to, gives the crucial word as "things," from the reading of the text that gives *deoi* here and not *dianoia*. Thus, our text does not correspond to the French edition of *Marges*, where the sentence in question would read, changing the one word: "What indeed would be the good of the speaker if his *thought* appeared in the required light even apart from anything he says?" Comparison with the Greek text used by Bywater (Becker's 1831 Quarto Text, also used in the Harvard University Press *Aristotle in Twenty-Three Volumes*, where Fyfe's translation of the *Poetics* occupies vol. 23, which is where I consulted it) shows that the Greek cited by Derrida here differs *only* as concerns this word. Even if Aristotle's text is corrupt here—which I am not competent to judge— Derrida has not falsified the *sense* of either citation in order to have it conform to his

not only due to the fact that the personage must be able to say something other than what he thinks. He exists and acts within tragedy only on the condition that he speaks.

So the discourse on metaphor belongs to a treatise *peri lexōs*. There is lexis, and within it metaphor, in the extent to which thought is not made manifest by itself, in the extent to which the meaning of what is said or thought is not a phenomenon of itself. *Dianoia* as such is not yet related to metaphor. There is metaphor only in the extent to which someone is supposed to make manifest, by means of statement, a given thought that of itself remains inapparent, hidden, or latent. Thought stumbles upon metaphor, or metaphor falls to thought at the moment when meaning attempts to emerge from itself in order to be stated, enunciated, brought to the light of language. And yet—such is our problem— the theory of metaphor remains a theory of *meaning* and posits a certain original *naturality* of this figure. How is this possible?

Aristotle has just set aside *dianoia*, sending it off into rhetoric. He then defines the components of *lexis*. Among them, the nominal, the noun. It is under this heading that he treats metaphor (*epiphora onomatos*). *Onoma* certainly has two values in this context. Sometimes it is opposed to the verb (*rhēma*), which implies an idea of time. Sometimes it covers the field of verbs, since metaphor, the displacement of nouns, also, in the examples given in the *Poetics,* plays upon verbs. This confusion is possible by virtue of the profound identity of the noun and the verb: what they have in common is that they are intelligible in and of themselves, have an immediate relation to an object or rather to a unity of meaning. They constitute the order of the *phōnē sēmantikē* from which are ex- cluded, as we will see, articles, conjunctions, prepositions, and in general all the elements of language which, according to Aristotle, have no meaning in themselves; in other words, which do not of themselves designate something. The adjective is capable of becoming substantive and nominal. To this extent it may belong to the *semantic* order. Therefore it seems that the field of *onoma*— and consequently that of metaphor, as the transport of names—is less that of the noun in the strict sense, (which it acquired very late in rhetoric), than that of the *nominalizable*. Every word which resists this nominalization would remain foreign to metaphor. Now, only that which claims—or henceforth claims—to have a complete and independent signification, that which is intelligible by itself, outside any syntactic relation, can be nominalized. To take up a traditional opposition that still will be in use in Husserl, metaphor would be a transport of categorematic and not of syncategorematic words *as such*. The *as such* must

---

argument, as Moore seems to suggest. It should be noted too that at least one other English translation of the *Poetics* (Butcher's in The Library of Liberal Arts volume, *Poetics and On Music*) gives the disputed word as *dianoia,* "thought." (My thanks to Richard Rand for his help here.)

be emphasized, since the syncategorem might itself also give rise to an operation of nominalization.[39]

Du Marsais had been tempted very literally to follow Aristotle in defining metaphor as "a figure by means of which the proper, literal meaning of a noun is transported." That he replaced *noun* by *word* from one edition to another, that his first gesture was criticized by both Laharpe and Fontanier, and that the latter systematically enlarges the field of metaphor to include all words—none of this, at least on this point, deeply disrupts the Aristotelian tradition. In effect, on the one hand, only "single word" tropes are "properly named" such, according to Fontanier. On the other hand, and consequently, after stating that all kinds of words can give rise to metaphors, Fontanier indeed must exclude from the enumeration which follows syncategorems, meanings said to be incomplete, the pivots of discourse: "*On the tropes by resemblance, that is, metaphors:*[40] Tropes by

39. Leibniz provides a remarkable example of this operation of *extension* and *extraction*. The issue is to unearth the hidden concept and name, the substantive idea dissimulated in every syntactic sign of relation. Thus, a particle is transformed into a complete signification. Again this is in a philosophical dialogue, and the subject treated is not very distant from the one in the *Garden of Epicurus*: "THEOPHILUS: I do not see why we could not say that there are *private* ideas, as there are negative truths, for the act of denial is positive . . . PHILALETHES: Without disputing about this point, it will be more useful to approach a little nearer the origins of all our notions and knowledge, to observe how the words employed to form actions and notions wholly removed from the senses, derive their *origin* from sensible ideas, whence they are *transferred* to significations more abstruse . . . Whence we may conjecture what kind of notions they had who spoke these first languages and how nature will suggest unexpectedly to men the origin and the principle of all their knowledge by the terms themselves. THEOPHILUS: . . . The fact is not always recognized because most frequently the true etymologies are lost . . . It will, however, be well to consider *this analogy of sensible and non-sensible things* which has served as the basis of *tropes:* a matter that you will understand the better by considering a very extended example such as is furnished by the use of *prepositions,* like *to, with, from, before, in, without, by, for, upon, towards,* which are all derived from place, from distance, and from motion, and afterwards transferred to every sort of change, order, sequence, difference, agreement. *To* signifies approach, as in the expression: I go *to* Rome. But as in order to attract anything we bring it near that to which we wish to unite it, we say that one thing is attached *to* another. And further, as there is, so to speak, an immaterial attachment." The demonstration is made for each preposition, and closes in this way: "and as these analogies are extremely variable and do not depend on any determinate notions, it thence comes that languages vary much in the use of these *particles* and *cases* which the prepositions govern, or rather in which they are found as things understood and virtually included." *New Essays Concerning Human Understanding,* trans. A. G. Langley (London, 1896), book 3, chap. 1, "Words," pp. 289–91. Du Marsais, *Traité des tropes:* "Each language has particular . . . proper . . . metaphors" (chap. 1, x). "Certain figures may vary from one language to another," as Fontanier will say, "and some do not even occur in every language." "Préface au Traité général des figures du discours autres que les tropes," in *Les Figures du Discours,* ed. Gérard Genette (Paris: Flammarion, 1968), p. 275.

Condillac, whom Fontanier judged to be as "strong" as Du Marsais (ibid., p. 276), also thought that "the same figures are not admitted to every language." *De l'art d'écrire,* in *Oeuvres Philosophiques* II, iv.

40. Fontanier, "Préface," p. 99. Resemblance or analogy: such is the distinctive source of metaphor, from Aristotle to Fontanier. Du Marsais, in defining metaphor, also spoke

resemblance consist in *presenting an idea under the sign of another idea that is more striking or better known, and which, moreover, has no other tie to the first idea than that of a certain conformity or analogy.* As a genre these tropes can be reduced to a single one, *Metaphor,* whose name, which is so well known, and perhaps better known than the thing itself, has lost, as Laharpe observes, all its scholarly import. *Metaphor* is not ordinarily distinguished into species, like *Metonymy* and *Synecdoche;* however it must not be thought that it has but a single form, a single aspect, and that it is the same in every case. On the contrary, it is quite varied, and doubtless extends further than *Metonymy* and *Synecdoche,* for not only the noun, but further the adjective, the participle, the verb, and finally all species of words belong to its domain. Thus all species of words can be employed, or in effect are employed, *metaphorically,* if not as *figures,* at least as *catachreses.* The species of words capable of being employed *metaphorically* as *figures* are the noun, the adjective, the participle, the verb, and perhaps also the adverb, although rather rarely" (p. 99).

Now, on the one hand, everything excluded from this list of words is reserved for the catachresis of metaphor, a "not true figure," which "embraces in its extension even the interjection." ("There are even very few words, in each species, not under its domination," p. 215. We will come back to this problem later.) True metaphor, therefore, keeps within the limits of the Aristotelian "noun." Which, on the other hand, appears to be confirmed throughout the entire system of distinctions proposed by Fontanier in his general definition of words. Among these words corresponding to "ideas of an object"—which naturally can be nominalized—are classed *nouns,* all words "employed substantively" (*the beautiful, the true, the just; eating, drinking, sleeping; the for, the against; the front, the back; the why, the how; the inside, the outside; the buts, the ifs, the whys, the wherefores*), and active or passive participles. The first group corresponds to *substantive* ideas of object, and the second to *concrete* ideas of object. Among the words corresponding to the "ideas of relationship" are classed the verb ("But by *verb,* here, I understand only the properly named verb, the verb *to be,* called

---

of a "comparison which is in the mind." It remains that Aristotle made of metaphor a rather extended genre, as we have seen, in order to cover every other nominal figure, including metonymy; that Fontanier restricts the field of metaphor (and therefore of analogy or of resemblance) in order to oppose it to metonymy; and that Du Marsais at first, by etymology, had loosened the limits of metonymy: "The word *metonymy* signifies transposition or changing of name, one name for another. In this sense, this figure includes all the other Tropes; for in all Tropes, a word not being taken in the meaning proper to it, it awakens an idea that might be expressed by another word. In what follows, we will notice what properly distinguishes metonymy from the other Tropes. The masters of the art restrict metonymy to the following uses:" (Du Marsais, II, 2). Condillac (whose philosophy, more than any other, or at least like every other, might be considered as a treatise on analogy) advances a symmetrically inverse proposition: "What we have said of comparisons must be applied to metaphors. I will bring to your attention only that if one consults etymology, all tropes are metaphors: for metaphor properly signifies a word transported from one meaning to an other" (*De l'art d'écrire* II, vi).

the *abstract verb* or substantive *verb;* and not those improperly named verbs, the *concrete* verbs which are formed by the combination of the verb *to be* with a participle: *I love, I read, I come* for *I am loving, I am reading, I am coming,"* p. 45), the preposition, the adverb, and the conjunction. The dissymmetry of these oppositions appears to be rather marked: the superiority of the ideas of object to the ideas of relation ("delicate ideas that we did not wish to separate from their signs, for fear that they escape us," p. 45), and the correlative superiority of the substantive. This superiority is apparent not only in the case of the verb *to be.* Among all other species of words, those which are subject to variations ("in their forms, in their inflections") are governed by the substantive idea ("But it is easy to see that they are dominated by the substantive idea to whose expression they all tend more or less directly," p. 46). The other species of words (preposition, conjunction, adverb, interjection) "do not vary at all, because they are not immediately tied to the substantive idea, and are even entirely detached and independent from it; and because they hardly seem tied, fundamentally, to anything other than the views of the mind, being only, as concerns it, ways of seeing" (p. 46).

Everything, in the theory of metaphor, that is coordinate to this system of distinctions or at least to its principle, seems to belong to the great immobile chain of Aristotelian ontology, with its theory of the analogy of Being, its logic, its epistemology, and more precisely its poetics and its rhetoric. In effect, let us consider the Aristotelian definition of the noun, that is, the element of metaphor. The noun is the first semantic unity. It is the smallest signifying element. It is a composite *phōnē sēmantikē,* each of whose elements is in itself insignificant (*asēmos*), without meaning. The noun shares this characteristic with the verb, from which it is distinguished only by its atemporality.

Before coming to the noun, Aristotle had enumerated all the elements of *lexis* which are constituted by sound without signification (*phōnē asēmos*). The letter, for example, the *stoikheion,* the ultimate element, is part of *lexis,* but has no meaning in itself. Here, the letter is not the graphic form, but the phonic element, the atom of the voice (*phōnē adiairetos*). Its insignificance is not indeterminate. The letter is not just any vocal emission without meaning. It is a vociferation which although without meaning, must nevertheless be capable of "naturally" entering into the formation or composition of a *phōnē sēmantikē (ex hēs pephuke sunetē gignesthai phōnē),* opening the possibility of a noun or a verb, contributing to *saying what is.* This is the difference between animals and man: according to Aristotle both can emit indivisible sounds, but only man can make of them a letter: "The Letter is an indivisible sound of a particular kind, one that may become a factor in an intelligible sound. Indivisible sounds are uttered by the brutes also, but no one of these is a Letter in our sense of the term" (*Poetics* 1456b22–25). Aristotle does not analyze this difference; he interprets it by teleological retrospection. No internal characteristic distinguishes the atom of animal sound and the letter, Thus, it is only on the basis of the signifying phonic composition, on the basis of meaning and reference, that the human voice should be distinguished from the call of an animal. Meaning and reference: that is, the possibility of signifying by means of a noun. What is proper to nouns is to signify something (*Ta de onomata sēmainei ti; Rhetoric* III, 10, 1410b11), an independent being identical to itself, conceived as such. It is at this point that the theory of the name, such as it is implied by the concept of metaphor, is articulated with ontology. Aside from the classical and dogmatically affirmed limit between the animal without *logos* and man as the *zōon logon ekhon*, what appears here is a certain systematic indissociability of the value of metaphor and the metaphysical chain holding together the values of discourse, voice, noun, signification, meaning, imitative representation, resemblance; or, in order to reduce what these translations import or deport, the values of *logos, phōnē sēmantikē, sēmainein, onoma, mimēsis, homoiosis*. The definition of metaphor is in its place in the *Poetics*, which opens as a treatise on *mimēsis*. *Mimēsis* is never without the *theoretical* perception of resemblance or similarity, that is, of that which always will be posited as the condition for metaphor. *Homoiosis* is not only constitutive of the value of truth (*alētheia*) which governs the entire chain; it is that without which the metaphorical operation is impossible: "To produce a good metaphor is to see a likeness" (*To gar eu metapherein to to homoion theōrein estin*. 1459a7–8). The condition for metaphor (for good and true metaphor) is the condition for truth. Therefore it is to be expected that the animal, deprived of *logos*, of *phonē sēmantikē*, of *stoikheion*, etc., also would be incapable of mimesis. *Mimēsis* thus determined belongs to *logos*, and is not animalistic aping, or gesticular mimicry; it is tied to the possibility of meaning and truth in discourse. At the beginning of the *Poetics mimēsis* in a way is posited as a possibility proper to *physis*. *Physis* is revealed in *mimēsis*, or in the poetry which is a species of *mimēsis*, by virtue of the hardly apparent structure which constrains *mimēsis* from carrying to the exterior the fold of its redoubling. It belongs to *physis*, or, if you will, *physis* includes its own exteriority and its double. In this sense, *mimēsis* is therefore a "natural" movement. This naturality is reduced and restricted to man's speech by Aristotle. But rather than a reduction, this constitutive gesture of metaphysics and of humanism is a teleological determination: naturality in general says itself, reassembles itself, knows itself, appears to itself, reflects itself, and "mimics" itself par excellence and *in truth* in human nature. *Mimēsis* is proper to man. Only man imitates properly. Man alone takes pleasure in imitating, man alone learns to imitate, man alone learns by imitation. The power of truth, as the unveiling of nature (*physis*) by *mimēsis*, congenitally belongs to the physics of man, to anthropophysics. Such is the natural origin of poetry, and such is the natural origin of metaphor: "It is clear that the general origin of poetry was due to two causes, each of them part of human nature (*physikai*). Imitation is natural (*symphyton*: innate, congenital) to man from childhood, one of his advantages over the lower animals being this, that he is the most imitative creature (*mimētikōtaton*) in the world and learns at first (*mathēseis prōtas*: first knowledge)

237

by imitation. And it is also natural for all to delight in works of imitation" (*Poetics*, 1448b4–9).

As these two sources of poetry confirm, *logos*, *mimēsis*, and *alētheia* here are one and the same possibility. And *logos* is in its element only in *phōnē*. It belongs there better than elsewhere. And this is always so according to a teleological determination: just as the destination of nature is to be mimed best in human nature, and just as man, more than any other animal, properly imitates (*mimetikōtaton*), so the voice is the organ most apt to imitate. This vocation of the voice is designated by the same word (*mimetikōtaton*) in book 3 of the *Rhetoric*: ". . . words (*onomata*) are imitations (*mimēmata*), and . . . the human voice . . . of all organs can best imitate things (*hē phōnē pantōn mimētikōtaton tōn moriōn*" [III, I, 1404a21–22; translation modified]).

Metaphor thus, as an effect of *mimēsis* and *homoiosis*, the manifestation of analogy, will be a means of knowledge, a means that is subordinate, but certain. One may say of it what is said of poetry: it is more philosophical and more serious (*philosophōteron kai spoudaioteron*) than history (*Poetics* 1451b5–6), since it recounts not only the particular, but also states the general, the probable and the necessary.[41] However, it is not as serious as philosophy itself, and apparently will conserve this intermediary status throughout the history of philosophy. Or rather, its ancillary status: metaphor, when well trained, must work in the service of truth, but the master is not to content himself with this, and must prefer the discourse of full truth to metaphor. For example, Aristotle reproaches Plato for being satisfied with "poetic metaphors" (*metaphoras legein poiētikas*) and for keeping to hollow language (*kenologein*) when he says that Ideas are the paradigms in which other things participate (*Metaphysics*, A9, 991a20, M5, 1079b25).

For the same reason, pleasure, the second "cause" of *mimēsis* and metaphor, is the pleasure of knowing, of learning by resemblance, of recognizing the same. The philosopher will be *more* apt at this than anyone else. He will be man par excellence: "The explanation is to be found in a further fact: to be learning something is the greatest of pleasures, not only to the philosopher, but to the rest of mankind, however small their capacity for it—the reason of the delight in seeing the picture (*eikonas*) is that one is at the same time learning, and deducing (*syllogizesthai*) what is represented" (*Poetics*, 1448b12–17). Book 3 of the *Rhetoric* specifies this idea, between a stalk and a flower: "We all naturally (*physei*) find it agreeable to get hold of new ideas easily: words (*onomata*) signify something (*sēmainei ti*), and therefore those words are the most agreeable which bring us knowledge of something new . . . From metaphor . . . we can best get hold of something fresh. When the poet calls old age a 'withered stalk' (*kalamēn*) he conveys a new idea, a new fact, to us by means of the general notion of 'lost

41. "Metaphors must be drawn, as has been said already, from things that are related to the original thing, and yet not obviously so related (*apo oikeiōn kei mē phanerōn*)—just as in philosophy also an acute mind will perceive resemblances (*to homoion . . . theōrein*) even in things far apart" (*Rhetoric* III, ii, 1412a9–12).

bloom' which is common to both things. The similes (*eikones*) of the poets do the same . . . The simile, as has been said before, is a metaphor, differing from it only in having a prefixed word (*prothesei*), and just because it is longer it is less attractive. Besides, it does not say outright that 'this' is 'that' " (*Rhetoric* III, 10, 1410b10–19). Thus, metaphor sets before us, vivaciously, what the comparison more haltingly reconstitutes indirectly. To set before us, to make a picture, to exercise a lively action—these are so many virtues that Aristotle attributes to the good metaphor, virtues that he regularly associates with the value of *energeia*, whose decisive role in Aristotelian metaphysics, in metaphysics, is well known. "We have still to explain what we mean by 'making a picture,' and what must be done to effect this. I say that an expression puts something before our eyes when it represents things as in a state of activity (*energounta sēmainei*). Thus to say that a good man is 'four-square' is certainly a metaphor; both the good man and the square are perfect; but the metaphor does not suggest activity (*ou sēmainei energeian*). On the other hand, in the expression 'with his vigour in full bloom' (*anthousan*) there is a notion of activity"[42] (*Rhetoric* III, II, 1411b22–29). Most often, this metaphorical activation or actualization consists in animating the inanimate, in transporting something into the "psychic" order (ibid., 1412a2). (The opposition animate/inanimate also governs Fontanier's entire classification of metaphors.)

A dividend of pleasure, therefore, is the recompense for the economic development of the syllogism hidden in metaphor, the theoretical perception of resemblance. But the energy of this operation supposes, nevertheless, that the resemblance is not an identity. *Mimēsis* yields pleasure only on the condition of giving us to see in action that which nonetheless is not to be seen in action, but only in its very resembling double, its *mimēma*. Let us leave open the question of this energetic absence, this enigmatic division, that is, the interval which makes scenes and tells tales.[43]

42. It indeed seems, in conformity with so many other convergent affirmations by Aristotle, that in the first case (" 'four-square' ") there is a metaphor, certainly, but a developed one, that is, a comparison, an image (*eikōn*) "preceded by a word."

43. The pleasure, here, comes from a syllogism—to be completed. Rhetoric must take it into account. "Since learning and wondering are pleasant, it follows that such things as acts of imitation must be pleasant—for instance painting, sculpture, poetry—and every product of skillful imitation; this latter, even if the object imitated (*auto to memimemēnon*) is not itself pleasant; for it is not the object itself which here gives delight; the spectator draws inferences (*syllogismoi*); 'that is a so-and-so,' and thus learns something fresh. Dramatic turns of fortune and hairbreadth escapes from perils are pleasant. Everything like (*homoion*) and akin (*sungenes*) to oneself is pleasant . . . And because we are all fond of ourselves (*philautoi*), it follows that what is our own is pleasant to all of us, as for instance our own deeds and words (*erga kai logous*). That is why we are usually fond of our flatterers, and honour; also of our children, for our children are our own work (*autōn gar ergon ta tekna*). It is also pleasant to complete what is defective (*ta ellipē*), for the whole thing thereupon becomes our own work . . . Similarly, since amusement and every kind of relaxation and laughter too belong to the class of pleasant things, it follows that ludicrous things are pleasant, whether men, words or deeds. We have discussed the ludicrous

The semantic system (the order of the *phōnē sēmantikē* with all its connected concepts) is not separated from its other by a simple and continuous line. The limit does not divide the human from the animal. Another division furrows the entirety of "human" language. This latter division is not homogenous, is not human in all its aspects, and to the same degree. The noun still remains the determining criterion: included in the literal elements, the asemantic vocal emissions, are not only letters themselves. The syllable belongs to *lexis*, but of course has no meaning in itself. Above all, there are whole "words" which play an indispensable role in the organization of discourse, but still remain, from Aristotle's point of view, totally without meaning. The conjunction (*sundesmos*)[44] is a *phōnē asēmos*. This holds equally for the article, for articulation in general (*arthron*), and for everything that functions *between* signifying members, between nouns, substantives, or verbs (*Poetics* 1456b38–1457a10). Articulation has no meaning because it makes no reference by means of a categoremic unity, to an independent unity, the unity of a substance or a being. Thus, it is excluded from the metaphorical field as the onomastic field. Henceforth, the annagrammatical,

---

separately (*chōris*) in the treatise on the Art of Poetry" (*Rhetoric* I, ii, 1371b4–1373a1).

According to the elliptical syllogism of *mimēsis*, the pleasure of knowing always accommodates itself to the marking absence of its object. It is even born of this accommodation. The *mimeme* is neither the thing itself nor something totally other. Nothing will upset the law of this pleasure according to the economy of the same and of difference, not even— especially not—the horror, ugliness, and unbearable obscenity of the imitated thing, as soon as it remains out of sight and out of reach, off stage. We would have to follow the chain of examples which have obsessed this classical *topos*, from Aristotle to Lessing. As always, when the mimetic ellipsis is in play, Oedipus, the serpent, and parricide are not far off. "Though the objects themselves may be painful to see, we delight to view the most realistic representations of them in art, the forms for example of the lowest animals and of dead bodies . . . the reason of the delight in seeing the picture is that one is at the same time learning and deducing (*manthanein kai syllogizesthai*) what is represented, for instance, that this figure is such and such a person" (*Poetics* 1448b10–17). "Il n'est point de serpent ni de monstre odieux / Qui par l'art imité, ne puisse plaire aux yeux: / D'un pinceau délicat l'artifice agréable / Du plus affreux objet fait un objet aimable. / Ainsi pour nous charmer, la Tragédie en pleurs / D'Oedipe tout sanglant fit parler des douleurs / D'Oreste parricide exprima les alarmes, / Et, pour nous divertir, nous arracha des larmes." Boileau, *Art Poétique*, Chant II, 1–8. ["There is no serpent or odious monster / That imitated by art cannot be pleasing to our eyes: /With a delicate brush agreeable artifice / Makes of the most frightful object a pleasing one. / Thus, for our pleasure, the tearful Tragedy / Of Oedipus, all bloody, spoke of sorrows / And of parricide Orestes sounded the alarum, / And, for our diversion, wrenched from us our tears."] Euripides' *Orestes* wished no longer to see in his dreams a head bristling with snakes. Longinus cited and commented on the lines of this scene; Boileau translated them. Within the same space, the same system, one can also refuse the unbearable pleasure of such a representation. From *La poétique* by Jules de la Mesnardière (1639): "Beautiful descriptions are certainly agreeable . . . But whatever powerful attractions these marvelous paintings might have, they should represent only things that are pleasant or at least bearable. A fine palette is to be employed for subjects that are not odious, and one should not work like those bizarre painters who put their entire science in the portrayal of a snake or some horrid reptile."

44. The *Rhetoric* also treats the good usage of the conjunction (III, v) and the effects of the asyndeton, the suppression of the conjunction (III, xii).

which functions with the aid of parts of nouns, dismembered nouns, is foreign to the metaphorical field in general, as is also the syntactic play of articulations.

Since this entire theory of the semantic, of *lexis,* and of the noun is implicated in metaphor, it is to be expected that the definition of metaphor would follow its exposition. This is the order of the *Poetics.* And that this definition should intervene immediately after that of the *phōnē semantikē* and the *phōnē asēmos,* is the index not only of a necessity, but also of a difficulty. Metaphor does not just illustrate the general possibilities thus described. It risks disrupting the semantic plenitude to which it should belong. Marking the moment of the turn or of the detour [*du tour ou du détour*] during which meaning might seem to venture forth alone, unloosed from the very thing it aims at however, from the truth which attunes it to its referent, metaphor also opens the wandering of the semantic. The sense of a noun, instead of designating the thing which the noun habitually must designate, carries itself elsewhere. If I say that the evening is the old age of the day, or that old age is the evening of life, "the evening," although having the same sense, will no longer designate the same things. By virtue of its power of metaphoric displacement, signification will be in a kind of state of availability, between the nonmeaning preceding language (which has a meaning) and the truth of language which would say the thing such as it is in itself, in act, properly. This truth is not certain. There can be bad metaphors. Are the latter metaphors? Only an axiology supported by a theory of truth can answer this question; and this axiology belongs to the interior of rhetoric. It cannot be neutral.

In nonmeaning, language has not yet been born. In the truth, language is to be filled, achieved, actualized, to the point of erasing itself, without any possible play, before the (thought) thing which is properly manifested in the truth. *Lexis* is itself, if we might put it thus, only at the stage when meaning has appeared, but when truth still might be missed, when the thing does not yet manifest itself in act in the truth. This is the moment of possible meaning as the possibility of non-truth. As the moment of the detour in which the truth might still be lost, metaphor indeed belongs to *mimēsis,* to the fold of *physis,* to the moment when nature, itself veiling itself, has not yet refound itself in its proper nudity, in the act of its propriety.

If metaphor, the chance and risk of *mimēsis,* can always miss the true, it is that metaphor must count with a determined absence. After the general definition, Aristotle distinguishes four kinds of metaphors. The apparently unsewn series of examples perhaps might follow the basting of an entire narrative. 1. Transport from genus to species (*genos* ——→ *eidos*): "Here stands my ship" (*Odyssey* I, 185). Instead of the word "stands," the more general word, the proper word would have been "anchored," its species. (A traditional recourse to the ship, to its movement, its oars, and its sails, in order to speak figuratively of the means of transport that the metaphorical figure is.) 2. Transport from species to genus: "Truly ten thousand good deeds has Ulysses wrought" (*Iliad* II, 272). "Ten thousand" is a specific member of the genus "large number." 3. Transport from species to species: " 'Drawing the life with bronze' " and " 'severing with the enduring bronze' " (doubtless from Empedocles' *Katharmoi*). "Drawing" and "severing" are two species of the general operation which consists in "taking away" (*aphelein*). 4. Analogy: when there are two terms two by two, analogy consists in stating the fourth instead of the second and the second instead of the fourth. The cup is to Dionysus what the shield is to Ares. "The shield of Dionysus" and "the cup of Ares" are metaphors by analogy. Old age and life, evening and day, yields for example in Empedocles, " 'the evening of life' " (*Poetics* 1457b10–25; *Rhetoric* III, chap. 4).

Analogy is metaphor par excellence. Aristotle emphasizes this point often in the *Rhetoric*. "Liveliness is got by using metaphor by analogy and by being graphic" (*Rhetoric* III, 11, 1411b21). "Of the four kinds of metaphor, the most taking is the metaphor by analogy (*kat' analogian*). Thus Pericles, for instance, said that the vanishing from their country of the young men who had fallen in the war was 'as if the spring were taken out of the year.' Leptines, speaking of the Lacedamonians, said that he would not have the Athenians let Greece 'lose one of her two eyes' " (*Rhetoric* III, 10, 1411a1). This privilege articulates Aristotle's entire metaphorology with his general theory of the analogy of Being.

In all these examples—in which it is so often a question of taking away, cutting off, severing (life, the eyes, etc.)—all the terms are nonetheless present or presentable. One can always convene four members, two by two, a kind of family whose relationships are evident and whose names are known. The hidden term is not anonymous, does not have to be invented; there is nothing hermetic or elliptical about the exchange. It is almost a comparison or a double comparison. Now, Aristotle remarks, there are cases in which one of the terms is missing. The term has to be invented then. More surprisingly, in these cases the impression is stronger and occasionally also truer, more poetic: the turn of speech is more generous, more generative, more ingenious. Aristotle illustrates this with an example: an example that is the most illustrious, that is illustrative par excellence, the most natural luster there is. It is as concerns this example's power to engender that the question of the missing name comes to be asked and that one of the members of the analogical square has to be supplemented.

(In the *Republic* (VI–VII), before and after the Line which presents ontology according to the analogies of proportionality, the sun appears. In order to disappear. It is there, but as the invisible source of light, in a kind of insistent eclipse, more than essential, producing the essence—Being and appearing—of what is. One looks at it directly on pain of blindness and death. Keeping itself beyond all that which is, it figures the Good of which the sensory sun is the son: the source of life and visibility, of seed and light.)

Here is the case of the Sun in the *Poetics* (1457b25–30): "It may be that some of the terms thus related have no special name of their own, but for all that they will be metaphorically described in just the same way. Thus to cast forth seed corn is called 'sowing' (*speirein*); but to cast forth its flame, as said of the sun, has no special name (*to de tēn phloga apo tou hēliou anōnymon*)." How is this anonymity to be supplemented? "This nameless act, however, stands in just the same relation (*homoiōs ekhei*) to its object, sunlight, as sowing to the seed-corn. Hence the expression in the poet 'sowing around a god-created flame' (*speirōn theoktistan phloga*)."

Where has it ever been *seen* that there is the same relation between the sun and its rays as between sowing and seeds? If this analogy imposes itself—and it does—then it is that within language the analogy itself is due to a long and hardly visible chain whose first link is quite difficult to exhibit, and not only for Aristotle. Rather than a metaphor, do we not have here an "enigma," a secret narrative, composed of several metaphors, a powerful asyndeton or dissimulated conjunction, whose essential characteristic is "to describe a fact in an impossible combination of words" (*ainigmatos te gar idea hautē esti, to legonta huparkhonta adunata sunapsai*)" (*Poetics*, 1458a26–27)?

If every metaphor is an elliptical comparison or analogy, in this case we are dealing with a metaphor par excellence, a metaphorical redoubling, an ellipsis of ellipsis. But the missing term calls for a noun which names something properly. The present terms (the sun, the rays, the act of sowing, the seed) are not in themselves, according to Aristotle, tropes. Here, the metaphor consists in a substitution of proper names having a fixed meaning and referent, especially when we are dealing with the sun whose referent has the originality of always being original, unique, and irreplaceable, at least in the representation we give of it. There is only one sun in this system. The proper name, here, is the nonmetaphorical prime mover of metaphor, the father of all figures. Everything turns around it, everything turns toward it.

And yet, in one sentence, in a parenthesis that is immediately closed, Aristotle incidentally invokes the case of a *lexis* that would be metaphorical in all its aspects. Or at least no proper name is present in it, is apparent as such. Immediately after the solar sowing, here is the "wineless cup": "There is also another form of qualified metaphor. Having given the thing the alien name, one may by a negative addition deny of it one of the attributes naturally associated with its new name. An instance of this would be to call the shield not 'the cup of *Ares*' as in the former case, but 'a cup that holds no wine' " (1457b30–33).

But this procedure can be pursued and complicated infinitely, although Aristotle does not say so. No reference properly being named in such a metaphor, the figure is carried off into the adventure of a long, implicit sentence, a secret narrative which nothing assures us will lead us back to the proper name. The metaphorization of metaphor, its bottomless overdeterminability, seems to be inscribed in the structure of metaphor, but as its negativity. As soon as one admits that all the terms in an analogical relation already are caught up, one by one, in a metaphorical relation, everything begins to function no longer as a sun, but as a star, the punctual source of truth or properness remaining invisible or nocturnal. Which refers, in any case, in Aristotle's text, to the problem of the proper name or the analogy of *Being*.[45]

If the sun can "sow," its name is inscribed in a system of relations that constitutes it. This name is no longer the proper name of a unique thing which metaphor would *overtake*; it already has begun to say the multiple, divided origin of all seed, of the eye, of invisibility, death, the father, the "proper name," etc. If Aristotle does not concern himself with this consequence of his theory, it is doubtless because it contradicts the philosophical value of *alētheia*, the proper appearing of the propriety of what is, the entire system of concepts which invest the philosopheme "metaphor," burden it in delimiting it. And do so by barring its movement: just as one represses by crossing out, or just as one governs the infinitely floating movement of a vessel in order to drop anchor where one will. All the onomatism which dominates the theory of metaphor, and the entire Aristotelian doctrine of simple names (*Poetics*, 1457a) is elaborated in order to assure harbors of truth and propriety.

Like *mimēsis*, metaphor *comes back* to *physis*, to its truth and its presence. There, nature always refinds its own, proper analogy, its own resemblance to itself, takes increase only from itself. Nature gives itself in metaphor. Which is why, moreover, the metaphoric capacity is a natural gift. In this sense, it is given to everyone[46] (*Rhetoric* III, II). But, following a framework we regularly come across, nature gives (itself) more to some than to others. More to men than to beasts, more to philosophers than to other men. Since the invention of metaphors is an innate, natural, congenital gift, it will also be a characteristic of genius. The notion of nature makes this contradiction tolerable. In nature each has his nature. Some have more nature than others, more genius, more generosity, more seed. If "the greatest thing by far is to be a master of metaphor," some have the genius of metaphor, know better than others to perceive resemblances and to unveil the truth of nature. An ungraspable resource. "To be a master of metaphor" "is the one thing that cannot be learnt from others and it is also a sign of genius" (*Poetics*, 1459a5–7; see also *Rhetoric* III, II). One knows or one does not know, one can or one cannot. The ungraspable is certainly a genius for perceiving the hidden resemblance, but it is also, consequently, the capacity to substitute one term for another. The genius of *mimēsis*, thus, can give rise to a language, a code

45. We cannot undertake this problem here. See, particularly, Pierre Aubenque, *Le problème de l'être chez Aristote* (Paris: Presses Universitaires de France, 1966), and J. Vuillemin, *De la logique à la théologie* (Paris: Flammarion, 1967).

46. "Boileau and Du Marsais have said, and it has been a thousand times repeated on their authority, that as concerns Tropes more are created in Les Halles on a market day than there are in the entire *Aeneid*, or than are created at the Académie in several consecutive sittings . . . Now is this not an obvious proof that Tropes are an essential part of the language of speech; and that like the language of speech, they have been given to us by nature in order to serve in the expression of our thoughts and feelings; and that consequently they have the same origin as this language and as languages in general?" (Fontanier, "Préface," p. 157).

of regulated substitutions, the talent and procedures of rhetoric, the imitation of genius, the mastery of the ungraspable. Henceforth, am I certain that everything can be taken from me except the power to replace? For example, that which is taken from me by something else? Under what conditions would one always have one more trick, one more turn, up one's sleeve, in one's sack? One more seed? And would the sun always be able to sow? and *physis* to sow itself?

The Flowers of Rhetoric:
The Heliotrope

Let us come back to philosophy, which requires arguments and not analogies.

Diderot, *Letter on the Deaf and Dumb*[47]

Mlle. de l'Espinasse: Why, I should think it's my head. Bordeu: Your whole head? Mlle. de l'Espinasse: No, but look here, Doctor, I'll have to give you a comparison if I am to make myself clear. Women and poets seem to reason mostly by comparisons. So imagine a spider . . . D'Alembert: Who's that? Is that you Mademoiselle de l'Espinasse?

Diderot, *D'Alembert's Dream*[48]

One day all that will be of just as much value, and no more, as the amount of belief existing today in the masculinity or femininity of the sun.

Nietzsche, *The Dawn of Day*[49]

The alternative "either-or" cannot be expressed in any way whatever . . . They [dreams] show a particular preference for combining contraries into a unity or for representing them as one and the same thing . . . The same blossoming branch (cf. *"des Mädchen's Blüten"* ["the maiden's blossoms"] in Goethe's poem *"Der Müllerin Verrat"*) represented both sexual innocence and its contrary . . . One and only one of these logical relations is very highly favoured by the mechanism of dream formation: namely the relation of similarity

47. TN. In *Diderot's Early Philosophical Works*, trans. Margaret Jourdain (Chicago: Open Court), p. 187.
48. TN. In *Rameau's Nephew and Other Works*, trans. Jacques Barzun and Ralph H. Bowen (New York: Doubleday, 1956), p. 127. Translation modified.
49. In *Complete Works*, vol. 9, trans. J. M. Kennedy, p. 12.

(*Ähnlichkeit*), consonance (*Über-einstimmung*) or approximation (*Berührung*)—the relation of "just as" (*gleichwie*). This relation, unlike any other, is capable of being represented in dreams in a variety of ways.* (**Note:* Cf. Aristotle's remark on the qualifications of a dream interpreter quoted above.)[50]

Aristotle remarked in this connection that the best interpreter of dreams was the man who could best grasp similarities (ibid., p. 97, n. 2). At this point, too, the words *"expensive flowers, one has to pay for them"* must have had what was no doubt literally a financial meaning.—Thus the flower symbolism in this dream included virginal femininity (*jung-fräulichweiblicher*), masculinity and an allusion to defloration by violence . . . She laid all the more emphasis on the preciousness of the *"centre"*—on another occasion she used the words, *"a centre-piece of flowers"*—that is to say, on her virginity . . . Later on the dreamer produced an addendum (*Nachtrag*) to the dream: . . . "there is a gap, a little space in the flowers"

(ibid., p. 376).

Metaphor then is what is proper to man. And more properly each man's, according to the measure of genius—of nature—that *dominates* in him. What of this domination? And what does "proper to man" mean here, when the issue is one of this kind of capacity?

The necessity of examining the history and system of the value of "properness" has become apparent to us. An immense task, which supposes the elaboration of an entire strategy of deconstruction and an entire protocol of reading. One can foresee that such a labor, however far off it may be, in one fashion or another will have to deal with what is translated by "proper" in the Aristotelian text. That is to say, with at least three meanings.

The Aristotelian problematic of metaphor does not recur to a very simple, very clear, i.e. central, opposition of what will be called proper, literal meaning/figurative meaning. Nothing prevents a metaphorical lexis from being proper, that is, appropriate (*prepon*), suitable, decent, proportionate, becoming, in re-

50. *SE* IV, 316–20. The next two citations from *The Interpretation of Dreams* are to this edition.

lation to the subject, situation, things.[51] It is true that this value of properness remains rather exterior to the form—metaphorical or not—of discourse. This no longer holds for the significations *kurion* and *idion,* which are both generally translated by the same word: *proper.*[52] Although the difference between *kurion* and *idion* is never given thematic exposition, it seems that *kurion,* more frequent in both the *Poetics* and the *Rhetoric,* designates the propriety of a name utilized in its dominant, master, capital sense. Let us not forget that this sense of sovereignty is also the tutelary sense of *kurion.* By extension, *kurion* is interpreted as the primitive (as opposed to derivative) sense, and sometimes is used as the equivalent of the usual, literal, familiar sense (*to de kurion kai to oikeion* [*Rhetoric,* III, II, 1404b6]): "By the ordinary word (*kurion*) I mean that in general use in a country" (*Poetics* 1457b3–4). *Kurion* is then distinguished, on the one hand, from the unusual, rare, idiomatic word (*glōtta*), and from metaphor, on the other. As for *idion,* which is much rarer in this context, it seems to participate in the two other meanings. More precisely, in the *Rhetoric* (III, V, 1407a31) to employ the proper name is to avoid the detour of periphrasis (*tois idiois onomasi legein, kai mē tois periekhousin*), which is the correct thing to do. The contamination of these three values seems already accomplished in the Ciceronian notion of *verba propria* as opposed to *verba translata* (*De oratore* 2.4).

However, the value of the *idion* seems to support this entire metaphorology, without occupying center stage. We know that in the *Topics,* for example, it is at the center of a theory of the proper, of essence, and of accident. Now, if metaphor (or *mimēsis* in general) aims at an effect of cognition, it cannot be treated without being placed in relation to a knowledge that bears on *definitions:* on what the thing of which one speaks is, properly, essentially, or accidentally. Certainly one may speak properly or improperly of what is not proper to the thing, its accident, for example. Here, the two values properness/improperness do not have the same locus of pertinence. Nevertheless, the ideal of every language, and in particular of metaphor, being to bring to knowledge the thing itself, the turn of speech will be better if it brings us closer to the thing's essential or proper truth. The space of language, the field of its divisions, is opened precisely by the difference between essence, the proper, and accident. Three reference points, preliminarily.

1. A noun is proper when it has but a single sense. Better, it is only in this case that it is properly a noun. Univocity is the essence, or better, the *telos* of language. No philosophy, as such, has ever renounced this Aristotelian ideal. This ideal is philosophy. Aristotle recognizes that a word may have several meanings. This is a fact. But this fact has right of entry into language only in the extent to which the polysemia is finite, the different significations are limited in number, and above all sufficiently *distinct,* each remaining one and identifi-

---

51. See, for example, *Rhetoric* III, 7. On the translation of *prepon* see Brunschwig's note to his edition of *Les Topiques d'Aristote* (Paris: Belles Lettres, 1966), p. 6, note 3.

52. TN. As will be seen in the next few citations from Aristotle, *kurion* and *idion* are *not* translated into English by the same word ("proper"), although they are in French. However, these concepts do belong to the system of concepts of the "proper" (literal, correct, usual, individual, particular, belonging) that Derrida is analyzing here.

able. Language is what it is, language, only insofar as it can then master and analyze polysemia. With no remainder. A nonmasterable dissemination is not even a polysemia, it belongs to what is outside language. "And it makes no difference even if one were to say a word has several meanings, if only they are limited in number; for to each formula there might be assigned a different word. For instance, we might say that 'man' has not one meaning but several, one of which would be defined as 'two-footed animal,' while there might be also several other formulae if only they were limited in number; for a peculiar name might be assigned to each of the formulae [what is translated by 'peculiar name' is precisely the 'proper' name, *idion onoma*; and 'formula' is *logos*]. If, however, they were not limited but one were to say that the word has an *infinite* number of meanings (*ei de mē (tetheiē) all' apeira sēmainein phaiē*), obviously reasoning [definition, discourse, *logos*] would be impossible; for not to have one meaning is to have no meaning (*to gar mē hen sēmainein outhen sēmainein estin*), and if words have no meaning, reasoning (*dialegesthai*) with other people, and indeed with oneself, has been annihilated; for it is impossible to think anything if we do not think one thing (*outhen gar endekhetai noein mē noounta hen*); but if this *is* possible, one name might be assigned to *this* thing. Let it be assumed then, as was said at the beginning, that the name has a meaning, and has one meaning (*sēmainon ti to onoma kai sēmainon hen*)" (*Metaphysics* 4, 1006a34–b13).[53]

Each time that polysemia is irreducible, when no unity of meaning is even promised to it, one is outside language. And consequently, outside humanity. What is proper to man is doubtless the capacity to make metaphors, but in order to mean some thing, and only one. In this sense, the philosopher, who ever has but one thing to say, is the man of man. Whoever does not subject equivocalness to this law is already a bit less than a man: a sophist, who in sum says nothing, nothing that can be reduced to a meaning.[54] At the limit of this "meaning-nothing," one is hardly an animal, but rather a plant, a reed, and not a thinking one: "We can however demonstrate negatively the impossibility of the same thing being and not being, if our opponent will only say something; and if he says nothing, it is absurd to attempt to reason with one who will not reason about anything, in so far as he refuses to reason. For such a man, as such, is

53. See also *Topics* I, 18. Du Marsais: "In a line of reasoning one must always take a word in the same sense as one has taken it initially, otherwise one is not reasoning correctly." Fontanier: "Words, in principle, cannot each signify but one single thing." Cited by Tzvetan Todorov, *Littérature et signification* (Paris: Larousse, 1967), pp. 109–10.

54. The poet stands between the two. He is the man of metaphor. While the philosopher is interested only in the truth of meaning, beyond even signs and names; and the sophist manipulates empty signs and draws his effects from the contingency of signifiers (whence his taste for equivocality, and primarily for homonymy, the deceptive identity of signifiers), the poet plays on the multiplicity of signifieds, but in order to return to the identity of meaning: "Homonyms are chiefly useful to enable the sophist to mislead his hearers. Synonyms are useful to the poet, by which I mean words whose ordinary meaning is the same (*kuria te kai sunōnuma*), e.g. *advancing* (*poreuesthai*) and *proceeding* (*badizein*); these two are ordinary words (*kuria*) and have the same meaning" (*Rhetoric* III s 1404b37–1405a1).

seen already to be no better than a mere vegetable (*homoios gar phutōi*)" (*Metaphysics* 1006a12–15). And such a metaphorical vegetable (*phutos*) no longer belongs completely to *physis* to the extent that it is presented, in truth, by *mimēsis*, *logos*, and the voice of man.

2. Although inseparable from essence, the proper is not to be confused with it. Doubtless this division is what permits the play of metaphor. The latter can manifest properties, can relate properties extracted from the essence of different things to each other, can make them known on the basis of their resemblance, but nonetheless without directly, fully, and properly stating essence itself, without bringing to light the truth of the thing itself.

The transported significations are those of attributed properties, not those of the thing itself, as subject or substance. Which causes metaphor to remain mediate and abstract. For metaphor to be possible, it is necessary, without involving the thing itself in a play of substitutions, that one be able to replace properties for one another, and that these properties belong to the same essence of the same thing, or that they be extracted from different essences. The necessary condition of these extractions and exchanges is that the essence of a concrete subject be capable of several properties, and then that a particular permutation between the essence and what is proper to (and inseparable from) it be possible, within the medium of a quasi-synonymy. This is what Aristotle calls the *antikatēgoreisthai*: the predicate of the essence and the predicate of the proper can be exchanged without the statement becoming false: "A property is something which does not show the essence of a thing, but belongs to it alone, and is predicated convertibly (*antikatēgoreitai*) of it."[55] We have been able to say, for example, that metaphor, the metaphoric capacity, is what is proper to man. In effect, given a concrete subject, Socrates, whose essence is humanity, one will have stated something proper each time that one will be able to say, "If Socrates is a man, he has logos," and reciprocally, "If Socrates has logos, he is a man"; or "If Socrates is capable of *mimēsis*, he is a man," and vice versa; or "If Socrates can make metaphors, he is a man" and vice versa, etc. The first example of the *antikatēgoreisthai* given by the *Topics* is grammar: what is proper to man is grammar, the capacity to learn to read and write. This property belongs to the chain of what is proper to man (*logos*, *phōnē sēmantikē*, *mimēsis*, *metaphora*, etc.). "For

55. Aristotle, *Topics* I, 5, 102a18–19, trans. E. S. Forster (Loeb Classical Library). Brunschwig's edition of the *Topics* contains a note that makes a point very important for us here: "Contrary to its traditional interpretation (but conforming to its etymological sense), the word *antikatēgoreisthai* does not designate the legitimacy of the *transposition of subject and predicate*, but rather the legitimacy of a *reciprocal substitution between two predicates* related to an identical concrete subject (designated by the words *tou pragmatos*). In other words, one can say that a predicate P is proper to a subject S not when one has '*S is P and P is S*,' but rather when one has '*for every concrete subject X, if X is S, X is P, and if X is P, X is S*.' " See also the following section of this note. And, on the different species of "proper" (proper in itself—"For example, the property of man as a mortal living creature receptive of knowledge,"—or relatively; perpetually or temporarily), see *Topics* V, i, 128b30–35.

example, it is a property of man to be capable of learning grammar (*hoion idion anthrōpou to grammatikēs einai dektikon*); for if a certain being is a man, he is capable of learning grammar, and if he is capable of learning grammar, he is a man."[56]

3. What is proper to the sun? The question is asked in the *Topics*, as an example. Is this by chance? Was this already insignificant in the *Poetics?* Unceasingly, unwillingly, we have been carried along by the movement which brings the sun to turn in metaphor; or have been attracted by what turned the philosophical metaphor toward the sun. Is not this flower of rhetoric (like) a sunflower? That is—but this is not exactly a synonym—analogous to the heliotrope?

Initially, of course, what will appear in the Aristotelian example is that heliotropic metaphors can be bad metaphors. In effect, it is difficult to know what is proper to the sun properly, literally named: the *sensory* sun. It follows that every metaphor which implies the sun (as tenor or vehicle) does not bring clear and certain knowledge: "Every object of sensation, when it passes outside the range of sensation, becomes obscure; for it is not clear whether it still exists, because it is comprehended only by sensation. This will be true of such attributes as do not necessarily and always attend upon the subject. For example, he who has stated that it is a property of the sun to be 'the brightest star that moves above the earth' has employed in the property something of a kind which is comprehensible only by sensation, namely 'moving above the earth'; and so the property of the sun would not have been correctly assigned, for it will not be manifest, when the sun sets, whether it is still moving above the earth, because sensation then fails us."[57]

This gives rise, apparently, to two consequences which might appear contradictory, but whose opposition in a way constructs the philosophical concept of metaphor, dividing it according to a law of ambiguity confirmed ceaselessly.

First consequence: Heliotropic metaphors are always imperfect metaphors. They provide us with too little knowledge, because one of the terms directly or indirectly implied in the substitution (the sensory sun) cannot be known in what is proper to it. Which also means that the sensory sun is always im-properly known, and therefore im-properly named. The sensory in general does not limit knowledge for reasons that are intrinsic to the *form of the presence* of the sensory thing; but first of all because the *aisthēton* can always *not* present itself, can hide itself, absent itself. It does not yield itself upon command, and its presence is not to be mastered. Now, from this point of view, the sun is the sensory object par excellence. It is the paradigm of the sensory *and* of metaphor: it regularly turns (itself) and hides (itself). As the metaphoric trope always implies a sensory kernel, or rather something like the sensory, which can always not be present

56. *Topics* I, 5, 102a20–22. See also Brunschwig's note.

57. *Topics* V, 3, 131b20–30. See also G. Verbeke, "La notion de propriété dans les To-piques," in *Aristotle on Dialectics: The Topics,* ed. G. E. L. Owen (Oxford, 1968). The author analyzes in particular the reasons for which " 'the proper' cannot be such that its belonging to the subject could be known uniquely by sensation" (p. 273).

in act and in person, and since the sun in this respect is the sensory signifier of the sensory par excellence, that is, the sensory model of the sensory (the Idea, paradigm, or parabola of the sensory), then the turning of the sun always will have been the trajectory of metaphor. Of bad metaphor, certainly, which furnishes only improper knowledge. But as the best metaphor is never absolutely good, without which it would not be a metaphor, does not the bad metaphor always yield the best example? Thus, metaphor means heliotrope, both a movement turned toward the sun and the turning movement of the sun.

But let us not hasten to make of this a truth of metaphor. Are you sure that you know what the heliotrope is?

The sun does not just provide an example, even if the most remarkable one, of sensory Being such that it can always disappear, keep out of sight, not be present. The very opposition of appearing and disappearing, the entire lexicon of the *phainesthai,* of *alētheia,* etc., of day and night, of the visible and the invisible, of the present and the absent—all this is possible only under the sun. Insofar as it structures the metaphorical space of philosophy, the sun represents what is natural in philosophical language. In every philosophical language, it is that which permits itself to be retained by natural language. In the metaphysical alternative which opposes formal or artificial language to natural language, "natural" should always lead us back to *physis* as a solar system, or, more precisely, to a certain history of the relationship earth/sun in the system of perception.

Second consequence: Something has been inverted in our discourse. Above we said that the sun is the unique, irreplaceable, natural referent, around which everything must turn, toward which everything must turn. Now, following the same route, however, we must reverse the proposition: the literally, properly named sun, the sensory sun, does not furnish poor knowledge solely because it furnishes poor metaphors, it is itself solely metaphorical. Since, as Aristotle tells us, we can no longer be certain of its sensory characteristics as of its "properties," the sun is never properly present in discourse. Each time that there is a metaphor, there is doubtless a sun somewhere; but each time that there is sun, metaphor has begun. If the sun is metaphorical always, already, it is no longer completely natural. It is always, already a luster, a chandelier, one might say an *artificial* construction, if one could still give credence to this signification when nature has disappeared. For if the sun is no longer completely natural, what in nature does remain natural? What is most natural in nature bears within itself the means to emerge from itself; it accommodates itself to "artificial" light, eclipses itself, ellipses itself, always has been other, itself: father, seed, fire, eye, egg, etc., that is, so many other things, providing moreover the measure of good and bad metaphors, clear and obscure metaphors; and then, at the limit, the measure of that which is worse or better than metaphor:

"One commonplace (*topos*) regarding obscurity is that you should see whether what is stated is equivocal with something else . . . Another commonplace is

251

to see whether he has spoken metaphorically, as, for example, if he has described knowledge as 'unshakeable' (*ametaptōton*), or the earth as a 'nurse' (*tithēnēn*) or temperance as a 'harmony' (*sumphōnian*); for metaphorical expressions are always obscure (*asaphes*; a metaphor in the qualification of metaphor). Also, it is possible to quibble against one who has spoken metaphorically, representing him as having used the word in its proper sense (*hōs kuriōs*); for then the definition given will not fit, as in the case of 'temperance' for 'harmony' is always used of sounds . . . Further, you must see if he uses terms of which the use is not well-established, as Plato calls the eye 'brow-shaded' . . . for unusual words are always obscure. Words are sometimes used neither equivocally, nor metaphorically, nor in their proper sense (*oute kuriōs*); for example, the law is said to be the 'measure' or 'image' (*metron ē eikōn*) of things naturally just. Such phrases are worse than metaphors; for a metaphor in a way adds to our knowledge of what is indicated (*to sēmainomenon*) on account of the similarity (*dia tēn homoiotēta*), for those who use metaphors always do so on account of some similarity. But the kind of phrase of which we are speaking does not add to our knowledge; for no similarity exists in virtue of which the law is a 'measure' or an 'image,' nor is the law usually described by these words in their proper sense. So, if anyone says that the law is a 'measure' or an 'image' in the proper sense of these words, he is lying; for an image is something whose coming into being is due to imitation (*dia mimēseōs*), and this does not apply to the law. If, however, he is not using the word in its proper sense, obviously he has spoken obscurely, and with worse effect than any kind of metaphorical language. Further, you must see whether the definition of the contrary fails to be clear from the description given; for correctly assigned definitions also indicate their contraries. Or, again, you must see whether, when it is stated by itself, it fails to show clearly what it is that it defines, just as in the words of the early painters, unless they were inscribed (*ei mē tis epegrapsen*), it was impossible to recognize what each figure represented" (*Topics* VI, 2, 139b19–140a23; see also IV, 3, 123a33).

The appeal to the criteria of clarity and obscurity would suffice to confirm what we stated above: this entire philosophical delimitation of metaphor already lends itself to being constructed and worked by "metaphors." How could a piece of knowledge or a language be properly clear or obscure? Now, all the concepts which have operated in the definition of metaphor always have an origin and an efficacy that are themselves "metaphorical," to use a word that this time, rigorously is no longer suitable to designate tropes that are as much defining as defined.[58] If we went back to each term in the definition proposed by the *Poetics*, we could recognize in it the mark of a figure (*metaphora* or *epiphora* is also

---

58. The general form of this inclusion is recognized by the *Topics*, and illustrated with this example: "Another way is when the term which is being defined is used in the definition itself. This passes unobserved when the actual name of the object which is being defined is not employed, for example, if one has defined the sun as 'a star appearing by day'; for in introducing the day, one introduces the sun" (VI, 4, 142a–142b).

a movement of spatial translation; *eidos* is also a visible figure, a contour and a form, the space of an aspect or of a species; *genos* is also an affiliation, the base of a birth, of an origin, of a family, etc.). All that these tropes maintain and sediment in the entangling of their roots is apparent. However, the issue is not to take the function of the concept back to the etymology of the noun along a straight line. We have been attentive to the internal, systematic, and synchronic articulation of the Aristotelian concepts in order to avoid this etymologism. Nevertheless, none of their names being a conventional and arbitrary *X*, the historical or genealogical (let us not say etymological) tie of the signified concept to its signifier (to language) is not a reducible contingency.

This implication of the defined in the definition, this abyss of metaphor will never cease to stratify itself, simultaneously widening and consolidating itself: the (artificial) light and (displaced) habitat of classical rhetoric.

Du Marsais illustrates his definition of metaphor this way:

"When one speaks of the *light of the spirit*, the word *light* is taken metaphorically; for, just as light in the literal, proper sense makes us see corporal objects, so the faculty of knowing and perceiving enlightens the spirit, and puts it in a condition to bear sound judgments. Metaphor is therefore a species of Trope; the word which one uses in the metaphor is taken in another than the literal, proper sense: *it is*, so to speak, *in a borrowed dwelling*, as one of the ancients says; which is common to and essential for all Tropes" (chap. 2, X).

These two examples—the light and the house—do not have the same function. Du Marsais believes that he can present the first metaphor as one example among others, as one metaphor among others. But we now have some reason to believe that this metaphor is indispensable to the general system in which the concept of metaphor is inscribed. Du Marsais does not give the other figure—the borrowed dwelling—as one metaphor among others; it is there in order to signify metaphor *itself*; it is a metaphor of metaphor; an expropriation, a being-outside-one's-own-residence, but still in a dwelling, outside its own residence but still in a residence in which one comes back to oneself, recognizes oneself, reassembles oneself or resembles oneself, outside oneself in oneself. This is the philosophical metaphor as a detour within (or in sight of) reappropriation, parousia, the self-presence of the idea in its own light. The metaphorical trajectory from the Platonic *eidos* to the Hegelian Idea.

The recourse to a metaphor in order to give the "idea" of metaphor: this is what prohibits a definition, but nevertheless metaphorically assigns a checkpoint, a limit, a fixed place: the metaphor/dwelling. That these two examples imposed themselves, fortuitously or not, upon Du Marsais, does not exclude that each metaphor can always be deciphered simultaneously as a particular figure and as a paradigm of the very process of metaphorization: *idealization* and *reappropriation*. Everything, in the discourse on metaphor, that passes through the sign *eidos*, with its entire system, is articulated with the analogy between the vision of the *nous* and sensory vision, between the intelligible sun and the

253

visible sun. The determination of the truth of Being in presence passes through the detour of this tropic system. The presence of *ousia* as *eidos* (to be placed before the metaphorical eye) or as *hupokeimenon* (to underlie visible phenomena or accidents) faces the theoretical organ; which, as Hegel's *Aesthetics* reminds us, has the power not to consume what it perceives and to let be the object of desire. Philosophy, as a theory of metaphor, first will have been a metaphor of theory. This circulation has not excluded but, on the contrary, has permitted and provoked the transformation of presence into self-presence, into the proximity or properness of subjectivity to and for itself. "It is the history of 'proper' meaning, as we said above, whose detour and return are to be followed."

The "idealizing" metaphor, which is constitutive of the philosopheme in general, opens Fontanier's *Figures of Discourse,* immediately providing him with the greatest generality of his theoretical space. In effect the entire treatise is rooted in the division between the signified and the signifier, sense and the sensory, thought and language, and primarily the division between the *idea* and the *word.* Fontanier recalls the etymology and buried origin of the word "idea," as if this were nothing at all, the very moment he opens his book and proposes his great distinction between words and ideas: "Thought is composed of ideas, and the expression of thought by speech is composed of words. First then, let us see what ideas are in themselves: following this we will see what words are relative to ideas, or, if you will, what ideas are as represented by words. A.—IDEAS. The word *Idea* (from the Greek *eidō,* to see) signifies relative to the objects seen by the spirit the same thing as *image*; and relative to the spirit which sees the same things as *seen* or *perception.* But the objects seen by our spirit are either physical and material objects that affect our senses, or metaphysical and purely intellectual objects completely above our senses" (p. 41). After which, Fontanier classes all ideas into physical or metaphysical (and moral) ideas, simple or complex ideas, etc. An entire stratification of metaphors and of philosophical interpretations therefore supports the concept of that which is called upon to precede language or words, that which is called upon to be previous, exterior, and superior to language and words, as meaning is to expressing, the represented to representation, *dianoia* to *lexis.* A metaphorical *lexis,* if you will, has intervened in the definition of *dianoia.* It has given the *idea.*

Here, in recalling the history of the signifier "idea," the issue is not to give in to the etymologism that we contested above. While acknowledging the specific function of a term within its system, we must not, however, take the signifier as perfectly conventional. Doubtless, Hegel's Idea, for example, is not Plato's Idea; doubtless the effects of the system are irreducible and must be read as such. But the word *Idea* is not an arbitrary *X,* and it bears a traditional burden that continues Plato's system in Hegel's system. It must also be examined as such, by means of a stratified reading: neither pure etymology nor a pure origin, neither a homogenous continuum nor an absolute synchronism or a simple interiority of a system to itself. Which implies a *simultaneous* critique of the model

254

of a transcendental history of philosophy and of the model of systematic structures perfectly closed over their technical and synchronic manipulation (which until now has been recognized only in bodies of work identified according to the "proper name" of a signature).

But, we were asking above, can these defining tropes that are prior to all philosophical rhetoric and that produce philosophemes still be called metaphors? This question could guide an entire reading of the analyses Fontanier reserves for catachresis in the *Supplement to the Theory of Tropes*.[59] Let us be content with indicating this reading. The *Supplement* concerns first the violent, forced, abusive inscription of a sign, the imposition of a sign upon a meaning which did not yet have its own proper sign in language. So much so that there is no substitution here, no transport of proper signs, but rather the irruptive extension of a sign proper to an idea, a meaning, deprived of their signifier. A "secondary origin":

"Nevertheless, since our principles concerning *Catachresis* serve as the foundation of our entire tropological system, we cannot but have the ardor to throw greater light on them, if possible. This is why we are going to add several new observations, here, to the very numerous ones already to be found in the *Commentary*.

"*Catachresis, in general, consists in a sign already affected with a first idea also being affected with a new idea, which itself had no sign at all, or no longer properly has any other in language.* Consequently, it is every Trope of forced and necessary usage, every Trope from which there results a purely *extensive sense*; this literal, proper sense of secondary origin, intermediate between the *primitive proper sense* and the *figurative sense* is closer to the first than to the second, although it could itself be *figurative* in principle. Now, the Tropes from which a purely *extensive meaning* results not only are three in number, like the Tropes from which a *figurative meaning* results, but they are determined by the same relationships as the latter: *correspondence, connection,* or *resemblance* between ideas; and they occur in the same fashion: by *metonymy, synecdoche,* or *metaphor.*"[60]

59. Fontanier, "Préface," pp. 207ff. "In this *supplement* will be found new, and doubtless rather illuminating, views on an important major point, *extensive* meaning or *Catachresis,* the subject of so many of the objections raised against Du Marsais in the *Commentary* on his Treatise. Also to be seen is how Tropes differ from the other forms of discourse called *figures;* consequently one will learn how better to distinguish these different forms from one another. But what this supplement quite particularly offers, and what Du Marsais's *Treatise* and the *Commentary* do not give the first idea about, is the art of recognizing and appreciating Tropes reduced to its principles and in practice" (p. 211).

60. Ibid., pp. 213–14. These definitions are illuminated and completed by the definitions of the three kinds of meaning (objective, literal, spiritual or intellectual) proposed in the first part. The literal seems to correspond rather well to the Aristotelian *kurion,* which can be either proper or tropological, and that is sometimes mistakenly translated as "proper." Here is Fontanier's definition. "The *literal sense* is the one which keeps to words taken literally, to words understood according to the acceptance in ordinary usage; consequently, it is the sense which immediately presents itself to the minds of those who understand a language. The *literal sense,* which keeps to a single word, is either *primitive, natural* and *proper,* or *derived,* if one must say so, and *tropological.* This last is due to *Tropes,* of which

255

Thus, Fontanier proposes a theoretical classification of all these irruptive tropes, these "nontrue figures" that no code of semantic substitution will have preceded. But this classification will borrow its types from the great, known norms. Whence a double gesture: setting catachresis completely apart, acknowledging its irreducibly original place, and yet bringing it into the shared taxonomy, seeing it as a phenomenon of usage (of abuse) rather than as a phenomenon of a code. Which is to be expected since the code is forced, but strange because the abuse is no more a form of usage than an application of the code: "There is a Trope that we have accepted, like Du Marsais, but to which we have neither assigned a rank, nor devoted an article in our *Theory*: this is *Catachresis*. In effect, we did not believe it necessary to treat this Trope more particularly, immediately that, far from making it a species apart, as does Du Marsais, and not only a species of Trope, but even of figure, we consider it only as the forced use, if not primitively, at least currently, of one or the other of the three great species we have already recognized" (p. 213).

In the supplement, the longest elaborations are granted to the catachresis of metaphor. Particularly because this time the order of the noun is largely surpassed. "Here, the examples would be innumerable, and it is not only nouns that could provide them, but all the species of words representative of ideas. *Metaphor-figure* hardly goes up to adverbs; but *metaphor-catachresis* includes in its extent even interjections. There are even very few words, in each species, that it has not subjected to its empire" (p. 215). It remains that the interpretation of the metaphor-catachreses of prepositions (*to*, for example) always consists in defining its meaning by means of the name of categoremes (disposition, site or place, time, posture, gesture, manner, animating cause, destination, etc.; cf. p. 219), and even by means of a single nominal signification, the "tendency," "as Condillac has shown so well in his Grammar."

As for nouns and verbs, the examples given by Fontanier are initially—and exclusively—those of metaphor-catachreses whose philosophical burden is the heaviest (light, blindness; to have, to be, to do, to take, to understand). The living body furnishes the "vehicle" for all the nominal examples in the physical order. *Light* is the first—and only—example chosen when one accedes to the moral

---

several genera and several species are to be distinguished. But *Tropes* occur, either by necessity and *extension*, in order to supplement the words for certain ideas which are missing from language, or by choice and *figure*, in order to present ideas with more vivid and striking images than their own signs. Whence two different kinds of *tropological sense*: the *extended tropological sense* and the *figurative tropological sense*. The first, as one can see, stands between the *primitive sense* and the *figurative* sense, and can hardly be regarded as anything but a new kind of *proper sense*" (pp. 57–58). What is interesting to us here, thus, is the production of a proper sense, a new kind of proper sense, by means of the violence of a catachresis whose intermediary status tends to escape the opposition of the primitive and the figurative, standing between them as a "middle." When the middle of an opposition is not the passageway of a mediation, there is every chance that the opposition is not pertinent. The consequences are boundless.

order: "Here are the ones in the moral order: *Light,* for clarity of spirit, for intelligence, or for enlightenment; *Blindness* for troubling or clouding of reason. The first *light* that we have known is doubtless the light of day, and it is for the latter that the word was created. But is not reason like a flame that the Author of nature has placed in us in order to enlighten our soul, and is not this flame for us exactly to the moral what the flame of day for us is to the physical? Thus a *light* necessarily has had to have been attributed to it, and we say, *The light of reason* just as we say *The light of day*" (p. 216).

After bringing to bear this analysis on the word *blindness,* Fontanier asks: "And how, without these *forced metaphors,* without these catachreses, could one have come to retrace these ideas?" (p. 217). These "ideas" already existed, Fontanier seems to think, were already in the mind like a grid without a word; but they could not have been retraced, tracked down, brought to daylight without the force of a twisting which goes *against usage,* without the infraction of a catachresis. The latter does not emerge from language, does not create new signs, does not enrich the code; and yet it transforms its functioning, producing, with the same material, new rules of exchange, new values. Philosophical language, a system of catachreses, a fund of "forced metaphors," would have this relation to the literality of natural language if, following Fontanier, some such thing existed. And when Fontanier nevertheless posits, presupposes the anteriority of the meaning or of the idea of the catachresis (which only comes back to an already present concept), he interprets this situation in philosophical terms; indeed, this is how philosophy traditionally has interpreted its powerful catachresis: the twisting return toward the already-there of a meaning, *production* (of signs, or rather of values), but as *revelation,* unveiling, bringing to light, truth. This is why "forced metaphors" may be, must be "correct and natural" (p. 216).

La métaphysique—relève de la métaphore[61]

And yet, though I am fully in favor of the positive use of metaphor, (this rhetorical figure does far more service to human aspirations towards the infinite than those who are riddled with prejudices and false ideas—which comes to the same thing—are prepared to acknowledge), it is nonetheless true that the risible mouths of these three peasants are still big enough to swallow three spermwhales. Let us shrink this comparison somewhat, let us be serious and content ourselves with saying that they were like three little elephants which have only just been born.

Lautréamont, *Maldoror* IV, 7[62]

It is generally speaking, a strange thing, this captivating tendency which leads us to seek out (and then to express) the resemblances and differences which are hidden in the most natural properties of objects which are sometimes the least apt to lend themselves to sympathetically curious combinations of this kind, which, on my word of honour, graciously enhance the style of the writer who treats himself to this personal satisfaction, giving him the ridiculous and unforgettable aspect of an eternally serious owl.

Ibid. V, 6[63]

Classical rhetoric, then, cannot dominate, being enmeshed within it, the mass out of which the philosophical text takes shape. Metaphor is less in the philosophical text (and in the rhetorical text coordinated with it) than the philosophical text is within metaphor. And the latter can no longer receive its name from metaphysics, except by a catachresis, if you will, that would retrace metaphor through its philosophical phantom: as "nontrue metaphor."

61. TN. This subtitle is untranslatable, at very least because of its double meaning. Derrida simultaneously uses *relève* as both noun and verb here. If *relève* is taken as a noun, the subtitle would read: "Metaphysics—the *relève*, the *Aufhebung* of metaphor." If *relève* is taken as a verb, which would be the usual reading, it can be understood in its usual sense, i.e. not as a translation of *Aufhebung*. Thus, the subtitle would read: "Metaphysics derives from, takes off from, metaphor." (Further, *relève* as a verb can also be taken as the translation of *Aufheben*, which gives a reading similar to the first one.) If one is attentive to the implications of this unstoppable alternation of meaning, along with the interplay of metaphysics, metaphor, and *relève*, one will have begun to grasp what Derrida is about in this essay. (For our system of notes on *relève*, see above, note 5.) See also below, note 73.

62. Lautréamont, *Maldoror and Poems,* trans. Paul Knight (Harmondsworth: Penguin Books, 1978), p. 172.

63. Ibid., p. 200.

For all that, can some metaphilosophy, a more general but still philosophical kind of discourse on the metaphors of the "first degree," the nontrue metaphors that opened philosophy, be dreamed of? The work to be undertaken under the heading of such a meta-metaphorics would not be without interest. In sum, it would amount to transporting into the philosophical order the Bachelardian program of a metapoetics (*Lautréamont*, p. 55).[64] What would the limits of such a transposition be?

Bachelard, on this point, is faithful to tradition: metaphor does not appear to him either simply or necessarily to constitute an obstacle to scientific or philosophical knowledge. It can work for the critical rectification of a concept, reveal a concept as a bad metaphor, or finally "illustrate" a new concept. In the process of scientific knowledge the "verbal obstacle" often has the form of metaphor ("metaphoric contrivance," "generalized image," "deficient metaphorical character of the explanation"[65] etc.), doubtless. And doubtless the domain of metaphor is extended even beyond language, taken in the strict sense of verbal "expression": "metaphors seduce reason."[66] But, on the one hand, the psychoanalysis of objective knowledge above all must denounce "immediate metaphors" ("The danger of immediate metaphors in the formation of the scientific spirit is that they are not always passing images; they push toward an autonomous kind of thought; they tend to completion and fulfillment in the domain of the image";[67] as we will see, it is the *system* of metaphors that interests Bachelard initially); and on the other hand, a nonimmediate, constructed metaphor is useful when it comes to "illustrate" knowledge wrested from bad metaphor. Its value is then essentially pedagogical: "A psychoanalysis of objective knowledge, then, must set itself to blanching, if not to erasing, these naive

64. Gaston Bachelard, *Lautréamont* (Paris: Corti, 1939; new ed., 1956).

65. Bachelard, *La Formation de l'esprit scientifique* (Paris: Corti, 1938), pp. 74–75. See also pp. 15, 194, 195.

66. Ibid., p. 78. Bachelard cites Van Swinden: " 'The expression that iron is a sponge of magnetic Fluid is therefore a *metaphor* that departs from the true: and yet all the explanations are founded on this expression used in the *proper, literal* sense. But as for myself, I think that it is not exact . . . to think that reason indicates that these expressions are erroneous, and nevertheless to use them in the explanation of Experiments' (1785). In a somewhat confused form, Van Swinden's thought is quite clear: one cannot so easily as is alleged confine metaphors only to the realm of expression. Whether one wishes it or not, metaphors seduce reason." Immediately afterward, Bachelard shows that "very great minds have been blocked, so to speak, in primary imagery." Thus, "Descartes's metaphysics of space" would be but a metaphorics of the sponge, "the metaphysics of the sponge" (p. 79).

67. Ibid., p. 81. On the contrary, however, the *Preliminary Discourse* of the work accredits the constructed and constructive metaphors, the metaphors of intermediary status which break with sensory immediacy and naive realism. They belong to the order of *"figurative quantity,* midway between the concrete and the abstract, in an intermediary zone." "Scientific thought then is drawn off in the direction of 'constructions' that are more metaphorical than real, 'spaces of configuration' whose sensory space, after all, is but an impoverished example" (p. 5).

images. When abstraction will have achieved this, it will be time to *illustrate* [Bachelard's italics] rational schemas. In short, the initial intuition is an obstacle to scientific thought; only an illustration working beyond the concept, putting a bit of color on the essential characteristics, can aid scientific thought."[68] One may reread, at the end of *La formation de l'esprit scientifique*, the most luminous examples with which the value of *illustration* illustrates itself: not only the example of the circle, of the egg, and the oval,[69] but also the examples of the sun and the focal point, the center, the circle, and the ellipse. Here, just the conclusion:

"Even in the simple domain of images, we have often usefully attempted conversions of values. Thus we developed the following antithesis in our teaching. For Aristotelian science, the ellipse is a poorly made circle, a flattened circle. For Newtonian science, the circle is an impoverished ellipse, an ellipse whose centers have been flattened one onto the other. I made myself the advocate of the ellipse: the center of the ellipse is useless because of its two distinct focal points; for the circle, the law of areas is a banality; for the ellipse, the law of areas is a discovery. Little by little, I slowly attempted to pry the mind loose from its attachment to privileged images . . . Also, I have little hesitation in presenting rigor as a psychoanalysis of intuition, and algebraic thought as a psychoanalysis of geometric thought. Even in the domain of the exact sciences, our imagination is a sublimation. It is useful, but it can fool us to the extent that we do not know what we sublimate and how we sublimate it. It is valid only insofar as one has psychoanalyzed the principle. Intuition must never be a given. It must always be an illustration."[70]

68. Ibid., p. 78. "Modern science employs the analogy of the pump in order to *illustrate* [Bachelard's italics] certain characteristics of electric generators, but does so in an attempt to clarify *abstract* ideas . . . Here one sees a vivid contrast of the two mentalities: in the scientific mentality the hydraulic analogy comes into play *after* the theory. It comes into play *before* in the prescientific mentality" (p. 80).

69. Ibid., pp. 233ff. This is surely the occasion to recall that in Bachelard's opinion the metaphoric obstacle is not only an epistemological obstacle due to the persistence, in the field of science, of nonscientific schema deriving from the popular imagination or from the philosophically imaginary. The metaphoric obstacle is sometimes a philosophical one, when scientific schema are imported into a philosophical domain without rhyme or reason. One might speak then of an *epistemologizing* obstacle. A certain naive scientism on the part of the philosopher can transform scientific discourse into a vast reservoir of metaphors or "models" for hurried theoreticians. "Science offers itself to the philosopher as a particularly rich collection of well constructed and well tied together knowledge. In other words, the philosopher simply demands *examples* of science." These examples "are always mentioned, never developed. Occasionally, the scientific examples are commented upon according to principles which are not scientific ones; they lead to metaphors, analogies, generalizations." *La Philosophie du non* (Paris, 1940), p. 3. In the same direction, see also the end of the chapter on "the diverse metaphysical explanations of a scientific concept," and what Bachelard says about the anagogical reverie as a mathematizing reverie, at the moment when the mathematical and the arithmetical intervene in the position of metaphors (pp. 38–40).

70. *La formation de l'esprit scientifique*, p. 237.

This epistemological ambivalence of metaphor, which always provokes, re-
tards, *follows* the movement of the concept, perhaps finds its chosen field in the
life sciences, which demand that one adapt an unceasing critique of teleological
judgment. In this field the animistic or (technical, social, cultural) analogy is *as*
at home as possible. Where else might one be so tempted *to take the metaphor for*
the concept? And what more urgent task for epistemology and for the critical
history of the sciences than to distinguish between the word, the metaphoric
vehicle, the thing and the concept? Among all the examples Georges Canguilhem
has analyzed, let us consider two. The first one concerns "the development of
cellular theory" over which "hover, more or less closely, affective and social
values of cooperation and association."[71]

"Concerning the cell, generally Hooke is granted too many honors. Certainly
it was he who discovered the thing, somewhat by chance, and due to the play
of a curiosity amused by the first revelations of the microscope. Having made
a fine section of a piece of cork, Hooke observed its compartmentalized structure.
It is he also, indeed, who invented the word, under the influence of an image,
by assimilating the vegetable object to a honeycomb, itself an animal labor
assimilated to human labor, for a cell is a small chamber. But Hooke's discovery
started nothing, is not a point of departure. The very word was lost, to be
rediscovered only a century later.

"This discovery of the thing and this invention of a word henceforth call for
some comments. With the cell, we are in the presence of a biological object
whose affective overdetermination is incontestable and considerable. The psychoanalysis of knowledge from now on may count among its happier successes
its pretension to the status of a genre to which several contributions may be
brought, even without systematic intention. Everyone will find among his mem-
ories of studying natural history the image of the cellular structure of living
beings. This image has an almost canonic constancy. The schematic representation of an epithelium is the image of the honeycomb. Cell is a word that does
not make us think of the monk or the prisoner, but of the bee. Haeckel has
pointed out that cells of wax filled with honey perfectly correspond to vegetable
cells filled with cellular essence. Nevertheless, the influence over the mind of
the notion of the cell does not appear to us to be due to the completeness of the
correspondence. Rather, who knows whether, in consciously borrowing from
the beehive the term cell in order to designate the element of the living organism,
the human mind has not also borrowed from the hive, almost unconsciously,
the notion of the cooperative work of which the honeycomb is the product? Just
as the alveolus is the element of an edifice, bees are, in Maeterlinck's expression,
individuals entirely absorbed by the republic. In fact, the cell is both an ana-

71. *La connaissance de la vie*, 2d ed. (Paris: Vrin, 1969), p. 49. On the problem of metaphor,
see also *Etudes d'histoire et de philosophie des sciences* (Paris: Vrin, 1968), most notably the
chapters entitled "Models and Analogies in Biological Discovery" and "Concept and Life"
(particularly pp. 358–60).

tomical and a functional notion, the notion of an elementary material and of a partial, subordinate individual labor."[72]

This animal metaphor of the hive, analyzed here in its determined effects on the development of a theory, is put into *abyme*[73] in a way by Nietzsche: in order to figure the metaphoricity of the concept, the metaphor of the metaphor, the metaphor of metaphoric productivity itself:

"Only out of the persistency of these primal forms the possibility explains itself, how afterwards, out of the metaphors themselves a structure of ideas could again be compiled. For the latter is an imitation of the relations of time, space and number in the realm of metaphors.

"As we say, it is *language* which has worked originally at the construction of ideas; in later times it is *science*. Just as the bee works at the same time at the cells and fills them with honey, thus science works irresistibly at the great columbarium of ideas, the cemetery of perceptions, builds ever newer and higher storeys; supports, purifies, renews the old cells, and endeavours above all to fill that gigantic framework and to arrange within it the whole of the empiric world, i.e., the anthropomorphic world. And as the man of action binds his life to reason and its ideas, in order to avoid being swept away and losing himself, so the seeker after truth builds his hut close to the towering edifice of science in order to collaborate with it and to find protection. And he needs protection. For there are awful powers which press continually upon him, and which hold out against the 'truth' of science 'truths' fashioned in quite another way, bearing devices of the most heterogeneous character."[74]

Nietzsche's procedure (the generalization of metaphoricity by putting into *abyme* one determined metaphor) is possible only if one takes the risk of a continuity between the metaphor and the concept, as between animal and man, instinct and knowledge.[75] In order not to wind up at an empiricist reduction of

---

72. *La connaissance de la vie*, pp. 48–49.

73. TN. *Mettre en abyme* (to put into *abyme*) is a heraldic term for the placement of a small escutcheon in the middle of a larger one. Derrida is playing on this old sense of *abyme*, with its connotation of infinite reflection, and the modern senses of *abîmer*, to ruin, and of *abîme*—abyss, chasm, depths, chaos, interval, difference, division, etc. As Derrida states two paragraphs below, he wishes to demonstrate both the generalization of metaphor, its infinitely reflective capacity, and the necessity of this (hidden) generalization in the production of so-called "nonmetaphoric" concepts, by means of the "ruination," the "plunging into the abyss" of a particular metaphor. We might think of what Derrida calls "the logic of the *abyme*" as the "figurative ruination" of logic as we know it, as for example when the distinction between the reflected and the reflecting falls apart. This is the "logic" implied by the double meaning of the title of this section: *la métaphysique—relève de la métaphore*. The double meaning of *relève*, infinitely reflecting itself in the same signifier, says that metaphysics' "derivation" from metaphor also produces its infinite attempt to "spiritualize," to negate-and-conserve (*Aufheben*) metaphor on a "higher" level, a purportedly nonmetaphoric level.

74. "On Truth and Falsity in Their Ultramoral Sense" (see note 14 above), pp. 187–88.

75. It is in order to mark this continuity that Nietzsche describes the metaphorical tissue produced by man ("solely in the . . . inviolability of the conceptions of time and space")

262

knowledge and a fantastic ideology of truth, one should surely substitute another articulation for the (maintained or erased) classical opposition of metaphor and concept. This new articulation, without importing all the metaphysics of the classical opposition, should also account for the specific divisions that epistemology cannot overlook, the divisions between what it calls metaphoric effects and scientific effects. The need for this new articulation has undoubtedly been called for by Nietzsche's discourse. It will have to provoke a displacement and an entire reinscription of the values of science and of truth, that is, of several others too.

Such a redistribution would have to permit the definition of the "figure" which necessarily continues to give its "sign" to a "concept" *after* rectification, after abandoning a given model "which perhaps, after all, was only a metaphor."[76]

Thus—second example—when the biological concept of *circulation* of the blood is substituted for the technical concept of *irrigation*,[77] the rectification has not reduced every figure of speech. Although not the irrigation of a garden, such as it is described in the *Timaeus*[78] or *De Partibus Animalium*, the "circulation" of

---

as a spider's web (ibid., p. 186). Again, re-mark and generalization of a particular metaphor, whose effects are determinable, for example in the history of the sciences. Georges Canguilhem writes, concerning Bichat's *Treatise on Membranes* (1800): "The term 'tissue' deserves to give us pause. Tissue comes, as is well known, from *tistre*, an archaic form of the verb *tisser*, to weave. If the word cell has appeared to be overburdened with implicit significations of an affective and social order, the word tissue appears no less burdened with extra-theoretical implications. Cell makes us think of the bee, and not of man. Tissue makes us think of man, and not of the spider. Tissue, a weave, is the human product *par excellence*" (*La connaissance de la vie*, pp. 64–65). See also Marx: "We have to consider labour in a form peculiar to the human species. A spider carries on operations resembling those of the weaver; and many a human architect is put to shame by the skill with which a bee constructs her cell. But what from the very first distinguishes the most incompetent architect from the best of bees, is that the architect has built a cell in his head before he constructs it in wax. The labour process ends in the creation of something which, when the process began, already existed in the worker's imagination, already existed in an ideal form. What happens is, not merely that the worker brings about a change of form in material objects, at the same time, in the nature that exists apart from himself, he realizes his own purpose, the purpose which gives the law to his activities, the purpose to which he has to subordinate his own will" (*Capital*, book 1, chap. 5, pp. 169–70).

76. "On this point, thus, experimental embryology and cytology have rectified the concept of organic structure that was too narrowly associated by Claude Bernard with a social model that perhaps, after all, was only a metaphor." "Le tout et la partie dans la pensée biologique," in *Études d'histoire et de philosophie des sciences*, p. 332.

77. See *La connaissance de la vie*, pp. 22–23.

78. From a purely rhetorical point of view, Condillac displays much severity concerning the figures of speech used by Plato ("the greatest philosopher and the greatest rhetorician") to describe the human body, which he makes into "a monster that escapes the imagination"; most notably when "he says that the blood is *the grazing ground of the flesh: and so*, he goes on, *that all the parts may receive nourishment, they have dug, as in a garden, several canals, so that the streams of the veins, emerging from the heart as from their source, can flow in these narrow channels of the human body.*" Condillac contrasts this with six lines from Rousseau, and comments on them thus: "The flowers which multiply on a stem watered by a pure stream are a beautiful image of what the love of glory produces in an elevated soul" ("De l'art d'écrire," in *Oeuvres philosophiques*, p. 555).

the blood does not properly travel in a circle. As soon as one retains only a predicate of the circle (for example, return to the point of departure, closing of the circuit), its signification is put into the position of a trope, of metonymy if not metaphor.

Is rectification henceforth the rectification of a metaphor by a concept? Are not all metaphors, strictly speaking, concepts, and is there *any sense* in setting metaphor against concept? Does not a scientific critique's rectification rather proceed from an inefficient tropic-concept that is poorly constructed, to an operative tropic-concept that is more refined and more powerful in a given field and at a determined phase of the scientific process? The criterion of this progress or mutation ("break," "remodeling," and many other forms that should be distinguished from each other), has not been defined, certainly, but a double certainty now seems problematic: 1. That this criterion must necessarily put to work a rhetorical evaluation ("from metaphor to concept," for example); 2. That tropes must necessarily belong to the prescientific phase of knowledge.

In other words, there is also a *concept of metaphor:* it too has a history, yields knowledge, demands from the epistemologist construction, rectifications, critical rules of importation and exportation.

We come back to our question: can one transport into the philosophical field the Bachelardian program of a metapoetics? Bachelard proposes to proceed by *groups* and *diagrams,* and this is what will retain us first. By *groups:*

"When one has meditated on the freedom of metaphors and on their limits, one perceives that certain poetic images are *projected* onto one another with certainty and exactitude, which amounts to saying that in *projective poetry* they are but one and the same image. In studying the Psychoanalysis of fire, we have perceived, for example, that all the 'images' of the internal fire, the hidden fire, the fire glowing beneath the embers, in short the unseen fire that consequently calls for metaphors, are 'images' of life. The projective link, then, is so primitive that one easily translates, certain of universal comprehension, images of life into images of fire, and vice versa. The deformation of the images then must designate, in a strictly mathematical way, the *group* of metaphors. Immediately that one can specify the diverse *groups* of metaphors of a particular poetry, one would perceive that occasionally certain metaphors fail because they have been added in defiance of the cohesion of the group. Naturally, sensitive poetic souls react by themselves to these erroneous additions, without needing the pedantic apparatus to which we are alluding. But it remains no less that a metapoetics will have to undertake a classification of metaphors, and that sooner or later it will have to adopt the only essential procedure of classification, the determination of groups."[79]

79. Gaston Bachelard, *Lautréamont,* pp. 54–55. Here, the *projective* model permits one to recognize not only the syntactic coherence of metaphors, but above all the original and final unity of their theme, their central semantic focal point. The demonstration of this point, moreover, is rather remarkable: the multiplicity of images (the images of fire, with which this metaphorology first had to concern itself) refers, while reflecting it, to the same

And then by *diagrams* (another mathematical metaphor, or more precisely, at least a geometrical metaphor, but this time garnished with a flower, in order to present the field of a meta-metaphorics): "If the present work could be retained as a basis for a physics or a chemistry of reverie, as the outline of a method for determining the objective conditions of reverie, it should offer new instruments for an objective literary criticism in the most precise sense of the term. It should demonstrate that metaphors are not simple idealizations which take off like rockets only to display their insignificance on bursting in the sky, but that on the contrary metaphors summon one another and are more coordinated than sensations, so much so that a poetic mind is purely and simply a syntax of metaphors. Each poet should then be represented by a *diagram* which would indicate the meaning and the symmetry of his metaphorical coordinations, exactly as the diagram of a flower fixes the meaning and the symmetries of its floral action. There is no *real flower* that does not have this geometrical pattern. Similarly, there can be no poetic flowering without a certain synthesis of poetic images. One should not, however, see in this thesis a desire to limit poetic liberty, to impose a logic or a reality (which is the same thing) on the poet's creation. It is objectively, after the event, after the full flowering, that we wish to discover the realism and the inner logic of a poetic work. At times some truly diverse images that one had considered to be quite opposed, incongruous and noncohesive, will come together and fuse into one charming image. The strangest mosaics of Surrealism will suddenly reveal a continuity of meaning."[80]

At the limit, is this very necessary attention to *syntax*, to the systematic logic of metaphoric productions, to "metaphors of metaphors" (p. 215), compatible with the concept of metaphor? Can one do it justice without putting into question the semantic, that is, monosemic point of view? Bachelard himself interprets syntactic coordination as a semantic or thematic sheaf. The multiplicity of metaphors is regulated with one's sights set on "one and the same image," whose

---

focal image ("one and the same image"): but the issue was one of the hidden fire "which is not seen, and which consequently demands metaphors." This "consequently" means that what is not seen demands a metaphor. Which seems to go without saying. But, if one follows the analogical equivalence in this case (covered fire = what is hidden = life), all metaphors are also metaphors of life, as the dissimulated focal point of all metaphors, metaphors of *physis*, the source and metaphor of metaphors. A circulation of meaning that does not get us very far but amounts to the metaphor of the same, whose shadow by now is familiar to us. This is why we insisted above on the necessity linking the values of life, of metaphor, and of the metaphor of metaphor. "The mind, then, is free for the *metaphor of metaphor*. This is the concept at which we wind up in our recent book on *The Psychoanalysis of Fire*. The long meditation of Lautréamont's work was undertaken with our sights set on a *Psychoanalysis of Life*" (p. 155). We must acknowledge, here, the strict constraints of a program. The respect for the "sensitive poetic souls" who "react by themselves" to metaphors that do not follow, also had long been prescribed in this program (from Aristotle to Condillac and Hegel), as is elsewhere prescribed the determination not "to limit poetic freedom" or "the creation of the poet."

80. Bachelard, *The Psychoanalysis of Fire*, trans. A. C. M. Ross (Boston: Beacon Press, 1964), pp. 109–10.

diffraction is but a projective system. Here, the unity and continuity of meaning dominates the play of syntax. We tried to demonstrate above that this subordination of the syntactic was inscribed in the most invariable characteristics of the concept of metaphor, and tried to show elsewhere[81] the essential limits of such a thematism.

Does not such a metaphorology, transported into the philosophical field, always, by destination, rediscover the same? The same *physis,* the same meaning (meaning of Being as presence or, *amounting to the same,* as presence/absence), the same circle, the same fire of the same light revealing/concealing itself, the same turn of the sun? What *other* than this return of the same is to be found when one seeks metaphor? that is, resemblance? and when one seeks to determine *the dominant* metaphor of a group, which is interesting by virtue of its power to assemble? What other is to be found if not the metaphor of *domination,* heightened by its power of dissimulation which permits it to escape mastery: God or the Sun?

For example, if one attempted to establish the diagram of the metaphorics proper (or presumed such) to Descartes, even supposing, *concesso non dato,* that one could strictly delimit the metaphoric corpus referring to this single signature, there still would be a need to point out, beneath the layer of apparently didactic metaphors (those indicated in Spoerri's psychological and empirical analysis: the ivy and the tree, the path, the house, the city, the machine, the foundation or the chain) another stratification, one that is less apparent but just as systematically organized, and that not only would be *beneath* the preceding one, but interwoven with it. Here we would encounter the wax and the pen, dress and nudity, the ship, the clock, seeds and the magnet, the book, the stick, etc. To reconstitute the grammar of these metaphors would be to articulate its logic with a discourse that presents itself as nonmetaphorical, which here is called the philosophical system, the meaning of concepts, and the order of reason, but it also would be to articulate it with schemas of continuity and permanence, with systems of longer sequences, the "same" metaphor being able to function differently here and there. But to respect above all else the philosophical specificity of this syntax is also to recognize its submission to sense, to meaning, to the truth of the philosophical concept, to the signified of philosophy. The tenor of the dominant metaphor will return always to this major signified of ontotheology: the circle of the heliotrope. Certainly the metaphors of light and the circle, which are so important in Descartes, are not organized as they are in Plato or Aristotle, in Hegel or Husserl. But if we put outselves at the most critical and most properly Cartesian point of the critical procedure, at the point of hyperbolic doubt and the hypothesis of the Evil Genius, at the point when doubt strikes not only ideas of sensory origin but also "clear and distinct" ideas and what is mathematically self-evident, we know that what permits the discourse

81. "The Double Session," sec. 2, in *Dissemination.*

to be picked up again and to be pursued, its ultimate resource, is designated as *lumen naturale*. Natural light, and all the axioms it brings into our field of vision, is never subjected to the most radical doubt. The latter unfolds *in* light: "for I cannot doubt that which the natural light causes me to believe to be true, as, for example, it has shown me that I am from the fact that I doubt."[82] Among the axioms that the natural light shows me to be true, there is, each time, at every stage, that which permits me to emerge from doubt and to progress within the order of reason, and in particular to prove the existence of a nondeceiving God ("Now it is manifest by the natural light that there must at least be as much reality in the efficient and total cause as in its effect," p. 162. "The light of nature shows us clearly that the distinction between creation and conservation is solely a distinction of the reason," p. 168. "From this it is manifest that He cannot be a deceiver, since the light of nature teaches us that fraud and deception necessarily proceed from some defect," p. 171). Prior to every determined presence, to every representative idea, natural light constitutes the very ether of thought and of its proper discourse. As natural, it has its source in God, in the God whose existence has been put into doubt and then demonstrated, *thanks to it.* "For I have certainly no cause to complain that God has not given me an intelligence which is more powerful, or a natural light which is stronger than that which I have received from Him" (*Meditation IV*, p. 177). In escaping from the logical circle that has so occupied him, Descartes all the while inscribes the chain of reason in the circle of the natural light that proceeds from God and returns to God.

This metaphorics is of course articulated in a specific syntax; but as a metaphorics it belongs to a more general syntax, to a more extended system that equally constrains Platonism; everything is illuminated by this system's sun, the sun of absence and of presence, blinding and luminous, dazzling. This is the end of *Meditation III*, when the existence of God has just been proved for the first time thanks to the natural light which he himself dispenses to us, pretending to disappear and to leave us to seek the blinding source of clarity: "It seems to me right to pause for a while in order to contemplate God Himself, to ponder at leisure His marvellous attributes, to consider and admire, and adore, the beauty of this light so resplendent, at least as far as the strength of my mind, which is in some measure dazzled by the sight, will allow me to do so" (p. 171).

Of course the adoration here is a philosopher's adoration, and since natural light is natural, Descartes does not take his discourse as a theologian's: that is, the discourse of someone who is satisfied with metaphors. And to whom one must leave them: "The author could explain in satisfactory manner, following his philosophy, the creation of the world, such as it is described in Genesis . . . ; the narrative of creation found there is perhaps metaphorical; thus, it must be

---

82. Descartes, *Meditations on First Philosophy,* in *The Philosophical Works of Descartes,* vol. 1, trans. Elizabeth Haldane and G. R. T. Ross (Cambridge: Cambridge University Press, 1970), p. 160. All further references to the *Meditations* will be to this edition.

left to the theologians . . . Why is it said, in effect, that darkness preceded light? . . . And as for the cataracts of the abyss, this is a metaphor, but this metaphor escapes us."[83]

Presence disappearing in its own radiance, the hidden source of light, of truth, and of meaning, the erasure of the visage of Being—such must be the insistent return of that which subjects metaphysics to metaphor.

To metaphors. The word is written only in the plural. If there were only one possible metaphor, the dream at the heart of philosophy, if one could reduce their play to the circle of a family or a group of metaphors, that is, to one "central," "fundamental," "principial" metaphor, there would be no more true metaphor, but only, through the one true metaphor, the assured legibility of the proper. Now, it is because the metaphoric is plural from the outset that it does not escape syntax; and that it gives rise, in philosophy too, to a *text* which is not exhausted in the history of its meaning (signified concept or metaphoric tenor: *thesis*), in the visible or invisible presence of its theme (meaning and truth of Being). But it is also because the metaphoric does not reduce syntax, and on the contrary organizes its divisions within syntax, that it gets carried away with itself, cannot be what it is except in erasing itself, indefinitely constructing its destruction.

This self-destruction always will have been able to take *two* courses which are almost tangent, and yet different, repeating, miming, and separating from each other according to certain laws. One of these courses follows the line of a resistance to the dissemination of the metaphorical in a syntactics that some-where, and initially, carries within itself an irreducible loss of meaning: this is the metaphysical *relève* of metaphor in the proper meaning of Being. The generalization of metaphor can signify this parousia. Metaphor then is included by metaphysics as that which must be carried off to a horizon or a proper ground, and which must finish by rediscovering the origin of its truth. The turn of the sun is interpreted then as a specular circle, a return to itself without loss of meaning, without irreversible expenditure. This *return to itself*—this interiori-zation—of the sun has marked not only Platonic, Aristotelian, Cartesian, and other kinds of discourse, not only the science of logic as the circle of circles, but also, and by the same token, the man of metaphysics. The sensory sun, which rises in the East, becomes interiorized, in the evening of its journey, in the eye and the heart of the Westerner. He summarizes, assumes, and achieves the essence of man, "illuminated by the true light" (*phōtizomenos phōti alēthinōi*).[84]

83. "Entretien avec Burman," in *Oeuvres complètes* (Paris: Pléiade, 1967), pp. 1387–88.
84. "In the geographical survey, the course of the World's History has been marked out in its general features. The *Sun*—the Light—rises in the East. Light is a simply self-involved existence; but though possessing thus in itself universality, it exists at the same time as an individuality in the Sun. Imagination has often pictured to itself the emotions of a blind man suddenly becoming possessed of sight, beholding the bright glimmering of the dawn,

Philosophical discourse—as such—describes a metaphor which is displaced and reabsorbed between two suns. This *end* of metaphor is not interpreted as a death or dislocation, but as an interiorizing anamnesis (*Erinnerung*), a recollection of meaning, a *relève* of living metaphoricity into a living state of properness. This is the irrepressible philosophical desire to summarize-interiorize-dialecticize-master-*relever* the metaphorical division between the origin and itself, the Oriental difference. In the world of this desire, metaphor is born in the East as soon as the latter sets itself to speak, to work, to write, suspending its pleasures, separating itself from itself and naming absence: that is, what is. Such at least is the philosophical proposition in its geotropic and historico-rhetorical enunciations. "As man's first motives for speaking were of the passions, his first expressions were tropes. Figurative language was the first to be born. Proper meaning was discovered last." And "the genius of the Oriental languages" is to be "vital and figurative."[85]

the growing light, and the flaming glory of the ascending Sun. The boundless forgetfulness of his individuality in this pure splendour, is his first feeling,—utter astonishment. But when the Sun is risen, this astonishment is diminished; objects around are perceived, and from them the individual proceeds to the contemplation of his own inner being, and thereby the advance is made to the perception of the relation between the two. Then inactive contemplation is quitted for activity; by the close of day man has erected a building constructed from his own inner Sun; and when in the evening he contemplates this, he esteems it more highly than the original external Sun. For now he stands in a *conscious relation* to his Spirit, and therefore a *free* relation. If we hold this image fast in mind, we shall find it symbolizing the course of History, the great Day's work of Spirit.

"The History of the World travels from East to West, for Europe is absolutely the end of History, Asia the beginning. The History of the World has an East *Kat' exochēn*, though the term East in itself is entirely relative; for although the Earth forms a sphere, History performs no circle round it, but has on the contrary a determinate East, v.z. Asia. Here rises the outward physical Sun, and in the West it sinks down: here consentaneously rises the Sun of self-consciousness, which diffuses a nobler brilliance. The History of the World is the discipline of the uncontrolled natural will, bringing it into obedience to a Universal principle and conferring subjective freedom." Hegel, Introduction, in *Lectures on the Philosophy of History*, trans. J. Sibree (New York: The Colonial Press, 1900), pp. 109–10.

85. Rousseau, *Essay on the Origin of Language*, trans. John Moran (New York: Frederick Ungar, 1966), pp. 12 and 11. See also, for example, Condillac, *Essai sur l'origine des connaissances humaines* II, 1, chap. 10, sec. 103, and especially *La logique:* "The generation of ideas and of the faculties of the soul must have been felt in these languages [the first vulgar languages] where the first acceptance of a word was known, and where one analogy provided all the others. In names were found again the ideas which escaped the senses, the very names of the sensory ideas from which they come; and, instead of seeing them as the proper names of these ideas, they were seen as figurative expressions which showed their origin. At this time, for example, it was not asked if the word *substance* meant something other than *that which is beneath;* if the word *pensée*, thought, meant other than *peser*, to weigh, to balance, to compare. In a word, one could not have imagined the questions that are asked today by metaphysicians: languages, which answered all of them in advance, did not yet permit them, and there was not yet any bad metaphysics. Good metaphysics began before languages; and languages owe to it what is best in them. But this metaphysics was then less a science than an instinct. It was nature which led men without their knowing it; and metaphysics became a science only when it ceased to be good." See, again, Fontanier, "Préface," p. 157.

"Not only the Greek philosophers, like Plato and Aristotle, or great historians and orators, like Thucydides and Demosthenes, but also the great poets, Homer and Sophocles, on the whole stick almost always to literal expressions (*eigentlichen Ausdrücken*), although similes (*Gleichnisse*) do also occur. Their plastic severity and solidity does not tolerate the sort of blending involved in metaphor or permit them to stray hither and thither away from the homogenous material and the simple, self-contained, complete cast, in order to gather up so-called 'flowers' of expression (*sogennante Blumen des Ausdrucks aufzulesen*) here and there. But metaphor is always an interruption of the course of ideas (*Vorstellungsganges*) . . . On the other hand, it is particularly the East, especially the later Mohammedan poetry, which uses figurative expressions and indeed has them of necessity."[86]

Metaphor, therefore, is determined by philosophy as a provisional loss of meaning, an economy of the proper without irreparable damage, a certainly inevitable detour, but also a history with its sights set on, and within the horizon of, the circular reappropriation of literal, proper meaning. This is why the philosophical evaluation of metaphor always has been ambiguous: metaphor is dangerous and foreign as concerns *intuition* (vision or contact), *concept* (the grasping or proper presence of the signified), and *consciousness* (proximity or self-presence); but it is in complicity with what it endangers, is necessary to it in the extent to which the de-tour is a re-turn guided by the function of resemblance (*mimēsis* or *homoiōsis*), under the law of the same. The opposition of intuition, the concept, and consciousness at this point no longer has any pertinence. These three values belong to the order and to the movement of meaning. Like metaphor.

Henceforth the entire teleology of meaning, which constructs the philosophical concept of metaphor, coordinates metaphor with the manifestation of truth, with the production of truth as presence without veil, with the reappropriation of a full language without syntax, with the vocation of a pure nomination: without differential syntax, or in any case without a properly *unnamable* articulation that is irreducible to the semantic *relève* or to dialectical interiorization.

The *other* self-destruction of metaphor thus *resembles* the philosophical one to the point of being taken for it. This time, then, in traversing and doubling the first self-destruction, it passes through a supplement of syntactic resistance, through everything (for example in modern linguistics) that disrupts the opposition of the semantic and the syntactic, and especially the philosophical hierarchy that submits the latter to the former. This self-destruction still has the form of a generalization, but this time it is no longer a question of extending and confirming a philosopheme, but rather, of unfolding it without limit, and wresting its borders of propriety from it. And consequently to explode the reassuring opposition of the metaphoric and the proper, the opposition in which

86. Hegel, *Aesthetics*, pp. 407–8.

the one and the other have never done anything but reflect and refer to each other in their radiance.

Metaphor, then, always carries its death within itself. And this death, surely, is also the death *of* philosophy. But the genitive is double. It is sometimes the death of philosophy, death of a genre belonging to philosophy which is thought and summarized within it, recognizing and fulfilling itself within philosophy; and sometimes the death of a philosophy which does not see itself die and is no longer to be refound within philosophy.

A homonymy in which Aristotle recognized—in the guise of the Sophist at this point—the very figure of that which doubles and endangers philosophy: these two deaths repeat and simulate one another in the heliotrope. The heliotrope of Plato or of Hegel on the one hand, the heliotrope of Nietzsche or Bataille[87] on the other, to use metonymic abbreviations here. Such a flower always bears its double within itself, whether it be seed or type, the chance of its program or the necessity of its diagram. The heliotrope can always be *relevé.* And it can always become a dried flower in a book. There is always, absent from every garden, a dried flower in a book; and by virtue of the repetition in which it endlessly puts itself into *abyme,*[88] no language can reduce into itself the structure of an anthology. This supplement of a code which traverses its own field, endlessly displaces its closure, breaks its line, opens its circle, and no ontology will have been able to reduce it.

Unless the anthology is also a lithography. Heliotrope also names a stone: a precious stone, greenish and streaked with red veins, a kind of oriental jasper.

87. See particularly, apart from Bataille's well known texts, certain of his first writings collected by Denis Hollier in volume 1 of the *Oeuvres complètes* (Paris: Gallimard, 1970): "L'Anus solaire," "Le langage des fleurs," "La mutilation sacrificielle de l'oreille coupée de Van Gogh," "Le bas matérialisme et la gnose," "Soleil pourri," "Corps celestes," etc.
88. TN. See above, note 73.

Qual Quelle:
Valéry's Sources[1]

A lecture given 6 November 1971 at the Johns Hopkins University on the centennial of Valéry's birth. I am indebted to Michel Lechantre's rereading of Valéry and his discovery of the *Cahiers*. The following pages therefore are naturally dedicated to him.

1. TN. As is so often the case for Derrida, this title has multiple meanings whose effects are disseminated throughout the essay. It must be understood that Derrida constantly plays on the meaning of "source" as both origin and as fountain or spring. The German *Quelle* has the same multiple meanings. The explanation of *qual quelle* will be found in note 12 below.

I—mark(s) first of all a division in what will have been able to appear in the beginning.

"Valéry's Sources," here, do not entitle those sources on which theses are written. What historians might name "influences" will not be followed upstream toward their hidden "sources," the near or distant, presumed or verified, origins of a "work," that is of a "thought" whose card in the catalogue thereby could be manipulated. Valéry himself warned of this in advance: concerning what is written here, the "discourse of history" would chatter on about heritages, readings, borrowings, biographical inner springs. The sources could multiply themselves infinitely, but as so many "sources of error and powers of falsifications."[2] We will not, as do positive historians, account for all that could have flowed into this text *from the outside.*

But—I mark(s) the division—by taking a different turn, by observing from an excentric place the logic of Valéry's aversions, why not ask outselves about another outside, about the *sources set aside,* the sources that Valéry could get a glimpse of only on the bias, as in a brief, or rather foreshortened, mirroring, just the time to recognize or reflect himself and immediately to turn away— quickly, decidedly, furtively too, like an about-face to be described according to the gesture of Narcissus. We will analyze this turning away only where it has left marks *within* Valéry's textual system, as a regular crinkling of every page. Here, for example, the names would be those of Nietzsche and Freud.

Further, under this heading one might also have expected a reading of "In Praise of Water," with which Valéry, in 1935, prefaced a collection of tributes to the *Source Perrier.*[3] Will academic accusations be made of the resources that Valéry more than once found for his talent? No moral or political lesson could be elaborated whose premises had not already infallibly been recognized by Valéry. In Mallarmé's wake, quite early on, he had analyzed the law that administers

2. TN. The following system of reference to Valéry's works will be employed. (*a*) References to Valéry's *Oeuvres* (Paris: Gallimard, 1957–60) will be given with a roman volume number (I or II) and a page number. Thus, the reference for this citation is *Discours de l'histoire,* I, 1130. (*b*) References to the *Cahiers* (Paris: Centre National de Recherche Scientifique, 1957) will be given by the letter C. followed by an arabic volume number, a page number, and a year. (*c*) References to works of Valéry translated into English will be to the thirteen-volume Bollingen series *The Collected Works of Paul Valéry,* ed. Jackson Mathews (New York: Bollingen Foundation, 1960–73). These will be indicated by an arabic volume number and a page number (e.g. 2, 11).

3. This booklet, published by the *Source Perrier* (2, 8ff., or II, 202ff.) contains "The History of a Source," by P. Reboux, "The Therapeutic Benefits of the Perrier Source," by Dr. Gervais, "How, and In What Circumstances, To Serve Perrier Water," by Baron Fouquier. In 1919 Gide had written to Valéry: "I cannot for an instant believe in the exhaustion of your resources or the drying up of your source: what is difficult is to bottle it, but there is nothing surprising about the fact that you find yourself worn out after the efforts of the winter," thereby describing everything at stake in the question that concerns us here. Without taking into account that by itself the name of the source in question, in a single word, reassembles the extensible length of a sentence. [*Perrier* in French is pronounced the same way as the sentence "Père y est"—"Father is there."]

the exchanges between the values of language, philosophy, or literature, for example, and those of political economy. The *Memoirs of the Poet* had compared the febrile agitation of Literature to that of the stock market.[4] And the trials to which he would be subjected still would derive from those "convictions . . . (that are) naively and secretly murderous" (I, 1129), and which he knew always explain "the deep meaning of speculative quarrels and even literary polemics" (ibid.).

But—again I mark(s) and multiply (multiplies) the division—we will not forget "In Praise of Water." Rather, in pretending that we abandon its subterranean discourse, perhaps we will see it reemerge, both itself and totally other, after several meanders. This discourse already entails that the "nymph and the spring stand at that holy place where life sits down and looks around her" (2, 10). Further, it announces that the water of the source holds up the tree on its own course. "Consider a plant, regard a mighty tree, and you will discern that it is none other than an upright river pouring into the air of the sky. By the tree WATER climbs to meet light" (2, 10). The "amorous form" of the source traverses and divides the tree in its ascent. In the course of his innumerable statements on the tree, the "supreme beech" [*hêtre suprême*], Valéry will have taken into account a "blind tree," and then a tree trembling in that "there are two *trees* within it."[5] This is the moment at which the erect, and thus divided, tree,

4. I, 1487. And elsewhere: "Every doctrine necessarily presents itself as a *scheme more advantageous* than the others. Therefore, it depends upon the others" (II, 690). "Thought is brutal—no taming it . . . What is more brutal than a thought?" (II, 694).

5. 2, 272 ("For Your 'Supreme' Beech"); 2, 161 ("Fragments of the Narcissus"). The dream of the tree always *returns* to a source ("Between them the pure air and a shrub contrive / A living spring (*source vive*)" from "The Spinner," 1, 3. "The tree dreams of being a stream / The tree dreams in the air of being a source" C. 9, p. 428, 1923). "The tree dreams of being a stream / *The tree dreams in the air of being a living source* . . . / And closer and closer, is changed into *poetry*, in a pure line" ("Arbre" in *Autres Rhumbs*, II, 659). "Today my soul is making itself into a tree. Yesterday I felt it to be a spring (*source*)" ("Dialogue of the Tree," 4, 154). We will retain from this work, aside from the play on *hêtre*—beech—and *être*—Being, that it posits, concerning the tree, "its desireful being, which is certainly feminine in essence," 4, 153; that it deciphers the tree as a petrification of disseminal waters ("the waters of the dense maternal earth, drawn from the depths for years on end, at last bring this hard substance to the light of day . . . TITYRUS. Substance as hard as stone, and fit like it to carve. LUCRETIUS. Ending in branches too, which end in leaves themselves, and then at last the mast which, fleeing far and wide, will scatter life abroad . . . TITYRUS. I see what you would say. LUCRETIUS. See then in this great being here a kind of river," 4, 157; "I have told you that I feel, born and growing in me, a Plantlike virtue, and I can merge myself in the thirst to exist of the hard-striving seed, moving towards an infinite number of other seeds throughout a plant's whole life," 4, 167; "What I was going to tell (perhaps to sing) to you would have, I think, dried up the spring (*source*) of words," 4, 167); that it asserts simultaneously that "There is no author, then . . . a work without an author is not impossible. No poet organized these phantasms for you," 4, 166, and that "In the beginning was the Fable," 4, 168. That division (itself) is marked in this dream ("And like a slow fiber / Which divides the moment") is what prohibits, for reasons to be seen in a moment, the *tree* from being constituted as a theme or a subject. Whence the trap and the irony of the *Notebooks*, when they underline, "The Tree—what a fine *subject!*" (C. 25, p. 118). P. Laurette cites them as epigraphs to his very rich polysemic inventory, *The Theme of the Tree in Paul Valéry* (Klincksieck, 1967).

separated from itself within itself, lets itself be cut off from the simple source. This is where we find the incision into the dream of the source. To be cut off from the source, as predicted finally by "In Praise of Water," is to let oneself be multiplied or divided by the difference of the other: to cease to be (a) *self*. The lure of the source ("Now comes the HOUR, the thirst, the spring (*la source*) and the siren" *Hour*, 1, 251): to become again present to oneself, to come back to oneself, to find again, along with the pure limpidity of water, the always efficient mirage of the point of emergence, the instant of welling up, the fountain or well surnamed Truth, which always speaks in order to say I: "Well one knows that pure thirst is quenched only in pure water. There is something exact and satisfactory in this matching of the real desire of the organism with the element of its origin. To thirst is to lack a part of oneself, and thus to dwindle into another. Then one must make good that lack, complete oneself again, by repairing to what all life demands. [*Etre altéré, c'est devenir autre: se corrompre. Il faut donc se desaltérer, redevenir, avoir recours à ce qu'exige tout ce qui vit. I*, 202] The very language is filled with the praise of WATER. We say that we THIRST FOR TRUTH. We speak of a LIMPID discourse" (2, 10–11). And when Valéry ends with an "I adore WATER," which resembles, for whoever would be taken in by it, an advertiser's platitude, he is speaking only of speech, insisting on the transition which puts water into the mouth, engenders discourse, oration, incantation.

What does the course of the source become when the course is made into discourse? What, then, of this turning away?

In letting oneself be carried along by the flow, one would rush, under the rubric of sources, toward a thematics of water, a semantics in "phenomenological" style or a psychoanalysis of material imagination, both spellbound by the unity, which is precisely originary, of a meaning or a theme flowing from the source and affecting itself with forms, modulations, and variations in a discourse. There would be no lack of material for such an inventory, which would filter almost the entirety of Valéry's text, ingenuously following the trail of the "MULTIFORM WATER" which from the source goes "down unconquerably to the ocean where she most abides" (2, 9). At the mouth again one would come back to the source of Paul Valéry himself, who often explained himself thus: "I was born in a port."

Without pretense of going any further than this thematic or semantic reading, rather let us attempt abstractly to complicate the question of meaning or of the theme; and of what happens to a text—as text—when the source is divided within it, and altered to the point of no longer rejoining the unity of the resources (the *s* divides itself again) that moreover it never will have been. In sum, repeating the critical question, Valéry's very insistent and very necessary question about *meaning* (theme, subject, content, etc.), we will bring the question to a certain heterogeneity of the source: and first, there are sources, the source is other and plural. But by means of this repetition we may be prepared to poison the question of meaning and to calculate the price that Valéry had to pay for the discredit that, to a certain extent and in a certain way, he justifiably threw on the value and authority of meaning. A repetition of Valéry's, doubtless, but perhaps we will not close this reflection in ring form. Or at least it will not return to where it was expected, to its origin, before leaving behind, thereby affecting and infecting itself, some hardly philosophical venom: thus giving us the sketch of a snake, amongst the tree, hissing with its double-edged tongue whose venom, however vile, leaves far behind the well tempered hemlock!

Rebound

I had not reread Valéry for a long time. And even long ago, I was far from having read all of Valéry. This is still true today. But in going back to the texts that I thought I knew, and in discovering others, especially in the *Notebooks*, naturally I asked myself in what ways a certain relationship had changed. Where had the displacement, which in a way prevented me from taking my bearings, been effected? What does this signify here, now? A banal question, a ring once more in the form of the return to the sources which always afflicts the rhetoric of the anniversaries of a birth: Valéry one hundred years later, Valéry for us, Valéry now, Valéry today, Valéry alive, Valéry dead—always the same code. What laws do these rebirths, rediscoveries, and occultations too, obey, the distancing or reevaluation of a text that one naively would like to believe, having put one's faith in a signature or an institution, always remains the same, constantly identical to itself? In sum a "corpus," and one whose self identity would be even less threatened than one's own body [*corps propre*]? What must a text be if it can, by itself in a way, turn itself in order to shine again, after an eclipse, with a different light, in a time that is no longer that of its productive source (and was it ever contemporaneous with it?), and then again repeat this resurgence after several deaths, counting, among several others, those of the author, and the simulacrum of a multiple extinction? Valéry also was interested in this power of regeneration. He thought that it—the possibility for a text to yield (itself) several times and several lives—calculates (itself). I am saying *it calculates itself:* such a ruse cannot be machinated in the brain of an author, quite simply, except if he is situated like a spider who is somewhat lost in a corner of its web, off to the side. The web very quickly becomes indifferent to the animal-source, who might very well die without even having understood what had happened. Long afterward, other animals again will come to be caught in its threads, speculating, in order to get out, on the first meaning of a weave, that is of a textual trap whose economy can always be abandoned to itself. This is called writing. It calculates itself, Valéry knew, and coming back to him, to the enormous cardboard web that literally bears his signature, I said to myself that it had, and not only in the form of the *Notebooks*, more than one certain return. Supposing, of course, that a return can ever be certain, which is precisely what is in question, as will be seen. In the calculation of this economy, for it to "work" (this is Valéry's expression), the price to be paid negotiates with death; with what cuts the *oeuvre* from its source ("thus there is no author"), henceforth imprinting on it a survival duration that is necessarily *discrete* and *discontinuous*. I am borrowing these qualifications from Valéry. When he analyzes what programs the duration and return of a writing, he never does so in terms of genius, meaning, or force, but in terms of "application of force."[6]

How does the return *of* the source negotiate—and dissociate—itself?

Let us repeat the question. Was the source a theme for Valéry? A great number of poems, analyses, meditations, and notes regularly seem to come back to the source as to their object or principal subject. There is here something like an overflow. And already, this thematic overabundance, in making the demonstration all too easy, makes us suspect confusion somewhere else. Here, the recurrence announces, as perhaps it always does, that one does not touch a theme, especially a principal theme. The compulsive obstinacy that always leads back toward a place, a locus, signifies that this topos cannot become a theme or the dwelling place of a rhetoric: it rejects any presentation, any representation. It can never be there, present, *posed* before a glance, facing it; it never constitutes a present or hidden unity, an object or a subject supporting, according to the occurrence or position of the theme, a system of variations, of modulations, of transformations whose meaning or substantial content at heart would remain identical to themselves.

The source for Valéry, then, must be that which never could become a theme. If we persist in considering it in this way, then at least we must specify from some angle or fold that this was the theme of that which cannot be thematized.

It is that the source cannot be reassembled into its originary unity. Because—first of all—it has no proper, literal meaning.

And yet if there is a word with a proper, literal meaning, is it not this one?

We are indeed certain that we know what the word *source* means before the intervention of all these metaphors, whose work was always remarked by Valéry.

Is not the source the origin, the point of formation, or rather emergence, of a flowing body of water, brook, stream, river? Nothing is more familiar to us than water, and than the very familiarity of the earth with water, which is sealed here and there, and unsealed in the *point d'eau*—incalculable syntagm[7]—that is called source: *origo fontium*.

But this meaning denominated as proper can appear for us within the element of familiarity only if we already know, or believe that we already know, what

---

6. "The duration of works is the duration of their utility. This is why it is discontinuous. There are centuries during which Virgil is useless" (II, 562). "To have 'genius' and to create a viable work are two profoundly different things. All the transports in the world yield only *discrete* elements. Without a fairly accurate reckoning, the work does not hold— does not *work*. An excellent poem supposes a mass of exact reasoning. A question not so much of forces, but of application of forces. And applied to whom?" (II, 566).

7. TN. *Point d'eau* is an incalculable—and untranslatable—syntagm because it means both a "source of water" and "no water at all." Derrida plays on this double meaning throughout this essay. Whenever he does so, *point* is left untranslated.

we are thinking when we say that the source is the *origin* of a body of water. If there were not an immemorial complicity with the meaning of the word *origin*, with the naked meaning of the word origin in general, could we ever come close to the determined origin that is a source (*origo fontium*), the birth of a body of water, its *nature*, that is the so-called *proper* and unique meaning of the word *source?* Therefore, we *already* would have to understand the meaning of the word *origin* when it designates something totally other than the welling up of a body of water, in order to gain access to that which nevertheless was proposed as the proper meaning of the source. One first would have to fix what *origo* means, the status of the origin or of the "source" in general, of the *departure* or beginning of anything at all, that is of the departure as ab-solute, of emergence unloosed from any determination, before coming back to what nevertheless would remain the proper meaning of the word *source*: the origin of a body of water, de-parture and *point d'eau;* locutions which are all very near to veering off, in a way that is not fortuitous, toward the figures of drought, the negative, and separation.

Therefore, we should not be surprised if generality (the origin in general) becomes the accomplice of metaphoricity, and if we learn from the trope about the status of literal, proper meaning, the status of that which *gives itself as* proper meaning.

But what is *to give itself,* what is the *as* when the issue is one of the proper (meaning)?

Proper meaning derives from derivation. The proper meaning or the primal meaning (of the word *source,* for example) is no longer simply the source, but the deported effect of a turn of speech, a return or detour. It is secondary in relation to that to which it seems to give birth, measuring a separation and a departure from it. The source itself is the effect of that (for) whose origin it passes. One no longer has the right to assimilate, as I have just pretended to do, the proper meaning and the primal meaning. That the proper is not the primal, that it is not at the source, is what Valéry gives us to read, thereby reawakening en route the debate to which this confusion of the proper and the primal gave rise in the history of classical rhetoric.

Therefore we will not listen to the source *itself* in order to learn what it is or what it means, but rather to the turns of speech, the allegories, figures, metaphors, as you will, into which the source has deviated, in order to lose it or rediscover it—which always amounts to the same.

Often designated as *source,* for Valéry the absolute origin first has the form of the *ego,* the *I,* the "most naked I," of "the pure *I,* that unique and monotonous element of each being, [that] is lost and recovered by itself, but inhabits our senses eternally" as "the fundamental permanence of a consciousness that depends on nothing" (*Note and Digression,* 8, 101–2). Nothing in the world, or at least nothing that is presented within it, appears as phenomenon, theme, or object, without first being for me, for (an) ego, and without coming back to me as to the opening, the very origin of the world: not as the cause of its existence, but as the origin of its presence, the point of source on whose basis *everything* takes on meaning, appears, delineates, and measures itself. Everything, that is to say everything that is not I. The non-I is *for* the I, appears as non-I for an I and on the basis of an I. Everything: which is to say that the I, the exception to and condition for everything that appears, does not appear. Never being present to itself, the source hardly exists. It is there for no one. For what Valéry here calls the pure I, and what philosophers usually name the transcendental *ego*, is not the "person," the ego or empirical consciousness of the psychologists. An unnamable, "unqualifiable" source, in effect it has no determinable character since it is not in the world and never presents itself.

Valéry encircles, or rather tracks down, this incessant disappearance, among other places, in the *Note and Digression* to the *Leonardo*: "But what he raises to this high degree is not his precious personal *self*, since he has renounced his personality by making it the object of his thought, and since he has given the place of *subject* to that unqualifiable *I* which has no name or history, which is neither more tangible nor less real than the center of gravity of a ring or that of a planetary system—but which results from the whole, whatever that whole may be" (8, 102–3, Valéry's italics).

The source results here. Valéry would probably have been *irritated* (I am borrowing this word from him for reasons to be given later) if he had been reminded that this proposition—the origin as result— is literally Hegelian, that it reassembles the essence of speculative dialectics whose proposition it properly is. Hegel does not by chance write it in Latin (*Der Anfang ist das Resultat*) at the beginning of the Greater Logic. In *Identity and Difference*, taking his departure from Hegel, Heidegger also analyzes this *ressaut* (*resultare, resilire, resalire*) of the origin in the result, of the founding proposition in the rebound or reflexive counter-motion (*Rückprall*).[8]

The pure I, the source of all presence, thus is reduced to an abstract point, to a pure form, stripped of all thickness, of all depth, without character, without quality, without property, without an assignable duration. This source therefore has no proper meaning. Nothing of that which proceeds from it belongs to it. *Point d'eau*—that is of it. Thus it has no proper name. It is so universal and so abstract a pronoun (*me, I*)[9] that it *replaces, stands for* no proper name of a person in particular: A universal pronoun, but of so singular a universality that it always remains, precisely, singular. The function of this source which *names itself I* is indeed, within and without language, that of a singular universal. In the same

8. TN. *Identity and Difference,* trans. Joan Stambaugh (New York: Harper and Row), p. 53.

9. TN. The translation of the critical words *moi* and *je* is particularly difficult in this essay. In general I have followed the practice of the translations of the *Collected Works*. It should be noted, however, that in French *le moi,* which in the term Valéry uses most frequently is variously translated as the I, the me, and the ego (in the psychoanalytic sense).

text, Valéry describes "the plurality of the singular, in the contradictory co-existence of mutually independent durations—as many of these as there are persons, *tot capita, tot tempora*—a problem comparable with that of *relativity* in physics, though incomparably more difficult" (8, 103). He also names, as if in resonance with the *Phenomenology of Spirit*, "the I, the universal pronoun, the appellation of which has no connection with a face" (8, 104).

That has no relation with a *face:* let us understand this equally as with a particular subject, empirically determined, and with the system which defines the face, to be reconsidered further on as a source which can also receive: the eyes, the mouth, the ears which yield (themselves to) sight, speech, hearing. This pure I which is the source, this singular universal above all does not amount to the individual. A pure consciousness, without the least psychic or physical determination, it "in an instant immolates its individuality" (8, 104). Like the transcendental consciousness described by Husserl, it is constituted, not being *in* the world, neither by a body, which goes without saying, nor even by a soul. The *psyche,* in effect, is a region of that which is in the world (the totality of that which is). But inversely, not being in the world, not belonging to the totality of the things which exist, which are maintained for and before it, this source is nothing, almost nothing. It would be experienced, if it were experienced, as the excess of everything that can be related to it. A relation of nothing to nothing, this relationship is barely a relation. Imagine the God of a negative theology attempting by himself to describe himself, to catch himself in the grid of a determining discourse: he will almost annihilate himself. "It [this consciousness] feels compelled to define itself by the sum total of things, as the *excess* over that totality of its own power of perception. In order to affirm itself, it had to begin by denying an infinite number of elements an infinite number of times, and by exhausting the objects of its power without exhausting that power—with the result that it differs from nothingness by the smallest possible margin" (8, 96).

Incapable of receiving the imprint of any characteristic, evading all predication, not permitting itself to be attributed any property, this source also will be able to lend itself without resistance to the most contradictory determinations. Valéry grants it, for example, a certain Being, but this is only to deny it all presence. Or almost, the *almost* imprinting with its regular cadence the play which dis-qualifies, and does so by arbitrating disqualification, confusing oppositions, and dissolving any ontological pertinence. In question is that which in "blending all the categories is something *that exists and does not exist*" (8, 137). Thus, this I is not an individual, is almost impersonal, very close to being a non-I. Of this consciousness which itself cannot posit itself, itself come before itself, become for itself a thesis or a theme, we cannot even say that it is present for-itself. This source which cannot be made a theme therefore is not a self consciousness, is hardly a consciousness. Is it not unconscious in a certain way or, barely to displace the citation, different from the unconscious by the smallest possible margin?

The analysis of consciousness, therefore, is not a sure thing. Let us not hasten to reproach Valéry for having limited himself to an analysis of consciousness. We are far from having finished with it. Freud says somewhere that what is most enigmatic, finally, is consciousness.

This I which is not an I, this unconscious consciousness, this X which properly has or is nothing, which is not what it is because it is pure, and which therefore is impure because it is pure—will it still be called a source? The source is, and it is in the world. Therefore, it is *for* the I that is called source. Therefore, it remains the deported metaphor of the I. But the I of which it would be the metaphor being intrinsically, properly, improper, that is, non-proper, impure to the extent that it is pure, it is nothing outside its metaphors, nothing except that which transports it outside itself and throws it outside itself at the instant of its birth, as the irruptive welling up, the sometimes discreet, but always violent effraction of the emerging source. As such, this source, in the purity of its waters, is always disseminated far from itself, and has no relation to itself as source. If pure consciousness and the pure I are *like* the source, it is in not being able to come back to it. In their perpetual and instantaneous loss of consciousness, they cannot become themes or give rise to proper or improper definitions, not even, if one might put it thus, to true tropes. Perhaps to the violence of catachreses, which Fontanier says are "not true figures."

And yet *there are* effects of theme, of meaning, of figure. The impossible is possible, by means of the abuse of the twisting which is not yet rhetoric in that it opens and furrows the space of rhetoric. The impossible is possible: the "source," for example, but equally everything that will place it in the position of a secondary proper meaning in order to bring back into it divisions and turns.

Der sich aufhebende Ursprung or
La Coupe de Source[10]

But how is the impossible possible? How can the source divide itself—the sources germinal from the title onward—and thus by itself separate from itself in order to be related to itself—which is, as a pure origin, the irreference to itself. And from as soon as the source begins its process, incising itself and escaping itself, is there a *first* metaphor of the origin? A properly originary metaphor? A metaphor in which the source loses itself less than in another metaphor? Or in which, losing itself *even more* it comes back to itself more certainly? In this procession—Plotinus's language imposes itself here—is there a first metaphoric emanation of the One which is the source?

The I has "no relation with a face." That which sees and is seen first of all, that which yields (itself to) seeing, the face, then, elevates the source into an

10. TN. This subtitle is a citation from Hegel, which is explained at the end of note 12 below.

initial displacement. In this figure an initial metaphoricity perhaps places on view that which has no *figure*.[11] Perhaps, but let us wait.

In the text to which I have referred, as in many others, the source (of the)— I is often described *as* a glance, as the site of the glance. The eye becomes simultaneously the division that opens and the substance of the source, the point of departure and the *point d'eau*. The allegory immediately becomes theatrical. Everything that separates itself from the source comes to be placed before it, a visible object on a stage. Facing the source in the light is everything that is presented to it which is not present to itself. Presence is objectivity. And if the source has no profile for itself, it is like an absolute glance which being always opened wide and thrown toward the visible, cannot itself perceive itself, never emerging from its night.

Incapable of putting itself onstage, pure consciousness therefore cannot give itself any image of itself; but this itself can be said only if, by means of an ancient and unperceived image, one already has made this consciousness into an eye and the source into a spectator. In order to speak of the source, which remains interdicted, first it has had to be *turned:* by means of a trope, it must yield to being seen and yield to seeing. The trope does not first consist of speaking, but of seeing. And more precisely, of seeing the invisible, that which only is said, in order blindly to say the interdicted.

Such is the reverie: "The image it brings to mind spontaneously is that of an invisible audience seated in a darkened theater—a presence that cannot observe itself and is condemned to watch the scene confronting it, yet can feel nevertheless how it creates all that breathless and invincibly oriented darkness" (8, 97–98; modified).

The invincible orient, always apprehended as such from its occidental other (*Orientem Versus*), is the source in that it can have but a single meaning. The eye is always turned in the same direction, toward the outside, and everything is related to this orient. Therefore, the misfortune is to have a meaning, a single invincible meaning. It is because it has a meaning that the source has nothing proper to it, a proper meaning permitting it to come back to and be equal to itself, to belong to itself. It is a kind of nature, or rather a threatened God, impoverished and impotent by virtue of its very originality and its independence from the source. As for this negativity which works upon and anguishes the generative god from within, a certain president, whom we are still leaving in the margin, may have shared knowledge of it with an entire mysticism, a theology, and a certain Hegelianism.[12] The text on the originary scene continues:

11. TN. *Figure* here has the double meaning of (1) figure of speech, and (2) face, visage.
12. [The "certain president" referred to is Schreber, whose memoirs of his mental illness were analyzed by Freud.] Hegel: "And this negativity, subjectivity, ego, freedom are the principles of evil and pain. Jacob Boehme viewed egoity (selfhood) as pain and torment (*Qual*), and as the fountain (*Quelle*, source) of nature and of spirit." *Hegel's Philosophy of Mind* (part 3 of the *Encyclopedia*), trans. William Wallace (Oxford: Clarendon Press, 1971),

"Nothing can be born or perish, exist in some degree, possess a time, a place, a meaning, a figure—except on this definite *stage*, which the fates have circumscribed, and which, having separated it from who knows what primordial chaos, as light was separated from darkness on the first day, they have opposed and subordinated to the condition of *being seen*" (8, 97; Valéry's italics).

For the source to become in turn an image, for it to become engaged in a tropic or fantastic system as well as to appear and to receive, for it to see itself as the glance of the origin, it must divide itself. Wherever the mirror intervenes, each time that Narcissus comes on stage in Valéry's text, the source can be found again as an effect of the mirror only by losing itself twice. The mirror, another unfindable theme (but it propagates itself like a theme that does not exist), manifests in this double loss the singular operation of a multiplying division which transforms the origin into effect, and the whole into a part. Valéry has recognized that the specular agency, far from constituting the I in its properness, immediately expropriates it in order not to halt its march. The imaginary is broken up rather than formed here.[13]

Glance of the figure, figure of the glance, the source is always divided, carried away outside itself: before the mirror it does not come back to itself, its consciousness is still a kind of unconscious. As soon as it performs Narcissus's turn, it no longer knows itself. It no longer belongs to itself. Narcissus defends himself from death only by living it, whether he distances himself from the "venerable

---

p. 232. In the *Lectures on the History of Philosophy,* after recalling that, for Boehme, negativity works upon and constitutes the source, and that in principle "God *is also* the Devil, each for itself," etc., Hegel writes this, which I don't attempt to translate: "*Ein Hauptbegriff ist die* Qualität. *Böhme fängt in der* Aurora (Morgenröte im Aufgang) *von den Qualitäten an. Die erste Bestimmung Böhmes, die der Qualität, ist Inqualieren, Qual, Quelle. In der* Aurora *sagt er:* 'Qualität ist die Beweglichkeit, Quallen (Quellen) oder Treiben eines Dinges' " (part 3, sec. 1, B. Jakob Böhme). It is within this context (negativity and division in the principle of things, in the mind or in God) that Hegel's well-known *ein sich Entzweiendes* (one dividing itself in two) also must be read. (See, for example, *Die Philosophie der Weltgeschichte, Allgemeine Einleitung,* II, 1 b.)

The law-of-the-proper, the *economy* of the source: the source is produced only in being cut off (*à se couper*) from itself, only in taking off in its *own* negativity, but equally, *and by the same token,* in reappropriating itself, in order to amortize its own, proper death, to rebound, *se relever.* Reckoning with absolute loss, that is, no longer reckoning, general economy does not cease to pass into the restricted economy of the source in order to permit itself to be encircled. Once more, here, we are reduced to the inexhaustible ruse of the *Aufhebung,* which is unceasingly examined, in these margins, along with Hegel, according to his text, against his text, within his boundary or interior limit: the absolute exterior which no longer permits itself to be internalized. We are led back to the question of dissemination: does semen permit itself to be *relevé?* Does the separation which cuts off the source permit itself to be thought as the *relève* of oneself? And how is what Hegel says of the child to be read in general: "Der sich aufhebende Ursprung" (*Realphilosophie d'Iena*) or "Trennung von dem Ursprung" (*Phenomenology of Spirit*)? [For our system of notes on *relève,* see above, "La différance," note 23.]

13. TN. The reference is to Lacan's theory linking the agency he calls the imaginary to the formation of the ego in the mirror stage.

fountain" ("Fountain, my fountain, water coldly present" 1, 151), or whether within it he unites himself to his own body in the moment of "extreme existence" in which the I loves itself to death:

> *I love, I love.* And who can love any other
> Than himself? . . .
> 　　　　　　　　You only, body mine, my dear body
> I love, the one alone who shields me from the dead!
> . . . .
>
> 　　　　　　　　　　. . . And soon let me break, kiss
> This frail defense against extreme existence
> This quivering, fragile and holy distance
> Between me and the surface . . .
>
> 　　　　　　　　　(*Fragments of the Narcissus,* 1, 158, 160)

Confronted with this menacing turn of the source, subjected to the contradiction of the apotropaic, desire cannot be simple. Implacable when he analyzes mortal division, Valéry is equally unalterable in his thirst for the origin: into which the analysis itself empties, if it decomposes only in going back toward the principle.

If the source cannot maintain itself, look at itself, present itself to itself in daylight, perhaps it lends itself to being heard. If one displaces the metaphor in order to write it according to other characteristics of the face, shutting the eye and the stage, perhaps the source will be permitted to return to itself: following another turn, another allegory of the origin, another *mythical* circuit from self to self. "In the Beginning Was the Fable."

Narcissus speaks. The poem that bears this title also says "the voice of the springs (*sources*)" and the shout "to the echoes." I do not see myself, said the source. But it says so at least, and thus hears itself. I say to myself that I do not see myself. I say to myself . . . perhaps again becoming myself between my direct and my indirect object, reassembling in this operation, virtually perfected, the subject, the object, the interlocutor—I, him, you. I—mark(s) the division.

Less well known, because Valéry devoted himself to them above all in the *Notebooks,* are the analyses reserved for the voice, the voice of the origin, the origin of the voice. The latter is heard as close as possible to the place where it sounds; it seems to do without the detour through the exteriority of the mirror or the water, the world, in order immediately to reflect itself in the intimate instantaneousness of resonance. Does not this echo without delay lift Narcissus from the death to which he was exposing himself? If the eye fails to institute itself as origin, perhaps the voice can produce itself, emerge from itself, all the while remaining or coming back to itself, without detour or organ, in the inner instance of what I propose to call "hearing oneself speak." Speech, then, would be the authentic exchange of the source with itself. Will it be said that the voice is finally the source? That it says the source? That it lets the source say itself? Or inversely that it produces only an effect of the source? And what does such an *effect* mean? We still must wait.

It belongs to the very structure of speech that it may be, or seem to be, immediately sensible from the source. What appears to be is not an accident here. It belongs to the very production of speech. Between what I say and what I hear myself say, no exteriority, no alterity, not even that of a mirror, seems to interpose itself. Mutism and deafness go hand in hand, and there is nothing less fortuitous. Hence, the interior speech that is not proffered, no longer would be a contingent event, occasionally occurring here or there: it is the condition for speech itself. The voice, it appears, therefore can accomplish the circular return of the origin to itself. In the circle the voice steps beyond the interdiction which made the eye blind to the eye. The true circle, the circle of the truth is therefore always an effect of speech. And Valéry recognized the immense bearing of this autonomous circuit of "hearing-oneself-speak," an apparently highly factual phenomenon, which always might be explained by the anatomical configuration of an animal in the world (but which produces, if one wishes to pursue its consequences, even the concept of an origin of the world, thereby disqualifying the alleged regional empiricity of the "physiological" explanation), and he did so better, without a doubt, than any traditional philosopher, better than Husserl,[14] and better than Hegel, who nevertheless had described phonic vibration as the element of temporality, of subjectivity, of interiorization, and of idealization in general, along with everything which thereby systemically lets itself be carried along in the circle of speculative dialectics.

But, like the lucid source, the sonorous source attempts to rejoin itself only by differentiating itself, dividing, differing, deferring without end. Quite simply, the lure of reappropriation this time becomes more interior, more twisted, more fatal. Valéry, as we will verify in an instant, did describe this movement which goes back to the source and which separates from the source or simultaneously interdicts the source. Which then occupies another position; it is no longer only that approaching which movement exhausts itself, but also that which somewhere eludes, always a bit further on, our grasp. It is born of this very eluding, like a situated mirage, a site inscribed in a directionless field. It is nothing before being sought, only an effect produced by the structure of movement. The source therefore is not the origin, it is neither at the departure or the arrival. Valéry marks in speech both the circle of hearing-oneself-speak, the lure of the source rejoined, and the law which makes such a return to itself an effect. An effect: simultaneously the derivation of that which is not *causa sui*, and the illusion, the trap, or the play of appearance.

Among many others, here are three fragments from the *Notebooks:*

14. See Michel Lechantre, "L'hiéroglyphe intérieur," in *Modern Language Notes*, 1972.

"Linguistics
I is an element of language linked to speech itself. All speech has its source which is an I. This *I* is ~~mine if~~ that of X if X ~~hears it~~ gives and receives this speech, and in receiving it recognizes himself as source, i.e. simultaneously an object among objects and a non-object, a space or world of objects.

"I, You, Him, this triangle—Trinity! The three roles of the same in relation to the verb, Mouth, ear, thing" (C. 11, p. 604, 1926). A very enigmatic sequence from 1910, in examining the "believer" who "believes he believes," proposed what is doubtless the most efficacious formula for every deviation of the source: "Thereby, change 3 to 4 in the Trinity" (II, 574).

In the return of the phonic circle, the source appears as such only at the moment, which is no longer a moment, the barely second second, of the instant emission in which the origin yields itself to receive what it produces. The source receives, receives itself, interrupts circulation only in order to saturate it. Would the circle disjoin itself only in the separation which is in sum undefinable, and hardly probable, between a voice of the interior and an effectively proffered voice? Such a separation in effect remains ungraspable in linguistic, poetic, or phenomenological terms. Neither in the form nor the content of a statement could we assign an intrinsic difference between the sentence I am pronouncing here, now, in my so-called speaking voice, which soon will return to the silence from which it proceeds, very low in my voice or on my page, and the *same* sentence retained in an inner instance, mine or yours. The two events are as different as possible as events, but in the qualitative description of events, in the determination of predicative traits, form or content, the principle of discernibility, the concept of difference evades us. Like the separation that disjoints the circle, a certain tangency here appears to be both nul and infinite. Another note from the *Notebooks*, concerning the *point de source*: ". . . no (*point de*) 'me' without 'you.' To each his Other, which is his Same. Or the *I is two*—by definition. If there is *voice*, there is ear. Internally there is voice, there is no sight of who is speaking, And who will describe, will define the *difference between the same sentence which is said* and *not pronounced*, and the *same sentence sounding in the air*. This identity and this difference are one of the essential secrets of the nature of the mind—and who has pointed it out? Who has 'exhibited' it? The same for sight. I believe that the relationship of these possibilities of double effect is in the power of motility, which will never sufficiently be thought about. Within it lies the mystery of time, i.e. the existence of that which is not. Potential and unactual" (C. 22, p. 304, 1939; Valéry's italics).

Not long after, still as a displacement but from whence the snake again is sketched in the form of circles drawn in the margin, we have from Valéry's hand: "There is nothing more astonishing than this 'interior' speech, which is heard without any noise and is articulated without movement. Like a closed circuit. Everything comes to be explained and thrashed out in this circle similar to the snake biting its tail. Sometimes the ring is broken and emits the internal speech.

Sometimes the communication between what is being born and the born is regular, regimented, and the distinction can no longer be felt. Sometimes the communication is only delayed, and the internal circuit serves as a preparation for a circuit of *external intention:* then there is emission to choice" (C. 24, p. 99, 1940).

The difference between internal speech and external speech therefore passes understanding. No concept can make it its own. Its reserve is almost unheard—with what ear could it be heard?—or in any event undescribable. Thirty years earlier: "How *to write* this singular difference rationally?" (C. 3, p. 483, 1905).[15] How to write it, in effect, if writing, phonetic writing above all, precisely has as its function the restitution of speech to the internal regime, and to act such that in its event effectively proffered speech is but an accident lost for reading? The regime, being regimented, in effect seems to insure the "normal" communication of the source with itself, thereby regularly circulating between the external event and the internal event, conferring upon the origin the invisible appearing, the calm being near to itself that the glance saw itself refused.

Now here, again, Valéry remarks a cutting difference: not the external prolation which accidentally would come to interrupt the circle, but already the circuit's return to itself: "Who speaks, who listens [in the interior speech]? It is not exactly the same . . . The existence of the speech from self to self is the sign of a *cut*" (C. 7, p. 615, 1920). The circle turns in order to annul the cut, and therefore, by the same token, unwittingly signifies it. The snake bites its tail, from which above all it does not follow that it finally rejoins itself without harm in this successful auto-fellatio of which we have been speaking all along, in truth.

15. "Ext. speech differs from secret speech only through the functions which are associated and co-ordinated with it—weighing it down with their inertia and their passive resistances, but making it subject to their more arduous and solid—more tied together—world. All exterior speech is reduced to an interior speech by creating these auxiliary functions: 0. This is a projection. But conversely, all int. speech cannot become exterior" (C. 3, p. 483, 1905). On the relationship mouth/ear, see, among other fragments, that of C. 24, p. 107, 1940 (which Valéry accompanies by sketches), and M. Lechantre's work cited above.

A Poet's Notebook, which joins an extreme formalism and a "verbal materialism" (7, 183), also analyzes poetics on the basis of the same functioning. For example: "So the poet at work is an expectation . . . He reconstructs what he desired. He reconstructs *quasi-mechanisms capable of giving back to him the energy they cost him and more* (for here the principles are apparently violated). *His ear speaks to him.*

"We wait for the unexpected word—which cannot be foreseen but must be awaited. We are the first to hear it.

"*To hear?* but that means *to speak.* One understands what one hears only if one has said it oneself from another motive.

"*To speak* is to hear.

"What is concerned, then, is a *twofold* attention. The state of being able to produce what is perceived admits of more or of less by reason of the number of elementary functions involved . . . One gets the idea of a reversible apparatus, like a telephone or a dynamo" (7, 174–75).

Cut off from the end as from the origin, the source is no longer anything but an effect of "reaction" or, if you will, of revolution, in a system that never will have obeyed it. "I speak *to myself*. The action formulated this way suggests a distinction. And in effect what one says (or shows) to the other *I* teaches the latter something—or rather excites a reaction—, which becomes an origin" (C. 15, p. 193, 1931). Earlier: "On the relations of the I and the me. If I *say* something *to myself*, what I say acts on what follows and modifies what I will say to myself—becomes an origin" (C. 12, p. 692, 1928).

The source having *become*—which is the unintelligible itself—time opens itself as the delay of the origin in relation to itself. Time is nothing other. "What comes to 'mind'—to the lips—modifies you yourself in return. What you have just emitted, emits toward you, and what you have produced fecundates you. In saying something without having foreseen it, you see it like a foreign fact, an *origin*—something you had not known. Thus you were delayed in relation to yourself" (C. 12, p. 24, 1926). And elsewhere: "We are made of two moments, and as if of the *delay* of a 'thing' for itself" (*Mauvaises pensées et autres* II, 885. Valéry's italics).

Thus, we have at our disposition, as a paradigm, all the movements by means of which Valéry could *track down* the source. And, for the very reason we have just analyzed, we no longer have to decide if this paradigm is an origin and a model or one example among others. To track down, to set out on the path on which the living signals death, is indeed to repeat without end the indestructible desire which comes back to the source as to the complicity or implicity of life and death. In the purity of the source the living is the dead. But to track down is also to disspell the illusion, to flush out all the questions and concepts of the origin. It is to unseal at the source the separation of an altering difference.

Among others, three fragments from the *Notebooks:* "Heaven preserve you from questions of origin" (C. 21, p. 275, 1938). "We are not origins, but the illusion of being so is with us" (C. 8, p. 895, 1922). "Some go to the furthest reach of the *origin*—which is the coincidence of *presence* and of the initial event—and attempt to go to find in this separation *gold, diamonds*" (C. 15, p. 526, 1931–32; Valéry's italics).

Point de philosophie[16]—Writing

The origin—coincidence of presence and the initial event. Perhaps I will let myself be guided now by the question put this way: can one dissociate the "initial event" from presence? Can one conceive of an initial event without presence, the value of a *first time* that cannot be thought in the form or category

16. TN. *Point de* must be understood in the double sense explained in note 7 above. Thus, simultaneously "point of, source of philosophy" and "no philosophy."

of presence? Would this be the impossible itself? And if so, impossible for whom, for what, according to what space?

Here we come to *philosophy*.

Valéry lays out his entire reading of the history of philosophy according to this snare. The philosopher—it is he of whom Valéry speaks, and whom Valéry summons to appear, rather than philosophy itself—is the person who wears himself out over vain questions of origin: an illusion both transcendental and natural, natural since it invincibly returns to the orient, to "nature," to birth, to the source. Everywhere that "nature" intervenes in philosophical discourse, that is everywhere, Valéry pursues it with ironic apostrophes that never aim at nature alone, but also the entire cortege of distinctions and oppositions that nature activates and regulates.[17]

Let us sketch out the scheme of this critical solicitation of philosophical discourse. It always insists upon a crisis of the origin.

Valéry reminds the philosopher that philosophy is written. And that the philosopher is a philosopher to the extent that he forgets this.

Philosophy is written—producing at least three consequences.

First of all, a break with the regime of hearing-oneself-speak, with self-presence in the meaning of a source whose truth continuously resources itself. Irreversibly, something of this presence of meaning, of this truth which nonetheless is the philosopher's great and only theme, is lost in writing. Hence the philosopher writes against writing, writes in order to make good the loss of writing, and by this very gesture forgets and denies what occurs by his hand. These two gestures must be kept together. As if unknown to each other, they cooperate as soon as one interprets writing as does Valéry in this context. The philosopher writes in order to keep himself within the logocentric circle. But also in order to reconstitute the circle, to interiorize a continuous and ideal presence which he knows, consciously or unconsciously—which does not matter since in any event he feels the effect—*already* to have been dispelled within the voice itself. Discontinuity, delay, heterogeneity, and alterity already were working upon the voice, producing it from its first breath as a system of differential traces, that is as writing before the letter. Philosophical writing, then, literally comes to bridge this gap, to close the dike, and to dream of virgin continuity.

Whence Valéry's apparently paradoxical argument, which opposes the continuousness of writing, or rather of the graphic, to the discontinuousness of speech. The philosopher intends to come back to the proximity of the speaking source, or rather to the source murmuring its interior speech, and to deny that he is writing. Terrified by the difference within hearing-oneself-speak, by the writing within speech, the philosopher writes—on the page—in order to erase and to forget that when he speaks the evil of the cipher is already there in germ. "But the nature of language is quite opposed to the happy outcome of this great

17. See e.g. *Orientem Versus* 10, 379ff. and II, 572.

endeavor to which all the philosophers have devoted themselves. The strongest of them have worn themselves out in the effort to *make their thoughts speak*. In vain have they created or transfigured certain words; they could not succeed in transmitting their inner reality. Whatever the words may be—Ideas or Dynamis or Being or Noumenon or Cogito or Ego—they are all *ciphers,* the meaning of which is determined solely by the context; and so it is finally by a sort of personal creation that their reader—as also happens with readers of poetry—gives the force of life to writings in which ordinary speech is contorted into expressing values that men cannot exchange and that do not exist in the realm of spoken words" (8, 150–51; Valéry's italics).

These philosophical ciphers formalize natural language and tend to forge, by means of the contract of their conventional formality, a kind of chain of security, of quasi-continuous plenitude which occasionally makes these ciphers resemble the thing itself. They tend to erase the breaks, the tremors working within speech and writing in what is called "natural language," which is also, from the start, a diastemic organization, a system of "arbitrary" signs, or in any event of discrete and diacritical signs. Now the paradoxical law that Valéry was able to recognize is that the more the graphic is formalized the more it is naturalized. As an artist of form, which is what he is from Valéry's point of view, the philosopher is still dreaming of nature. Here we might elaborate the motif of a critique of formalist illusion which would complicate what is often considered to be Valéry's formalism somewhat. The complication is due to the fact that formality, far from simply being *opposed* to it, *simultaneously* produces and destroys the naturalist, "originarist" illusion. Always insufficiently formalized, still too embroiled in natural language, in natural language's vagueness, equivocalness, and metaphoricity, philosophical writing does not support comparison with its model: the rigor and exactitude of a purely formal language. Valéry has just recalled the effort of the philosopher wearing himself out in *making his thoughts speak:* "Today, in a number of truly remarkable cases, even the expression of things by means of discrete signs, arbitrarily chosen, has given way to lines traced by the things themselves, or to transpositions or inscriptions directly derived from them. The great invention that consists in making the laws of science visible to the eyes and, as it were, readable on sight has been incorporated into knowledge; and it has in some sort *doubled* the world of experience with a visible world of curves, surfaces, and diagrams that translate properties into forms whose inflexions we can follow with our eyes, thus by our consciousness of this movement gaining an impression of values in transition. The *graphic* has a continuity of movement that cannot be rendered in speech, and it is superior to speech in immediacy and precision. Doubtless it was speech that commanded the method to exist; doubtless it is now speech that assigns a meaning to the graphisms and interprets them; but it is no longer by speech that the act of mental possession is consummated. Something new is little by little taking shape under our eyes; a sort of ideography of plotted and diagrammed relations between qualities and quantities, a language that has for grammar a body of preliminary conventions (scales, axes, grids, etc.)" (8, 152–53; modified).[18]

Philosophy is written—second consequence—so that it must reckon with a formal instance, reckon with form, is unable to get away from it: "I said one day before philosophers: philosophy is an affair of form."[19]

A task is then prescribed: to study the philosophical text in its formal structure, in its rhetorical organization, in the specificity and diversity of its textual types, in its models of exposition and production—beyond what previously were called genres—and also in the space of its mises en scène, in a syntax which would be not only the articulation of its signifieds, its references to Being or to truth, but also the handling of its proceedings, and of everything invested in them. In a word, the task is to consider philosophy also as a "particular literary genre," drawing upon the reserves of a language, cultivating, forcing, or making deviate a set of tropic resources[20] older than philosophy itself. Here we are quite close to Nietzsche, but let us not hasten to compare: "What becomes of it (philosophy) when—in addition to feeling beset, overrun, and dismayed at every turn by the

18. "It is the vice of the ordinary philosophical vocabulary that though it must necessarily put on the appearances of technical language, it is nonetheless necessarily lacking in really precise definitions: for the only precise definitions are *instrumental* (that is to say, reducible to acts, such as pointing at an object or carrying out an operation). It is impossible to convince ourselves that words like *reason, universe, cause, matter,* or *idea* possess single, uniform, unchanging meanings. What usually happens is that every attempt to make the meaning of such terms clearer leads to introducing under the same name a fresh object of thought *which differs from the original object in so far as it is new*" (*Swedenborg*, 9, 118).

19. "I meant to talk of philosophers—and to philosophers.

"I wanted to show that it would be of the greatest profit to them to practice this labor of poetry which leads insensibly to the study of word combinations, not so much through the conformity of the meanings of these groups to an idea or thought that one thinks should be *expressed*, as, on the contrary, through their effects once they are formed, from which one chooses.

"Generally one tries to 'express one's thought,' that is, to pass from an *impure* form, a mixture of all the resources of the mind, to a *pure* form, that is, one solely verbal and organized, amounting to a system of arranged acts or contrasts.

"But the art of poetry is alone in leading one to envisage pure forms in themselves" (7, 178).

On philosophical writing and the philosophical spider, see also *My Faust*, 3, 123–24.

20. "But up to the present, literature has not, so far as I am aware, paid much attention to this immense treasure house of subjects and situations . . . What are we to make of terms that cannot be precisely defined unless we re-create them? *Thought, mind* itself, *reason, intelligence, understanding, intuition,* or *inspiration?* . . . Each of these terms is both a means and an end in turn, a problem and a solution, a state and an idea; and each of them, in each of us, is adequate or inadequate according to the function which circumstances impose on it. You are aware that at this point the philosopher becomes a poet, and often a great poet: he borrows metaphor from us and, by means of splendid images which we might well envy, he draws on all nature for the expression of his profoundest thought.

"The poet is not so fortunate when he tries the corresponding procedure" (9, 19).

"Philosophy is reduced to a logic and to a rhetoric or poetics" (C. 8, p. 911, 1922). (See also the entirety of *Leonardo and the Philosophers* 8, 110ff.)

furious activity of the physical sciences—it is also disturbed and menaced in its most ancient, most tenacious (and perhaps least regrettable) habits by the slow and meticulous work of the philologists and semanticists? What becomes of the philosopher's *I think*, and what becomes of his *I am*? What becomes, or rebecomes, of that neutral and mysterious verb TO BE, which has had such a grand career in the void? From those modest syllables, released to a peculiar fortune by the loss or attrition of their original meaning, artists of great subtlety have drawn an infinite number of answers.

"If, then, we take no account of our habitual thinking and confine ourselves to what is revealed by a glance at the present state of intellectual affairs, we can easily observe that philosophy as defined by its product, which is *in writing*, is objectively a particular branch of literature . . . we are forced to assign it a place not far from poetry . . .

"But the artists of whom I was speaking fail to recognize themselves as artists and do not wish to be such. Doubtless their art, unlike that of the poets, is not the art of exploiting the sound values of words; it speculates on a certain faith in the existence of an absolute value that can be isolated from their meaning. 'What is reality?' the philosopher asks, or likewise, 'What is liberty?' Setting aside and ignoring the partly metaphorical, partly social, and partly statistical origin of these nouns, his mind, by taking advantage of their tendency to slip into indefinable meanings, will be able to produce combinations of extreme depth and delicacy" (8, 139–40).[21]

Perhaps I will be able to state further on how the critical necessity of this aesthetics, of this formalism or conventionalism, if adhered to otherwise than with controlled insistence and a calculated strategic reaction, would risk just as surely leading us back to the places in question.

Philosophy is written—third consequence—as soon as its forms and operations are not only oriented and watched over by the law of meaning, thought, and Being, which speaks in order to say I, and does so as close as possible to the source or the well.

Of this proposition, as of its simulacrum, Descartes here is exemplary. Valéry does not cease to question him, never leaves him; and if his reading of Descartes at the very least might appear uneven to the historians of philosophy, the fact was not unforeseen by Valéry, who interpreted it in advance. We will concern ourselves with this for a while.

What is the operation of the I in the Cogito? To assure itself of the source in the certitude of an invincible self presence, even in the figure—always paternal, Freud tells us—of the devil. This time a *power*[22] is gained in the course of a movement in grand style which takes the risk of enunciating and writing itself. Valéry very quickly suggests that truth is Descartes's last concern. The words

21. See also 7, 180; and on prose as the erasure of metaphor, 7, 177.
22. Elsewhere, philosophy is considered precisely as the loss of power; or at least it does not lead to "establishing any power" (8, 139).

"truth" and "reality" are once again in quotation marks, advanced as effects of language and as simple citations. But if the "I think therefore I am" "has no meaning whatever,"[23] and a fortiori no truth, it has "a very great value," and like the style is "entirely characteristic of the man himself." This value is that of a shattering blow, a quasi-arbitrary affirmation of mastery by means of the exercise of a style, the egotistic impression of a form, the stratagem of a mise en scène powerful enough to do without truth, a mise en scène keeping that much less to truth in its laying of truth as a trap, a trap into which generations of servile fetishists will come to be caught, thereby acknowledging the law of the master, of I, René Descartes.

Valéry insists upon the style: "It is precisely this that I think I see in the *Cogito*. Neither a syllogism nor even meaning in the literal sense; but a reflex action of the man, or more accurately, the explosion of an act, a shattering blow. There is, in any thinker of such intellectual power, what might be described as a home policy and a foreign policy of thought; he sets up certain 'reasons of state' against which nothing can prevail . . . Never, until he came, had a philosopher so deliberately exhibited himself on the stage of his own thought, risking his own neck, daring to write 'I' for whole pages on end; he does it above all, and in an admirable style, when writing the *Meditations* . . . I have called his style admirable" (9, 55–56).

Further on, and elsewhere, Valéry associates style with the "timbre" of the voice. Descartes could assert himself, posit his mastery, only by "paying with his person," exposing himself in a theater, putting himself on stage and into play "by risking the *I*." And henceforth at issue are the *style* of his writing and the *timbre* of his voice.

How are we to reassemble these propositions? Will it be said that Descartes, by means of what is inimitable in his text (timbre and style), has succeeded in imposing the source, in restoring the presence of the origin that is so implacably set aside by the play of signification?

23. "At this point I am going to take a considerable risk. I say that we can consider it from a very different point of view—we can assert that this brief and pregnant expression of its author's personality *has no meaning whatever*. But I must add that it has *a very great value*, entirely characteristic of the man himself.

"I maintain that *Cogito ergo sum* has no meaning because that little word *sum* has no meaning. No one dreams of saying or needs to say 'I am' unless he is taken for dead and wants to protest that he is not. In any case he would say 'I'm alive.' But a cry or the slightest movement would be quite sufficient. No, 'I am' cannot tell anyone anything and is no answer to any intelligible question. But the remark does correspond here to something else, which I shall explain presently. Furthermore, what meaning can be attributed to a proposition whose negative form would express its content just as well as the positive? If 'I am' means anything, 'I am not' tells us neither more nor less" (9, 54). In the *Address to the Congress of Surgeons*, Valéry scans the formula: "At one moment I think; at another I am" (11, 139).

I have proposed elsewhere an interpretation of the equivalence, "I am": "I am living": "I am dead." Although made from a very different point of view, this interpretation nevertheless seems to me to intersect with Valéry's. Cf. *Speech and Phenomena*.

Not at all, and such is the risk of what is at stake. In order to understand this, we must recall that the concepts of style and timbre have a rigorous definition in Valéry's analyses. In its irreplaceable quality, the timbre of the voice marks the event of language. By virtue of this fact, timbre has greater import than the *form* of signs and the *content* of meaning. In any event, timbre cannot be summarized by form and content, since at the very least they share the capacity to be repeated, to be imitated in their identity as objects, that is, in their ideality. ("Now, as far as you are concerned, all I need do is watch you talk, listen to your timbre, the excitement in your voice. The way people talk tells you more than what they say . . . The content in itself has no . . . essential importance. —Odd. That's one theory of poetry," *Idée Fixe*, 5, 106.) Numerous notes in the *Notebooks* confirm this point. Not lending itself to substitution, is not timbre on the order of a pure event, a singular presence, the very upsurge [*sourdre*] of the source? And is not style the equivalent of this unique vibration in writing? *If there is* one poetic event, it sounds in timbre; *if there is* one literary event, it is inscribed by style. "Literature, style—it is to write that which will supplement for the absence of the author, for the silence of the absent, for the inertia of the written thing" (C. 12, p. 10, 1926). This proposition, and others[24] along the same lines, appear to be quite classical, and doubtless are so up to a certain point: style, supplementing timbre, tends to repeat the event of pure presence, the singularity of the source present in what it produces, supposing again that the unity of a timbre—immediately it is identifiable—ever has the purity of an event. But, if style supplements timbre, nothing, it appears, can supplement their unique exchange, nothing can repeat the pure event (if at least there is something like the purity of a style and a timbre, which for me remains quite a hypothesis) that style and timbre constitute.

But, if there is a timbre and a style, will it be concluded that here the source *presents itself?*

Point. And this is why *I* loses itself here, or in any event exposes itself in the operation of mastery. The timbre of my voice, the style of my writing are that which for (a) me never will have been present. I neither hear nor recognize the timbre of my voice. If my style marks itself, it is only on a surface which remains invisible and illegible for me. *Point* of *speculum:* here I am blind to my style, deaf to what is most spontaneous in my voice. It is, to take up again the formulation from above, and to make it deviate toward a lexicographical monstrosity, the *sourdre* of the source.[25] The spontaneous can emerge as the pure initiality of the

24. On voice, writing, and literature, see also II, 549.

25. [Derrida's "lexicographical monstrosity" involves a play on the word *sourdre* which means to well up, to surge up, as when a source emerges from underground. In this context, i.e. the discussion of being *"deaf* to what is most spontaneous in my voice," Derrida is playing on the *sourd,* deaf, in *sourdre.* He is forcing *sourdre* to mean "to make deaf" (which it does not), at the same time as it means to well up, and is playing on the consequences of this "monstrous" double meaning.]

Once more, then, the value of the origin must be dissociated from the value of the event only on the condition that it does not itself *present itself*, on the condition of this inconceivable and *irrelevable*[26] passivity in which nothing can present itself to itself. Here we are in need of a paradoxical logic of the event as a *source which cannot present itself, happen to itself*. The value of the event is perhaps indissociable from that of presence; it remains rigorously incompatible with that of self-presence.

The Event and the Regime of the Other:
Timbre

To hear oneself is the most normal and the most impossible experience. One might conclude from this, first, that the source is always other, and that whatever hears itself, not itself hearing itself, always comes from elsewhere, from outside and afar. The lure of the I, of consciousness as hearing-oneself-speak would consist in dreaming of an operation of ideal and idealizing mastery, transforming hetero-affection into auto-affection, heteronomy into autonomy. Within this process of appropriation somehow would be lodged a "regime" of normal hallucination. When I speak (to myself) without moving tongue and lips, I believe that I hear myself, although the source is other; or I believe that we are two, although everything is happening "in me." Supported by a very ancient history, traversing all the stations of the relation to the self (sucking, masturbation, touching/touched, etc.), this possibility of a "normal" double hallucination permits me to give myself to hear what I desire to hear, to believe in the spontaneity of the power which needs no one in order to give pleasure to itself. Valéry

---

source. "One must go back to the *source*—which is not the *origin*. The *origin*, in all, is *imaginary*. The *source* is the fact within which the imaginary is proposed: water wells up there. Beneath, I do not know what takes place?" (C. 23, p. 592, 1940).

Beneath, I do not know what takes place. Although we cannot follow all the implications here, let us indicate that which, within the trope, both retains and brings to the surface what is most strange beneath the most familiar (*heimlich/unheimlich*). Two examples, themselves cited as examples: 1. "When, seeking to explain the generation of the operations of the soul, you say, Monseigneur, that they have their source in sensation, and that attention flows into comparison, comparison into judgment, etc., you are comparing all these operation to streams, and the words *source* and *flow* are tropes, which convey your thought in sensory fashion. We use this language on all occasions which present themselves, and you experience daily to what extent it is proper to enlighten you." (Condillac, *De l'art d'écrire*, in *Oeuvres philosophiques*, ed. Georges Le Roy (Paris: Presses Universitaires de France, 1947), pp. 560–61.) It will have been noticed, among other things, that here the *source* is a trope and a comparison which is possible not at the source of the operations, but at a moment which itself is determinate, derived from the course (of what is compared): comparison. 2. "Compare: 'The Zecks are all "heimlich." ' ' "Heimlich?" . . . *What do you understand by "heimlich"*?' 'Well, . . . they are like a buried spring (*zugegrabenen Brunnen*) or a dried-up pond. One cannot walk over it without always having the feeling that water might come up there again.' 'Oh, we call it "*unheimlich*." ' " Freud, *The Uncanny*, in SE XVII, 223.

26. TN. *Irrelevable*, i.e. that which cannot be *relevé*, subjected to the Hegelian operation of the *Aufhebung*.

perhaps has read into this the essence of poetic power. "A Poet's Notebook" opens with these words: "Poetry. Is it impossible, given time, care, skill, and desire, to proceed in an orderly way to arrive at poetry? To end by *hearing* exactly what one wished to hear by means of a skillful and patient management of that same desire?" (7, 173).

At a certain moment in history, for reasons to be analyzed, the poet ceased being considered the prey of a foreign voice, in mania, delirium, enthusiasm, or inspiration. Poetic "hallucination" is then accommodated under the rubric of the "regime": a simple elaboration of hearing-oneself-speak, a regulated, normed exchange of the same and the other, within the limits tolerated by a kind of general organization, that is, an individual, social, historical system, etc.

But what happens when this organization, still intolerant somewhere, incriminates "literally" abnormal hallucination? What happens, for example, when someone hears voices that he *remains alone* to hear, and that he perceives as a foreign source, which proceeds, as is said, from his own interior? Can one settle this problem as being the poet's? Can one content oneself with saying that since the source is transcendentally other, in sum, this hallucination too is normal, more or less, i.e. an exaggeration hardly baring the truth that would be the essential heterogeneity of the source?

Here is announced the question of psychoanalysis. In one of the *Notebooks* of 1918–21, concerning silent discourse, Valéry noted: "This voice (morbidly) might become entirely foreign" (C. 7, p. 615, 1920). And, during the course of an analysis that is systematically, in detail, to be collated with Freud's analysis of Schreber's *Memoirs*, Valéry slips in, without pausing, an allusion to Swedenborg's father. Then, like Freud, setting aside the hypothesis of a purely delirious disorder, Valéry wonders: "*How is a Swedenborg possible?*" Making his question explicit, he almost could be speaking of Schreber: "From what premises must we start when we come to study the coexistence in the same person of a scientist and engineer, a high official, a man at once wise in practical affairs and learned in everything, who yet had the characteristics of an Illuminatus, who did not hesitate to write and publish an account of his visions, and who claimed to have been visited by the inhabitants of another world, to be in touch with them, and to have spent part of his life in their mysterious company?" (9, 123).

Valéry indeed must admit that if the source is always other, the alterity of the source, in the case of the mystic or the hallucinated, is of an other alterity; it is no longer the source which "normally" divides and constitutes the I, if we might put it thus, although for Valéry, as for Freud, the notion of normality appears to be "cursory and too simple." Therefore, he takes into account this surplus heterogeneity of alterity. And the word "source" imposes itself upon Valéry several times.

In the "normal" regime, the I controls the distinction between an internal alterity, in some way, and an external alterity. Above all, it does not transform "deviations" that it may "attribute" to an "intimate and functional origin" (9,

120; modified) into an absolutely external source. It recognizes what comes from its own desire. "The mystic, on the contrary, has a sense of the exteriority, or rather extraneousness, of the *source* of the images, emotions, words, and impulses which reach him through some inner channel" (9, 121; Valéry's italics). The question then becomes one of this alienation of the source, the becoming-exterior of an intimate source: "How can we conceive that a man like Swedenborg, a highly cultivated man . . . could have failed to perceive the part played by his own mind in producing the images, admonitions, 'truths' which came to him as though from some secret source?" (9, 121). And of course Valéry also leads these phenomena of the alienation or alteration of the source back to a certain desire of Swedenborg's: he receives from an "external source" something "intensely desired" (9, 125).[27]

But here we have only the principle of a description. There is still nothing to permit us to explain the difference between the state of the hallucinated or the mystic and, for example, the state of the poet, that is, whoever finishes "by *hearing* precisely what he had desired to hear." Now, Valéry knew that Swedenborg's experience was not homogenous with "poetic" experience, that is, with the experience of the alterity of the "regimented" source. Valéry recognizes this clearly, and even goes to the extent of indicating that the " 'subjective' events which were, strictly speaking, hallucinatory," as narrated by Swedenborg, "cannot be reduced either to mystic vision or to the admitted existence of a certain *sign*" (9, 125–26).

The Implex (Question of Formalisms): Nietzsche and Freud

At this point, ceasing to describe, but also renouncing any attempt at explanation, Valéry in his last three pages proposes a purely negative and polemical discourse which can be summarized as a principled objection to any hypothesis of the psychoanalytic type in the name of the ineffable. The central nerve of the argument is the following: one gains access to these hallucinatory or oniric phenomena only by means of a narrative discourse, a discrete and relational verbal chain of ex post facto descriptions, of transcriptions, of translations of transcriptions, etc. which always leave the experience itself out of reach, the experience being *"something which is nameless"* (9, 127; Valéry's italics). And, before coming to any conclusions on what he dubiously calls the "Swedenborg Mystery," Valéry had written: "That is why I am very far from putting confidence in the pretended analysis of dreams which is so fashionable at the present time and in which we seem to have forged a new Key to Dreams" (9, 126).

27. This is the analysis that Valéry proposes of Swedenborg's "sign." And, in this case at least, he excludes the hypothesis "of a vast lie in the grand manner" (9, 124).

Here the question of psychoanalysis imposes itself. All the motifs I have emphasized, and still others, to a certain point are in agreement, in any event in their principles, with Freud's motifs: redefinition of the I (the ego) and consciousness as effects in a system, development of the logic of a primary narcissism in relation to a death drive, systematic interest in everything that escapes the control of waking consciousness (Valéry's meditation on dreams was unceasing), etc. One could pursue the correspondence of the two texts a long way. I do not know whether Freud read Valéry, and since it is not his birthday, I leave suspended the question of knowing why, and above all if he can be excused for this. But why did Valéry so nervously reject psychoanalysis? Why did he seize upon the argument of the unnamable that he just as summarily could have used against all science? The connotation of nervousness, of precipitation, and of spasm are not insignificant. Valéry could have offered arguments, showed his disagreement, asked epistemological questions, differentiated his criticisms, vigilantly examined what then could be seen of psychoanalysis: but he did so only by opposing his formalist point of view—which therefore produces an effect of obscurantism here—to what he considered to be Freud's semantic, "significative" point of view about dreams.[28] But why talk about Freud's "stupidity"? Why multiply sarcastic remarks against those whom he names "Freud and Co."? Most often it is the insistence on sexuality that infuriates him, and without recognizing, wanting or being able to recognize, that Freud's "sexualism" is

28. For example: "I have been concerned with dreams for centuries. Since then have come the theses of Freud and Co., which are completely different—because it is the possibility and intrinsic characteristics of the phen. which interest me; while for them, it is its meaning, its relation to the subject's history—which I am not worried about." Valéry had just written: "The small child of two years is transparent. Its impressions, its psyche, and its acts have very few *waystations*" (C. 19, p. 456, 1936).
"My theories of the dream are completely opposed to those of the day. They are completely 'formal,' while the latter are completely 'significative' " (C. 17, p. 766, 1935). "Now, I am inclined to think that these words have *no meaning*, that it is useless to look for meaning in them, vain to give them meaning. And the reflex acts of the sleeper are only *linear* responses. The sleeper discharges himself through the brain as through the limbs— without past or future—without additivity. For my way of thinking, it is a mistake to approach dreams by way of the *significative*" (ibid., p. 771). See also p. 770, and the entire chapter "Le rêve et l'analyse de la conscience," in Judith Robinson, *L'analyse de l'esprit dans les Cahiers de Valéry* (Paris: Corti, 1963). This semanticist error, if we may put it thus, is what from Valéry's point of view deprives psychoanalysis of all scientificity, if not all efficacity. "If Freud's theories have therapeutic value, it is highly probable that they have no *scientific* value" (C. 11, p. 476, 1926). "There are authors (and therefore theories at their service) whose works, consciously founded on the unconscious, are comparable finally to the Flea Market" (C. 17, p. 515, 1934).
As is inevitable in this situation of misconstruing, Valéry, who calls himself "the least Freudian of men" (cited by Robinson, *L'analyse,* p. 105), occasionally makes statements that Freud would not simply have rejected, at the very moment when it is believed that these statements are in opposition to him. Thus: "Freud's theories are repulsive to my way of thinking, which would have it that in dreams the ideas of the most *insignificant* things from waking life play a role equal to that played by things which are moving, or would be the most moving" (C. 11, p. 621, 1925–26).

much more complex and problematical than it appears, Valéry often gets carried away, losing his *teste*[29] so to speak, when confronted by what he calls the "dirty ins and outs." Unless M. Teste's strong point, his cold and pure intellectuality ("Stupidity is not my strong point"), somewhere is constructed in order to resist a certain psychoanalytic "stupidity." One also might reread *Idée Fixe* with one's sights set in this direction, on Valéry's rejection; in an instant I will indicate why. Concerning dreams and psychoanalysis, we may point out the following in particular: "My dear man, I'm so fed up with the whole story and all its dirty ins and outs . . . I've been stuffed to the skin with incestuous narcoses!" (5, 41). And the "Propositions Concerning Me" close the door on Proust and Freud with a redoubled negation at odds with "absurd" analyses, which moreover are reproached for being too "significant": "No! no! I do not at all like to find myself once more in mind of the ancient pathways of my life. I will not track down Things Past! And even less would I approve of those absurd analyses which inculcate in people the most obscene rebuses, that they are already to have composed at their mothers' breasts" (II, 1506). And in the *Notebooks*, concerning love: "What is more stupid than Freud's inventions on these matters?" (C. 22, p. 201, 1939).

Here I am setting aside two questions. Not that I judge them to be without interest or without pertinence, but in the small amount of time given us here, they might distract us from a reading which appears more urgent. In the first place, the issue will not be to improvise by tinkering with something which might resemble a psychoanalysis of Valéry's resistance to psychoanalysis. In the conditions under which this might be done, it would be very naive, and would fall well within Valéry's text, and the problems it elaborates, the questions it puts to a psychoanalysis of the text, to a psychoanalysis in the text, neither of which have come close to being articulated, or could not be, except by means of major transformations. Second, the issue will not be of a historical analysis explaining why Valéry, at a given date, could not read Freud,[30] read him as we

29. [Derrida is playing on *tête*, head, and *teste*, the Latin root of the word, and the name of Valéry's most famous character. Valéry himself plays on this word as will be seen in the citation below.] Rather than play upon the word *testis*, let us cite several lines from "Sketches for a Portrait of Monsieur Teste": "Monsieur Teste is the witness.

"That in us which causes *everything* and therefore nothing—reaction itself, pure recoil . . .

"Conscious—Teste, Testis.

"Given an 'eternal' observer whose role is limited to repeating and rehearsing the system of which the *Self* is that instantaneous part which believes it is the Whole.

"The Self (*le Moi*) could never engage itself if it did not believe—it is all.

"Suddenly the *suavis mamilla* that he touches becomes nothing more than what it is.

"The sun itself . . .

"The 'stupidity' of everything makes itself felt. Stupidity—that is, particularity opposed to generality. 'Smaller than' becomes the terrible sign of the mind" (6, 68).

"The game played with oneself . . . The essential is against life." ("A Few of Monsieur Teste's Thoughts," 6, 72, and 78.)

30. Cf. Judith Robinson, *L'analyse*, p. 105, n. 2.

301

read him now, or will read him henceforth. One would have to take into account a large number of elements—the state of the translation and introduction of Freud in France and elsewhere, a general weave of resistances, and their relation to a certain state of Freudian theory, the heterogeneity of the psychoanalytic text in general, etc. It is not certain that Valéry simply participated in this closing off, that is, that he simply consolidated it. Valéry's work, his attention to language, to rhetoric, to formal agencies, to the paradoxes of narcissism, his distrust concerning naive semanticism, etc. all have probably contributed, or in any event belonged, to an entire groundswell which, after the war, carried along a particular rereading of Freud. As for the irony directed against the psychoanalytic "fashion," the ingenuous rush toward a mono- or pansexual semanticism for Parisian parlor games or literary futilities (Valéry at the time was thinking primarily of the Surrealists), nothing could appear less anti-Freudian, whatever Valéry may have thought himself, and nothing could be more needed.

Having reserved these two questions, we will ask, then, which concepts and which internal marks are the means with which to recognize, in Valéry's textual system, a certain division and a certain conflict of forces between two critical operations, at the sharpest and most novel point of two necessarily heterogeneous discourses: Valéry's and Freud's.

Here we must content ourselves with the most schematic reading. Thus, without pretending to determine any center in Valéry's text, without defining some closed fist that everything in a powerful, open, and ceaselessly questioning work renders improbable, I nevertheless will venture to localize a concept, and even a word, that nothing in what I have read seems to contradict. In question is a focal point of great economic density, the intersection of a great circulation, rather than some theological principle. Implied everywhere, never surprised or exceeded, this focal point seems to bring everything back to itself as if to a source. Thus, you will very quickly be tempted to object: aren't you going to reduce a text to its thematic or semantic center, to its final truth, etc.? I will adduce the singular form of this word-concept, which precisely marks an implication that is not one, an implication that cannot be reduced to anything simple, an implication and complication of the source that in a certain way cannot be disimplicated: thus, the IMPLEX.

The implex: that which cannot be simplex. It marks the limit of every analytic reduction to the simple element of the point. An implication-complication, a complication of the same and the other which never permits itself to be undone, it divides or equally multiplies infinitely the simplicity of every source, every origin, every presence. Throughout the numerous variations and contextual transpositions to which Valéry submits this concept, the same structure is always sketched out: the impossibility for a present, for the presence of a present, to *present itself as a source:* simple, actual, punctual, instantaneous. The implex is a complex of the present always enveloping the nonpresent and the other present in the simple appearance of its pointed identity. It is the potentiality or rather the power, the dynamis and mathematical exponentiality of the value of presence, of everything the value of presence supports, that is of everything—that *is*. Among many possible citations, let us focus upon *Idée Fixe*. In question is the present and that which the "popular conception," that is philosophy, discerns as past, present, future: "Thus if you stick the point of the *present* into the actual moment . . . You create the present tense of the present, which you express as: *I am in the process of* . . . You create the future tense of the present: *I am just about to* . . . And so on. The present tense of the present of the present tense, the present tense of the future of the past pluperfect, and so on . . . You could refine on that. A mathematician could . . . You've started exponentiating all by yourself . . . To sum up, what I signify by *Implex* is that by which, and in virtue of which we remain contingent, conditional" (5, 57–58).

This value of contingency, eventuality, describes what is at stake in the concept. The implex, a nonpresence, nonconsciousness, an alterity folded over in the *sourdre* of the source,[31] envelops the possible of what it is not yet, the virtual capacity of that which presently it is not in act. ". . . Now what about that word, that name? . . .—My name for all that inner potentiality that we were talking about is: the IMPLEX . . . No, the Implex is not an activity. Quite the contrary. It's a *capacity*" (5, 55–56).

This nonconsciousness or nonpresence, this nonsimplicity is *the same as* that which it actually is not; it is homogenous with present consciousness, that is with the self presence whose dynamic virtuality it opens. Even if, at the limit, it were impossible to make it explicit, it relates perception to self-consciousness as potentiality to act. It belongs to the same system as that which would remain, at the limit, always doubled over within it. Such a system covers that of the classical philosopheme of *dynamis*.

This limit is precisely the one which seems to pass between Valéry's critique of consciousness and Freudian psychoanalysis. The unconscious, that which Freud names in this way, is not a virtual consciousness; its alterity is not homogenous with the alterity lodged in the implex. Here the *sourdre* is entirely other. And the operation that Freud calls repression, which seems to have no specific place in Valéry's analysis, would introduce, if some such thing exists, a difference irreducible to the difference between the virtual and the actual; even if this virtuality must remain an undecomposable implex. This is what, from the outset, would separate the analysis of Swedenborg from the analysis of Schreber.

But would this be teaching Valéry anything? He indeed knew that such was the site of his resistance to psychoanalysis. If I have chosen to remain within *Idée Fixe*, it is that in this text everything seems to be edified around this center, like a system of fortifications impenetrable by psychoanalysis. The implex represents the major device here. From this strong point, one can throw psychoanalysis back where it comes from, that is, from the sea, into the sea, a movement

31. TN. See above, note 25.

which could not have been simple for Valéry—such occasionally seems to be the obsidional operation of the *Idée Fixe* itself. When the interlocutor, imprudent soul, proposes to "open up the Implex," even risking a rapprochement between the implex and the unconscious, he is simply threatened with being thrown into the sea. All the criticisms that have been addressed to psychoanalysis in France for fifty years, find their resources here: "We'll have to open up the *Implex*. But wait a moment. Does this Implex of yours amount to any more than what vulgar, common mortals, the masses, philosophers, psychologists, psychopaths, the non-Crusoes—the herd, in fact—call quite simply and crudely the 'unconscious' or the 'subconscious.'?

"—Do you want me to pitch you into the sea? . . . Don't you know I detest such dirty words? . . . And anyhow, it isn't the same thing at all. They are meant to signify some inconceivable hidden springs of action—at times they stand for sly little inner goblins, marvelous tricksters, who can guess riddles, read the future, see through brick walls, and carry on the most amazing industry inside our hidden workings" (5, 55–56).

Immediately afterward defining the implex as virtuality and general *capacity* ("for feeling, reacting, doing, and understanding"), it is true that Valéry adds to the end of the list the "capacity for resistance": "To all that we must add our capacity for resistance" (5, 56).

We will not ask what the *meaning* of this resistance is before pointing out that what Valéry intends to resist is meaning itself. What he reproaches psycho-analysis for is not that it interprets in such or such a fashion, but quite simply that it interprets at all, that it is an interpretation, that it is interested above all in signification, in meaning, and in some principial unity—here, a sexual unity—of meaning. He reproaches psychoanalysis for being a "symbolics"—this is what he names it—a hermeneutism, a semanticism. Is there not, henceforth, a place where all of Valéry's poetic and linguistic formalism, his very necessary critique of thematicist or semanticist spontaneity, in literature and elsewhere, all the irony with which he paralyzed the prejudices of meaning, theme, subject, con-tent, etc., a place, then, where all of these come to be articulated systematically with his compulsive and obstinate rejection of psychoanalysis, a rejection op-erating as close as possible to psychoanalysis, and completely opposed to it? Was there not in meaning, to the extent that it is worked upon and afterward constituted by repression, something which above all had not to be dealt with? Something which formally had to be thrown back into the sea?

Above all I will not conclude that this hypothesis disqualifies Valéry's critical formalism. Something within it remains necessary and must be maintained, it seems to me, in opposition to all precritical semanticisms. The psychoanalytic discourses known to us are far from being exempt from this semanticism. Per-haps we here are touching upon a limit at which the opposition of form and meaning, along with all the divisions coordinated to it, loses its pertinence, and calls for an entirely other elaboration.

This elaboration would pass through the rereading of all these texts, of course, and of several others. It demands that one become engaged in it without endlessly circling around the form of these texts, that one decipher the law of their internal conflicts, of their heterogeneity, of their contradictions, and that one not simply cast an aesthete's glance over the philosophical discourse which carries within it the history of the oppositions in which are displaced, although often under cover, both critical formalism and psychoanalytic hermeneutics.

Like Nietzsche, reinterpret interpretation.

I proposed that Nietzsche may have been Valéry's other set-aside source. Everything should have led Valéry back to him: the systematic mistrust as concerns the entirety of metaphysics, the formal vision of philosophical discourse, the concept of the philosopher-artist, the rhetorical and philological questions put to the history of philosophy, the suspiciousness concerning the values of truth ("a well applied convention"),[32] of meaning and of Being, of the "meaning of Being," the attention to the economic phenomena of force and of the difference of forces, etc.

Valéry no doubt sensed this perhaps excessive proximity. He was ready to associate Nietzsche with Poe (I, 1781). And yet, in certain letters (see, for example, I, 855), after having rendered homage to Nietzsche, he explains why Nietzsche "shocked" him, "irritated" him (this is often his reaction to philosophy). In the course of a rather summary argumentation, he accuses Nietzsche of being "contradictory," of being a "metaphysician," and of "seeking to create a philosophy of violence." Elsewhere, in the form of a parody, he composes a false letter by Nietzsche, marked, if one may put it thus, by a Teutonic accent, in which the stiffest, and also most ardent, seriousness seems to be more on Valéry's side (I, 1781–83).

Why does M. Teste again permit himself to be irritated here? Why did Valéry not want, not want to be able, to read Nietzsche? Did he consider him threatening? And why? Too close? And in what way? These two hypotheses are not any more mutually exclusive than the for or the against. Did not Valéry push away Nietzsche for the same reason that made him push away Freud?

This is what Freud thought, and he was well placed to know so. Freud in advance knew that if Valéry could not acknowledge Nietzsche, it is because Nietzsche resembled Freud too much. And he had said so around 1925, or rather whispered it, with an imperturbable confidence.

For one to admire the wicked ruse of a certain *igitur (ja)*, it suffices to make psychoanalysis probable from the very fact of its own *mise en scène (Selbstdar-*

32. I, 1748. "Truth is a means. It is not the only one" (I, 380).

stellung): "Nietzsche, another philosopher whose guesses and intuitions often agree in the most astonishing way with the laborious findings of psycho-analysis, was for a long time avoided by me on that very account; I was less concerned with the question of priority than with keeping my mind unembarrassed."[33]

33. [*An Autobiographical Study*, SE XX, 60. The title of this work in German is *Selbstdarstellung*, literally "self-representation," although representation here has a theatrical sense of *mise en scène*, direction, that Derrida plays upon here.] *Selbstdarstellung*, 1925, *Gesammelte Werke* (Frankfurt: Fischer Verlag, 1967), vol. 14, p. 86. ("*Nietzsche, den anderen Philosophen, dessen Ahnungen und Einsichten sich oft in der erstaunlichsten Weise mit den mühsamen Ergebnissen der Psychoanalyse decken, habe ich gerade darum lange gemieden; an der Priorität lag mir ja weniger als an der Erhaltung meiner Unbefangenheit.*")

Signature Event
Context

A communication to the Congrès international des Sociétés de philosophie de langue française, Montreal, August 1971. The theme of the colloquium was "Communication."

Still confining ourselves, for simplicity, to *spoken* utterance.
Austin, *How to Do Things with Words*, p. 113 n. 2.

Is it certain that there corresponds to the word *communication* a unique, univocal concept, a concept that can be rigorously grasped and transmitted: a communicable concept? Following a strange figure of discourse, one first must ask whether the word or signifier "communication" communicates a determined content, an identifiable meaning, a describable value. But in order to articulate and to propose this question, I already had to anticipate the meaning of the word *communication:* I have had to predetermine communication as the vehicle, transport, or site of passage of a *meaning,* and of a meaning that is *one.* If *communication* had several meanings, and if this plurality could not be reduced, then from the outset it would not be justified to define communication *itself* as the transmission of a meaning, assuming that we are capable of understanding one another as concerns each of these words (transmission, meaning, etc.). Now, the word *communication,* which nothing initially authorizes us to overlook as a word, and to impoverish as a polysemic word, opens a semantic field which precisely is not limited to semantics, semiotics, and even less to linguistics. To the semantic field of the word *communication* belongs the fact that it also designates nonsemantic movements. Here at least provisional recourse to ordinary language and to the equivocalities of natural language teaches us that one may, for example, *communicate a movement,* or that a tremor, a shock, a displacement of *force* can be communicated—that is, propagated, transmitted. It is also said that different or distant places can communicate between each other by means of a given passageway or opening. What happens in this case, what is transmitted or communicated, are not phenomena of meaning or signification. In these cases we are dealing neither with a semantic or conceptual content, nor with a semiotic operation, and even less with a linguistic exchange.

Nevertheless, we will not say that this nonsemiotic sense of the word *communication,* such as it is at work in ordinary language, in one or several of the so-called natural languages, constitutes the *proper* or *primitive* meaning, and that consequently the semantic, semiotic, or linguistic meaning corresponds to a derivation, an extension or a reduction, a metaphoric displacement. We will not say, as one might be tempted to do, that semiolinguistic communication is *more metaphorico* entitled "communication," because by analogy with "physical" or "real" communication it gives passage, transports, transmits something, gives access to something. We will not say so:

1. because the value of literal, *proper meaning* appears more problematical than ever,

309

2. because the value of displacement, of transport, etc., is constitutive of the very concept of metaphor by means of which one allegedly understands the semantic displacement which is operated from communication as a nonsemiolinguistic phenomenon to communication as a semiolinguistic phenomenon.

(I note here between parentheses that in this communication the issue will be, already is, the problem of polysemia and communication, of dissemination—which I will oppose to polysemia—and communication. In a moment, a certain concept of writing is bound to intervene, in order to transform itself, and perhaps in order to transform the problematic.)

It seems to go without saying that the field of equivocality covered by the word *communication* permits itself to be reduced massively by the limits of what is called a *context* (and I announce, again between parentheses, that the issue will be, in this communication, the problem of context, and of finding out about writing as concerns context in general). For example, in a *colloquium* of *philosophy* in the *French language*, a conventional context, produced by a kind of implicit but structurally vague consensus, seems to prescribe that one propose "communications" on communication, communications in discursive form, colloquial, oral communications destined to be understood and to open or pursue dialogues within the horizon of an intelligibility and truth of meaning, such that in principle a general agreement may finally be established. These communications are to remain within the element of a determined "natural" language, which is called French, and which commands certain very particular uses of the word *communication*. Above all, the object of these communications should be organized, by priority or by privilege, around communication as *discourse*, or in any event as signification. Without exhausting all the implications and the entire structure of an "event" like this one, which would merit a very long preliminary analysis, the prerequisite I have just recalled appears evident; and for anyone who doubts this, it would suffice to consult our schedule in order to be certain of it.

But are the prerequisites of a context ever absolutely determinable? Fundamentally, this is the most general question I would like to attempt to elaborate. Is there a rigorous and scientific concept of the *context*? Does not the notion of context harbor, behind a certain confusion, very determined philosophical presuppositions? To state it now in the most summary fashion, I would like to demonstrate why a context is never absolutely determinable, or rather in what way its determination is never certain or saturated. This structural nonsaturation would have as its double effect:

1. a marking of the theoretical insufficiency of the *usual concept of* (the linguistic or nonlinguistic) *context* such as it is accepted in numerous fields of investigation, along with all the other concepts with which it is systematically associated;

2. a rendering necessary of a certain generalization and a certain displacement of the concept of writing. The latter could no longer, henceforth, be included in the category of communication, at least if communication is understood in the restricted sense of the transmission of meaning. Conversely, it is within the

general field of writing thus defined that the effects of semantic communication will be able to be determined as particular, secondary, inscribed, supplementary effects.

Writing and Telecommunication

If one takes the notion of writing in its usually accepted sense—which above all does not mean an innocent, primitive, or natural sense—one indeed must see it as a *means of communication.* One must even acknowledge it as a powerful means of communication which *extends* very far, if not infinitely, the field of oral or gestural communication. This is banally self-evident, and agreement on the matter seems easy. I will not describe all the *modes* of this extension in time and in space. On the other hand I will pause over the value of *extension* to which I have just had recourse. When we say that writing *extends* the field and powers of a locutionary or gestural communication, are we not presupposing a kind of *homogenous* space of communication? The range of the voice or of gesture certainly appears to encounter a factual limit here, an empirical boundary in the form of space and time; and writing, within the same time, within the same space, manages to loosen the limits, to open the *same field* to a much greater range. Meaning, the content of the semantic message, is thus transmitted, *communicated,* by different *means,* by technically more powerful mediations, over a much greater distance, but within a milieu that is fundamentally continuous and equal to itself, within a homogenous element across which the unity and integrity of meaning is not affected in an essential way. Here, all affection is accidental.

The system of this interpretation (which is also in a way *the* system of interpretation, or in any event of an entire interpretation of hermeneutics), although it is the usual one, or to the extent that it is as usual as common sense, has been *represented* in the entire history of philosophy. I will say that it is even, fundamentally, the properly philosophical interpretation of writing. I will take a single example, but I do not believe one could find, in the entire history of philosophy as such, a single counterexample, a single analysis that essentially contradicts the one proposed by Condillac, inspired, strictly speaking, by Warburton, in the *Essay on the Origin of Human Knowledge (Essai sur l'origine des connaissances humaines).*[1] I have chosen this example because an *explicit* reflection on the origin and function of the written (this explicitness is not encountered in all philosophy, and one should examine the conditions of its emergence or occultation) is organized within a philosophical discourse which like all philosophy presupposes the simplicity of the origin and the continuity of every derivation, every production, every analysis, the homogeneity of all orders. Analogy is a major con-

1. TN. *Essai sur l'origine des connaissances humaines,* with an introductory essay by Jacques Derrida (Paris: Galilée, 1973).

cept in Condillac's thought. I choose this example also because the analysis which "retraces" the origin and function of writing is placed, in a kind of noncritical way, *under the authority of the category of communication.*[2] If men write, it is (1) because they have something to communicate; (2) because what they have to communicate is their "thought," their "ideas," their representations. Representative thought precedes and governs communication which transports the "idea," the signified content; (3) because men are *already* capable of communicating and of communicating their thought to each other when, in continuous fashion, they invent the means of communication that is writing. Here is a passage from chapter 13 of part 2 ("On Language and On Method"), section 1 ("On the Origin and Progress of Language"), (writing is thus a modality of language and marks a continuous progress in a communication of linguistic essence), section 13, "On Writing": "Men capable of communicating their thoughts to each other by sounds felt the necessity of imagining new signs apt to perpetuate them and to make them *known* to *absent* persons" (I italicize this value of *absence,* which, if newly reexamined, will risk introducing a certain break in the homogeneity of the system). As soon as men are capable of "communicating their thoughts," and of doing so by sounds (which is, according to Condillac, a secondary stage, articulated language coming to "supplement" the language of action, the unique and radical principle of all language), the birth and progress of writing will follow a direct, simple, and continuous line. The history of writing will conform to a law of mechanical economy: to gain the most space and time by means of the most convenient abbreviation; it will never have the least effect on the structure and content of the meaning (of ideas) that it will have to vehiculate. The same content, previously communicated by gestures and sounds, henceforth will be transmitted by writing, and successively by different modes of notation, from pictographic writing up to alphabetic writing, passing through the hieroglyphic writing of the Egyptians and the ideographic writing of the Chinese. Condillac continues: "Imagination then will represent but the *same* images that they had already expressed by actions and words, and which had, from the beginnings, made language figurative and metaphoric. *The most natural means* was therefore to draw the pictures of things. To *express the idea* of a man or a horse the form of one or the other will be represented, and the first attempt at writing was but a simple painting" (p. 252; my italics).

The representative character of written communication—writing as picture, reproduction, imitation of its content—will be the invariable trait of all the progress to come. The concept of *representation* is indissociable here from the concepts of *communication* and *expression* that I have underlined in Condillac's text. Representation, certainly, will be complicated, will be given supplementary way-stations and stages, will become the representation of representation in

2. Rousseau's theory of language and writing is also proposed under the general rubric of *communication.* ("On the Various Means of Communicating Our Thoughts" is the title of the first chapter of the *Essay on the Origin of Languages.*)

312

hieroglyphic and ideographic writing, and then in phonetic-alphabetic writing, but the representative structure which marks the first stage of expressive communication, the idea/sign relationship, will never be suppressed or transformed. Describing the history of the kinds of writing, their continuous derivation on the basis of a common radical which is never displaced and which procures a kind of community of analogical participation between all the forms of writing, Condillac concludes (and this is practically a citation of Warburton, as is almost the entire chapter): "This is the general history of writing conveyed by a *simple gradation* from the state of painting through that of the letter; for letters are *the last steps* which remain to be taken after the Chinese marks, which partake of letters precisely as hieroglyphs partake equally of Mexican paintings and of Chinese characters. These characters are so close to our writing that an alphabet *simply diminishes* the confusion of their number, and is their *succinct abbreviation*" (pp. 254–53).

Having placed in evidence the motif of the economic, *homogenous, and mechanical* reduction, let us now come back to the notion of *absence* that I noted in passing in Condillac's text. How is it determined?

1. First, it is the absence of the addressee. One writes in order to communicate something to those who are absent. The absence of the sender, the addressor, from the marks that he abandons, which are cut off from him and continue to produce effects beyond his presence and beyond the present actuality of his meaning, that is, beyond his life itself, this absence, which however belongs to the structure of all writing—and I will add, further on, of all language in general—this absence is never examined by Condillac.

2. The absence of which Condillac speaks is determined in the most classical fashion as a continuous modification, a progressive extenuation of presence. Representation regularly *supplements* presence. But this operation of supplementation ("To supplement" is one of the most decisive and frequently employed operative concepts on Condillac's *Essai*)[3] is not exhibited as a break in presence, but rather as a reparation and a continuous, homogenous modification of presence in representation.

Here, I cannot analyze everything that this concept of absence as a modification of presence presupposes, in Condillac's philosophy and elsewhere. Let us note merely that it governs another equally decisive operative concept (here I am classically, and for convenience, opposing *operative* to *thematic*) of the *Essai: to trace* and *to retrace*. Like the concept of supplementing, the concept of trace could be determined otherwise than in the way Condillac determines it. According to him, to trace means "to express," "to represent," "to recall," "to make present" ("in all likelihood painting owes its origin to the necessity of thus tracing our thoughts, and this necessity has doubtless contributed to conserving the lan-

---

3. Language supplements action or perception, articulated language supplements the language of action, writing supplements articulated language, etc.

guage of action, as that which could paint the most easily," p. 253). The sign is born at the same time as imagination and memory, at the moment when it is demanded by the absence of the object for present perception ("Memory, as we have seen, consists only in the power of reminding ourselves of the signs of our ideas, or the circumstances which accompanied them; and this capacity occurs only by virtue of the *analogy of signs* (my italics; this concept of analogy, which organizes Condillac's entire system, in general makes certain all the continuities, particularly the continuity of presence to absence) that we have chosen, and by virtue of the order that we have put between our ideas, the objects that we wish to retrace have to do with several of our present needs" (p. 129). This is true of all the orders of signs distinguished by Condillac (arbitrary, accidental, and even natural signs, a distinction which Condillac nuances, and on certain points, puts back into question in his Letters to Cramer). The philosophical operation that Condillac also calls "to retrace" consists in traveling back, by way of analysis and continuous decomposition, along the movement of genetic derivation which leads from simple sensation and present perception to the complex edifice of representation: from original presence to the most formal language of calculation.

It would be simple to show that, essentially, this kind of analysis of written signification neither begins nor ends with Condillac. If we say now that this analysis is "ideological," it is not primarily in order to contrast its notions to "scientific" concepts, or in order to refer to the often dogmatic—one could also say "ideological"—use made of the word ideology, which today is so rarely examined for its possibility and history. If I define notions of Condillac's kind as ideological, it is that against the background of a vast, powerful, and systematic philosophical tradition dominated by the self-evidence of the *idea (eidos, idea)*, they delineate the field of reflection of the French "ideologues" who, in Condillac's wake, elaborated a theory of the sign as a representation of the idea, which itself represents the perceived thing. Communication, hence, vehiculates a representation as an ideal content (which will be called meaning); and writing is a species of this general communication. A species: a communication having a relative specificity within a genus.

If we ask ourselves now what, in this analysis, is the essential predicate of this *specific difference*, we once again find *absence*.

Here I advance the following two propositions or hypotheses:

1. Since every sign, as much in the "language of action" as in articulated language (even before the intervention of writing in the classical sense), supposes a certain absence (to be determined), it must be because absence in the field of writing is of an original kind if any specificity whatsoever of the written sign is to be acknowledged.

2. If, perchance, the predicate thus assumed to characterize the absence proper to writing were itself found to suit every species of sign and communication, there would follow a general displacement: writing no longer would be a species of communication, and all the concepts to whose generality writing was sub-

314

ordinated (the concept itself as meaning, idea, or grasp of meaning and idea, the concept of communication, of sign, etc.) would appear as noncritical, ill-formed concepts, or rather as concepts destined to ensure the authority and force of a certain historic discourse.

Let us attempt then, while continuing to take our point of departure from this classical discourse, to characterize the absence which seems to intervene in a fashion specific to the functioning of writing.

A written sign is proffered in the absence of the addressee. How is this absence to be qualified? One might say that at the moment when I write, the addressee may be absent from my field of present perception. But is not this absence only a presence that is distant, delayed, or, in one form or another, idealized in its representation? It does not seem so, or at very least this distance, division, delay, *différance*[4] must be capable of being brought to a certain absolute degree of absence for the structure of writing, supposing that writing exists, to be constituted. It is here that *différance* as writing could no longer (be) an (ontological) modification of presence. My "written communication" must, if you will, remain legible despite the absolute disappearance of every determined addressee in general for it to function as writing, that is, for it to be legible. It must be repeatable—iterable—in the absolute absence of the addressee or of the empirically determinable set of addressees. This iterability (*iter*, once again, comes from *itara*, *other* in Sanskrit, and everything that follows may be read as the exploitation of the logic which links repetition to alterity), structures the mark of writing itself, and does so moreover for no matter what type of writing (pictographic, hieroglyphic, ideographic, phonetic, alphabetic, to use the old categories). A writing that was not structurally legible—iterable—beyond the death of the addressee would not be writing. Although all this appears self-evident, I do not want it to be assumed as such, and will examine the ultimate objection that might be made to this proposition. Let us imagine a writing with a code idiomatic enough to have been founded and known, as a secret cipher, only by two "subjects." Can it still be said that upon the death of the addressee, that is, of the two partners, the mark left by one of them is still a writing? Yes, to the extent to which, governed by a code, even if unknown and nonlinguistic, it is constituted, in its identity as a mark, by its iterability in the absence of whoever, and therefore ultimately in the absence of every empirically determinable "subject." This implies that there is no code—an organon of iterability—that is structurally secret. The possibility of repeating, and therefore of identifying, marks is implied in every code, making of it a communicable, transmittable, decipherable grid that is iterable for a third party, and thus for any possible user in general. All writing, therefore, in order to be what it is, must be able to function in the radical absence of every empirically determined

4. TN. On the concept of *différance*, see "La différance," above, and my notes 7, 8, 9, and 10.

addressee in general. And this absence is not a continuous modification of presence; it is a break in presence, "death," or the possibility of the "death" of the addressee, inscribed in the structure of the mark (and it is at this point, I note in passing, that the value or effect of transcendentality is linked necessarily to the possibility of writing and of "death" analyzed in this way). A perhaps paradoxical consequence of the recourse I am taking to iteration and to the code: the disruption, in the last analysis, of the authority of the code as a finite system of rules; the radical destruction, by the same token, of every context as a protocol of a code. We will come to this in a moment.

What holds for the addressee holds also, for the same reasons, for the sender or the producer. To write is to produce a mark that will constitute a kind of machine that is in turn productive, that my future disappearance in principle will not prevent from functioning and from yielding, and yielding itself to, reading and rewriting. When I say "my future disappearance," I do so to make this proposition more immediately acceptable. I must be able simply to say my disappearance, my nonpresence in general, for example the nonpresence of my meaning, of my intention-to-signify, of my wanting-to-communicate-this, from the emission or production of the mark. For the written to be the written, it must continue to "act" and to be legible even if what is called the author of the writing no longer answers for what he has written, for what he seems to have signed, whether he is provisionally absent, or if he is dead, or if in general he does not support, with his absolutely current and present intention or attention, the plenitude of his meaning, of that very thing which seems to be written "in his name." Here, we could reelaborate the analysis sketched out above for the addressee. The situation of the scribe and of the subscriber, as concerns the written, is fundamentally the same as that of the reader. This essential drifting, due to writing as an iterative structure cut off from all absolute responsibility, from *consciousness* as the authority of the last analysis, writing orphaned, and separated at birth from the assistance of its father, is indeed what Plato condemned in the *Phaedrus*. If Plato's gesture is, as I believe, the philosophical movement par excellence, one realizes what is at stake here.

Before specifying the inevitable consequences of these nuclear traits of all writing—to wit: (1) the break with the horizon of communication as the communication of consciousnesses or presences, and as the linguistic or semantic transport of meaning; (2) the subtraction of all writing from the semantic horizon or the hermeneutic horizon which, at least as a horizon of meaning, lets itself be punctured by writing; (3) the necessity of, in a way, *separating* the concept of polysemia from the concept I have elsewhere named *dissemination*, which is also the concept of writing; (4) the disqualification or the limit of the concept of the "real" or "linguistic" context, whose theoretical determination or empirical saturation are, strictly speaking, rendered impossible or insufficient by writing—I would like to demonstrate that the recognizable traits of the classical and narrowly defined concept of writing are generalizable. They would be valid not only for all the orders of "signs" and for all languages in general, but even, beyond semiolinguistic communication, for the entire field of what philosophy would call experience, that is, the experience of Being: so-called "presence."

In effect, what are the essential predicates in a minimal determination of the classical concept of writing?

1. A written sign, in the usual sense of the word, is therefore a mark which remains, which is not exhausted in the present of its inscription, and which can give rise to an iteration both in the absence of and beyond the presence of the empirically determined subject who, in a given context, has emitted or produced it. This is how, traditionally at least, "written communication" is distinguished from "spoken communication."

2. By the same token, a written sign carries with it a force of breaking with its context, that is, the set of presences which organize the moment of its inscription. This force of breaking is not an accidental predicate, but the very structure of the written. If the issue is one of the so-called "real" context, what I have just proposed is too obvious. Are part of this alleged real context a certain "present" of inscription, the presence of the scriptor in what he has written, the entire environment and horizon of his experience, and above all the intention, the meaning which at a given moment would animate his inscription. By all rights, it belongs to the sign to be legible, even if the moment of its production is irremediably lost, and even if I do not know what its alleged author-scriptor meant consciously and intentionally at the moment he wrote it, that is abandoned it to its essential drifting. Turning now to the semiotic and internal context, there is no less a force of breaking by virtue of its essential iterability; one can always lift a written syntagma from the interlocking chain in which it is caught or given without making it lose every possibility of functioning, if not every possibility of "communicating," precisely. Eventually, one may recognize other such possibilities in it by inscribing or *grafting* it into other chains. No context can enclose it. Nor can any code, the code being here both the possibility and impossibility of writing, of its essential iterability (repetition/alterity).

3. This force of rupture is due to the spacing which constitutes the written sign: the spacing which separates it from other elements of the internal contextual chain (the always open possibility of its extraction and grafting), but also from all the forms of a present referent (past or to come in the modified form of the present past or to come) that is objective or subjective. This spacing is not the simple negativity of a lack, but the emergence of the mark. However, it is not the work of the negative in the service of meaning, or of the living concept, the *telos*, which remains *relevable* and reducible in the *Aufhebung* of a dialectics.[5]

Are these three predicates, along with the entire system joined to them, reserved, as is so often believed, for "written" communication, in the narrow

5. TN. On Derrida's translation of *Aufheben* as *relever*, and my maintenance of the French term, see note 23 to "La différance," above, for a system of references.

sense of the word? Are they not also to be found in all language, for example in spoken language, and ultimately in the totality of "experience," to the extent that it is not separated from the field of the mark, that is, the grid of erasure and of difference, of unities of iterability, of unities separable from their internal or external context, and separable from themselves, to the extent that the very iterability which constitutes their identity never permits them to be a unity of self-identity?

Let us consider any element of spoken language, a large or small unity. First condition for it to function: its situation as concerns a certain code; but I prefer not to get too involved here with the concept of code, which does not appear certain to me; let us say that a certain self-identity of this element (mark, sign, etc.) must permit its recognition and repetition. Across empirical variations of tone, of voice, etc., eventually of a certain accent, for example, one must be able to recognize the identity, shall we say, of a signifying form. Why is this identity paradoxically the division or dissociation from itself which will make of this phonic sign a grapheme? It is because this unity of the signifying form is constituted only by its iterability, by the possibility of being repeated in the absence not only of its referent, which goes without saying, but of a determined signified or current intention of signification, as of every present intention of communication. This structural possibility of being severed from its referent or signified (and therefore from communication and its context) seems to me to make of every mark, even if oral, a grapheme in general, that is, as we have seen, the nonpresent *remaining* of a differential mark cut off from its alleged "production" or origin. And I will extend this law even to all "experience" in general, if it is granted that there is no experience of *pure* presence, but only chains of differential marks.

Let us remain at this point for a while, and come back to the absence of the referent and even of the signified sense, and therefore of the correlative intention of signification. The absence of the referent is a possibility rather easily admitted today. This possibility is not only an empirical eventuality. It constructs the mark; and the eventual presence of the referent at the moment when it is designated changes nothing about the structure of a mark which implies that it can do without the referent. Husserl, in the *Logical Investigations*, had very rigorously analyzed this possibility. It is double:

1. A statement whose object is not impossible but only possible might very well be proffered and understood without its real object (its referent) being present, whether for the person who produces the statement, or for the one who receives it. If I say, while looking out the window, "The sky is blue," the statement will be intelligible (let us provisionally say, if you will, communicable), even if the interlocutor does not see the sky; even if I do not see it myself, if I see it poorly, if I am mistaken, or if I wish to trick my interlocutor. Not that it is always thus; but the structure of possibility of this statement includes the capability of being formed and of functioning either as an empty reference, or

cut off from its referent. Without this possibility, which is also the general, generalizable, and generalizing iteration of every mark, there would be no statements.

2. The absence of the signified. Husserl analyzes this too. He considers it always possible, even if, according to the axiology and teleology which govern his analysis, he deems this possibility inferior, dangerous, or "critical": it opens the phenomenon of the *crisis* of meaning. This absence of meaning can be layered according to three forms:

a. I can manipulate symbols without in active and current fashion animating them with my attention and intention to signify (the crisis of mathematical symbolism, according to Husserl). Husserl indeed stresses the fact that this does not prevent the sign from functioning: the crisis or vacuity of mathematical meaning does not limit technical progress. (The intervention of writing is decisive here, as Husserl himself notes in *The Origin of Geometry*.)

b. Certain statements can have a meaning, although they are without *objective* signification. "The circle is square" is a proposition invested with meaning. It has enough meaning for me to be able to judge it false or contradictory (*widersinnig* and not *sinnlos*, says Husserl). I am placing this example under the category of the absence of the signified, although the tripartition signifier/signified/referent does not pertinently account for Husserl's analysis. "Square circle" marks the absence of a referent, certainly, and also the absence of a certain signified, but not the absence of meaning. In these two cases, the crisis of meaning (nonpresence in general, absence as the absence of the referent—of perception— or of meaning—of the actual intention to signify) is always linked to the essential possibility of writing; and this crisis is not an accident, a factual and empirical anomaly of spoken language, but also the positive possibility and "internal" structure of spoken language, from a certain outside.

c. Finally there is what Husserl calls *Sinnlosigkeit* or agrammaticality. For example, "green is or" or "abracadabra." In the latter cases, as far as Husserl is concerned, there is no more language, or at least no more "logical" language, no more language of knowledge as Husserl understands it in teleological fashion, no more language attuned to the possibility of the intuition of objects given in person and signified in *truth*. Here, we are confronted with a decisive difficulty. Before pausing over it, I note, as a point which touches upon our debate on communication, that the primary interest of the Husserlian analysis to which I am referring here (precisely by extracting it, up to a certain point, from its teleological and metaphysical context and horizon, an operation about which we must ask how and why it is always possible) is that it alleges, and it seems to me arrives at, a rigorous dissociation of the analysis of the sign or expression (*Ausdruck*) as a signifying sign, a sign meaning something (*bedeutsame Zeichen*), from all phenomena of communication.[6]

6. "So far we have considered expressions as used in communication, which last depends essentially on the fact that they operate indicatively. But expressions also play a

Let us take once more the case of agrammatical *Sinnlosigkeit*. What interests Husserl in the *Logical Investigations* is the system of rules of a universal grammar, not from a linguistic point of view, but from a logical and epistemological point of view. In an important note from the second edition,[7] he specifies that from his point of view the issue is indeed one of a purely *logical* grammar, that is the universal conditions of possibility for a morphology of significations in the relation of knowledge to a possible object, and not of a pure grammar in *general*, considered from a psychological or linguistic point of view. Therefore, it is only in a context determined by a will to know, by an epistemic intention, by a conscious relation to the object as an object of knowledge within a horizon of truth—it is in this oriented contextual field that "green is or" is unacceptable. But, since "green is or" or "abracadabra" do not constitute their context in themselves, nothing prevents their functioning in another context as signifying marks (or indices, as Husserl would say). Not only in the contingent case in which, by means of the translation of German into French "le vert est ou" might be endowed with grammaticality, *ou* (*oder*, or) becoming when heard *où* (where, the mark of place): "Where has the green (of the grass) gone (*le vert est où*)?," "Where has the glass in which I wished to give you something to drink gone (*le verre est où*)." But even "green is or" still signifies an *example of agrammaticality*. This is the possibility on which I wish to insist: the possibility of extraction and of citational grafting which belongs to the structure of every mark, spoken or written, and which constitutes every mark as writing even before and outside every horizon of semiolinguistic communication; as writing, that is, as a possibility of functioning cut off, at a certain point, from its "original" meaning and from its belonging to a saturable and constraining context. Every sign, linguistic or nonlinguistic, spoken or written (in the usual sense of this opposition), as a small or large unity, can be *cited*, put between quotation marks; thereby it can break with every given context, and engender infinitely new contexts in an absolutely nonsaturable fashion. This does not suppose that the mark is valid outside its context, but on the contrary that there are only contexts without any center of absolute anchoring. This citationality, duplication, or duplicity, this

---

great part in uncommunicated, interior mental life. This change in function plainly has nothing to do with whatever makes an expression an expression. Expressions continue to have *Bedeutungen* as they had before, and the same *Bedeutungen* as in dialogue." *Logical Investigations*, trans. J. N. Findlay (London: Routledge and Kegan Paul, 1970), p. 278. What I am asserting here implies the interpretation I proposed of Husserlian procedure on this point. Therefore, I permit myself to refer to *Speech and Phenomena*.

7. "In the First Edition I spoke of 'pure grammar,' a name conceived and expressly devised to be analogous to Kant's 'pure science of nature.' Since it cannot, however, be said that pure formal semantic theory comprehends the entire *a priori* of general grammar—there is, e.g., a peculiar *a priori* governing relations of mutual understanding among minded persons, relations very important for grammar—talk of pure logical grammar is to be preferred." *Logical Investigations*, vol. 2, p. 527. [In the paragraph that follows I have maintained Findlay's translation of the phrase Derrida plays upon, i.e. "green is or," and have given the French necessary to comprehend this passage in parentheses.]

iterability of the mark is not an accident or an anomaly, but is that (normal/ abnormal) without which a mark could no longer even have a so-called "normal" functioning. What would a mark be that one could not cite? And whose origin could not be lost on the way?

The Parasites. Iter, of Writing: That Perhaps It Does Not Exist

I now propose to elaborate this question a little further with help from—but in order to go beyond it too—the problematic of the *performative*. It has several claims to our interest here.

1. Austin,[8] by his emphasis on the analysis of perlocution and especially illocution, indeed seems to consider acts of discourse only as acts of communication. This is what his French translator notes, citing Austin himself: "It is by comparing the *constative* utterance (that is, the classical 'assertion,' most often conceived as a true or false 'description' of the facts) with the *performative* utterance (from the English *performative*, that is, the utterance which allows us to do something by means of speech itself) that Austin has been led to consider *every* utterance worthy of the name (that is, destined to *communicate*, which would exclude, for example, reflex-exclamations) as being first and foremost a *speech act* produced in the *total* situation in which the interlocutors find themselves (*How to Do Things With Words*, p. 147)."[9]

2. This category of communication is relatively original. Austin's notions of illocution and perlocution do not designate the transport or passage of a content of meaning, but in a way the communication of an original movement (to be defined in a *general theory of action*), an operation, and the production of an effect. To communicate, in the case of the performative, if in all rigor and purity some such thing exists (for the moment I am placing myself within this hypothesis and at this stage of the analysis), would be to communicate a force by the impetus of a mark.

3. Differing from the classical assertion, from the constative utterance, the performative's referent (although the word is inappropriate here, no doubt, such is the interest of Austin's finding) is not outside it, or in any case preceding it or before it. It does not describe something which exists outside and before language. It produces or transforms a situation, it operates; and if it can be said that a constative utterance also effectuates something and always transforms a situation, it cannot be said that this constitutes its internal structure, its manifest function or destination, as in the case of the performative.

8. TN. J. L. Austin, *How to Do Things with Words* (New York: Oxford University Press, 1962). Throughout this section I have followed the standard procedure of translating *enoncé* as statement, and *énonciation* as utterance.
9. G. Lane, Introduction to the French translation of *How to Do Things with Words*.

4. Austin had to free the analysis of the performative from the authority of the *value of truth*, from the opposition true/false,[10] at least in its classical form, occasionally substituting for it the value of force, of difference of force (*illocutionary or perlocutionary force*). (It is this, in a thought which is nothing less than Nietzschean, which seems to me to beckon toward Nietzsche; who often recognized in himself a certain affinity with a vein of English thought.)

For these four reasons, at least, it could appear that Austin has exploded the concept of communication as a purely semiotic, linguistic, or symbolic concept. The performative is a "communication" which does not essentially limit itself to transporting an already constituted semantic content guarded by its own aiming at truth (truth as an *unveiling* of that which is in its Being, or as an *adequation* between a judicative statement and the thing itself).

And yet—at least this is what I would like to attempt to indicate now—all the difficulties encountered by Austin in an analysis that is patient, open, aporetic, in constant transformation, often more fruitful in the recognition of its impasses than in its positions, seem to me to have a common root. It is this: Austin has not taken into account that which in the structure of *locution* (and therefore before any illocutory or perlocutory determination) already bears within itself the system of predicates that I call *graphematic in general*, which therefore confuses all the ulterior oppositions whose pertinence, purity, and rigor Austin sought to establish in vain.

In order to show this, I must take as known and granted that Austin's analyses permanently demand a value of *context*, and even of an exhaustively determinable context, whether de jure or teleologically; and the long list of "infelicities" of variable type which might affect the event of the performative always returns to an element of what Austin calls the total context.[11] One of these essential elements—and not one among others—classically remains consciousness, the conscious presence of the intention of the speaking subject for the totality of his locutory act. Thereby, performative communication once more becomes the communication of an intentional meaning,[12] even if this meaning has no referent in the form of a prior or exterior thing or state of things. This conscious presence of the speakers or receivers who participate in the effecting of a performative, their conscious and intentional presence in the totality of the operation, implies teleologically that no *remainder* escapes the present totalization. No remainder, whether in the definition of the requisite conventions, or the internal and linguistic context, or the grammatical form or semantic determination of the words used; no irreducible polysemia, that is no "dissemination" escaping the horizon of the unity of meaning. I cite the first two lectures of *How to Do Things with*

10. ". . . two fetishes which I admit to an inclination to play Old Harry with, viz., 1) the true/false fetish, 2) the value/fact fetish" (p. 150).
11. See e.g. pp. 52 and 147.
12. Which sometimes compels Austin to reintroduce the criterion of truth into the description of performatives. See e.g. pp. 51–52 and 89–90.

Words: "Speaking generally, it is always necessary that the *circumstances* in which the words are uttered should be in some way, or ways, *appropriate*, and it is very commonly necessary that either the speaker himself or other persons should *also* perform certain *other* actions, whether 'physical' or 'mental' actions or even acts of uttering further words. Thus, for naming the ship, it is essential that I should be the person appointed to name her, for (Christian) marrying, it is essential that I should not be already married with a wife living, sane and undivorced, and so on; for a bet to have been made, it is generally necessary for the offer of the bet to have been accepted by a taker (who must have done something, such as to say 'Done'), and it is hardly a gift if I *say* 'I give it you' but never hand it over. So far, well and good" (pp. 8–9).

In the Second Lecture, after having in his habitual fashion set aside the grammatical criterion, Austin examines the possibility and origin of the failures or "infelicities" of the performative utterance. He then defines the six indispensable, if not sufficient, conditions for success. Through the values of "conventionality," "correctness," and "completeness" that intervene in the definition, we necessarily again find those of an exhaustively definable context, of a free consciousness present for the totality of the operation, of an absolutely full meaning that is master of itself: the teleological jurisdiction of a total field whose *intention* remains the organizing center (pp. 12–16). Austin's procedure is rather remarkable, and typical of the philosophical tradition that he prefers to have little to do with. It consists in recognizing that the possibility of the negative (here, the *infelicities*) is certainly a structural possibility, that failure is an essential risk in the operations under consideration; and then, with an almost *immediately simultaneous* gesture made in the name of a kind of ideal regulation, an exclusion of this risk as an accidental, exterior one that teaches us nothing about the language phenomenon under consideration. This is all the more curious, and actually rigorously untenable, in that Austin denounces with irony the "fetish" of opposition *value/fact.*

Thus, for example, concerning the conventionality without which there is no performative, Austin recognizes that *all* conventional acts are *exposed* to failure: "It seems clear in the first place that, although it has excited us (or failed to excite us) in connexion with certain acts which are or are in part acts of *uttering words*, infelicity is an ill to which *all* acts are heir which have the general character of ritual or ceremonial, all *conventional* acts: not indeed that *every* ritual is liable to every form of infelicity (but then nor is every performative utterance)" (pp. 18–19; Austin's italics).

Aside from all the questions posed by the very historically sedimented notion of "convention," we must notice here: (1) That in this specific place Austin seems to consider only the conventionality that forms the *circumstance* of the statement, its contextual surroundings, and not a certain intrinsic conventionality of that which constitutes locution itself, that is, everything that might quickly be summarized under the problematic heading of the "arbitrariness of the sign"; which extends, aggravates, and radicalizes the difficulty. Ritual is not an eventuality, but, as iterability, is a structural characteristic of every mark. (2) That the value of risk or of being open to failure, although it might, as Austin recognizes, affect the totality of conventional acts, is not examined as an essential predicate or *law*. Austin does not ask himself what consequences derive from the fact that something possible—a possible risk—is *always* possible, is somehow a necessary possibility. And if, such a necessary possibility of failure being granted, it still constitutes an accident. What is a success when the possibility of failure continues to constitute its structure?

Therefore the opposition of the success/failure of illocution or perlocution here seems quite insufficient or derivative. It presupposes a general and systematic elaboration of the structure of locution which avoids the endless alternation of essence and accident. Now, it is very significant that Austin rejects this "general theory," defers it on two occasions, notably in the Second Lecture. I leave aside the first exclusion. ("I am not going into the general doctrine here: in many such cases we may even say the act was 'void' (or voidable for duress or undue influence) and so forth. Now I suppose that some very general high-level doctrine might embrace both what we have called infelicities *and* these other 'unhappy' features of the doing of actions—in our case actions containing a performative utterance—in a single doctrine: but we are not including this kind of unhappiness—we must just remember, though, that features of this sort can and do *constantly obtrude* into any case we are discussing. Features of this sort would normally come under the heading of 'extenuating circumstances' or of 'factors reducing or abrogating the agent's responsibility,' and so on"; p. 21; my italics). The second gesture of exclusion concerns us more directly here. In question, precisely, is the possibility that every performative utterance (and a priori every other utterance) may be "cited." Now, Austin excludes this eventuality (and the general doctrine which would account for it) with a kind of lateral persistence, all the more significant in its off-sidedness. He insists upon the fact that this possibility remains *abnormal, parasitical,* that it constitutes a kind of extenuation, that is an agony of language that must firmly be kept at a distance, or from which one must resolutely turn away. And the concept of the "ordinary," and therefore of "ordinary language," to which he then has recourse is indeed marked by this exclusion. This makes it all the more problematic, and before demonstrating this, it would be better to read a paragraph from this Second Lecture:

"(ii) Secondly, as *utterances* our performatives are *also* heir to certain other kinds of ill which infect *all* utterances. And these likewise, though again they might be brought into a more general account, we are deliberately at present excluding. I mean, for example, the following: a performative utterance will, for example, be *in a peculiar way* hollow or void if said by an actor on the stage, or if introduced in a poem, or spoken in soliloquy. This applies in a similar manner to any and every utterance—a sea-change in special circumstances. Language in such circumstances is in special ways—intelligibly—used not *seriously* [I am italicizing here, J.D.], but in ways *parasitic* upon its normal use—ways which fall under the doctrine of the *etiolations* of language. All this we are *excluding* from consideration. Our performative utterances, felicitous or not, are to be understood as issued in ordinary circumstances" (pp. 21–22). Austin therefore excludes, along with what he calls the *sea-change*, the "non-serious," the "parasitic," the "etiolations," the "non-ordinary" (and with them the general theory which in accounting for these oppositions no longer would be governed by them), which he nevertheless recognizes as the possibility to which every utterance is open. It is also as a "parasite" that writing has always been treated by the philosophical tradition, and the rapprochement, here, is not at all fortuitous.

Therefore, I ask the following question: is this general possibility necessarily that of a failure or a trap into which language might *fall*, or in which language might lose itself, as if in an abyss situated outside or in front of it? What about *parasitism?* In other words, does the generality of the risk admitted by Austin *surround* language like a kind of *ditch*, a place of external perdition into which locution might never venture, that it might avoid by remaining at home, in itself, sheltered by its essence or *telos?* Or indeed is this risk, on the contrary, its internal and positive condition of possibility? this outside its inside? the very force and law of its emergence? In this last case, what would an "ordinary" language defined by the very law of language signify? Is it that in excluding the general theory of this structural parasitism, Austin, who nevertheless pretends to describe the facts and events of ordinary language, makes us accept as ordinary a teleological and ethical determination (the univocality of the statement—which he recognizes elsewhere remains a philosophical "ideal," pp. 72–73—the self-presence of a total context, the transparency of intentions, the presence of meaning for the absolutely singular oneness of a speech act, etc.)?

For, finally, is not what Austin excludes as anomalous, exceptional, "non-serious,"[13] that is, *citation* (on the stage, in a poem, or in a soliloquy), the determined modification of a general citationality—or rather, a general iterability—without which there would not even be a "successful" performative? Such that—a paradoxical, but inevitable consequence—a successful performative is necessarily an "impure" performative, to use the word that Austin will employ later on when he recognizes that there is no "pure" performative.[14]

13. The very suspect value of the "non-serious" is a frequent reference (see e.g. pp. 104, 121). It has an essential link with what Austin says elsewhere about the *oratio obliqua* (pp. 70–71) and about *mime*.

14. From this point of view one might examine the fact recognized by Austin that "the *same* sentence is used on different occasions of utterance in *both* ways, performative and constative. The thing seems hopeless from the start, if we are to leave utterances *as they stand* and seek for a criterion" (p. 67). It is the graphematic root of citationality (iterability) that provokes this confusion, and makes it "not possible," as Austin says, "to lay down even a list of all possible criteria" (ibid.).

Now I will take things from the side of positive possibility, and no longer only from the side of failure: would a performative statement be possible if a citational doubling did not eventually split, dissociate from itself the pure singularity of the event? I am asking the question in this form in order to forestall an objection. In effect, it might be said to me: you cannot allege that you account for the so-called graphematic structure of locution solely on the basis of the occurrence of failures of the performative, however real these failures might be, and however effective or general their possibility. You cannot deny that there are also performatives that succeed, and they must be accounted for: sessions are opened, as Paul Ricoeur did yesterday, one says "I ask a question," one bets, one challenges, boats are launched, and one even marries occasionally. Such events, it appears, have occurred. And were a single one of them to have taken place a single time, it would still have to be accounted for.

I will say "perhaps." Here, we must first agree upon what the "occurring" or the eventhood of an event consists in, when the event supposes in its allegedly present and singular intervention a statement which in itself can be only of a repetitive or citational structure, or rather, since these last words lead to confusion, of an iterable structure. Therefore, I come back to the point which seems fundamental to me, and which now concerns the status of the event in general, of the event of speech or by speech, of the strange logic it supposes, and which often remains unperceived.

Could a performative statement succeed if its formulation did not repeat a "coded" or iterable statement, in other words if the expressions I use to open a meeting, launch a ship or a marriage were not identifiable as *conforming* to an iterable model, and therefore if they were not identifiable in a way as "citation"? Not that citationality here is of the same type as in a play, a philosophical reference, or the recitation of a poem. This is why there is a relative specificity, as Austin says, a "relative purity" of performatives. But this relative purity is not constructed *against* citationality or iterability, but against other kinds of iteration within a general iterability which is the effraction into the allegedly rigorous purity of every event of discourse or every speech act. Thus, one must less oppose citation or iteration to the noniteration of an event, than construct a differential typology of forms of iteration, supposing that this is a tenable project that can give rise to an exhaustive program, a question I am holding off on here. In this typology, the category of intention will not disappear; it will have its place, but from this place it will no longer be able to govern the entire scene and the entire system of utterances. Above all, one then would be concerned with different types of marks or chains of iterable marks, and not with an opposition between citational statements on the one hand, and singular and original statement-events on the other. The first consequence of this would be the following: given this structure of iteration, the intention which animates utterance will never be completely present in itself and its content. The iteration which structures it a priori introduces an essential dehiscence and demarcation.

326

One will no longer be able to exclude, as Austin wishes, the "non-serious," the *oratio obliqua*, from "ordinary" language. And if it is alleged that ordinary language, or the ordinary circumstance of language, excludes citationality or general iterability, does this not signify that the "ordinariness" in question, the thing and the notion, harbors a lure, the teleological lure of consciousness whose motivations, indestructible necessity, and systematic effects remain to be analyzed? Especially since this essential absence of intention for the actuality of the statement, this structural unconsciousness if you will, prohibits every saturation of a context. For a context to be exhaustively determinable, in the sense demanded by Austin, it at least would be necessary for the conscious intention to be totally present and actually transparent for itself and others, since it is a determining focal point of the context. The concept of or quest for the "context" therefore seems to suffer here from the same theoretical and motivated uncertainty as the concept of the "ordinary," from the same metaphysical origins: an ethical and teleological discourse of consciousness. This time, a reading of the connotations of Austin's text would confirm the reading of its descriptions; I have just indicated the principle of this reading.

Différance, the irreducible absence of intention or assistance from the performative statement, from the most "event-like" statement possible, is what authorizes me, taking into account the predicates mentioned just now, to posit the general graphematic structure of every "communication." Above all, I will not conclude from this that there is no relative specificity of the effects of consciousness, of the effects of speech (in opposition to writing in the traditional sense), that there is no effect of the performative, no effect of ordinary language, no effect of presence and of speech acts. It is simply that these effects do not exclude what is generally opposed to them term by term, but on the contrary presuppose it in dyssemtrical fashion, as the general space of their possibility.

Signatures

This general space is first of all spacing as the disruption of presence in the mark, what here I am calling writing. That all the difficulties encountered by Austin intersect at the point at which both presence and writing are in question, is indicated for me by a passage from the Fifth Lecture in which the divided agency of the legal *signature* emerges.

Is it by chance that Austin must note at this point: "I must explain again that we are floundering here. To feel the firm ground of prejudice slipping away is exhilirating, but brings its revenges" (p. 61). Only a little earlier an "impasse" had appeared, the impasse one comes to each time "any *single simple* criterion of grammar or vocabulary" is sought in order to distinguish between performative or constative statements. (I must say that this critique of linguisticism and of the authority of the code, a critique executed on the basis of an analysis of language, is what most interested me and convinced me in Austin's enterprise.) He then attempts to justify, with nonlinguistic reasons, the preference he has shown until now for the forms of the first-person present indicative in the active voice in the analysis of the performative. The justification of last appeal is that in these forms reference is made to what Austin calls the *source* (origin) of the utterance. This notion of the *source*—whose stakes are so evident—often reappears in what follows, and it governs the entire analysis in the phase we are examining. Not only does Austin not doubt that the source of an oral statement in the first person present indicative (active voice) is *present* in the utterance and in the statement, (I have attempted to explain why we had reasons not to believe so), but he no more doubts that the equivalent of this link to the source in written utterances is simply evident and ascertained in the *signature:* "Where there is *not,* in the verbal formula of the utterance, a reference to the person doing the uttering, and so the acting, by means of the pronoun 'I' (or by his personal name), then in fact he will be 'referred to' in one of two ways:

"(a) In verbal utterances, *by his being the person who does* the uttering—what we may call the utterance-*origin* which is used generally in any system of verbal reference-co-ordinates.

"(b) In written utterances (or 'inscriptions'), *by his appending his signature* (this has to be done because, of course, written utterances are not tethered to their origin in the way spoken ones are)" (pp. 60–61). Austin acknowledges an analogous function in the expression "hereby" used in official protocols.

Let us attempt to analyze the signature from this point of view, its relation to the present and to the source. I take it as henceforth implied in this analysis that all the established predicates will hold also for the oral "signature" that is, or allegedly is, the presence of the "author" as the "person who does the uttering," as the "origin," the source, in the production of the statement.

By definition, a written signature implies the actual or empirical nonpresence of the signer. But, it will be said, it also marks and retains his having-been present in a past now, which will remain a future now, and therefore in a now in general, in the transcendental form of nowness (*maintenance*). This general *maintenance* is somehow inscribed, stapled to present punctuality, always evident and always singular, in the form of the signature. This is the enigmatic originality of every paraph. For the attachment to the source to occur, the absolute singularity of an event of the signature and of a form of the signature must be retained: the pure reproducibility of a pure event.

Is there some such thing? Does the absolute singularity of an event of the signature ever occur? Are there signatures?

Yes, of course, every day. The effects of signature are the most ordinary thing in the world. The condition of possibility for these effects is simultaneously, once again, the condition of their impossibility, of the impossibility of their rigorous purity. In order to function, that is, in order to be legible, a signature must have a repeatable, iterable, imitable form; it must be able to detach itself from the present and singular intention of its production. It is its sameness which, in altering its identity and singularity, divides the seal. I have already indicated the principle of the analysis above.

To conclude this very *dry*[15] discourse:

1. As writing, communication, if one insists upon maintaining the word, is not the means of transport of sense, the exchange of intentions and meanings, the discourse and "communication of consciousnesses." We are not witnessing an end of writing which, to follow McLuhan's ideological representation, would restore a transparency or immediacy of social relations; but indeed a more and more powerful historical unfolding of a general writing of which the system of speech, consciousness, meaning, presence, truth, etc., would only be an effect, to be analyzed as such. It is this questioned effect that I have elsewhere called *logocentrism*.

2. The semantic horizon which habitually governs the notion of communication is exceeded or punctured by the intervention of writing, that is of a *dissemination* which cannot be reduced to a *polysemia*. Writing is read, and "in the last analysis" does not give rise to a hermeneutic deciphering, to the decoding of a meaning or truth.

3. Despite the general displacement of the classical, "philosophical," Western, etc., concept of writing, it appears necessary, provisionally and strategically, to conserve the *old name*. This implies an entire logic of *paleonymy* which I do not wish to elaborate here.[16] Very schematically: an opposition of metaphysical concepts (for example, speech/writing, presence/absence, etc.) is never the face-to-face of two terms, but a hierarchy and an order of subordination. Deconstruction cannot limit itself or proceed immediately to a neutralization: it must, by means of a double gesture, a double science, a double writing, practice an *overturning* of the classical opposition *and* a general *displacement* of the system. It is only on this condition that deconstruction will provide itself the means with which to *intervene* in the field of oppositions that it criticizes, which is also a field of nondiscursive forces. Each concept, moreover, belongs to a systematic chain, and itself constitutes a system of predicates. There is no metaphysical concept in and of itself. There is a work—metaphysical or not—on conceptual systems. Deconstruction does not consist in passing from one concept to another, but in overturning and displacing a conceptual order, as well as the nonconceptual order with which the conceptual order is articulated. For example, writing, as a classical concept, carries with it predicates which have been subordinated, excluded, or held in reserve by forces and according to necessities to be analyzed. It is these predicates (I have mentioned some) whose force of generality, generalization, and generativity find themselves liberated, grafted onto a "new" concept of writing which also corresponds to whatever always has *resisted* the former organization of forces, which always has constituted the *remainder* irre-

15. TN. Derrida's word here is *sec*, combining the initial letters of three words that form his title, signature, event, context.
16. See *Dissemination* and *Positions*.

ducible to the dominant force which organized the—to say it quickly—logocentric hierarchy. To leave to this new concept the old name of writing is to maintain the structure of the graft, the transition and indispensable adherence to an effective *intervention* in the constituted historic field. And it is also to give their chance and their force, their power of *communication*, to everything played out in the operations of deconstruction.

But what goes without saying will quickly have been understood, especially in a philosophical colloquium: as a disseminating operation *separated* from presence (of Being) according to all its modifications, writing, if there is any, perhaps communicates, but does not exist, surely. Or barely, hereby, in the form of the most improbable signature.

(*Remark:* the—written—text of this—oral—communication was to have been addressed to the *Association of French Speaking Societies of Philosophy* before the meeting. Such a missive therefore had to be signed. Which I did, and counterfeit here. Where? There. J.D.)

J. DERRIDA

330